Celts in the Americas

Michael Newton, Editor

CAPE BRETON UNIVERSITY PRESS
SYDNEY, NOVA SCOTIA

Copyright 2013 - Cape Breton University Press

All rights reserved. No part of this work may be reproduced or used in any form or by any means, electronic or mechanical, including photocopying, recording or any information storage or retrieval system, without the prior written permission of the publisher. Responsibility for the research and the permissions obtained for this publication rests with the authors.

Canada Council for the Arts / Conseil des Arts du Canada

Cape Breton University Press recognizes the support of the Province of Nova Scotia, through the Department of Communities, Culture and Heritage and the support received for its publishing program from the Canada Council for the Arts Block Grants Program. We are pleased to work in partnership with these bodies to develop and promote our cultural resources.

NOVA SCOTIA
Communities, Culture and Heritage

Cover images: (clockwise from upper right) Welshmen in Patagonia (see p. 256); High cross, Québec City (see p. 63); Breton demonstration (see p. 31); Welsh gravestone (see p. 103)
Cover design: Cathy MacLean Design, Pleasant Bay, NS
Layout: Laura Bast, Sydney, NS
First printed in Canada

Library and Archives Canada Cataloguing in Publication

Celts in the Americas / edited by Michael Newton.
Based on papers presented at a conference held at St. Francis Xavier University, June 29-July 2, 2011.
Includes bibliographical references and index.
ISBN 978-1-897009-75-8

1. Celts--America--Congresses. 2. Civilization, Celtic--Congresses.
I. Newton, Michael Steven, 1965-

CB206.C44 2013 909'.04916 C2013-901416-0

Cape Breton University Press
PO Box 5300
1250 Grand Lake Road
Sydney, NS B1P 6L2 CA
www.cbu.ca/press

Table of Contents

5   **Michael Newton, Robert Dunbar, Gearóid Ó hAllmhuráin and Daniel G. Williams**
Introduction: The Past and Future Celt

Part I: Overviews of Celtic Peoples

18   **Éva Guillorel and Josette Jouas**
Fishermen and Farmers, Priests and Poets: The Bretons in North America

39   **Bernard Deacon**
Chameleon Celts: The Cornish in the Americas

56   **Tomás Ó h-Íde**
Emancipation through Exile: Irish Speakers in the Americas

76   **Michael Newton**
Bards of the Forests, Prairies and Skyscrapers: Scottish Gaels in the Americas

94   **Gethin Matthews**
Miners, Methodists and Minstrels: The Welsh in the Americas and their Legacy

Part II: Language

117   **Robert Dunbar**
Understanding Canadian Multiculturalism and Cultural Diversity in a 21st-Century Context from a "Celtic" Perspective

145   **Ian Johnson**
Revitalizing Welsh in the Chubut Province, Argentina: The Role of the Welsh Language Project

160   **Emily McEwan-Fujita**
Gaelic Revitalization Efforts in Nova Scotia: Reversing Language Shift in the 21st Century

Part III: Cultural Expression

187 **Gearóid Ó hAllmhuráin**
The Stranger's Land: Historical Traditions and Postmodern Temptations in the Celtic Soundscapes of North America

209 **Shamus Y. MacDonald**
Micro-Toponymy in Gaelic Nova Scotia: Some examples from Central Cape Breton

218 **Natasha Sumner**
The Ceudach Tale in Scotland and Cape Breton

Part IV: Identity and Race

248 **Paul W. Birt**
The Earth in a Suitcase: Cultural Hybridization in the Welsh and Cornish Diasporas

270 **Rhiannon Heledd Williams**
Whose Friend from the Old Country? The Welsh-Language American Press and National Identity in the 19th Century

283 **Michael Newton**
How Scottish Highlanders Became White: The Introduction of Racialism to Gaelic Literature and Culture

298 **C. Alexander MacLennan**
The "Good Indian" stories in Mac-Talla

Part V: Interethnic Interactions

305 **Daniel G. Williams**
Is the "Pan-" in Pan-Celticism the "Pan-" in Pan-Africanism? Language, Race and Diaspora

323 **Simon Brooks**
The Indigenous Atlantic: Welsh-Language Poetry and Indigenous Peoples in the Americas

335 **Éva Guillorel**
Speaking Mi'kmaw or Gaelic? The Linguistic Policy of the Catholic Church toward Missionaries Sent to Eastern Canada, 17th-19th Centuries

349 **Notes on Contributors**
354 **Other Conference Abstracts**
371 **Index**

Michael Newton, Robert Dunbar, Gearóid Ó hAllmhuráin and Daniel Williams

Introduction: The Past and Future Celt

Lost Legacies

As subjects of jealously hegemonic rulers, the monolithic term "British" (or "French" in the case of the Bretons) has obscured and eclipsed the identity and historical experiences of Celtic-speaking peoples in the Americas. As colonial offshoots of an essentially English empire, most scholars of Canadian and American history have been content to perpetuate an anglocentric master narrative. R. R. Davies has pointed out that

> this essentially Anglocentric approach has been in effect the dominant historiographic tradition in England from at least the twelfth century to the twentieth centuries. Furthermore it has been, and remains, the determining paradigm in historical writing about the British Isles generally. (2000: 2)

Despite the efforts of the English Crown to impose a single anglocentric identity upon the various peoples it claimed as subjects, the British Isles have never been a homogenous cultural entity. Celtic languages and cultures have persisted to the present, even if driven to the margins. "As late as 1500, about half the geographical area of the British Isles was still predominantly Celtic speaking" (Ellis 2004: 223).

Within Celtic studies, Celticity is not framed in geographical or racial terms—it is, rather, an abstraction for peoples speaking languages derived from a common ancestor and sharing cultural features that are directly related to this ancestral cultural core, regardless of their genetic makeup or territory (Koch 2003). Just as it is not possible to simply be an Indigenous

American without being a member of a more specific nation, so too it is impossible to be merely "Celtic" without being a member of a particular regional and linguistic identity and cultural milieu: Breton, Cornish, Irish, Manx, Scottish Gaelic or Welsh. The success of any endeavour to chart Celtic diasporic legacies will be determined based on the degree to which such an endeavour is grounded in the language and culture of a specific Celtic community. This fact is why this volume opens with chapters providing overviews of most of these individual nations.[1]

Many previous investigations into Celts in the Americas have foundered on the rocks of a false essentialism. Some have equated Celticity with rusticity, unaware of the sophisticated élite cultures of Celtic peoples that were annihilated as a consequence of cultural conquest. The attempt to derive the "cracker culture" of the American South from Celts, and thus distinguish it from that of the North in the pre-Civil War era, was plagued by this error (Berthoff 1986; Newton 2006). Some have attributed Celtic origins to cultural features that once enjoyed much wider currency, even in anglophone societies. Few aficionados of what generally passes as "Celtic music" appreciate that it is a very modern medley of elements and that much of what has been preserved in the "Celtic fringe" had very close counterparts in England and elsewhere before being obscured and eclipsed by industrialization (Chapman 1994; Roberts 2012). Indeed, as Ó hAllmhuráin's chapter in this volume adeptly explains, "Celtic music" has accumulated numerous layers of global "flows" of various sorts. Finally, some scholars have associated Celticity with entire nations—Ireland, Scotland or Wales, for example—even though they have all had settler colonies since the high medieval period which cannot be properly considered Celtic. Thus, characterizing all Scottish emigrants as "Celtic," for example, creates the fallacious categorization of Lowland features (many having Germanic origins) as Celtic, thus leading to further miscalculations.

Although it is a secondary phenomenon, one of the common formative experiences of Celtic communities (with the exception of the Bretons) has been conflict with an aggressively expansionist anglophone state. It is ironic that cultures that have spent centuries in opposition to English hegemony should be represented as synonymous to it in mainstream discourse. Michael Kennedy notes that

> within Canada's "two founding nations" model, a cultural group once considered nearly antithetical to North American "English" culture has been redefined as somehow inherently English. As an ethnic group, Scottish Gaels quite simply do not exist within the context of Canadian cultural history. (2002: 28)

The efforts of Celtic studies scholars and advocates of various Celtic heritages notwithstanding, government publications articulating national narratives still reiterate these telescoped imperial identities. For example, the current handbook about Canadian history and identity for those aspiring to become Canadian citizens states:

> The basic way of life in English-speaking areas was established by hundreds of thousands of English, Welsh, Scottish and Irish settlers, soldiers and migrants from the 1600s to the 20th century. Generations of pioneers and builders of British origins, as well as other groups, invested and endured hardship in laying the foundations of our country. This helps explain why Anglophones (English speakers) are generally referred to as English Canadians. (Minister of Citizenship and Immigration Canada 2011: 12)

A recognition of the social construction of knowledge will help us to make sense of the discrepancies between these historiographic fictions and historical reality (a topic further explored by Dunbar in this volume). Educational institutions were not established as unbiased centres of purely objective intellectual exploration but were inextricably tied to the ideologies of the empires and nation-states who built and ran them. The "knowledge" they produced was part of the enterprise of the domination of populations. Linguistic and cultural diversity was perceived as destabilizing and threatening in both British and French Empires, and so, until recently, official institutions, including those of education, rarely encouraged Celtic languages and cultures to be living entities. Being members of subordinated societies impeded the establishment of institutions representative of the Celts' own cultures empowered to act on their own behalf, whether in European homelands or in diasporic contexts.

Even in the present, significant elements of the British academy resist a dissolution of the imperial facade that would expose the suppressed Celtic elements. Antoinette Burton observes that some of the most problematic assumptions of British historiography have eluded attempts to deconstruct them:

> Through what kinds of practices is it possible to practice "British" history so that it does not continue to act as a colonial form of knowledge? ... The tenacity of the nation in debates about remaking British history signals an historically and culturally specific kind of attachment to the project of linear progress—even as it dramatizes how imperial traditions have shaped that investment and, finally, how tenuous the stability of "national" culture really is. (2000: 143, 144)

The conceit of linear progress is worth stressing, for it sanctions both the impetus of education and the ideology of imperialism. In the mid-12th century, English writers were depicting history as a progression from barbarity to civilization, claiming cultural, intellectual and moral superiority over their Celtic neighbours—tropes already present in Greek and Roman texts (Gillingham 1992; Davies 2000; Stroh 2011). Although the means of asserting political and economic dominance over Celtic peoples evolved continuously over the following centuries, proponents of English supremacy returned time and again to these assertions of inherent superiority, whether through the discourse of civility, the Enlightenment's theories of stadial social evolution or racialism of the modern era (Kidd 1995; Patterson 1995-1996). Silke Stroh demonstrates that anglophone discourse about Celtic peoples is not so different from that of other colonial subjects:

> Ideological aspects which have been identified as being comparable to overseas colonial ones include various patterns of othering and the construction of the Scottish, Irish or Welsh subject as a binary opposite to the English "coloniser." ... The representation of the peripheral subject has often been characterised by the discursive hegemony of externally constructed stereotypes that are often informed by a universalist teleology of progress.... The centre (typically anglophone England, sometimes also Lowland Scotland) is associated with culture, order, control, lawfulness, diligence, cleanliness, rationality, intellect, reality/realism, constancy, regularity and dynamic progress. The savage or barbarian periphery is credited with the exact opposites of the centre's traits, i.e. lack of culture or cultivation, disorder, lack of control, lawlessness, laziness, dirtiness, irrationality, unreality, dreams, ghosts, superstition, emotion, a passionate temper, violence, immorality, inconstancy, unreliability, stasis and parochialism. (2011: 22-23)

Intellectual institutions were necessarily complicit in such ideological formations which have been unconsciously absorbed into educational communities, who in turn often assume that Celtic societies were simply undeveloped peasant groups waiting to be civilized and integrated by superior societies and therefore do not merit special consideration on their own terms. Although such ethnocentric pretensions have now been rightfully overturned in the case of many other minoritized peoples, Celtic peoples are still engaged in questions of cultural authority and legitimacy.

Each immigrant community has had its own set of geographical, social, economic and cultural features that determined the channels and rate of assimilation. Unlike much of the rest of Europe, none of the Celtic-speaking communities had the experience or benefit of formal institutions that enshrined, normalized and developed their languages and cultures within a nation-state (with the late and limited exception of the Republic of Ireland). Additionally, centuries of marginalization and stigmatization weakened the collective willpower to oppose monocultural hegemony and to ensure cultural reproduction. The path to assimilation and the lure of racial dividends slowly undermined Celtic distinctiveness. Celtic immigrant communities were safely subsumed within the bounds of "whiteness" by the Civil Rights era, when intellectual institutions realigned their goals toward issues of social justice. Celtic peoples have thus not been able to benefit to any substantial degree from the modern liberalization of North American academia and have not formed a lobbying group pressing for greater representation in the curriculum or national discourse.

It would be remiss not to celebrate the establishment of the Chair of Gaelic Studies at St. Francis Xavier University, the Chair of Irish Studies at St. Mary's University, and the Chair of Celtic Studies at the University of Ottawa, an accomplishment put in full context in the chapter by Dunbar. It is very difficult, however, for a few isolated Chairs, without considerable additional support, to train new generations of scholars fully and to make an impact large enough to move the academy, with its discipline-specific silos, out of old ruts. Scholarly endeavours of this nature need to be connected to communities who sustain patronage for their work, mobilize the results effectively and advocate the importance of such efforts.

Although Celtic studies has been developing for several generations in the European homelands, the immigrant legacy has hardly merited a footnote. One reason for this silence may be the false perception that emigration was a sign of weakness and decline, and that upon leaving their homelands Celtic peoples became quickly assimilated. The chapters in this volume will contradict the assumption, implicit in the lack of appearance of a Celtic narrative in the standard historiography, that

> the vast majority of them, for obvious historic reasons, either were
> bilingual or spoke English exclusively before they migrated to
> this country, and it was easy and natural for them to speak only
> English in their new homeland. Thus, despite their numbers, it is a
> reasonable assumption that Irish, Scottish-Gaelic, and Welsh had a
> far less vigorous and enduring life after migration here than did the
> speeches of other linguistic groups. (Blenner-Hassett 1954: 5)

Decolonizing the "Western Canon"

If we are committed to cultural diversity in the present, why is this ideal so seldom applied to our understanding of the past? Why is the history of "Western civilization" still so dominated by a monolithic and empire-centric narrative (from Sumerians to Egyptians, Greeks, Romans, Anglo-Saxons, etc.), when we say that we value the many different contributions of many different peoples in the present? Is the desire for a simple, single-threaded historical narrative so strong as to deny the validity of previous human cultures which did not emerge as the "winners" of history?

By any objective measure, Celtic-speaking peoples played a vital role in the history of Europe and North America. They formed a substantial majority of the population of western Europe during Classical Antiquity and laid many of the foundations for medieval European civilization (Koch 2007). They continued to constitute a significant proportion of the population of the British Isles into the period of colonization, and, as this volume amply demonstrates, immigrant Celtic communities in the Americas enjoyed many accomplishments worth commemorating: continuing literary traditions, printing written literature in journals and books reflecting their new conditions, establishing organizations and facilities to represent their origins and concerns.

In spite of these indisputable facts, Celtic-speaking peoples are not reflected in academic institutions or standard educational materials in proportion either to their numbers or to their cultural and intellectual achievements. Even in the most up-to-date and open-minded of standard university textbooks on "Western civilization," for example, if Celts appear at all, they make only brief cameos as exotic barbarians hovering on the edges of civilizations in order to threaten them and act as anti-images of cultural sophistication. In many cases, Celtic features and innovations have been falsely attributed to Romans or Germanic peoples (especially Anglo-Saxons), and "Celtic" and "civilization" are essentialized so as to remain mutually exclusive (Patterson 1995-1996, 1996; Little 2004; Hammond 2006; Newton 2011).

Likewise, standard anthologies of World or British Literature rarely give voice to the vigorous Celtic literary traditions that preceded English literature and influenced European traditions, much to the detriment of a balanced understanding of contemporary realities (Dooley 2003: 68-69; Boyd forthcoming). As the historical narrative of English literature has a huge impact on the popular understanding of both history and literature, for example, we should be concerned that even current scholarship is commonly conducted without taking interactions and influences of Celtic neighbours into consideration:

> Most scholars continue to operate from the assumption that Anglo-Saxon studies is a Germanic discipline, and only vernacular literature in Old English, Old Norse or Old German can be relevant to their researches. What this otherwise excellent collection of essays points out is the need for Anglo-Saxonists to expand their interdisciplinary investigations to include Welsh and Irish cultures, including both Latin and vernacular literatures. (Ireland 2010: 337-38)

The importance of Celtic materials has long been recognized by a small circle of scholars. Over half-a-century ago, an American scholar surveyed with optimism the many fertile fields waiting to be examined and the ways in which Celtic studies could enrich the academy:

> A whole world of imaginative accomplishment in the Celtic literature[s] awaits the attention of the student of *belles-lettres* who masters one or more of the languages.... Opportunities for the folklorist in Celtic are almost unlimited.... Innumerable opportunities await the historical scholar trained in one or more of the Celtic languages. Because of the vicissitudes of past events, the histories of the Celtic peoples have rarely been written by historians conversant with Celtic and hence able to examine and evaluate documents and other primary source materials in Celtic.... considerable light remains to be shed on the history of races whose destinies so far have been chronicled and interpreted largely by writers unable to speak or read the languages of these peoples. For instance, much valuable work remains to be accomplished in revealing the importance of Celtic—particularly Irish—influences on early medieval European history and culture.... Anthropologists, archeologists, numismatists, students of personal names and place-names, historians of philosophy, theology, and comparative religion—all can, to some extent, benefit considerably from a study of Celtic. (Blenner-Hassett 1954: 11, 12)

The potential for revising the "Western canon" so that Celtic peoples are given their due place in the narrative—as other minoritized peoples have been in recent years—has been thwarted by bootstrapping problems: Celtic studies is still an underdeveloped field on the margins of North American academia; its under-representation in academic activity makes it difficult to make an impact on mainstream academic discourse; authors responsible for standard curricula have been trained in disciplines with little or no awareness of Celtic studies; the absence of Celtic materials in such texts (not to mention the shortage of institutional positions) limits scholars and students from pursuing research in Celtic studies and including it in standard narratives; and so on.

The Future of Celtic Studies in North America

Celtic studies was developed formally during the 19th century as an outgrowth of philology, Classical Studies and the study of the medieval past (Tymoczko 2002: 13-15; Dooley 2003). Some academic institutions around the turn of the 20th century supported Celtic studies in response to the demands of local Celtic-speaking communities who wished to see their heritage represented in the curriculum and felt that the prestige lent by higher education would enhance their cultural capital (Newton 2003; Linkletter 2009). On the whole, however, Celtic studies in North America, especially in recent generations, has followed antiquarian tendencies rather than involving itself with living speech communities and championing their cultural legacies.

While philology, Classical antiquity and the medieval period are stimulating and underdeveloped fields of enquiry that deserve to be studied and cultivated, support for them within universities has been plummeting in recent decades. Celtic studies has been affected correspondingly. As Tymoczko warns, "There are signs of the waning of scholarly and administrative support for the field [of Celtic studies], with fewer appointments in the field, fewer library resources allocated, and so forth" (Tymoczko 2002: 19). She notes that disciplines such as Celtic studies "find it difficult to compete with more 'glitzy' fields in the humanities in the attempt to secure scarce resources" (19).

Celtic studies could reinvigorate itself in the Americas by addressing those issues of greatest relevance and interest in this geographical and cultural context: race, ethnicity, immigration, imperialism, (post)colonialism, linguistic revitalization, etc. In fact, greater awareness of and engagement with these issues in the North American academy could result in a significant contribution to the revitalization of the Celtic languages and cultures not just in the Americas but in the Celtic homelands as well (Koch 2003: 77-80). Doing so will require a shift in emphasis from the tools and methods of the medievalist—the current staple of Celtic studies—to those of modern critical cultural studies. As Stroh points out,

> Many Celtic Studies scholars prefer more traditional methods and concerns, such as textual criticism, close reading, detailed author- or at most period-specific studies, biographical approaches, assessments of literary "merit," general overviews of literary history, or folklore studies.... Increased dialogue with other disciplines and greater openness to recent trends in literary and cultural studies might make some small contribution to changing this reductive and derogatory image of backward-looking parochialism. (Stroh 2011: 34)

Many of the chapters in this volume offer excellent models for future research informed by current practices in a number of different disciplines and subject areas, models that extend far beyond the conventional framework of the field of Celtic studies, while being firmly rooted in the languages and cultural expressions of Celtic communities.

Exactly how to constitute Celtic studies—or to frame research focused on its constituent peoples—within the context of the history of the

Americas is no trivial matter. By the time that the various Celtic peoples—Bretons, Cornish, Irish Gaels, Manx, Scottish Gaels and Welsh—came to the Americas, they had been developing independently for many centuries: their languages had diverged and their cultural expressions had evolved into distinctively different forms. Although, as demonstrated by this volume, the heritages of Celtic-speaking immigrant communities in the Americas are directly derived from the medieval period, to study Old Gaelic and Old Welsh might be pushing the horizon too far back. Would it be more sensible to reconceptualize groupings such as Brythonic Studies or Goidelic Studies? While this question was raised at the concluding round table of the Celts in the Americas conference, we did not come to a clear resolution.

The current dispensation is clearly inadequate. For the most part, the legacy of Celtic-speaking peoples is claimed by scholars trained in anglocentric (or francocentric) fields, and such training perpetuates the asymmetries and distortions of the imperial era. All too often, if Celtic-speaking communities are studied at all, they are framed primarily within texts and perspectives produced by the external, anglocentric observer. Celtic communities are not allowed to have an autonomous, internal life of their own in their own languages—this would threaten the authority of the non-Celtic specialist and the canonized heroes of the imperial age. That which is specific to the Celtic languages and expressed in them (especially sources derived from oral tradition) is too often snubbed by people who do not speak them as though they were delusions as unsubstantial as the "fairies" that Celts were supposedly predisposed to see. Unless stakeholders lobby against such disparities, they are likely to continue. The chapters by Brooks, MacDonald, MacLennan, Newton, Sumner and Rhiannon Williams suggest the rewards that result from understanding the cultural expressions of Celtic-speaking immigrant communities within their own linguistic, literary, historical and epistemological frameworks.

The degree to which Celtic languages are still spoken in the Americas and are subjects of personal and community interest is not widely recognized. Besides the celebrated cases of Scottish Gaelic in eastern Nova Scotia and of Welsh in Patagonia (discussed by McEwan-Fujita and Johnson respectively), there are vestiges of these and other Celtic languages scattered through communities from coast to coast and speakers of Celtic languages continue to migrate to the Americas. There is significant zeal to acquire these languages and use them in a variety of contexts, as demonstrated by associated university courses, formal organizations and informal practices. Like other so-called heritage languages, they continue to have a contemporary relevance to many as a means of communication, as carriers of culture and, indeed, as markers of identity in societies that allow for the freedom to choose an eclectic set of multiple identities. Just as departments of Celtic studies in the Celtic homelands prioritize their national languages and cultures, so should scholars of Celtic studies give special consideration to connections with the diasporic communities and languages of their region.

Celtic languages continue to attract the attention of policy-makers, most notably in Nova Scotia through the Office of Gaelic Affairs, but also intermittently over the years via different multicultural programs in Canada. In this regard, the Canadian Supreme Court has indicated that a commitment to multiculturalism is a fundamental unwritten principle underlying the Canadian constitution, and speakers of Celtic languages can and should be expected to contribute in a dynamic way to defining (and constantly redefining) what this commitment implies for linguistic and cultural diversity in Canada, as discussed in the chapter by Dunbar. Cross-cultural collaboration with the indigenous peoples of the Americas and New Zealand has resulted from efforts to revitalize Celtic languages in their European homelands and immigrant communities.

The complex relations between Celtic immigrants and peoples of indigenous American or African ancestry often reflect the ambiguous and subordinate status of Celtic peoples. The historical and literary record offers plentiful scope for the study of the interactions (real and imagined) between Celtic-speaking peoples and various ethnic groups throughout the Americas, as demonstrated in the chapters by Birt, Brooks, Guillorel, MacLennan, Newton and Daniel Williams. These contributions also substantiate the idea that historians of the British Empire should not deny the role of Celtic peoples as the first subjects of its "laboratory for empire," but neither should they whitewash the complicity of Celtic peoples in assuming the role of colonizer.

Scholars working in the Americas can be facilitated by fostering connections to centres of study in Celtic countries, where there are signs of growing interest in the diasporic experience. Immigrant communities have preserved aspects of the cultural legacy lost in their homelands, but they also created ongoing links through which ideas and material resources were exchanged in both directions. The social processes surrounding the migration of Celtic peoples to the Americas—imperialism, the plight of refugees, globalization, identity politics, economic and cultural marginalization, the immigrant experience, etc.—continue to be relevant issues on a large scale in both Europe and the Americas.

Acknowledgments

We would first of all like to acknowledge the contributions of the authors of this volume. We have every confidence that the labour, originality and insights of the scholars who have invested their research in this effort will be recognized as constituting a milestone in the field of Celtic studies in the "New World" context. Thanks to Pádraig Ó Siadhail for assistance on the Irish chapters and to Mike Hunter for his work as general editor and to Laura Bast, production coordinator at CBU Press.

Other than the overview histories of the Celtic peoples which begin this volume, these chapters were first presented as talks at the Celts in the Americas conference hosted at St. Francis Xavier University, Antigonish, Nova Scotia (and co-hosted by the Centre for Cape Breton Studies at Cape Breton University) June 29-July 2, 2011. Our gathering was attended by an enthusiastic audience of scholars and members of the public.

The conference could not have happened without support, especially financial, from many quarters. We were fortunate enough to receive a grant from the Social Sciences and Humanities Research Council of Canada. It was further underwritten by institutional funding from the Centre for Cape Breton Studies at Cape Breton University and the Office of the Academic Vice-President of St. Francis Xavier University. Local investment in the topics explored at the conference was also demonstrated by generous donations made by local organizations and individuals: the MacLeod Group (Antigonish), Harbourview Properties (Antigonish), The Charitable Irish Society of Halifax, John Hamilton (Antigonish), and the Office of Gaelic Affairs, Nova Scotia.

This volume is dedicated to the memory of Kenneth Nilsen, whose untimely death came during its preparation. His illness prevented him from contributing the chapter he had planned and was uniquely qualified to write. Ken was a rarely gifted linguist who spoke many languages, including Breton, Irish, Scottish Gaelic and Welsh. He conducted fieldwork and collected oral tradition in Irish, Scottish Gaelic and Welsh from native speakers all around North America (Nilsen 1988). He occupied the Chair of Celtic Studies at St. Francis Xavier University for twenty-eight years and inspired many students with his passion for Celtic Studies. *Clach air a chàrn.*

Notes

1. It is regrettable that no suitable scholar could be found to discuss the history of Manx immigrants. Several excellent resources originally published in the *Proceedings of the Isle of Man Natural History and Antiquarian Society* have been made available on the website http://www.isle-of-man.com. Probably the best of these is Kinvig 1955.

References

Berthoff, Rowland. 1986. Celtic Mist over the South. *Journal of Southern History* 52 (4): 523-46.

Blenner-Hassett, Roland. 1954. A Brief History of Celtic Studies in North America. *Proceedings of the Modern Language Association* 69 (4.2): 3-21.

Boyd, Matthieu. Forthcoming. The Languages of British Literature and the Stakes of Anthologies. *Pedagogy*.

Burton, Antoinette. 2000. Who needs the nation? Interrogating "British" history. In *Cultures of Empire: A Reader*, ed. Catherine Hall, 137-53. New York: Routledge.

Chapman, Malcolm. 1994. Thoughts on Celtic Music. In *Ethnicity, Identity and Music: The Musical Construction of Place*, ed. Martin Stokes, 29-44. Oxford: Berg.

Davies, R. R. 2000. *The First English Empire: Power and Identities in the British Isles 1093-1343*. Oxford: Oxford University Press.

Dooley, Ann. 2003. A view from North America: obstacles and opportunities for Celtic studies. In *Retrospect and Prospect in Celtic Studies*, ed. Máire Herbert and Kevin Murray, 59-73. Dublin: Four Courts Press.

Ellis, Steven. 2004. Why the History of "the Celtic Fringe" Remains Unwritten. *European Review of History: Revue europeenne d'histoire* 10:221-31.

Gillingham, John. 1992. The Beginnings of English Imperialism. *Journal of Historical Sociology* 5 (4): 392-409.

Hammond, Matthew. 2006. Ethnicity and the Writing of Medieval Scottish History. *The Scottish Historical Review* 85 (1): 1-27.

Ireland, Colin. 2010. Review of *Cædmon's Hymn and material culture in the world of Bede*. *Peritia* 21:330-38.

Kennedy, Michael. 2002. *Gaelic Nova Scotia: An economic, cultural, and social impact study*. Halifax: Nova Scotia Museum.

Kidd, Colin. 1995. Teutonic Ethnology and Scottish Nationalist Inhibition, 1780-1880. *The Scottish Historical Review* 74 (1): 45-68.

Kinvig, R. J. 1955. Manx Settlement in the United States of America. *Proceedings of Isle of Man Natural History and Antiquarian Society* 5 (4): 436-55.

Koch, John. 2003. Some thoughts on ethnic identity, cultural pluralism, and the future of Celtic Studies. In *Retrospect and Prospect in Celtic Studies*, ed. Máire Herbert and Kevin Murray, 75-92. Dublin: Four Courts Press.

———. 2007. *An Atlas for Celtic Studies: Archaeology and Names in Ancient Europe and Early Medieval Ireland, Britain, and Brittany*. Oxford: Oxbow.

Linkletter, Michael. 2009. The Early Establishment of Celtic Studies in North American Universities. *Proceedings of the Harvard Celtic Colloquium* 29:138-53.

Little, Lester. 2004. Cypress Beams, Kufic Script, and Cut Stone: Rebuilding the Master Narrative of European History. *Speculum* 79:909-28.

Minister of Citizenship and Immigration Canada. 2011. *Discover Canada: The Rights and Responsibilities of Citizenship*. http://www.cic.gc.ca/english/pdf/pub/discover.pdf (accessed 6 June 2012).

Newton, Michael. 2003. "Becoming Cold-Hearted Like the Gentiles Around Them": Scottish Gaelic in the United States 1872-1912. *eKeltoi* 2:63-131.

———. 2006. Review essay of *How Celtic Culture Invented Southern Literature*. *eKeltoi* 1:10-16.

———. 2011. "Western Civilization" as seen by the Celtic West. http://people.stfx.ca/mnewton/westernciv7celts.pdf (accessed 9 November 2012).

Nilsen, Kenneth. 1988. Collecting Celtic Folklore in the United States. *Proceedings of the First North American Congress of Celtic Studies*, ed. Gordon MacLennan, 55-74. Ottawa: University of Ottawa.

Patterson, Nerys. 1995-1996. The English Just Are—1. *Planet: The Welsh Internationalist* 114:72-77.

———. 1996. The English Just Are—2. *Planet: The Welsh Internationalist* 115:84-90.

Roberts, Paul. 2012. The Village Music Project. http://www.village-music-project.org.uk/ (accessed 28 June 2012).

Stroh, Silke. 2011. *Uneasy Subjects: Postcolonialism and Scottish Gaelic Poetry*. Amsterdam and New York: Rodopi.

Tymoczko, Maria. 2002. What Questions Should We Ask in Celtic Studies in the New Millennium? In *Identifying the "Celtic": CSANA Yearbook 2*, ed. Joseph Nagy, 10-29. Dublin: Four Courts Press.

Part I: Overviews of Celtic Peoples

Éva Guillorel and Josette Jouas

Fishermen and Farmers, Priests and Poets: The Bretons in North America

The phenomenon of migration is essential in the study of economic, social and cultural dynamics in Brittany. Since the 1960s, immigration into Brittany has reversed longstanding trends, thanks to a newfound interest in this region (Cassard et al. 2008: 253-54). Even more than immigration into Brittany, however, emigration has transformed it. The massive Breton emigration to Paris prompted a number of studies (Gauthier 1953; Violain 1997; Tardieu 2003), but it must not overshadow the importance of migrations beyond France, which started with the deployment of French colonialism in the 16th century. North America occupies a privileged place in the history of Breton departures from the homeland.

Before describing these five centuries of Breton migration, heritage and identity in North America, we must clarify what we mean by "Bretons." Since late Antiquity, Brittany (a province of France since the 16th century) has been split into two linguistic zones: Lower Brittany (*Basse-Bretagne*), the western and Breton-speaking part influenced by a Celtic heritage, is distinct from Upper Brittany (*Haute-Bretagne*), the eastern and French-speaking part (Broudic 1995). Nevertheless, many texts about the Bretons in America do not make a distinction between Breton and French speakers. While providing an overview of Breton immigrant history as a whole, this chapter will give prominence to the Bretons of the west.

The First Migrants: From Brittany to New France

Bretons were in North America as early as 1504. Written sources mentioned their leaving from Saint-Malo and Paimpol for the cod-fishing season. In a letter dated 1540, the Spanish ambassador in France mentioned that some Bretons claimed that they had been going to the Grand Banks of Newfoundland since 1462 (Fournier 2005: 57). The importance of fishing in Newfoundland was such that the *Dictionnaire François-Celtique* published by Grégoire de Rostrenen in 1732, provided specific Breton words describing the fishing boats.[1] Between 1534 and 1542, the French king entrusted a Breton, Jacques Cartier from Saint-Malo, with making three voyages that led to the exploration of the Gulf of St. Lawrence, which he followed to what is today Montréal (Trudel 2000a). Between 1578 and 1598, Troïlus Mesgouez de la Roche, from Morlaix, was named "Viceroy of Newfound Lands." He tried several times to colonize the country, but failed (Trudel 1963: 231-38; Lanctot 2000). François Gravé du Pont, also from Saint-Malo, made his first trip to Tadoussac in 1600, before participating in the colonization of Acadia several years later (Trudel 2000b).

Other than these famous men (mainly from the French-speaking part of Brittany), the real Breton demographic weight in American colonization is subject to diverging interpretations. The argument that prevailed up to the beginning of the 20th century was that of a massive proportion of Bretons and Normans in New France. This view was integrated in a historiography of ecclesiastical and conservative inspiration, which saw in Brittany an attractive motherland strongly influenced by Catholicism (Simard 1995: 55-56; Fournier 1981: 8-11). It also emphasized Jacques Cartier's role as the Frenchman who officially discovered Canada.

Newer demographic research has since revised the estimated number of Breton immigrants significantly. In 1946, Archange Godbout estimated the total number of Bretons to be at only 4.6 per cent of the original immigrant population between 1600 and 1765, placing Brittany in fifth place among provinces that sent over colonists. Sixty years later, Marcel Fournier estimated that 5 per cent of the colonial population was Breton (Godbout 1946; Fournier 2005: 60). As for Marcel Trudel, he placed Brittany in only eleventh place for the number of colonists present in 1663, which emphasizes the small proportion of Bretons settled during the first decades of colonization (Trudel 1973: 35). However, these calculations concern only the colonists established in America, neglecting those who returned to Europe after several months or several years. After taking into account the temporary migrants and seasonal workers (many navy seamen, fishermen and soldiers did not settle permanently in New France), Leslie Choquette recently estimated that Brittany did, indeed, contribute the greatest number of migrants under the French regime with 16.7 per cent of the total number (Boleda 1984; Choquette 1997: 29-33).

Whatever the calculations and the numbers, all the demographers agree on the disparity in distribution between Upper and Lower Brittany. Nearly two thirds of the migrants came from the French part of Brittany; this rises to 70 per cent if seasonal migrants are included. The difference can be explained by the force of attraction of two ports in French-speaking Brittany, which were first in line for Atlantic exchanges under the French regime: Saint-Malo in the 16th century, and Nantes during the 17th century. In Breton-speaking Brittany, the migrants also came mainly from ports such as Vannes or Brest, while the inland was less mobile before the 19th century (Fournier 1981: 26; Choquette 1997: 56-60; Mimeault 1999).

There is, however, a category of migrants in which western Brittany strongly asserted itself: the clergy. With a long-standing tradition of training and sending priests abroad (Croix 1993: 354-57), Breton-speaking Brittany, especially the northwest (Léon), logically participated in the missionary effort in Canada. The Jesuits Jean-Pierre Daniellou and Joseph-Pierre de Bonnécamp taught at Québec College in the 18th century. Bonnécamp also participated as hydrographer during an expedition in the Ohio Valley in 1742 (Fournier 2005: 108-109, 474-75). In Acadia, priests Jean Manach, Jean-Louis Le Loutre and François Le Guerne, served the Mi'kmaq and Acadians during the troubled years of the 1750s. Le Loutre played an important political role in the resistance to the English, before helping to welcome the Acadian population exiled to France, specifically to the isle of Belle-Île in the south of Brittany (Dumont-Johnson 1970; David 1931-1932). In 1753, Joseph Gueguen was sent to Acadia as a child to become familiar with Native American languages with the intention of training him as a missionary, but he was wounded and his plans had to change. He turned to fur trading, became one of the richest Frenchmen in New Brunswick and left numerous descendants (Brun 1984).

The 18th century was marked by a continuous French expansion across North American territory. According to demographic research by Marcel Fournier, Brittany was the second most active province in sending permanent migrants, through marriage, to Louisiana between 1720 and 1770. Moreover, Louis Billouart de Kerlérec, a Breton nobleman from Quimper, was appointed Governor of Louisiana between 1752 and 1763 (Fournier 2005: 40-43).

Breton Migrations in the 19th and 20th Centuries

In the sixty years following the Treaty of Paris (1763) and the conquest of New France by the British Crown, Breton migration—and, to a larger extent, French migration—to the Americas stopped almost entirely (Frenette 2008: 310-312).

Emigration resumed in the 19th century, with the Breton clergy playing leading roles. A countless number of priests, nuns or missionaries were sent to North America to found missions: the Eudists among the Acadians in the Maritime Provinces from 1830 and the Missionary Oblates of Mary Immaculate among the First Nations in northern Canada from 1841 (Michel 1997: 248). It can easily be said that from 1870 to 1930, French settlement in western Canada was dominated by the Roman Catholic Church (Lalonde 1993). Missionaries were learned men who documented the landscapes and wildlife they saw and the customs and languages of the different populations they encountered. One such Breton clergyman was Auguste Le Corre, born in Inzinzac. He was sent by the Missionary Oblates to the north of Canada in 1872 and spent nearly fifty years travelling thousands of kilometres in his ash-bark canoe. His journal remains an interesting work of ethnography (Duchaussois 1934).

In the beginning of the 20th century, Breton priests and nuns founded congregations in North America. In 1905, the French Assembly approved the law on the *Separation of Church and State*, thereby inciting the clergy to assert their faith more freely elsewhere. The new religious communities worked with underprivileged populations, as nurses in poor neighbourhoods or as teachers in orphanages or girls' refuges. One such congregation was the Filles du Saint-Esprit. Six nuns left Brittany in 1902 for Hartford, Connecticut and, once in their convents, learned the English language in eight months (Congrégation des Filles du Saint-Esprit 1912: 21).

Other ecclesiastics took the role of recruiters. Between 1880 and 1910, Brittany was in a period of rural overpopulation, with farms too small to feed the large families (eight to twelve children) on them. Craftsmen, such as weavers, could not compete with the more industrialized regions of France and England and found themselves out of work. Unemployment became pervasive. The manufacturing of sail-cloth met with British competition, and cotton took the place of linen. The closing of unprofitable mines and slate quarries obliged workers to find work elsewhere. Poverty increased and many of those not fit for emigration joined the large body of beggars (Patault 1967; Cariou 1987).

In 1870, the Canadian government strongly encouraged clergy to recruit French speakers to ensure the survival of a French presence in the new territory colonized by Canada, but soon it became obvious that their efforts went unanswered. Climatic conditions in the west were not very inviting, but, more to the point, several of the Canadian priests had been appointed because of political reasons, not because of their dynamism. The priests themselves were pessimistic about the future. In 1890, the archbishop of St. Boniface turned to Europe—France, Belgium and Switzerland in particular—for a solution (Lalonde 1993: 103-104). Because of the economic situation in Brittany, the Breton clergy had no difficulty convincing their parishioners to migrate to Canada since they were guaranteed a strong adherence to Catholicism. The vast prairies promised to be a land of plenty for agrarian Bretons. Free land was given by the government on the condition that the farmers labour the land and build their homes. In Brittany, Father Paul Le Floch convinced a colony of three hundred people to found St. Brieux in Saskatchewan; Father Hervé Péran went to Saint-Laurent, Manitoba, with 150 colonists. During the 19th and 20th centuries, most migrants came from the Breton-speaking part of Brittany, contrary to the former period (Flatrès 1959: 106; Le Clec'h 1969, 1974). Private initiatives resulted in the founding of Gourin City in the province of Alberta, while the Rannou families settled in Ville-Marie in Québec, and the Bourhis family in Hazelwood (Jouas, Le Corre and Jamet 2005: 45-50).

It must be stressed, however, that the greatest number of Breton-speaking missionaries did not land in either Canada or the United States, but on the island of Haiti. In 1860, Pope Pius IX appointed Monseigneur Testard du Cosquer, a Breton from Lesneven, as first Archbishop of Port-au-Prince. For a long time, this choice made Haiti the spiritual daughter of Brittany, attracting missionaries by the hundreds throughout the 19th and 20th centuries. The island came to be called "black Brittany" (Michel 1997: 92-100; Delisle 2003).

In the civilian domain, certain Breton migrants stood out because of their unusual careers in America, among them several women. Countess Geneviève de Méhérenc de St. Pierre, or Véfa de St. Pierre, as she was called by the Bretons, was born in Brittany in 1872. She had a liberal upbringing influenced by her grandfather, a naval officer who had participated in battles during the American Revolutionary War. She learned the Breton language from domestic servants and English from her tutors. She was interested in photography and worked as a journalist. In Canada, she became a Breton ambassador and attempted to meet all the Breton colonists. She collected and published an abundance of ethnographical information on First Nations and continued to travel throughout the world as an explorer and writer. Later in life, she financially aided the Breton regionalist movement (Méhérenc de Saint-Pierre 1908: 56-76; Arlaux 1995).

Another Breton woman also travelled throughout North America, but in the realm of the cinema. Countess de Grandsaignes d'Hauterives, more commonly called Marie de Kerstrat, was born in Briec. In 1896, at the age of 55, she decided to follow her son to bring the new moving pictures to the masses, from the inhospitable north of Canada to the St. Louis World Fair in the United States (Duigou and Lacasse 1987). Also notable was Théodore Botrel, the famous Breton chansonnier, born in Dinan in 1868. He enjoyed great success during several trips performing in Canada, where his music is still part of the *bonnes chansons* in Québec.

The Breton Language in America

Contrary to Welsh, Irish and Scottish Gaelic, the Breton language had no well-established presence in North America, nor a multigenerational transmission in the heart of large communities, even if the language was, and continues to be, spoken in the restrained context of family and friends.

There are a number of reasons why linguists do not acknowledge the existence of Breton-language speakers in North America. Most of the migrants in New France were already French speakers before they left. Originating mainly from the northern and French part of the country, they had an urban background and were more literate than average, making them better equipped to master French. Before the 19th century, furthermore, Breton-speaking communities did not emigrate en masse or settle in homogenous enclaves which could have continued to use and transmit the language. On the contrary, the intermixing of migrants from different regions of France reinforced the use of French as a *lingua franca* (Barbaud 1984; Mougeon and Beniak 1994; Morin 2002). Even in the smaller fishing communities of the coast, with a less mixed population, the Bretons, unlike the Basques,[2] did not seem to leave a durable linguistic imprint. Thus, no reference to the Breton language is made by the main observers under the French or English regimes (Caron-Leclerc 1998), and only brief mentions of Breton by certain migrants have been collected haphazardly. Yves Phlem, a surgeon from Morlaix, in a report published in 1737, explains the difficulty he had in carrying out his profession on his arrival in New France in 1720, for he only spoke Breton (Memoire instructif 1737; Douville 1975: 6-7). In 1735, the missionary Jean-Louis Le Loutre made a parallel between the pronunciation of his Breton language and that of the Mi'kmaq he was evangelizing in Acadia (Le Loutre 1738).

We must wait until the first years of the 20th century and great waves of Breton emigration to find any tangible traces of structured Breton communities. On the Canadian prairies, family transmission of the language was attested in certain areas. The transmission was facilitated by the isolation of these areas, and also by the fact that entire families emigrated (Le Clec'h 1954-1955: 46). In Connecticut, Jean Le Dour, born in 1904 of parents born in Langonnet, was raised in Breton and still spoke the language when his family returned to Breton-speaking Brittany in 1912 (Plourin and Cadic 1985-1986: 82). It was claimed in the mid-20th century that "in and around Montreal there are several thousand Bretons, many of whom speak Breton exclusively in their homes" (Blenner-Hassett 1954: 7). The Breton language was also present in Newfoundland in the 1950s, thanks to the migration of several families from Breton-speaking Brittany (Brasseur 2001: x-xi). In the communities of Milltown, New Jersey, and Lenox Dale, Massachusetts, Breton was spoken by families from 1910 to 1935. Later, in New York, by far the largest community, Breton was regularly heard in some families from the 1950s to 1980s.

An interesting anecdote is that of a Breton couple who emigrated in the 1950s from Gourin to New York. She was from Gourin town, he from the Gourin countryside. She spoke French, he spoke Breton and French. In New York, she learned to speak Breton with her husband, and they both became trilingual (Jouas, Le Corre and Jamet 2005: 110). An inventory was taken in the United States in 1970 and stated that 32,722 people residing in the country declared to have Breton as their mother tongue, of whom a little less than half were born in the United States, suggesting a strong family transmission of the language (Fishman et al. 1982: 48-49).

Such figures, however, seem to be high compared to the personal accounts of Bretons established in North America at the same period, which stress the lack of transmission of Breton to the second and third generations. Breton speakers continued to speak their mother tongue with their husband or wife and their immediate circle of family and friends, but for the sake of integration, they spoke English or French to their children. The Carduner family, who emigrated to Saskatchewan in 1912, is a significant example of loss of mother tongue. Before they had decided to leave, the family spoke Breton but had a solid knowledge of French. The father had already studied with priests and he insisted his elder sons do the same, which made them perfectly bilingual. But arriving in Canada, their English environment quickly obliged them to learn the new language and they could communicate more easily with the other French immigrants in French. Therefore, teaching Breton to the smaller children seemed inappropriate. Cut off from their homeland and their roots, their mother tongue slowly dwindled to set expressions such as *un grand blavez d'eorch tout* (a grand year to all), *madé* (okay), and *kenavo* (goodbye) (Le Bihan 1997). Several accounts, collected from Breton-speaking emigrants to the United States who returned to Brittany on retirement, reveal influences from French and English on Breton morphology (Plourin and Cadic 1985-1986: 83-86).

The Michelin factory in Milltown, New Jersey (1907-1930) maintained a French school for its employees, but it mainly catered to the directors and heads of departments, who were not Breton. The workers, who very often spoke Breton among themselves, sent their children to the Milltown Public School. This was important for them, since they had had so little schooling back home and wanted their children to "advance in life." In the year 1929 alone, there were at least twenty-three Breton families represented from kindergarten to eighth grade (Jouas, Le Corre and Jamet 2005: 69).

Another interesting example is the case of Marie-Anne Hillion. After landing at Ellis Island from the centre of Brittany in 1924, she started to learn English the very first day she set foot in New York. Although she could not read English, she bought the newspaper to know the exchange

MOUEZ AR VRETONED

"Voix des Bretons"

BULLETIN DE L'ASSOCIATION BRETONNE AUX ETATS-UNIS

Nouvelle Série No. 3 — Siège Social : 145 East 45th Street, New York 17, N. Y. — Avril 1956

BAL DES AJONCS D'OR

Comme chaque année les Bretons et amis des Bretons sont venus très nombreux danser et s'amuser au Manhattan Center. Nous ne pouvons nier que le défilé des costumes et l'exhibition des danses de chez nous, par leur richesse et leur diversité, sont très appréciés à New-York et nous attirent chaque année une foule plus nombreuse d'amis.

Nous remercions ici les joueurs de binious, Georges Cariou et Guy Chevalier, et les danseurs du groupe "Bleun Brug" sous la direction de Gérard Martin, car cette soirée représente de la fatigue et un surcroît de travail. Notre gracieuse Duchesse Anne 1956, Mademoiselle Annie Caro, entourée de ses demoiselles d'honneur Annick Guillerm et Elaine Le Goff, et des pages, a bien représenté notre Bretagne. Nous espérons qu'elle continuera la tradition de notre Duchesse Anne de l'an dernier Mlle Annick Corre, secrétaire de l'Association, qui a beaucoup travaillé au succès de notre groupe. Nous remercions aussi le groupe d'enfants, sous la direction de Mme Georges Capgras, qui si fièrement portait le costume du vieux pays et qui fut bien applaudie par toute la salle.

Après les discours d'usage et le couronnement de notre Duchesse Anne par Monsieur Jean de Lagarde, Ministre Plénipotentiaire et Consul Général de France à New-York, nous avons eu l'agréable surprise de l'entendre nous souhaiter en breton—une agréable soirée. Ça c'est chic et tout à l'honneur de la Franche-Comté. Merci Monsieur de Lagarde et permettez-nous d'espérer que vous serez toujours des nôtres.

Merci aussi à Monsieur James O'Brien, un fidèle ami de toujours, à Monsieur Jean Hesse, président du Comité Central et des Vétérans Français, qui a fait un si grand éloge des soldats bretons qu'il a commandés, et M. Goiran du French Folklore, M. Télémaque des Coloniaux, M. Hertrich de la Sté Culinaire Philanthropique, M. Grenier de la Ligue St. Joseph, Mme Bosquer du Vatel Club, Mme Bertini de l'Union Alsacienne, et Mlle Marie Andrée Haan, Miss France d'Amérique, pour nous avoir honorés de leur présence.

Merci encore à *France-Amérique* qui, par l'intermédiaire de son directeur M. Jacques Habert, nous réserve toujours ses colonnes pour la diffusion de nos nouvelles. Merci à tous ceux que nous pourrions oublier et qui ont contribué au succès de notre 6e Grand Bal des Ajoncs d'Or par leur travail. Disons à l'année prochaine.

Réunion du Comité de Direction, 31 Octobre 1955

La séance est ouverte par Mme Daniel, présidente.

Les minutes de l'Assemblée générale du 22 octobre 1955, sont lues par la secrétaire; ces minutes sont approuvées. Les dispositions habituelles sont prises pour notre soirée dansante au "French Chef" le 19 nov. 1955. Le Comité décide de ne pas avoir de tombola pour notre première danse, et décide aussi de ne pas avoir de soirée le 10 déc. 1955, cette date étant trop proche de nos fêtes de Noël et du 1er de l'An.

L'Arbre de Noël pour les enfants de nos membres aura lieu le dimanche 18 déc. au "French Chef." La présidente et Mme Le Berre se chargent de l'achat des jouets. Le Réveillon de la St. Sylvestre aura lieu au "French Chef" le 31 déc. au prix de $4.00 comme les années précédentes. A cette soirée, les jeunes filles désirant se faire inscrire comme candidates pour la Duchesse Anne devront donner leurs noms au Comité. Mention est faite que si l'année est profitable, une soirée gratuite pourrait être offerte, aux membres en règle, plus tard dans la saison; aucune décision n'est prise à ce sujet.

A. Kervran, du Comité des Fêtes, se charge de faire imprimer les contrats de publicité, ainsi que les affiches pour notre Grand Bal du 11 février. Georges Cariou et les "Korrigans" doivent être avisés pour nos futures danses. Le Comité décide de réserver une loge au Bal de l'Armistice le 11 novembre. Une discussion s'ensuit au sujet du Stade Breton. Y prennent part F. Cloitre et J. Le Bris, la majorité des membres du Stade Breton ne faisant pas parti de l'Association, aucune décision n'est prise à ce sujet, mais le Comité promets notre collaboration, et notre appui moral au nouveau groupement breton. — La séance est levée à 11:45 P. M.

Réunion du Comité de Direction, 6 Décembre 1955

La séance est ouverte par Mme Daniel, présidente.

Les minutes du 31 oct. 1955, sont lues et approuvées.

Les derniers arrangements sont faits pour les fêtes de l'Arbre de Noël et du Réveillon du 31 déc. 1955.

Les dispositions pour l'élection de la Duchesse Anne et l'Assemblée générale du 20 janvier 1956 au "French Chef" sont prises. L'élection sera faite par courrier comme l'année précédente.

La séance est levée à 11:30 P. M.

Figure 1. Voice of the Bretons, *journal of one of the Breton associations in New York, 1956. (Josette Jouas)*

rate of the dollar. She managed to communicate thanks to a dictionary and later went to English classes offered to the immigrants in Lenox Dale. Although she continued to speak Breton with her husband and family, she wrote in French and spoke English at work. At the age of ninety-five, she still read in Breton, French and English (Boropert 1995).

Few vestiges of Breton remain today in North America. In the United States, the census after 1970 no longer mentions Breton speakers, although Welsh, Scottish Gaelic and Irish, are still represented.[3] There seems to be a renewed interest for the language among the younger generations of Breton origin, however, echoing the revitalization in Brittany from the 1970s. For example, Breton classes are currently offered by Breton associations in Montréal (Guidroux 2011: 309-13).

Integration into a new linguistic environment is often linked with loss of traditional clothing. The Breton migrants left behind their *coiffes* and clogs, and very few of their personal photographs show any sign of the traditional Breton costume in North America. Before leaving for Canada, Jean Carduner's wife sold her *coiffe* to buy her family new clothes (Le Bihan 1997). The Coyet family emigrated to the States in 1906. When the family returned to Gourin in 1914 because of the war, Jean-Marie's wife immediately took up her Breton costume. In 1919, he returned to Lenox Dale. His two daughters soon joined him, but they did not buy new clothes in Brittany before leaving because they would not reflect American fashion (Jouas, Le Corre and Jamet 2005).

The presence of Breton speakers on North American territory is also revealed through onomastics. During his first voyage, Jacques Cartier mentioned names of towns or islands of Brittany already used for the Breton fishing communities in Newfoundland in the first half of the 16th century. They are then found on numerous maps drawn up in the 16th and 17th centuries (Litalien, Palomino and Vaugeois 2007: 210; Le Nail 2001: 11-13). Many Breton place names have been subsequently anglicized or Frenchified. The Terre des Bretons, mentioned by Samuel de Champlain in 1612, was soon renamed Acadie, while the Île du Cap Breton (on maps of the first half of the 16th century) became l'Île Royale under the French regime (even if the name of Cape Breton came back under the English regime).

The list of Breton-based place names expanded again during the 19th and 20th centuries with the coming of the clergy and colonization in the west of Canada. Villages were given names such as Quimper, Folgoët, Kermaria, Vannes, Sainte-Anne and Saint-Malo (Jouas, Le Corre and Jamet 2005: 45-50). In the second half of the 20th century, in Québec, successive toponymy commissions, concerned about the enhancement of the French past in the province, produced other Breton names (Le Nail 2001).

As to family names, there is little evidence of them from Breton-speaking Brittany, whether at the beginning of the colonies or today. No Breton-sounding name is found among the 100 most frequent family names in the province of Québec (Duchesne 2006: 10-12). One must, however, also take into account Breton names that were Frenchified: certain names, even before emigration, were hardly recognizable. For example, the name

"Legault" was derived from the name "Le Goff," a soldier from Irvillac, who served in the Navy and emigrated in 1689 (Fournier 2005: 208-209). Others were less common, but today well known thanks to the fame of their bearers, such as "Kerouac," derived from the Breton *Kervoac* (Picard 2010: xxiii; Dagier and Quéméner 1999). A parallel phenomenon of anglicization occurred in the United States. Pierre Even, from Leuhan, emigrated in 1912 and spoke only Breton. When he went through the customary steps at Ellis Island, he gave the Breton pronunciation of his name which was recorded as Haven.

Breton Literature in America

The first Breton-language literary source accurately describing Breton fishermen in North America was written by Jean Conan (1765-1834), a weaver from Guingamp. At the end of his life, he wrote *Avanturio*, an autobiography in 7,054 rhyming verses (Conan 1990). One of the first memories he described was the cod fishing season in which he participated in 1787. Leaving Paimpol in the spring, he was shipwrecked on the ice of Newfoundland, and was saved, with several of his companions, by a group of Aboriginals with whom they shared their daily lives for a period of time. His account is exceptional in more than one respect. Firstly, it is a rare example of Breton secular literature from the 18th century, written by an author from a modest background and of republican sympathies. He drew a precise picture (although romanticized) of a voyage to North America, which is, in part, representative of the countless cod fishermen on the Grand Banks of Newfoundland since the 16th century. He attested to the usage of Breton on boats, but also to the necessity of multilingualism in a transnational context. During his trip, he encountered boats from Normandy, England and Holland. Finally, the descriptions of his different encounters with Béothuks, Montagnais and Inuits are of great ethnographic and historical value (Bakker and Drapeau 1994).

Jean Conan's account is all the more invaluable since no other written work in Breton concerning immigrants in North America survives from before the French Revolution: no letter, book nor written or published document circulating in New France has been found. We can, however, mention a reference to Newfoundland in several songs in Breton, collected from oral tradition in Brittany, which refer in some cases to the *Ancien Régime* (Guillorel 2010: 352-53; Jézéquel and Giraudon 1987). America, in particular Newfoundland, is also represented, without surprise, in the French sea faring repertoire collected in Brittany, which reflects the flourishing fishing activity of the Bretons up until the 1960s (Chants des marins bretons 2007).

In the 19th century, the development of a Breton literature reaching a large audience is linked to the increase in allusions to America. *Feiz ha Breiz* (Faith and Brittany), a weekly journal published between 1865 and 1884, is the best example of the use of the Breton language to promote religious edification. It published the correspondence of Breton-speaking missionaries and moralizing stories of their religious work, and valourized Catholic missions throughout the world. There were approximately 2,000 Breton-speaking subscribers in 1875, who, in turn, relayed the journal's contents orally to their families and neighbours. *Feiz ha Breiz* contributed to spreading a heroic image of missions and an exotic vision of an America inhabited by indigenous peoples of primitive and stereotyped customs (Choplin 2011). Along the same lines, other Breton poetic compositions spoke of the saintly lives of missionaries, some of which integrated oral traditions. Thus was found a lament on the agony of Félix Poullaouec, a missionary who died of fever in Haiti, and whose body was repatriated to his hometown of Ploumoguer in 1873. The same song was found in the repertoire of a singer on the isle of Ouessant and collected in 1906 (Guillorel 2013: 298-300).

It is in the 20th century, however, that one can speak of a genuine Breton literature written by emigrants to the United States and Canada. Three of the most important Breton writers in the second half of the 20th century lived in North America. Jakez Konan, who emigrated first to Québec, and then lived in Ontario between 1952 and 1973, found there inspiration for many of his literary productions (Favereau 2008: 166-68). Reun ar C'halan, who moved to Connecticut and then to Massachusetts, is an author of fiction as well as of academic scholarship. But it is, by far, Youenn Gwernig who represents the prolific encounter between Breton literature and emigration to America. Born in Scaër in 1925, he was a poet, writer, singer, musician, composer and woodcarver who counted among his friends other renowned artists on both sides of the Atlantic. If Jack Kerouac was a personal friend and member of the Beat Generation, Youenn belonged to the Breiz Generation, along with Glenmor, Alan Stivell or Gilles Servat—all of whom expressed, through their music, their pride of being Breton. Like many children at that time, Youenn had been humiliated in school because he spoke his parent's tongue. In the 1940s, he composed and sang in Breton. In 1957, Youenn was drawn to New York. While he continued to carve wood for a living, he played bagpipes with the *Association Bretonne*. He discovered he could access many books written in Breton and started writing himself—in three languages. *Al Liamm* (the Link), a Parisian Breton magazine, published some of his works. After fifteen years on American soil, Youenn returned to Brittany, where society and culture had changed: Breton music and literature abounded, *festoù-noz* (dances) were popular, Celtic dance groups were created in every town or village, and bilingual schools (*Diwan*) were opening, but there were

Figure 2. Breton Annual Ball, New York, 1964. (Josette Jouas)

still projects to be carried out. Youenn joined other Breton personalities to create Breton programs on radio and TV. Meanwhile, he continued to write, compose and sing in Breton, French and English with his daughters. His life in New York and the weight of exile pervaded all of his works (Gwernig 1982, 1997).

We must not overlook francophone literature written by Bretons about migration to and settlement in North America. The observations made in the 19th century by François-René de Chateaubriand or Jules Verne during their voyages to the United States—landscapes, Native American populations, technological innovations—were rendered in many of the works of both these authors (Jouas, Le Corre and Jamet 2005: 22, 25). In the beginning of the 20th century, Louis Hémon (1921) wrote *Maria Chapdelaine* during his stay in Québec, inspired by the stories he heard relating the customs of earlier French Canadians. It was a big success in Canada, as well as in France. At the same period, Marie Le Franc, who lived between Brittany and Canada, was inspired by the grandiose landscapes and wrote about the people of the Laurentian forests and the fishermen of Gaspesia. In the 1970s, poet and playwright Paol Keineg lived between California and Brittany before settling permanently on the coast of the United States.

Social Institutions and Cultural Identity

Social and cultural organizations played an essential role in facilitating migration to America and in helping to preserve the links of the Bretons with their homeland and customs, especially in the 20th century.

The Michelin factory had already established a social organization for their workers which fostered a strong sense of belonging: workers and their families worked, lived, played and prayed together (the first couple to celebrate their wedding in the new Catholic Church was Breton). From the 1950s to the 1970s in New York City, two Breton clubs or associations played an important role in the development of the Breton community. In 1948, the *Association Bretonne* assembled members around the music, dances (with the folkloric group *Bleun Brug*) and costumes of Brittany. They elected their *Duchesse Anne* (Duchess of Brittany) from the young girls of Breton origin. The *Stade Breton* was a sports-oriented club of men who gathered and played soccer on Sundays. They became the embryo of a club started in 1955 which grew to be one of the first soccer teams among the foreign communities in the city. A cycling and *pétanque* section was added to diversify and meet the needs of the newer members. Their colours were black and white (like the Breton flag) and their motto was "tenacity and loyalty."

In the United States, there was no financial security for those who did not work. These Breton clubs offered social and economic aid for those who were in hospital, helped pay for medication and organized the donation of blood. Newcomers needing lodging or a job would immediately be taken care of. They both published a bulletin to keep the community informed of births, weddings, deaths and trips to Brittany and welcomed newcomers from the homeland. They helped with judicial, economic and social issues (military service, dual driver's licences, etc.). Each one held an annual picnic and ball, which allowed the community to come together, dance, play soccer or just catch up on news of family and friends on both sides of the Atlantic. They later chartered planes in the summer to facilitate visits to families left behind (Jouas, Le Corre and Jamet 2005: 113-15).

In Canada, the *Amicale Armor*, which became *l'Union des Bretons*, started after the Second World War in Montréal. It is still an active Breton association that celebrates the Feast of St. Yves (the patron saint of Brittany) and holds other events and dances. In memory of the culinary specialties of their ancestors, the Bretons serve *charcuterie*, crepes, *kouign-amann* and cider. Their bulletin, *An Amzer* (The Time), contains cultural, social and economic news of Bretons living in Canada.

Figure 3. Breton demonstration in Montréal in 1967. (Roger Moride, courtesy of the Union des Bretons du Canada)

As in the United States, there are Breton entrepreneurs who have set up factories to produce, package, transport, sell and/or export Breton cakes and pancakes. Over the years, a Breton culinary specialty, crepes, has encouraged many Bretons to open their crêperies, both in Canada and the United States, which have become a big success (Hamon and Mauras 1997; Jouas, Le Corre and Jamet 2005: 106; Guidroux 2011: 264-96).

By allowing the Bretons to assemble, such organizations give the Bretons a better visibility in Canadian society, including in the political domain. In the 1960s and 1970s, certain Bretons confronted the federal Canadian government in the struggle for an independent French Québec, making an explicit parallel with the Breton situation in France. In 1967, the day after French President General De Gaulle's visit, placards, making the comparisons between the two cultural zones, were brandished near the Montréal Town Hall, where he pronounced his famous words, *"Vive le Québec libre!"* (Guidroux 2011: 130-32).

The bonds the associations generated were also the basis of the transmission of Breton heritage today. Charles Kergaravat, President of Bzh-NY (Bzh is short for *Breizh* [Brittany]), is one of the children born in the United States to Breton parents. He and his dynamic team perpetuate the same spirit as the associations of the 1950s, 1960s and 1970s but using modern technology (Twitter, Facebook, blogs) to stay in contact with other Breton associations of the world (Bretons of Japan, of China, etc.). All together, they gather the Bretons dispersed throughout the world in a gigantic cyber-*fest-noz*. Each year in New York, there is a Breton *bagad* (pipe band) and dance group invited to take part in the famous St. Patrick's Day Parade, while a *fest-noz* is organized yearly by the Québec Celtic Festival, amid Irish and Scottish cultural activities.

Due to better communication between Brittany, Canada and the United States, contacts are still very strong today, thanks to two men in particular, Jean Montaufray and Jean Pengloan. Montaufray was a former immigrant to Canada who, upon returning to Brittany (Gourin), founded the *Amicale des Parents d'Emigrés en Amérique du Nord*. Pengloan (also from Gourin) was the charismatic President of the *Stade Breton*. They both worked hard to strengthen the ties among the three countries, organizing exchanges, celebrations and gatherings. Today, Bretagne TransAmerica (BTA), in Gourin, continues the transmission of Breton collective memory. This association organizes a permanent exhibition open to the public, retracing the footsteps of Breton immigration to North America throughout the centuries. It has collected documents, photographs, personal stories and histories concerning the thousands of Bretons who decided one day to leave their homeland. Its vocation is to illustrate the different facets of immigration (discovery, colonization, military recruitment, emigration) at different periods of time in history. Gourin (and its immediate surroundings) is a town whose members have been highly affected by emigration to North America, whether through their own direct personal experience or that of close friends and family. A replica of the Statue of Liberty stands proudly in the centre of town, evidence of its past and present link to the United States. As for Canada, in 2012, Acadia was the cultural region chosen to be the honoured guest at the renowned *Festival Interceltique* in Lorient.

Conclusion

Five centuries of contact between Brittany and North America have left noticeable and durable traces on both sides of the Atlantic Ocean. The existence of Breton communities in Canada and in the United States, and the—sometimes—strong links they have with their original country, invite us to wonder about the nature of their identities. What is it to be Breton in America? Why be Breton and how does one assert it?

Jean Le Bihan's study of a Breton family who emigrated to Saskatchewan speaks rightly of identity in terms of remembrance, loss, recollection (Le Bihan 1997: 99-101). The first years of immigration are a time of confused and conflicting coexistence of identities, cultures, traditions, languages. The old country is present in the mind; everything recalls the old life. It is also a time of transition towards the new, the future. The second stage is acceptance of loss, which allows rebirth to other values and ideas and another identity. Accepting the fact that they are no longer living in a foreign land, but in their own country, the immigrants are no longer Breton Canadians or Canadian Bretons, but Canadians of Breton origin. Letters once written regularly to the family in the homeland become letters of good wishes for the New Year, or ones announcing a death, wedding or birth. Voyages once made for important events are no longer necessary. The elders become out of touch with their native country and the young do not feel concerned. The third stage is recollection. The elders on both sides of the Atlantic pass away, only cousins remain. The former emotions, good and bad feelings towards close relations, no longer exist. Memory is limited and less important, but it becomes a moment of commemoration of times of endurance and merit, of family myths and a basis for genealogical research. Despite this loss of ancestral identity over several generations, which is linked to the cultural integration into the host country, many inhabitants of the United States and Canada still claim a Breton identity today. This claim is regularly fuelled by new waves of immigrants coming from Brittany. These Bretons in the Americas unavoidably live with multiple identities that intertwine with, complement or confront each other.

Much research on the Bretons in North America remains to be carried out. Studies to better understand the paths of the emigrants, whether as individuals or families, have intensified in recent years because of the increasing interest in issues of genealogy, identity and memory (Le Bihan 1997; Fournier 2005; Jouas, Le Corre and Jamet 2005; Guidroux 2011). No in-depth work concerning Breton-speaking Brittany, however, has yet concentrated on linguistic dimensions of the immigrant experience. We know very little concerning the number of Breton speakers in North America throughout the centuries, the strategies of transmission or non-transmission of the language and the context of its practice. In general, the under-representation of the Breton cultural domain in Celtic studies in North American academia is a serious challenge. With rare exceptions, Breton is not taught in Celtic studies or modern language departments. Irish and Welsh, and sometimes Scottish Gaelic, cultural domains get the majority of researchers' attention, while the influence of Breton scholars is limited outside of Brittany. We can only hope that in the future there will be a renewed interest in research on Brittany and the Bretons of North America and that it will find its place in international Celtic studies.

Notes

We wish to thank Francis Favereau and Rénald Lessard for their help on this chapter.

1. "Amérique, une des quatre parties de monde, doüar-nèvez – Vaisseau qui va ou qui vient d'Amérique, doüar-nevezyad, pl. doüar-nevezys, doüar-nevezydi" (Grégoire de Rostrenen 1732: 33, 917).

2. The Basque language was incorporated into the language of several Algonquin languages, such as Mi'kmaw and Montagnais, to form pidgins useful in commercial exchanges between the 17th and 18th centuries (Bakker 1989; Bakker and Grant 1996: 1150-51).

3. According to the information given by the Census of Population: Social and Economic Characteristics for the censuses of 1980, 1990, 2000 and 2005.

References

1980 Census of Population. 1982. Social and Economic Characteristics. Washington. U.S. Dept. of Commerce, Economics and Statistics Administration.

1990 Census of Population. 1993. Social and Economic Characteristics. Washington. U.S. Dept. of Commerce, Economics and Statistics Administration.

2000 Census of Population. *Modern Language Association.* http://www.mla.org/map_data_results&mode=lang_tops&SRVY_YEAR=2000&lang_id=634 (accessed 7 August 2012).

2005 Census of Population. Most spoken languages in the entire U.S. in 2005. *Modern Language Association.* http://www.mla.org/map_data_results&SRVY_YEAR=2005&geo=us&state_id=&county_id=&mode=geographic&lang_id=&zip=&place_id=&cty_id=&region_id=&division_id=&a=&ea=&order=&ll=all&pc=1 (accessed 14 November 2012).

Arlaux, Claire. 1995. *Une Amazone Bretonne, Véfa de Saint-Pierre*. Spézet: Coop Breizh.

Bakker, Peter. 1989. "The Language of the Coast Tribes is Half Basque": A Basque-American Indian Pidgin in Use between Europeans and Native Americans in North America, ca. 1540-ca. 1640. *Anthropological Linguistics* 31 (3-4): 117-47

Bakker, Peter and Lynn Drapeau. 1994. Adventures with the Beothuks in 1787: A Testimony from Jean Conan's Autobiography. In *Actes du vingt-cinquième congrès des Algonquinistes*, ed. William Cowan, 32-45. Ottawa: Carleton University.

Bakker, Peter and Anthony P. Grant. 1996. Interethnic communication in Canada, Alaska and adjacent areas. In *Atlas of Languages of Intercultural Communication in the Pacific, Asia, and the Americas*, ed. Stephen A. Wurms, Peter Mühlhäuser and Darrell T. Tryon, 1107-69. The Hague: Mouton de Gruyter.

Barbaud, Philippe. 1984. *Le choc des patois en Nouvelle-France: Essai sur l'histoire de la francisation du Canada*. Sillery: Presses universitaires du Québec.

Blenner-Hassett, Roland. 1954. A Brief History of Celtic Studies in North America. *Proceedings of the Modern Language Association* 69 (4): 3-21.

Boleda, Mario. 1984. Les migrations au Canada sous le régime français (1608-1760). *Cahiers québécois de démographie* 13 (1): 23-39.

Boropert, M. A. 1995. Interview by Josette Jouas. Loudéac.

Brasseur, Patrice. 2001. *Dictionnaire des régionalismes du français de Terre-Neuve*. Tübingen: Max Niemeyer Verlag.

Broudic, Fañch. 1995. *À la recherche de la frontière: La limite linguistique entre Haute et Basse-Bretagne au XIXe et XXe siècle*. Brest: Ar Skol Vrezoneg, Emgleo Breiz.

Brun, Régis. 1984. *Pionnier de la nouvelle Acadie, Joseph Gueguen, 1741-1825*. Ottawa: Éditions d'Acadie.

Cariou, Martine. 1987. From Brittany to America 1820-1939. MA thesis, Université Catholique de l'Ouest.

Caron-Leclerc, Marie-France. 1998. Les témoignages anciens sur le français du Canada (du XVIIe au XIXe siècle): édition critique et analyse. PhD diss., Université Laval.

Cassard, Jean-Christophe, Alain Croix, Jean-René Le Quéau and Jean-Yves Veillard. 2008. *Dictionnaire d'histoire de Bretagne*. Morlaix: Skol Vreizh.

Chants des marins bretons de Cancale à Paimpol. 2007. Phare Ouest/Musique des gens de Mer. CD-PO123505.

Choplin, Cédric. 2011. *Le chouan et le sauvage. La représentation des peuples exotiques et des missions dans Feiz ha Breiz (1865-1884)*. Rennes: Tir.

Choquette, Leslie. 1997. *Frenchmen into Peasants. Modernity and Tradition in the Peopling of French Canada*. Cambridge, MA: Harvard University Press.

Conan, Jean. 1990. *Avanturio ar citoien Jean Conan a Voengamb/Les aventures du citoyen Jean Conan de Guingamp*. Morlaix: Skol Vreizh.

Congrégation des Filles du Saint-Esprit: État actuel de la Colonie des États-Unis d'Amérique. 1912. Hartford: The Plimpton Press.

Croix, Alain. 1993. *L'âge d'or de la Bretagne: 1532-1675*. Rennes: Ouest-France.

Dagier, Patricia and Hervé Quéméner. 1999. *Jack Kerouac. Au bout de la route... La Bretagne*. Le Relec-Kerhuon: An Here.

David, Albert. 1931-1932. L'abbé Le Loutre. *Revue de l'Université d'Ottawa* 1 (4): 474-85 and 2 (1): 65-75.

Delisle, Philippe. 2003. *Le catholicisme en Haïti au XIXe siècle: Le rêve d'une « Bretagne noire » (1860-1915)*. Paris: Karthala.

Douville, Raymond. 1975. *Les tribulations d'un guérisseur à Sainte-Anne-de-la-Pérade au 18e siècle : Yves Phlem, ancêtre des familles Hivon*. Collection Nos vieilles familles 3.

Duchaussois, Pierre. 1934. *Aventures canadiennes des Sœurs grises*. Paris: Flammarion.

Duchesne, Louis. 2006. *Les noms de famille au Québec: aspects statistiques et distribution spatiale*. Québec: Institut de la statistique du Québec.

Duigou, Serge and Germain Lacasse. 1987. *Marie de Kerstrat, l'aristocrate du cinématographe*. Quimper, France: Ressac.

Dumont-Johnson, Micheline. 1970. *Apôtres ou agitateurs: la France missionnaire en Acadie*. Trois-Rivières, QC: Boréal.

Favereau, Francis. 2008. *Anthologie de la littérature bretonne au XXe siècle*. Vol. 3, 1945-1968. Morlaix, France: Skol Vreizh.

Fishman, Joshua A., Michael Gertner, Esther Lowy and William Milan. 1982. Maintien des langues, « renouveau ethnique » et diglossie aux États-Unis. *La linguistique* 18 (1): 45-64.

Flatrès, Pierre. 1959. Bretagne et Canada: quelques aspects de l'émigration bretonne au Canada. *Cahiers de géographie du Québec* 3 (6): 103-13.

Fournier, Marcel. 1981. *Dictionnaire biographique des Bretons en Nouvelle-France, 1600-1765*. No. 4 of *Collection Études et recherches archivistiques*. Québec: Ministère des affaires culturelles/Archives nationales du Québec.

———. 2005. *Les Bretons en Amérique française, 1504-2004*. Rennes: Les portes du large.

Frenette, Yves. 2008. L'apport des immigrants français aux francophonies canadiennes. *Francophonies d'Amérique* 26:309-30.

Gauthier, Élie. 1953. *L'émigration bretonne*. Paris: Bulletin de l'entr'aide bretonne de la région parisienne.

Godbout, Archange. 1946. Nos hérédités provinciales françaises. *Les Archives de folklore* 1:26-40.

Grégoire de Rostrenen. 1732. *Dictionnaire françois-celtique, ou françois-breton*. Rennes: Julien Vatar.

Guidroux, Linda. 2011. Appartenances culturelles et ethnologie des migrations. Les Bretons émigrants au Québec depuis 1950. PhD diss., Université Laval, Université de Bretagne occidentale.

Guillorel, Éva. 2010. *La complainte et la plainte. Chanson, justice, cultures en Bretagne (XVIe-XVIIIe siècles)*. Rennes, Brest: Presses universitaires de Rennes, Dastum, Centre de recherche bretonne et celtique.

———, ed. 2013. *Barzaz Bro-Leon. Une expérience inédite de collecte en Bretagne*. Rennes: Presses universitaires de Rennes.

Gwernig, Youenn. 1982. *La Grande Tribu*. Paris: Grasset.

———. 1997. *Un dornad plu/A handful of feathers*. Brest: Al Liamm.

Hamon, Olivier and Véronique Mauras. 1997. *Ces Bretons du Canada*. Saint-Thonan, France: Cloître imprimeurs.

Hémon, Louis. 1921. *Maria Chapdelaine*. Paris: Grasset.

Jézéquel, Yves and Daniel Giraudon. 1987. Terre-Neuviers victimes des Barbaresques au XVIIe siècle. Gwerz Itron Varia a Bennwern. *Musique Bretonne* 73:5-10.

Jouas, Josette, Christian Le Corre and Christiane Jamet. 2005. *Ces Bretons d'Amérique du Nord*. Rennes: Ouest-France.

Lalonde, André. 1993. The French Canadians of the West: Hope, Tragedy, Uncertainty. In *French America: mobility, identity, and minority experience accross the continent*, ed. Dean R. Leader and Eric Waddell, 100-16. Baton Rouge: Louisiana State University Press.

Lanctot, Gustave. 2000. La Roche de Mesgouez, Troilus de. *Dictionary of Canadian Biography Online*. University of Toronto, Université Laval. http://www.biographi.ca/009004-119.01-e.php?&id_nbr=395 (accessed 30 August 2012).

Le Bihan, Jean. 1997. Enquête sur une famille bretonne émigrée au Canada (1903-1920). *Prairie Forum: The Journal of the Canadian Plains Research Center* 22 (1): 73-102.

Le Clec'h, Grégoire. 1954-1955. Sur la piste des émigrants bretons en Amérique. *Penn ar Bed* 4-5:36-49.

———. 1969. Quelques figures de pionniers de l'émigration bretonne au Canada et aux États-Unis. *Bulletin de la société archéologique du Finistère* 95:277-304.

———. 1974. La fondation de la paroisse de Saint-Brieux, Saskatchewan (Canada) en 1904. *Bulletin de la Société archéologique du Finistère* 102:110-29.

Le Loutre, Jean-Louis. 1738. Letter, 1 October. Centre de référence de l'Amérique Française, Archives du Séminaire de Québec, sme 2.1/r/087.

Le Nail, Bernard. 2001. *Noms de lieux bretons à travers le monde*. Rennes: Les portes du large.

Litalien, Raymonde, Jean-François Palomino and Denis Vaugeois. 2007. *Mapping a Continent: Historical Atlas of North America, 1492-1814*. Trans. Kathe Röth. Georgetown, QC: Presses de l'Université McGill, Queen's University Press, Septentrion.

Méhérenc de Saint-Pierre, Comtesse G. de. 1908. En dehors de la Civilisation. *Le Mois Littéraire et Pittoresque* 10 (20): 56-76.

Memoire instructif contenant griefs et moyens d'appel pour le sieur Yves Phlem, chirurgien etabli sur le fief de Ste Anne près Batiscan, appelant. 1737. Bibliothèque et Archives nationales du Québec, TL5, D1145, pièce 1145-24.

Michel, Joseph. 1997. *Missionnaires bretons d'outre-mer: XIXe-XXe siècles.* Rennes: Presses universitaires de Rennes.

Mimeault, Mario. 1999. Bretons. Encyclopedia of Canada's Peoples. *Multicultural Canada.* http://www.multiculturalcanada.ca/Encyclopedia/A-Z/b7 (accessed 21 September 2012).

Morin, Yves-Charles. 2002. Les premiers immigrants et la prononciation du français au Québec. *Revue québécoise de linguistique* 31 (1): 39-78.

Mougeon, Raymond and Édouard Beniak. 1994. *Les origines du français québécois.* Sainte-Foy: Presses de l'Université Laval.

Patault, M. V. 1967. Breton Emigration to the United States. MA thesis, Université de Rennes.

Picard, Marc. 2010. *Dictionnaire des noms de famille du Canada français: anthroponymie et généalogie.* Sainte-Foy: Presses de l'Université Laval.

Plourin, Jean-Yves and Mireille Cadic. 1985-1986. Aspects linguistiques de l'émigration langonnetaise vers l'Amérique. *La Bretagne Linguistique* 2:82-86.

Simard, Jean. 1995. Le modèle breton. *Les Cahiers des Dix* 50:55-70.

Tardieu, Marc. 2003. *Les Bretons à Paris: de 1900 à nos jours.* Paris: Éditions du Rocher.

Trudel, Marcel. 1963. *Histoire de la Nouvelle-France: I-Les vaines tentatives 1524-1603.* Montréal: Fides.

———. 1973. *La population du Canada en 1663.* Montréal: Fides.

———. 2000a. Cartier, Jacques. *Dictionary of Canadian Biography Online.* University of Toronto, Université Laval. http://www.biographi.ca/009004-119.01-e.php?&id_nbr=107 (accessed 30 August 2012).

———. 2000b. Gravé Du Pont, François. *Dictionary of Canadian Biography Online.* University of Toronto, Université Laval. http://www.biographi.ca/009004-119.01-e.php?&id_nbr=321 (accessed 30 August 2012).

Violain, Didier. 1997. *Bretons de Paris: des exilés en capitale.* Paris: Parigramme.

Bernard Deacon

Chameleon Celts: The Cornish in the Americas

Cornwall is an ambiguous place. Geographically at the edge of Europe, it balances precariously between continental land mass and Atlantic Ocean. Politically part of the English state since medieval times, its people look back to cultural roots in a non-English and Celtic past. Narratives of the Cornish past echo this ambiguity. One such narrative, prominent among the Cornish themselves, is a tale of worldliness, of an industrial rise and fall. Another, more familiar outside Cornwall, is etched with distinctly otherworldly mystery, magic and romance. Yet, these stories are on closer inspection less starkly opposed than they first appear. Indeed, the same element can appear in both narratives. Physical artifacts of the Cornish landscape move from stony realism to subtle representation, their meaning transformed in the process. For instance, the buildings housing the steam engines that pumped Cornwall's mines, hoisted its minerals and stamped its ores were classic parts of realist Cornwall. But they are now also part of romantic Cornwall. Their bleak ruins point to a long-lost golden age. Rather than distinct and separate, the realist and romantic narratives within which the Cornish have been located are themselves hybrid and ambiguous, with movement across blurred borders. Furthermore, just as narratives of the Cornish oscillate between gritty realism and ethereal romanticism, so too the Cornish have sometimes integrated with their English neighbours, but at other times loudly proclaimed their difference from them.

The emigration of thousands of Cornish people in the 19th century is often designated with the descriptor "great" and given upper case letters. This "Great Migration" has not escaped a typically Cornish ambivalence. At the time it was viewed as a great accomplishment, as the Cornish helped to wrest "civilization" out of the "wilderness." But it was also seen, then and increasingly later, as a symptom of Cornwall's decline. The exodus of the brightest and best of its people was a journey of loss and decay (Payton 1999: 17). Ambiguous or not, Cornwall's emigrants were firmly set within a realist narrative. Histories were solidly economic and social in orientation, focusing on heroic family sagas and individual epics, the emigrants' contributions to their receiving societies (Rowe 1974; Rowse 1967; Todd 1966). Yet this economic and social narrative came at the expense of the cultural. According to Rowse, the Cornish "have not been much a writing folk—more expert with pick and shovel than with the pen" (1967: 18). Only recently have rich veins of hidden literature been exposed and the literary life of the Cornish overseas re-introduced to the folk back home.

Back there—"over home" as Cornish emigrants in 19th-century America would have said—the traces of the "Great Migration" are "the defining trait of modern Cornish identity" (James-Korany 1993; Kent 2000: 223). For the modern Cornish person, locked into a politically ignored territory undergoing rapid anglicization, emigrant forebears offer a way of escaping an ambiguous location either as an indistinguishable part of England or an often-overlooked minor player in a Celtic symphony. The international links forged by past generations in the Americas, Australasia and South Africa open the horizons of those Cornish left in Cornwall. They speak of an outward-looking, international aspect to Cornishness, an added layer to its Celticity and a potential release from the confines of its constrained contemporary political and cultural dilemma.

This chapter will attempt to bring together the hitherto separate strands of the Cornish migration experience—the realist focus on the course, causes and contribution of Cornish migrants and the representations of themselves that the resultant transplanted communities created. It first outlines the context for the chameleon-like character of the Cornish in the so-called New World, the continuation of an ambiguity that can be traced throughout its history (for hybridity in Cornwall, see Deacon 2007a; Kent 2010). Second, it focuses on the course and causes of Cornish migration to the Americas, before identifying the characteristics of visibly Cornish communities. Third, it synthesizes the evidence for the presence of the Cornish language in North America, but first argues that the real contribution of the Cornish linguistically was not via its former Celtic language but its post-Celtic Cornu-English dialect. Finally, it notes the astonishing rebirth of a hybrid Cornish American ethnicity and the reappearance of the Cornish language on the western side of the "herring pond" before concluding with some suggestions for further work on the Cornish in the Americas.

A Rational Ethnicity?

The Cornish perpetually hover on the brink of invisibility. To a large degree this is a function of size. Even in the 21st century, the 540,000 people who live in Cornwall, not all of them Cornish, make up less than 1 per cent of the population of Great Britain. This was equally so in the 19th century when Cornwall's population peaked somewhere around 370,000 in the mid-1860s. That figure was around a quarter of the population of Wales, a ninth of that of Scotland and a mere fifteenth of the size of the Irish population even after its depopulation following the Famine (Woods 1995: 10).

Numerically challenged, the Cornish could seem invisible on the Celtic stage for other reasons. First and foremost was language. In 1901 the Pan Celtic Congress voted to postpone admittance of Cornwall on the grounds that Cornish, a Brythonic language closest to Breton, was no longer a living Celtic language, having ceased to be used as an everyday means of communication at the very end of the 18th century. Nonetheless, almost as soon as it was decently dead and buried, antiquarians had begun to try to bring the corpse back to life by collecting and publishing its fragments. This eventually led to attempts to revive a version of the spoken language and the appearance of a Cornish grammar in 1904, which belatedly convinced the Pan Celtic Congress meeting at Caernarfon to accord Cornwall membership (Williams 2004: 96-97). Although "perhaps the most obscure of Celts" (James 1994: 34), the loss of their language had not prevented some Cornish from stubbornly maintaining a Celtic status in the face of skepticism from their bigger siblings. In fact, the term "Celtic" had been used in Cornwall as a self-descriptor from the 18th century and was given greater impetus in the middle of the 19th century after the idea of a "Celtic" literature emerged and Cornwall's archaeological remains began to be described as "Celtic" (Naylor 2003).

If the status of Cornwall was and is indistinct in Britain, sometimes a Celtic country, at other times an English county, the ethnic status of its emigrants is also unclear. A series of books on the ethnic groups of the Pacific North West published in 1981, for example, includes the Scots, Germans and Chinese, among others, but the Cornish are subsumed as part of the "English" (Green 1981). On the other hand Calhoon (1986), when listing the various ethnic groups in early California, separated the Cousin Jacks (as the Cornish were commonly known) from the English. The manner in which the Cornish in the States seemed content enough to join civic associations such as the Sons of St. George, restricted to those of "English" ancestry, added to the ambiguity surrounding their ethnicity (Ewart 1998: 35). This ambiguity continued a familiar theme back in Cornwall. Sometimes the Cornish would be English but, when it suited them, not of England.

There were advantages to this flexible strategy, especially for a small, vulnerable group living next to a powerful and often aggressive neighbour. There were also advantages after migration. Todd has called the Cornish in America "at one and the same time the most and least American of all the emigrants for they could don and doff the costume of a new people almost at will"(1966: 26). The Cornish were able, perhaps more than others, to choose their ethnicity. Mulligan pointed out how the Cornish were an "extreme case" of Charlotte Erickson's invisible English immigrants in the U.S. English-speaking, Protestant and with economically saleable skills, they were "able to enter American society with few difficulties" (1958: vii). Others have more recently built on this insight. The Cornish could choose whether to "perpetuate their ethnic character." Often they did so as a strategy "to secure preferential employment in the mines" (James 1994). At other times and in non-mining contexts there was no occupational advantage to be gained from stressing their separate ethnicity. In such cases, as in Victoria, British Columbia, "the non-mining Cornish exhibited few of the ethnic group behaviours" of their mining compatriots (Mindenhall 2000). The visible Cornish were a particular variety of Cornish, the Cousin Jacks of the mining communities. To understand their distinct culture we have to first place them in the broader context of Cornwall's migration experience.

Miners on the Move: From Cornwall to Little Cornwalls

By the end of the 1860s homogenously Cornish communities could be found scattered across the globe. The two most clearly Cornish places were the northern Yorke peninsula of South Australia and Grass Valley in California. Grass Valley grew during the 1850s as streaming for gold was supplanted by deep mining and Cornish miners flocked to a district where their expertise found a ready market. While these were the epicentres of a global Cornish identity, there were other recognizably Cornish communities. The Cornish had arrived in the upper peninsula of Michigan on the northernmost edge of the U.S. in the 1840s and soon made it home. In the same decade, the lead mining region of southwest Wisconsin around Mineral Point contained distinct Cornish communities, as did towns like Virginia City, Colorado, and Butte, Montana, later in the century.

What produced these Little Cornwalls? Mass emigration from Cornwall became the norm in the 1840s and continued into the middle years of the 20th century. We can calculate from census records that there was a net emigration flow of around 144,000 from Cornwall overseas in the second half of the 19th century, 80 per cent direct from Cornwall and 20 per cent via intermediate places in England and Wales (Deacon 2007b). If we assume a return rate of 30 to 40 per cent this suggests a gross migration of between 185,000 and 200,000 in the years before 1900. At least half of these, perhaps as many as two thirds, must have gone to the Americas. This was a considerable number in relative terms given that Cornwall's 19th-century population never exceeded 370,000. Indeed, Cornwall has been described as "an emigration region comparable with any in Europe" at this time (Baines 1985: 157). Nevertheless, while relatively important, Cornish emigrants made up only a small minority of the estimated four million emigrants from "England" and in absolute terms hardly compared with the seven million who left Ireland (Richards 2004: 6). A small group of this size could easily have been lost among the millions heading west, especially given that the Cornish seemed pre-programmed to become Americans. In 1842 it was reported of the mining communities of west Cornwall that there was "a character of independence – something American – to this population" (Barham 1842: 759). While the geographical distance between Cornwall and North America was considerable, the cultural distance was less so.

The reason the thousands who left Cornwall for the Americas were not irrecoverably lost in that melting pot was not because they were a culturally distinct Celtic people but because they made up an occupationally distinct group. By the late 18th century the Cornish economy was moving to the rhythm of international metal markets. By the 1850s around a third of Cornish men were directly employed in the tin, copper and silver/lead mines of Cornwall. Miners followed the mines, determined to pursue their occupational calling rather than try something new (Burt and Kippen 2001). The vicissitudes of the mining industry structured the geography of Cornish settlement and concentrated sufficient Cornish folk in certain places to produce the Little Cornwalls that mimicked the mining communities of home.

The characteristics of migration from Cornwall also changed over time. When large-scale flows began at the very end of the 1830s, farmers and labourers from agricultural parts of Cornwall were prominent. Much of these were to Canada, although that migration stream tapered off rapidly in the late 1850s. That first flow of free migrants joined a separate and slightly earlier movement of miners contracted to open up metal mines in Mexico, Chile and Brazil from the 1820s. Migrants continued to move to Latin America into the mid-century and afterwards. Indeed, Pachuca in Mexico attained "Little Cornwall" status for a time in the third quarter of the 19th century (Schwartz 2005). During the 1840s, however, these dispersed flows gave way first to a focus on the lead mining region of southern Wisconsin around Mineral Point and then the copper and iron mines of the Keweenaw Peninsula of upper Michigan. Nonetheless, in the 1840s, migrants from Cornwall remained a mix of agriculturists and miners.

That changed after the discovery of gold in California. By the 1860s, destinations shifted westwards, first to California and then in the 1870s and 1880s to the states of Colorado, Nevada, Utah, Montana and Arizona, which joined Michigan as favoured destinations. The discovery of the Comstock lode in western Nevada in 1859 heralded new opportunities in western mining for the "Cornish expert, self-trained and uninhibited, who formed the backbone of practical mine management during the entire period" (Spence 1958: 13). Later in the century there is evidence that the proportion of women among emigrants to the U.S. fell—from around half the number of men at mid-century to between 30 and 40 per cent by the 1890s, a far lower proportion than English and Scottish migrants (Gabaccio 1996). This indicates a migration stream characterized more by the classic single roaming miner than families. It also hints at a greater likelihood of return migration, something supported by a rapid growth in remittances from the States back to Britain from the late 1870s to the 1910s (Magee and Thompson 2005). Meanwhile, in the later 1850s migration from agricultural districts suddenly declined and Cornish emigrants were increasingly likely to be miners and their families. By the 1880s the highest numbers of emigrants set out from the mining parishes of Redruth, Camborne, Breage, Crowan, St. Agnes, Lelant and St. Ives. This occupationally concentrated migration stream culturally replenished the transplanted Cornish communities dominated by mining overseas.

What caused this outpouring from Cornwall? On the surface the explanation looks straightforward, a simple case of the movement of miners from a declining mining region with a shrinking labour force to new regions with higher pay. Baines asserts that the quantity of emigration from Cornwall was "obviously connected with the decline of copper and tin mining after the crisis of 1866" (1985: 159). "Connected" perhaps but not quite so "obviously." For migration was already running at a high level before the late 1860s, during the relatively prosperous years of the 1850s. Moreover, the detailed chronology of migration suggests that it may have been at its peak when mining was booming at home, rather than in crisis (Schwartz 2005). It was precisely then that demand for skilled miners within a global labour market was greatest. Having established a myth of Cousin Jack's mining expertise, by the 1830s Cornwall was a "major reserve of skilled mining labour" (Richards 2004: 133). The early emergence of a global labour market in mining had also produced what Payton (1995) terms an emigration trade, as emigration agents found profitable business in Cornwall. Their activities reinforced migration chains already forged and a cultural context predisposed to look favourably on emigration. These overcame the poverty constraint on migration from an early point, with virtually all Cornish migration to North America being self-financed or aided by remittances from previous migrants.

Later there was less choice. Then, according to Schwartz (2002), a strategy of individual and family advancement gave way to one of risk diversification as younger male members of the family migrated, often roaming vast distances and between continents as they pursued the mining frontiers in order to mobilize financial remittances. Schwartz's important critique seeks to replace an explanation of Cornish emigration that stresses push factors and the collective tragedy of a diasporic scattering with a more flexible, less pessimistic and less structural view of Cornish migration. This intervention serves to qualify earlier reliance on more structural models of a flexible reserve army of labour (Burke 1984) or the inherently peripheral location of the Cornish economy within the British state (Payton 1992). It does not necessarily replace those broader explanations but can be combined with them, reminding us of elements of the migration story missing in previous accounts—for example, the role of remittances in Cornwall, the role of women in a traditionally extremely male-biased narrative and the extent of return migration, especially in the later phases of migration.

Women played a critical role in the maintenance and reproduction of the values characteristic of the Little Cornwalls. Much of their activity would have been outside the formal associational networks that bound male Cornish migrants together. These latter would have included freemasons' lodges (Burt 2003), which Payton argues functioned as surrogate Cornish associations in many places (1999: 37). Later, in the 1890s, formal Cornish associations arose, but these tended to become nostalgic reminders of home with a limited rather than mass membership (Payton 1999: 378; Schwartz 2006). But perhaps the most ubiquitous social institution colouring the lives of the Cornish was one more likely to have involved women in its activities: the Methodist church. Wherever the Cornish roamed, they invariably recorded the building of Methodist chapels. Methodism and the round of religious life was a world within which women played a critical role, although it remains an under-researched one. Their Methodist allegiance was one part of the "cultural baggage" that the Cornish brought with them (Langton 1997: 63). Accompanying it were distinct foods, notably the meat-, potato- and turnip-filled pasties that were a mainstay of the Cornish diet, and folklore such as the underground tommyknockers, spirits who, like the Cornish, exercised their cultural sway underground (Manning 2005). The Methodist heritage included hymn-singing, and this gave rise to a stereotype of the Cornish as an especially musical people. Brass and silver bands were commonly encountered in mining communities, but perhaps the best-known Cornish musical contribution was their love of choral music and particular carols. These contributions achieved their institutional expression in the annual Christmas carol-singing at Grass Valley (McKinney 2001). Other cultural activities flourished in the Americas to a later date than in Cornwall itself. Wrestling was one, with well-attended wrestling tournaments recorded on the Keweenaw peninsula into the 1930s (Thurner 1994: 253).

Whenever Little Cornwalls arose, this mix of cultural activities and the Cornish monopoly of the better-paid, supervisory jobs at many mines helped to give rise to a very common stereotype of Cornish clannishness. In the 1860s it was stated that on the Keweenaw peninsula "the Cousin Jacks have everything sewed up" (Thurner 1994: 155). A Grass Valley newspaper of 1871 described the Cornish as "more clannish than any other foreigners" (qtd. in Payton 1999: 216). Residential segregation, occupational exclusivity, religious homogeneity and cultural particularity were the everyday aspects of Cornish immigrant mining communities:

> The Cornish took with them an American frontier version of their Cousin Jack (and Cousin Jenny) ethnic identity, one moulded in Wisconsin, honed on the Lakes and given expression in a score of western mining camps from Grass Valley to Virginia City to Leadville, Nevadaville and Butte. (Payton 1999: 160)

Cornish control of the best-paid mining jobs and their confusing chameleon identity—sometimes Cornish, sometimes English—led to longstanding animosity from the Irish, which was fully reciprocated. There is little evidence of any inter-Celtic solidarity in the behaviour of these groups on the western mining frontiers of the 19th century or on Michigan's Keweenaw peninsula. In the 1860s it was reported from Hancock that the "Cornish-hating Irish ... viewed all English as inveterate enemies" (Thurner 1994: 77). Economic competition combined with religious difference to reinforce the mutual suspicion of Cornish and Irish, a suspicion that on many occasions spilled over into violence. Conflict reached a head in the early 1890s when the Western Federation of Miners was fatally "handicapped by chronic Irish-Cornish feuding within the Butte Union" (Payton 1999: 337).

Talking Cousin Jack: Cornish emigrants and their language

An occupationally specific people who were technological leaders in their chosen field could be expected to contribute much to the technical language of that economic sector. And so it was. Perhaps the Cornish emigrants' greatest contribution was to provide "a language that became a lingua franca in mining camps the world over" (Todd 1966: 16). As miners scattered across the globe they took with them their specialized vocabulary of mining, a vocabulary infused with older words, some of which had their origin in the Cornish language.

While their vocabulary dominated underground, dialect terms and Cornish intonation would have been commonplace in the Little Cornwalls overground for a couple of generations at least. The final oft-commented-upon characteristic of the Cornish in the Americas was their dialect of English. In 1880 the folklorist William Bottrell wrote of the "ancient Cornish language in the colonies" but he was referring not to Cornwall's Celtic language but to the way Cornu-English dialect was deliberately deployed by Cornishmen to ensure jobs went to Cousin Jacks. The Cornish could always find work in Butte for example provided they "spoke the right spoke" (Hand 1946: 175). Meanwhile, in Grass Valley in 1911, where it was estimated "three quarters of the people were of Cornish birth or descent" their dialect was described as "almost unintelligible" (McKinney 2009: 293). Even as late as the 1930s it was reported that "you couldn't get a job unless you talked 'Cousin Jack' [Cornish dialect]" (McKinney 2009: 272). Yet, even here we might suspect that dialect was sometimes deliberately employed instrumentally as part of a conscious ethnic display for economic advantage, for there is contradictory evidence of the motives for employing such dialects. A boy arriving at Grass valley from St. Austell in Cornwall in 1885 dropped his accent because "everyone" at his school made fun of his "heavy Cornish accent" (Ewart 1998: 45).

More generally, dialect was a "signifier of Cornish difference" (Kent 2004: 124). Thurner reports that a key element in that difference was a "practical joke, for the Cornish played them often, with subtle sardonicism" (1994: 136). What was noted in upper Michigan reappeared in Montana where Cornish miners were described as possessing "delightful humour and colourful speech" (Hand 1946: 174). The humour was most effective in short, pithy tales with a punch line that worked by playing on misplaced words and malapropisms. A tendency to mix up pronouns was evident. As the common Cousin Jack story tells us, "We do call anything 'she' excepting a tomcat, and we call 'er "e'" (qtd. in Kent 2004: 130). The Cornish did not hesitate to poke fun at themselves; their humour contained a strong element of the in-joke, not always easily decoded by outsiders. Many of these tales were originally part of an oral tradition, the extension, argues Kent, of a Cornish droll-telling tradition back home that was fast dying out in the mid-19th century. This was overlain in turn by written dialect tales, a popular commercial genre of later 19th-century Cornwall. Kent likens the droll-telling tradition to the travelling storytellers of Gaelic Ireland and Scotland, although James (2010) reminds us that, unlike the conservatism of the Gaelic version, the Cornish drolls were spontaneous and innovative, changing form and content to suit their audience.

With a uniformly mining metaphorical base (exactly reflecting dialect tales in Cornwall) many of the Cousin Jack narratives of North America were committed to paper in the 1920s and 1930s. The stories of D. A. Charlton and the recently rediscovered collection of Walter Gries from upper Michigan supplied a "new droll of modernism" (Kent and McKinney 2008: 20). For Kent this is "a vital literary form, uniquely linked to industrial experience" and "perhaps our finest representation of industrial Celtic culture" (20). The 1930s and 1940s were not only the great age of the Cousin Jack narratives but also "the golden age of the great novels of the Cornish emigration experience" (21). Interestingly, they were written about a generation later than a wave of indigenous novels in Cornwall chronicling industrial Cornwall. These had appeared as the sun was most definitely setting on the great days of Cornish mining and engine houses were fast joining Celtic standing stones or medieval castles as romantic ruins. However, the survival of mining communities into the inter-war period overseas postponed the demise of the Cornish culture there by a few decades.

Timing was not the only difference between the novels of Cornwall and the Cornish novels of America. While literature at home was suffused with fatalism and loss and increasingly introverted, that in America contained a strong theme of accomplishment and achievement (Payton 1999: 378). Jim Holman, the central character in Newton G. Thomas's *The Long Winter Ends* (1941), about a year in the life of an immigrant on the Keweenaw peninsula, charts his gradual realization that his future lies in America as he abandons his original intention of returning. By implication, his hope of preserving Cornish traditions in America is replaced by an optimism induced by becoming American. Both Cousin Jack narratives and Cornish-American novels creatively used Cornu-English, a genre that in the last decade Alan Kent has done much to rehabilitate to its proper place in the Cornish literary tradition.

Nonetheless, while containing the odd survival from Celtic Cornish, this was a literature written in a variety of English. But is there any evidence of traces of Cornwall's Celtic language in the Americas? As Mulligan (1958: vii) observed, the Cornish had seen "their distinct language all but disappear before they began large-scale migration to America in the 1840s." That has not stopped considerable speculation about individual emigrants carrying that language over the Atlantic with them (Kent 2007). Clearly, in the 16th century, when up to half the Cornish population spoke Cornish, it is almost certain that some emigrants would have been Cornish speakers. There was Cornish involvement in the doomed Roanake colony of the 1580s, but it seems to have been mainly from eastern, English-speaking Cornwall. A more likely colonization venture to include Cornish speakers would have been the second Virginia charter of 1609, when some Western landlords were involved. While this may have provided an "early tight window of opportunity" for the Cornish language in America (Kent 2007), that window closed very quickly in the 17th century. Moreover, migrants at this time tended to be part of wider groups more likely to be bound together by religion than ethnicity. The dominant means of communication was no doubt English, so even families whose home language was Cornish would have been forced to employ English to communicate with other settlers.

Much has been made of a letter written in Cornish in 1710 by the early 18th-century revivalist William Gwavas. It was addressed to *"An poble hui, en pow America"* (you people in America) and contained a simplified version of the Apostles' Creed in Cornish. Nance, the leading early 20th-century language revivalist, viewed this letter "as a specimen of the language" sent "to some persons or group of persons in America" (1925: 37). Others have been less cautious. Pool states that the letter implies "that some Cornish speakers had emigrated and that the language was spoken, or at least understood, in America" (1982: 16-17). Ellis went even further, saying that "these letters [sic] were sent to exiled Cornishmen who had taken their knowledge of the language with them" (1974: 100). But as Kent observes, "most Cornish-language scholarship has failed to grasp the nettle of this text" (2007: 202). In reality, the letter tells us nothing at all about anyone's ability to speak Cornish. All it suggests is that some person or persons read a Cornish text in the Americas. It is likely that Gwavas sent it to one of his antiquarian correspondents in the thirteen colonies as an example of written Cornish, an extension of his activities in Cornwall. The intended recipient may have had some knowledge of spoken Cornish or may have been a non-speaker interested in seeing an example of the written language. We do not even know if they were Cornish.

While Gwavas addressed his letter to people *"uncuth dho nei"* (strangers to us), we do know the name of one individual emigrant recorded as being able to converse in Cornish. In the 1770s the English antiquarian Daines Barrington visited Cornwall seeking evidence of the Cornish language. In addition to the famed fishwife of Mousehole, Dolly Pentreath—reputed almost certainly erroneously to be the last speaker of Cornish—Barrington mentioned a John Nancarrow. Nancarrow emigrated from Marazion to Philadelphia in 1774 and was "one of the few persons who could speak Cornish; he having learned it from the country-folk in his youth," which would have been around the 1750s (Anon. 1932). He was last heard of alive in New York in 1804 after a number of unsuccessful business ventures. Even in the case of the elusive Nancarrow, keeping one step ahead of his creditors, "the extent of his ability to speak [Cornish] remains a mystery" (Jeffery 1985: 35).

Nevertheless, Nancarrow may have a claim to be the last Cornish speaker in the Americas. One further possibility remains. William Rowe was a farmer in the St. Just district in the far west of Cornwall who set out in the late 17th century to translate parts of the Bible into Cornish, getting as far as one chapter of the Book of Genesis and two of Matthew. Some of Rowe's descendants were known to have emigrated to North America from Sancreed and it has been suggested that they may have taken some of Rowe's Cornish language work with them. However, this remains speculative and perhaps is best seen as an example of the wishful thinking of a modern Cornish revivalist movement desperate to uncover any evidence for use of the language into the 19th century.

Rediscovering Cornish Roots: Cornishness in Present-Day North America

As Cornish language enthusiasts in Cornwall continued to hunt for specimens of the language, the vibrant Cornu-English communities and Cornish culture of the Little Cornwalls in the States began to wither. Formally, few Cornish associations survived the Second World War. Informally, the second and third generations of migrants lost their distinctive accent. Sometimes, this process was encouraged by the first generation. Harvey Wearne's parents migrated to Grass Valley in the 1910s. He recalled,

> [my parents] raised their children as Americans.... My father got rid of his brogue as soon as he arrived in this country, and when I went back to England for a visit and learned the brogue and brought it back with me, he told me "You've had your fun, now knock it off." (qtd. in Kent and McKinney 2008: 253)

Although Grass Valley—where mining survived into the early 1950s—was perhaps the last place to retain a distinctive Cornish ambience, even here its "unofficial designation as the Cornish capital of America" was fading (McKinney 2009: 293). By 1953 it was reported that it was "becom[ing] increasingly difficult to tell who's a Cousin Jack or a 'Cousin Jenny'" (qtd. in Schwartz 2006: 176). By mid-century, both here and in upper Michigan, the two epicentres of Cornish culture in the Americas, "many Cornish cultural events were increasingly stage-managed," and, "as Americanization proceeded, the descendants of the Cornish became even more self-conscious of their culture" (Thurner 1994: 138). Sometimes, memories had all but dissipated completely. Donald Rickard was proud to assert his Cornish antecedents when at school in Wisconsin in the early 20th century but "[they] had no idea what Cornish was [and] were never able to find out anyone very interested or willing to be aware of its importance" (Payton 1999: 143).

Cornishness was slipping apparently inevitably into the mists of memory, doomed to oblivion as the mining communities of old became monuments to an age of industry fast being replaced by financial services and shopping malls. With the decline of industry there seemed no place left for the industrial Celt. But then the unexpected happened. At some point in the late 1960s or 1970s people began to turn to their Cornish roots with greater enthusiasm; by the 1980s "the Cornish had suddenly re-emerged, as if from nowhere" (Payton 1999: 392; Birt in this volume). This soon took institutional form. The first Cornish association reappeared in North America in the Cornish Heritage Society, formed in Illinois in 1982. This was stimulated by an earlier re-emergence of Cornish societies and festivals in Australia in the 1970s. The Cornish Heritage Society organized two Cornish Gatherings in 1982 at Detroit and Mineral Point, before settling into a regular biennial gathering. By the sixth Cornish Gathering at Victoria in British Columbia in 1991, thirty-eight Cornish associations were represented and people attended from Australia and Cornwall. Cornish associations possibly peaked in activity at the turn of the millennium, but many remain active, notably at Keweenaw, Milwaukee, southwest Wisconsin, Chicago, New Jersey, Pennsylvania, California and Toronto. With a few exceptions, their geography reflects that of Cornish settlement, with half of the sixteen Cornish Gatherings from 1982 to 2011 hosted on Michigan's upper peninsula, southwest Wisconsin or California.

In addition to restoring respect for the Cousin Jack culture of the 19th century, such associations unselfconsciously embrace a "Celtic" self-definition. According to the Cornish American Heritage Society, Cornwall is "a land of mystery, myth and magic" populated by a Celtic people (Cornish American Heritage Society). Payton notes how a new synthesis of Celtic revivalist and traditional culture has occurred, reflecting a process observed in Cornwall itself since the 1970s. Some Cornish-Americans even set about learning a revived Cornish language based on the Cornish of the 14th and 15th centuries; in the land of hyper-modernity people turned to pre-modernity. A trickle of Americans are regularly made language bards by the Cornish Gorseth, which has itself held mini-Gorseths on North American soil, the first at Vancouver in 1991. Kent (2007) notes how this renewed assertion of Celtic Cornishness acts as a "cultural delineator" but in doing so also adopts an over-romanticized iconography, drawing uncritically from often externally generated representations of the Cornish Celt. Nevertheless, the growth of "New World Celts" parallels the rise of a pan-Celtic consciousness and feeds back to Cornwall (see Hale and Payton 2000: 95). Perhaps most importantly, it heralds the demise of the chameleon Celt. The Cornish no longer hover on the brink of ambiguity these days but throw their hats more unreservedly into the Celtic ring.

Future Research

It only remains to suggest some avenues of research on the Cornish in North America worthy of further attention. As we have seen, the possibilities of pursuing the role of the Cornish language after migration are limited. But Kent's preliminary work on the Cornu-English Cousin Jack narratives would benefit from comparative research, exploring links with the narratives of other Celtic countries both past and present. They could also fruitfully be cross-referenced to similar Cornish drolls across the world and with the dialect tale genre in Cornwall. Three other areas remain under-researched. First, the construction and reproduction of Cornish identity in the Americas, both its presence in traditional Cornish communities and its modern re-assertion and transformation via the transregional public sphere of the Internet, need more detailed analyses (for some pointers see Schwartz 2006 and Deacon and Schwartz 2007). Second, the role of women in reproducing the everyday values of Cornish communities and the ongoing synthesis of host and transplanted communities calls for further exploration (Trotter 2011). Finally, there remains the possibility of work on non-mining migrants, on Cornish immigrants in farming communities and others outside the mining Little Cornwalls. In the history of the chameleon Cornish Celt of the 19th century those who chose to remain invisible within an English identity may tell us something of value about those who did not.

References

Anon. 1932. Paul Burall's Journal. *Old Cornwall* 2 (4): 34.

Baines, Dudley. 1985. *Migration in a Mature Economy: Emigration and Internal Migration in England and Wales, 1861-1900.* Cambridge: Cambridge University Press.

Barham, Charles. 1842. *Report on the Employment of Children and Young Persons in the Mines of Cornwall and Devonshire ... to the Children's Employment Commission.* London: British Parliamentary Papers.

Burke, Gill. 1984. The Cornish Diaspora of the Nineteenth Century. In *International Labour Migration: Historical Perspectives*, ed. Shula Marks and Peter Richardson, 57-75. London: Temple Smith.

Burt, Roger. 2003. Freemasonry and Business Networking During the Victorian Period. *Economic History Review* 56 (4): 657-88.

Burt, Roger and Sandra Kippen. 2001. Rational Choice and a Lifetime in Metal Mining: Employment Decisions by Nineteenth-Century Cornish Miners. *International Review of Social History* 46:46-75.

Calhoon, F. D. 1986. *Coolies, Kanakas and Cousin Jacks and eleven other ethnic groups who populated the West during the Gold Rush years.* Sacramento: F. D. Calhoon.

Cornish American Heritage Society. Who We Are. http//www.cousinjack.org (accessed 10 February 2012).

Deacon, Bernard. 2007a. *Cornwall: A Concise History.* Cardiff: University of Wales Press.

———. 2007b. "We Don't Travel Much, Only to South Africa": Reconstructing Nineteenth-Century Cornish Migration Patterns. In *Cornish Studies Fifteen*, ed. Philip Payton, 90-117. Exeter: University of Exeter Press.

Deacon, Bernard and Sharron Schwartz. 2007. Cornish Identities and Migration: A Multi-Scalar Approach. *Global Networks* 7 (3): 289-306.

Ellis, Peter Beresford. 1974. *The Cornish Language and its Literature*. London: Routledge and Kegan Paul.

Ewart, Shirley with Harold T. George. 1998. *Highly Respectable Families: The Cornish of Grass Valley California 1854-1954*. Grass Valley: Comstock Bonanza Press.

Gabaccio, Donna. 1996. Women of the Mass Migrations: From Minority to Majority, 1820-1930. In *European Migrants: Global and local Perspectives*, ed. Dirk Hoerder and Leslie Page Moch, 90-111. Boston: Northeastern University Press.

Green, Frank L. 1981. *Captains, Curates and Cockneys: The English in the Pacific Northwest*. Tacoma: Washington State Historical Society.

Hale, Amy and Philip Payton, eds. 2000. *New Directions in Celtic Studies*. Exeter: University of Exeter Press.

Hand, Wayland. 1946. The Folklore, Customs and Traditions of the Butte Miner. *California Folklore Quarterly* 5 (2): 153-78.

James, Ronald M. 1994. Defining the Group: Nineteenth-Century Cornish on the North American Mining Frontier. In *Cornish Studies Two*, ed. Philip Payton, 32-47. Exeter: University of Exeter Press.

———. 2010. Cornish Folklore: Context and Opportunity. In *Cornish Studies Eighteen*, ed. Philip Payton, 121-40. Exeter: University of Exeter Press.

James-Korany, Margaret. 1993. "Blue Books" as a Source for Cornish Emigration History. In *Cornish Studies One*, ed. Philip Payton, 31-45. Exeter: University of Exeter Press.

Jeffery, C. 1985. John Nancarrow Jr. *Old Cornwall* 10 (1): 31-35.

Kent, Alan M. 2000. *The Literature of Cornwall: Continuity, Identity, Difference 1000-2000*. Bristol: Redcliffe Press.

———. 2004. "Drill Cores": a Newly Found Manuscript of Cousin Jack Narratives from the Upper Peninsula of Michigan, USA. In *Cornish Studies Twelve*, ed. Philip Payton, 106-43. Exeter: University of Exeter Press.

———. 2007. "Mozeying on Down ...": The Cornish Language in North America. In *The Celtic Languages in Contact*, ed. Hildegaard L.C. Tristram, 193-216. Potsdam: Universitatsverlag Potsdam.

———. 2010. *The Theatre of Cornwall: Space, Place, Performance*. Bristol: Redcliffe Press/Westcliffe Books.

Kent, Alan M. and Gage McKinney, eds. 2008. *The Busy Earth: A Reader in Global Cornish Literature 1700-2000*. St. Austell: Cornish Hillside Publications.

Langton, Larry. 1997. *Beyond the Boundaries: Life and Landscape at the Lake Superior Copper Mines 1840-1875*. Oxford: Oxford University Press.

McKinney, Gage. 2001. *When Miners Sang: The Grass Valley Carol Choir*. Grass Valley: Comstock Bonanza Press.

———. 2009. *The 1930s: No Depression Here*. Grass Valley: Comstock Bonanza Press.

Magee, Gary and Andrew Thompson. 2005. Remittances Revisited: a Case Study of South Africa and the Cornish Migrants, c.1870-1914. In *Cornish Studies Thirteen*, ed. Philip Payton, 288-306. Exeter: University of Exeter Press.

Manning, Paul. 2005. Jewish Ghosts, Knackers, Tommyknockers, and Other Sprites of Capitalism in the Cornish Mines. In *Cornish Studies Thirteen*, ed. Philip Payton, 216-55. Exeter: University of Exeter Press.

Mindenhall, Dorothy. 2000. Choosing the Group: Nineteenth-Century Non-Mining Cornish in British Columbia. In *Cornish Studies Eight*, ed. Philip Payton, 40-53. Exeter: University of Exeter Press.

Mulligan, William H. 1958. Introduction to *The Long Winter Ends*, Newton G. Thomas. Detroit: Wayne State University Press.

Nance, Robert Morton. 1925. The Cornish Language in America. *Old Cornwall* 1 (1): 37.

Naylor, Simon. 2003. Collecting quoits: field cultures in the history of Cornish antiquarianism. *Cultural Geographies* 10 (3): 309-33.

Payton, Philip. 1992. *The Making of Modern Cornwall*. Redruth: Dyllansow Truran.

———. 1995. Cornish Emigration in Response to Changes in the International Copper Market in the 1860s. In *Cornish Studies Three*, ed. Philip Payton, 60-82. Exeter: University of Exeter Press.

———. 1999. *The Cornish Overseas*. Fowey: Alexander Associates.

Pool, P. A. S. 1982. *The Death of Cornish (1600-1800)*. Penzance: Cornish Language Board.

Richards, Eric. 2004. *Britannia's Children: Emigration from England, Scotland, Wales and Ireland Since 1600*. London: Hambledon and Loudon.

Rowe, John. 1974. *The Hard Rock Men: Cornish Immigrants and the North American Mining Frontier*. Liverpool: Liverpool University Press.

Rowse, A. L. 1967. *The Cornish in America*. London: Macmillan.

Schwartz, Sharron. 2002. Cornish Migration Studies: an Epistemological and Paradigmatic Critique. In *Cornish Studies Ten*, ed. Philip Payton, 136-65. Exeter: University of Exeter Press.

———. 2005. Migration Networks and the Transnationalization of Social Capital: Cornish Migration to Latin America, a Case Study. In *Cornish Studies Thirteen*, ed. Philip Payton, 256-87. Exeter: University of Exeter Press.

———. 2006. Bridging "The Great Divide": The Evolution and impact of Cornish translocalism in Britain and the USA. *Journal of American Ethnic History* 25 (2/3): 169-89.

Spence, Clark C. 1958. *British Investments and the American Mining Frontier, 1860-1901*. Ithaca: Cornell University Press.

Thomas, Newton G. 1941. *The Long Winter Ends*. New York: The Macmillan Company.

Thurner, Arthur W. 1994. *Strangers and Sojourners: A History of Michigan's Keweenaw Peninsula*. Detroit: Wayne State University Press.

Todd, Arthur Cecil. 1966. *The Cornish Miner in America*. Truro, U.K.: D. Bradford Barton.

Trotter, Lesley. 2011. Desperate? Destitute? Deserted? Questioning Perceptions of Miners' Wives in Cornwall during the Great Emigration, 1851-1891. In *Cornish Studies Nineteen*, ed. Philip Payton, 195-224. Exeter: University of Exeter Press.

Williams, Derek R. 2004. Henry Jenner, F.S.A: City Scholar and Local Patriot. In *Henry and Katharine Jenner: A Celebration of Cornwall's Culture, Language and Identity*, ed. Derek R. Williams, 70-110. London: Francis Boutle.

Woods, Robert. 1995. *The population of Britain in the nineteenth century*. Cambridge: Cambridge University Press.

Tomás Ó h-Íde

Emancipation through Exile: Irish Speakers in the Americas

The presence of Irish speakers can be documented throughout the colonial history of the Americas to the present from Argentina through to Canada. Data on individual Irish speakers living in the Americas is more frequent than descriptions of immigrant communities of Irish speakers. However, much can be inferred from individual data when taking into consideration the general patterns of immigration from specific counties of Ireland.

One challenge with which the researcher is presented is identifying who exactly Irish speakers are; it is a question which standard accounts of the Irish diaspora typically ignore. As McMonagle points out, "historians of the Irish in Canada have shown a similar reluctance to investigate language issues, and in some instances may even be charged with denying the arrival of Irish speakers" (2012: 138). With the focus of this volume being on Celtic-speaking communities, this chapter will not attempt to chronicle the activities of language activists and their efforts in language promotion and language preservation if those efforts were not tied to dominant (or bilingual) Irish speakers. Ample discussion of Irish language classes and publications for non-dominant Irish speakers can be found in recent articles (McGowan 1994; Nilsen 1996; Ihde 2005, 2008). Likewise, isolated references to the Irish language in legal or political affairs from the mid-1850s on, such as the Fenian Trials in 1866 in Sweetsburgh, Québec, where one of the accused, Michael Crowley, attempted to use Irish in the court proceedings (Sweetsburgh 1866; Preparation 1866), will not be considered.

What is meant by dominant (or bilingual) Irish speakers is crucial to this chapter. In the 17th and 18th century, dominant Irish language speakers would be those individuals who were raised speaking Irish at home and in their community. As the English language grew in influence, many individuals, especially in the 19th century, would gain varying degrees of English fluency while Irish still remained the home and, to varying extents, the community language. Those who did acquire English while continuing to speak Irish are referred to here as bilingual. Clearly, in the 19th and 20th century, a bilingual individual may have found it easier to use Irish at home (relationships, household tasks, religious practices, etc.) and at work (fishing and farming) but English at school, at the shops and with strangers. Yet these individuals would still be identified as dominant Irish speakers. Although there was a strong correlation between religious affiliation, cultural makeup and language use, it must be remembered that knowledge of the Irish language was not confined to Catholics (McMonagle 2012: 140, 145).

From the mid-19th century, the Irish language was promoted as the "native" language of all Irishmen and women regardless of their first language. The Gaelic revival in Ireland that aided in bringing about a new national identity in the mid- to late 19th century and early 20th century through the teaching of the Irish language and promoting native sports, music and dance served to instill a positive attitude toward this Celtic language. However, as a result, identifying dominant (or bilingual) Irish-language speakers from the students of the language, in for example census data from Ireland or language organization reports, continues to be difficult to this day.

An additional challenge hinted at above relates to the changing language patterns among the Irish not only in the Americas but in the home country as well. At the turn of the 19th century, several counties arguably still had a majority of Irish speakers. However, that percentage fell quickly with the Great Famine, marking a significant loss of language dominance. Antiquarian organizations quickly attempted to save the relics of the past, including the rich literary legacy, although the large monolingual Irish-speaking population continued to be neglected. With the introduction of English-language education in the 1800s, the Irish language continued to lose ground at an alarming rate.

Lastly, it should be noted that it would be an oversimplification to identify certain groups of individuals as emigrating to New York and others emigrating to Buenos Aires in a straightforward fashion. In reality, Irish speakers often did not travel to just one location, nor did they just travel to one continent. For example, many Donegal Irish speakers emigrated to Scotland before attempting to travel across the Atlantic. Many Galway Irish speakers emigrated to London, England, before making it to Boston in the United States. Emigrants were not necessarily wedded to a single target destination but travelled between cities, islands and countries.

This chapter will look at several historical periods of immigration to the present day, considering migratory patterns, the survival of the language, literature and publication production and social institutions that supported Irish-speaking communities. Before beginning, let us consider a couple of immigrant profiles to put a face on this story.

Anne McDonagh was born in An Cheathrú Rua (Carraroe), Co. Galway. She does not appear in the 1901 census but is recorded in the 1911 census. In 1901, her parents Kate and Coleman are reported as monolingual Irish speakers, as is the youngest child of the family who was eight years of age. Uí Fhlannagáin points out that schooling was reported to take place from nine to eighteen years of age in one Galway case which would explain monolingualism in an eight-year-old (1990: 12). Older children who could read and write in the McDonagh family are noted as bilingual. By the 1911 census, Anne appears as twelve years of age, is able to read and write, and is noted to be bilingual. However, unlike in 1901, her parents are now noted as bilingual. Cladhnach (Clynagh), An Cheathrú Rua in Connemara, Co. Galway, and all of the Crumpaun (An Crompán) District Electoral Division (DED) as well as neighbouring DEDs, was identified as part of the Fíor-Ghaeltacht, a truly Irish-speaking region, by the Government of Ireland in 1926. While English was making its inroads into this region, especially through the education system, this remote community still remains strongly Irish speaking to this day: schools have taught through the medium of Irish since the establishment of the Free State, and it was accorded Category "A" status in 2007 for having 80 per cent or higher of first-language Irish speakers (Ó Giollagáin et al. 2007: 18). It is reported that Anne immigrated to Boston. It appears that most of her six siblings that are noted in the 1901 and 1911 censuses immigrated to the Boston area as well with the exception of Peter (Peadar) who moved with his family to Ráth Chairn (Rathcarran) in County Meath in the 1930s (Thomas Griffin, personal communication, 16 July 2012).

It is expected that Anne and her siblings were able to join the large Irish-speaking community in Boston and that their children would have been able to at least acquire a passive knowledge of the Irish language if so inclined. To this day, one can meet up with native Irish speakers in South Boston, and the language remains strong in the home region, of course, thus enabling frequent Irish-language exchanges between the Boston and Connemara peoples.

Thomas Malley used the name "Thomas O'Malley" after immigrating to the United States. Born in 1878 in County Galway and raised on the eastern shores of Loch Corrib, his community was also identified as a Fíor-Ghaeltacht by the Government of Ireland in 1926. However, by 1956, we no longer see this region listed in the *Gaeltacht Areas Order* as the Irish language in the Killursa (Cill Fhursa) DED is assumed to have died out as a community language a generation or two after being included in that initial survey. The Irish Census for 1901 identifies Thomas Malley as a bilingual speaker of Irish and English and notes that his father, Peter Malley, is a monolingual Irish speaker, while his mother, Winnie, is bilingual. The father's monolingual status is reaffirmed in the 1911 census in which Peter is once again identified as able to speak Irish only. It is interesting to note that in 1901 Peter is one of three inhabitants of the village of Cloononaghaun (Cluain Onchon) who is reported as a monolingual speaker; all others are identified as bilingual. By 1911, he is the last surviving monolingual speaker of the village. In 1901 and 1911, in villages off the Headford Road from Galway City to the Mayo border, we find again and again at most a handful of monolingual Irish speakers in each village whose ages attest that they are Great Famine survivors. This is truly a region in transition. Occasionally, though rarely, we do have a boarder in a bilingual household reported to know English only. These English reportings, along with the monolingual Irish reportings, strengthen the credibility of the Galway data collected.

Immigrating to Philadelphia at the turn of the last century, Thomas soon settled in New Jersey and married an English-speaking Monaghan woman. They raised a family of eight children through the English language. Anecdotal reports indicate that Thomas did have occasion to use the Irish language with his siblings who also immigrated. As would be expected with assimilation in a new culture and language-use in a home where primarily English was spoken, the Irish language for the most part died with that generation. There is no evidence that Thomas sought out fellow Irish-language speakers to maintain Irish-language community ties although this may have happened to a lesser extent with membership in the Ancient Order of Hibernians. Thomas's case is typical of this time period in that we see a first-language Irish speaker immigrating, occasionally using the language in America and not passing it on to the next generation. However, not only did the language die out in that New Jersey home, but, as indicated above, the language also died out in his native Killursa community.

With these profiles in mind, we now turn to a broader overview of Irish speakers in the Americas throughout the centuries.

17th Century

Based on the widespread dominance of the Irish language in the 17th century, we can assume that most of the Irish that arrived in the Caribbean as indentured servants or forced labourers were monolingual Irish speakers. Transportation to the islands of Barbados, Montserrat and Jamaica, among others, was notable during the Cromwellian conquest of Ireland. The island of Bermuda has a similar history. Recent films regarding populations referred to as "Redlegs" have further fuelled interest in these descendants of the Irish in the Americas (2012). Irish speakers moved from the islands of the Caribbean to the North American mainland and vice versa. One such Irishwoman from the 17th century who was sold into slavery in the Bahamas and later ended up in Massachusetts was Anne "Goody" Glover. It is reported that she requested interpreters at her witch trial in court (Mac Aonghusa 1979: 14).

> It was not long before the Witch thus in the Trap, was brought upon her Tryal; at which, thro' the Efficacy of a Charm, I suppose, used upon her, by one or some of her Crue the Court could receive Answers from her in one but the Irish, which was her Native Language; altho she understood the English very well, and had accustomed her whole Family to none but that Language in her former Conversation; and therefore the Communication between the Bench and the Bar, was now cheefly convey'd by two honest and faithful men that were interpreters. (Mather 1914: 103-104)

One of the successful attempts to develop a fishing colony in Newfoundland in the 17th century involved seasonal and permanent workers from Ireland and Wales. The Irish language flourished in this isolated community (Byrne 1988; Ó hEadhra 1997; Ó Liatháin 2011). Baile Sheáin (a translation of "St. John's") and Talamh an Éisc (literally "Land of the Fish," referring to Newfoundland) are among the few North American place names to have their own Irish versions recorded in history and which can still be found in Irish atlases today (Roinn Oideachais 1978: 38-39). References to the use of Irish in courts and by the clergy attest to its survival in that part of British North America into the 19th century. Donnchadh Rua Mac Conmara composed poems in mid-18th-century Newfoundland that seem to be the earliest Irish-language literary works composed in North America to have survived (Ó Laoire 2009).

18th Century and First Half of 19th Century

Many inhabitants of the previously mentioned islands in the Americas today proudly trace their heritage to both Ireland and Africa. Of course, the language of the plantation masters dominated this disparate mixture and lessened the probability that traces of Irish and other languages would remain. The 18th century also saw increases in voluntary immigration (as opposed to transportation). Plantations depended less on European indentured servants and white and Native American forced labourers, and more on slaves from Africa. While North America had been used as a penal colony by the British in the 17th and early 18th century, Australia was used for this purpose soon after the American Revolution.

In the 1700s, we see Irish emigrants voluntarily travelling to North American locations such as Pennsylvania, among others (Callahan 1994). The Gaelic literati in Ireland composed poetry, particularly in the *aisling* literary genre, commenting on the American Revolutionary War, expressing their hopes that Britain would be defeated and Ireland would benefit (Morley 2007). It is not clear whether such poems reached the colonies in written or oral form, but these and other texts evince a keen interest in international politics and the desire to adapt native literary forms to discuss them. There are occasional clues about Irish speakers around the era of the Revolutionary War in North America itself. Colonial newspapers printed occasional notices of Irish-speaking indentured servants on the run, and in 1784 a speaker in the House of Commons blamed the loss of the American colonies on Irish emigrants who joined George Washington's troops, many of whom were said to speak Irish. Charles Whelan, the first Catholic pastor to serve in New York after the Revolution, was said to have been better at speaking Gaelic and French than English (Nilsen 2002b: 191-92).

By the early 1800s we see immigration to South America while immigration to North America continued to increase. During these pre-Great Famine years, Ulster Scots-Irish immigrants outnumbered native Irish immigrants; the percentage of native Irish immigrants in Pennsylvania, Delaware, Virginia, North Carolina, South Carolina and Georgia was about 9 per cent of the white population of those states in 1790. At the same time, percentages were lower in New York (4.9 per cent) and New

Table 1: Estimated Irish Percentage of White Population in Selected States (1790)				
	Ulster Scots Irish	Ulster native Irish	Non-Ulster Irish	Total Irish
New York	8.3	1.9	3.0	12.1
New Jersey	9.0	3.5	3.2	15.2
Pennsylvania	16.6	5.5	3.5	23.6
Delaware	8.0	4.5	5.4	17.7
Maryland	7.6	4.0	6.5	17.1
Virginia	9.0	3.4	6.2	17.9
North Carolina	8.1	3.3	5.4	17.1
South Carolina	13.6	5.3	4.4	25.8
Georgia	17.0	6.0	3.8	26.3

Source: Kallen 1994: 29. Based on Doyle 1981: 75. See Doyle for detailed notes concerning calculation of each column.

Jersey (6.7 per cent). The total Ulster Scots and native Irish immigrants from all provinces ranged from 12 per cent to 26 per cent, depending on the state.

However, the numbers of immigrants from Ireland would significantly increase to somewhere between 38 per cent to 50 per cent of all European immigration in the years before the Great Famine, that is, in the early 1800s (Kallen 1994: 30).

One of the social institutions at this time to leave evidence of addressing the needs of those in the Irish-speaking communities was the Catholic Church. Accounts of the existence and need for Irish-speaking priests in the Americas provide clues as to the location and survival of the language during the 18th and the first half of the 19th century. As regards the family, with the exception of the case of Newfoundland cited above, there is little evidence to demonstrate Irish being passed on to subsequent generations in the Americas.

Some evidence survives of literary activity in Irish from this era in the United States. Matthias O'Conway (Maitias Ó Conmhidhe), who settled in Philadelphia, began putting together an English-Irish dictionary in the early 1800s (McGowan 1994: 5; Kallen 1994: 34). Pádraig Phiarais Cúndún (Patrick Condon), a Cork farmer and poet who immigrated to New York in 1826 and settled in Utica, wrote letters in Irish between the 1830s and 1850s (Ó Foghludha 1932; Ó Buachalla 1979) and composed poems in Irish about his experiences in the U.S., some of them in the *aisling* tradition (Nilsen 2002b: 194). At this time we also see one of the earliest attempts to republish material from Ireland in Irish, a practice that became much more common in the late 1800s (Kallen 1994: 32).

Dr. William James MacNeven, an Irish speaker who arrived in New York in 1805, translated Ossianic tales from Irish to English before emigrating (Nilsen 1996: 254). He may have been one of a number of immigrants bringing Irish manuscripts with them to the Americas during this period, since individuals such as Patrick Ferriter (Pádraig Feiritéar), who immigrated at the end of the 19th century, found manuscripts already in North America in collections such as that in the Boston Athenaeum (Ó Diollúin 2009: 12).

Great Famine Immigration

One of the greatest blows for the Irish language in Ireland was the Great Famine, known in Irish as *An Gorta Mór*, or alternatively (and euphemistically) *An Drochshaol* ("the bad life"), which had marked economic, religious and linguistic characteristics:

It has been estimated that one and a half million people died during the Famine and between 1846 and 1851 a million emigrated. It is not unreasonable to assume that a great proportion of these were Irish speakers. The poorest districts, from which the greatest flow of emigration has continued ever since, have been, in general, the districts which were predominantly Irish-speaking. (Wall 1969: 87)

Most monolingual Irish speakers immigrating at this time were also illiterate and hence left little trace of their language.

Most important, although in prior decades most Catholic emigrants had come from English-speaking or rapidly Anglicizing districts in eastern and central Ireland, the Famine exodus had a decidedly Gaelic character. Munster and Connaught, where in 1841 over half the inhabitants spoke Irish, contributed at least 50 percent of the

Figure 1. High cross memorial of Great Famine in Ireland erected in 2000 in Québec City, with inscription in Irish. (Michael Newton)

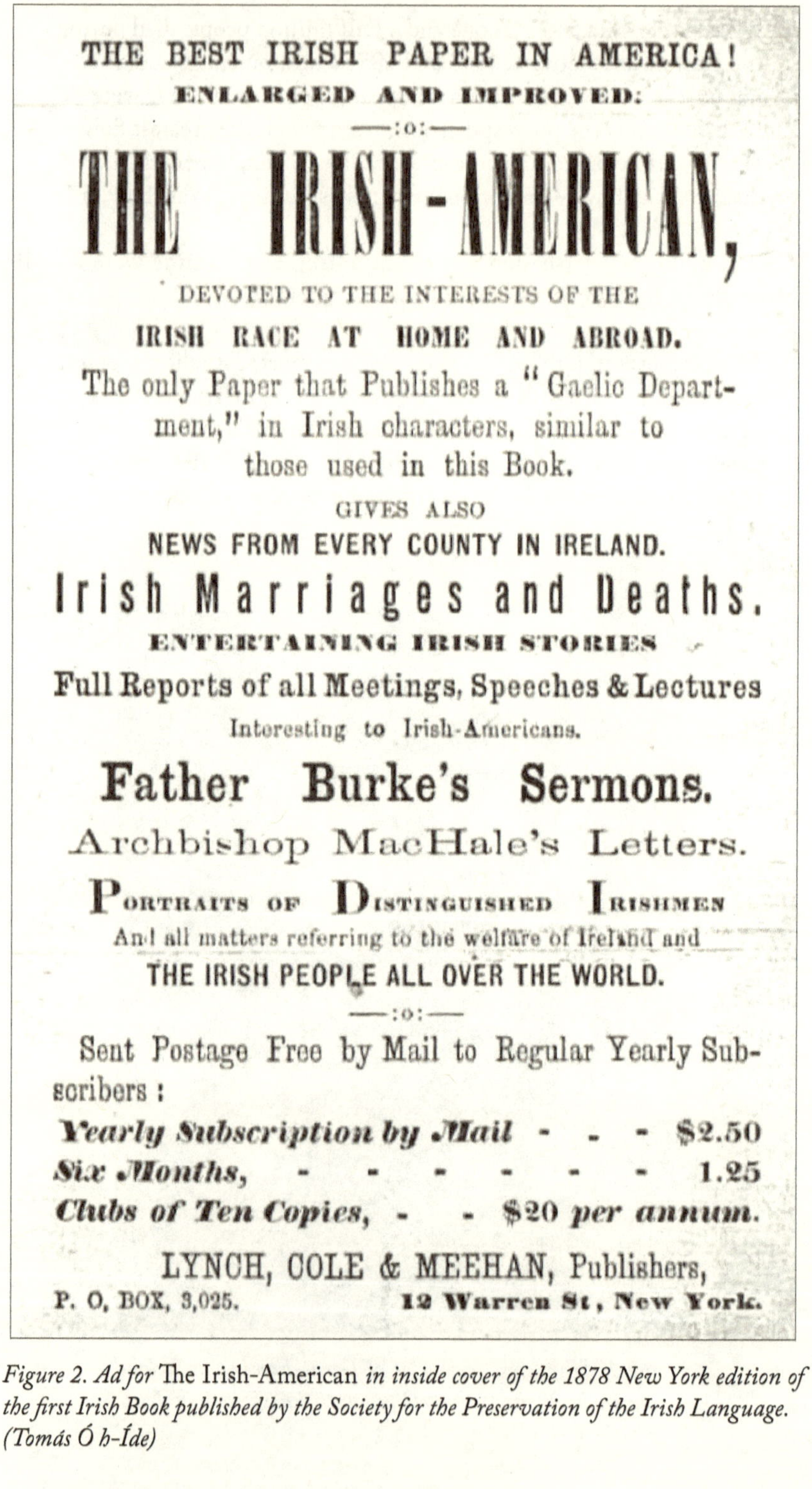

> **THE BEST IRISH PAPER IN AMERICA!**
> **ENLARGED AND IMPROVED:**
>
> # THE IRISH-AMERICAN,
>
> DEVOTED TO THE INTERESTS OF THE
>
> **IRISH RACE AT HOME AND ABROAD.**
>
> The only Paper that Publishes a "Gaelic Department," in Irish characters, similar to those used in this Book.
>
> GIVES ALSO
>
> **NEWS FROM EVERY COUNTY IN IRELAND.**
>
> **Irish Marriages and Deaths.**
>
> **ENTERTAINING IRISH STORIES**
>
> Full Reports of all Meetings, Speeches & Lectures
>
> Interesting to Irish-Americans.
>
> **Father Burke's Sermons.**
>
> Archbishop MacHale's Letters.
>
> Portraits of Distinguished Irishmen
>
> And all matters referring to the welfare of Ireland and
>
> **THE IRISH PEOPLE ALL OVER THE WORLD.**
>
> Sent Postage Free by Mail to Regular Yearly Subscribers :
>
> *Yearly Subscription by Mail* - - - $2.50
> *Six Months,* - - - - - - 1.25
> *Clubs of Ten Copies,* - - $20 *per annum.*
>
> LYNCH, COLE & MEEHAN, Publishers,
> P. O. BOX, 3,025.   **12 Warren St, New York.**

Figure 2. Ad for The Irish-American *in inside cover of the 1878 New York edition of the first Irish Book published by the Society for the Preservation of the Irish Language. (Tomás Ó h-Íde)*

Famine emigrants. About 40 percent came from Munster and from Galway, Mayo, and Sligo in Connaught, areas where a large majority were Irish-speakers. Almost 15 percent more left Leitrim and Roscommon in Connaught, Donegal in west Ulster, and Kilkenny and Louth in Leinster-counties where a least a fifth of the inhabitants spoke Irish. In short, about 54 percent of the Famine emigrants had lived in regions where Irish was still in the majority, or at least a strong minority, language; in addition, large numbers also left south Ulster and Leinster counties such as Meath and Westmeath, where perhaps 10 percent spoke Irish.... Perhaps a fourth to a third of all Famine emigrants—as many as half a million people—were Irish-speakers. (Miller 1985: 297)

Newspapers in America took note of the decline of the Irish language. For example, in 1857 one could read, "Within the memory of man, the Irish language was the daily tongue of between two and three millions of people in Ireland—now, only about one fifth of the population can understand Irish at all" (Celtic Race 1857). And yet another American newspaper declared in the same year, "It appears by the census of Ireland that the old Irish language is going out of use. Less than five hundredths of the people are ignorant of English, and not one-fourth of the whole can speak the original Irish" (Johnson 1857: 1).

Emigrants travelled to Scotland, England, Canada, the United States and Australia. Significant numbers perished on the journey. The largest Great Famine burial site in the Americas is located at Grosse-Île, Québec, Canada. Notable numbers of immigrants made their way to ports all over Canada, from the port of Saint John, New Brunswick, to the major towns and cities along the St. Lawrence River and the far side of Lake Ontario. Integration into francophone Canada was facilitated through a common adherence to Catholicism: French Catholics adopted many orphaned children and many French and Irish families intermarried, their descendants often becoming francophone (McMonagle 2012: 143-44).

In the United States, the ports of the eastern seaboard also saw substantial famine immigration. The number of Irish speakers concentrated in the cities of North America must have peaked during this period. In the press of the day, for example in New York state, we see accounts of Irish-language use. References to the language in Ireland show a growing awareness of the presence of the language of the masses pouring into North American ports. A column in the *Oneida Morning Herald* at the height of the Famine publishes an impression of Ireland as Irish speaking:

> Some idea of the tone and spirit of a portion of the press of Ireland, in the present condition of Irish affairs, may be obtained from the

following remarks of the *Nation*, published at Dublin. It is highly probable that the English people understand the Irish language sufficiently well to apprehend the meaning of such talk as this without the aid of interpreters or translators:—"We Spit upon the English Charity." (German and Colston 1847: 1)

Likewise in 1848 an article in the *Mohawk Courier* (NY) recounts an execution in Clonmel in South Tipperary, Ireland, with reference to the language.

Curses loud and deep were vociferated during this awful scene, which continued for twenty-seven minutes. "Revenge" was sworn to audibly and determinedly in the Irish language, and imprecations awful to mention, were levelled at the aiders and abetters of this most frightful and horrible scene. (Johnson 1848)

Such outbursts in the Irish language would be replayed on the stage in New York, for example in *Peep O'Day* at the Laura Keene's Theatre, where "An Irruption of Irish Language" was included in the murder trial (Laura Keene's Theatre 1862). Jokes recounted at the expense of Irish-language speakers could be read as well, as in the story of the three sons in Connemara with only a handful of English words, and they did not understand even those. The story was printed in stage Irish English dialect (with even one line in Irish) in the Long Island, NY, newspaper *The Corrector* on August 1, 1857.

There is evidence of the use of Irish by the religious institutions that attempted to serve Irish immigrants. In the 1840s, Reverend Joseph Burke, an Irish-speaking Catholic priest from Ireland, helped to build St. Columba Church in New York City. He is reported to have preached in Irish in his New York parish (McGowan 1994: 5). In his 1846 letter of farewell to the parish published in the *New York Herald* he mentions returning to Ireland where he would minister to the poor peasants in their "vernacular tongue," a practice which he undoubtedly did in New York as well (Burke 1912: 214). Additionally, we see an advertisement in the *New York Sun* regarding a lecture by Father Meehan to be given in the Irish language at St. Anne's Church in Brooklyn (Society Notices 1865).

Likewise, other faith traditions sought to serve the religious needs of the high number of Irish-speaking immigrants at this time. A report of a meeting of the Irish Society held at Astor Place in New York City in 1859 indicated that "among the influences which helped the Society on was the possession of the Scriptures in the Irish language" (Meeting 1859). In a sermon delivered in 1860 at Trinity Church in New York City, Rev. George Gough Gibbins claimed that the Irish of the west of Ireland

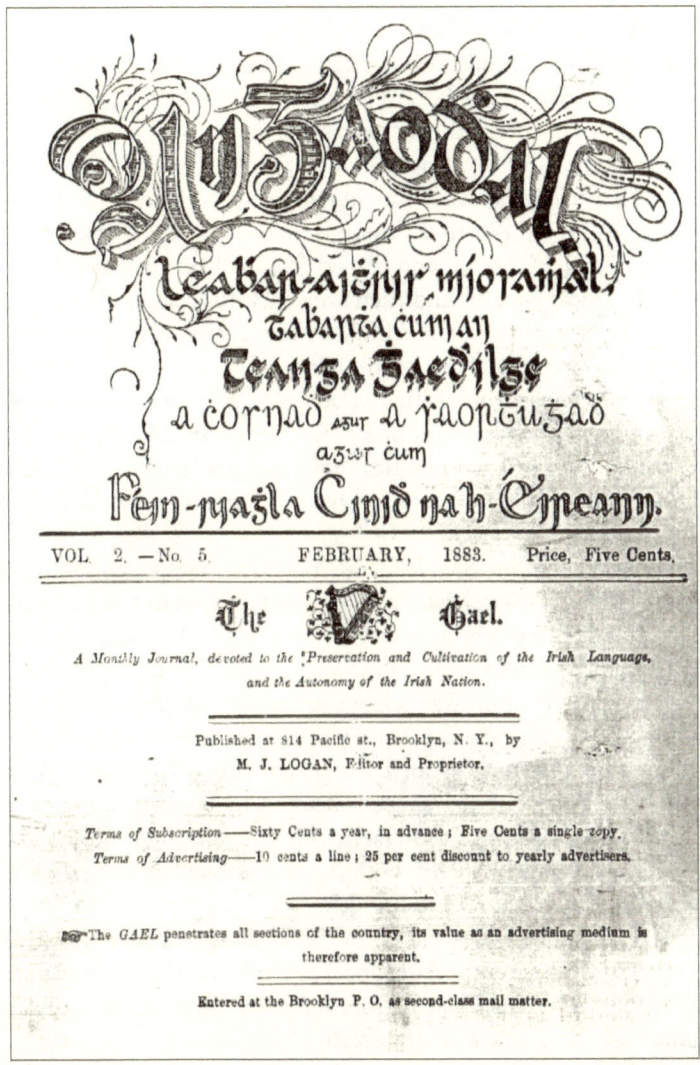

Figure 2. An Gaodhal *newspaper title page, 1883. (Tomás Ó h-Íde)*

would make better immigrants to America if they were evangelized in their native Irish tongue before immigrating, rather than in the English language, which they could not comprehend (Local Intelligence 1860). In addition to religious institutions, we see discussion at the local government level addressing the language needs of these immigrants. Proposals at a New York City Council meeting on October 27, 1863 suggested that equal numbers of the election pamphlet, "Practical Directions for the Holding of Elections, and the Canvassing of Votes under the new Election Law, principally applicable to the City of New York," be produced in the German and Irish languages (Sweeny 1864: 1).

While the height of publication in the Irish language in North America would not be experienced until the late 1800s with the founding of the newspaper *An Gaodhal/The Gael* in Brooklyn, New York, Irish literati were preserving manuscripts and contributing Irish texts to English-language newspapers soon after the Great Famine. Both Thomas Norris (Tomás D. de Norradh) and Patrick Ferriter actively collected Irish-language manuscripts in North America. These were brought from Ireland, bought and sold in North America, and copied from collections already resident in North America. Most found their way back to Ireland after the deaths of these collectors (Ó Diollúin 2009). Additionally, Ferriter was actively writing original works in Irish at this time.

The translation and publishing of one notable manuscript took place at this time, namely Geoffrey Keating's *Foras Feasa ar Eirinn*, translated by John O'Mahony from Irish-language manuscripts that Michael Sheehan, John H. Maume and Mrs. James O'Dwyer (resident in the United States) lent him (Keating 1866: 17).

Nilsen notes that in 1851 *The Irish-American* newspaper published one of its first contributions in Irish, "a three-stanza poem in Irish in praise of a tavern on Duane Street run by James O'Dwyer" (2002a: 60), but it was not until 1857 that the newspaper established a regular Irish-language column. The timing of the column was related to the newspaper's commissioning and acquiring an Irish typeface, since publishers were strongly discouraged from using Roman typefaces for Irish at that time (1996: 261). Although based in New York, the newspaper clearly circulated in Canada, as the "first five original poems of the Gaelic column were sent in by two Irishmen living in Canada" (2002b: 202). After the death of Pádraig Cúndún in 1857, his son Pierce moved to Brooklyn and brought his father's writings with him. His poems were printed in the *Irish-American* in 1858 (2002a: 58). Some 450 Irish columns had appeared in the newspaper by 1881, connecting readers and contributors from locations as far afield as Alabama, Louisiana and San Francisco (2002b: 207).

Other newspapers of this period, including the *Phoenix* and *The Irish People*, printed Irish-language contributions in their pages (2002a: 60-61). Traditional songs and poetry formed the bulk of Irish material that appeared in the newspapers, some of which came from the many manuscripts in the United States.

1870s-1930s

The end of the 19th century saw an alarming drop in the number of native Irish speakers in Ireland, a decline that has continued into recent years. Because Irish was not typically passed on from one generation to the next in the diaspora, the probability that immigrants would have been dominant or bilingual Irish speakers during this period is also low. Similar to the generation before them, few of those who were Irish speaking were literate in the language. In one collection of letters from the McGee brothers in America sent home to Donegal during this period we see that all of the letters were written in English, but there are references that others had to write these letters for them with lines like "Daniel Ferry wrote this letter" and "These lines were written by young Grace Ferry" (Ó Dúill 1994: 60, 65).

Members of the Irish-language revival and preservation organizations of this time included native Irish speakers and fluent learners, but the reader of contemporary accounts usually has to infer such distinctions. For example, the "Philo-Celts" attendance notes from the February 1883 issue of *An Gaodhal* state, "Mrs. Masterson (nee Miss Fanny Slattery) has got the best conventional knowledge of the language of any one we know, of those who did not speak it from infancy. However she had an excellent preceptor in Miss Annie Fitzgerald" (Ó Lócháin 1883: 189). The implication is that other members did speak it from infancy.

The goal of the many organizations that followed in the steps of the Philo-Celtic Society was to support language revival in Ireland rather than fostering dominant Irish speakers in the Americas. During this period, as the examples at the beginning of this chapter illustrate, the default immigration pattern was to transition to English and to raise children in English. Once the goal of establishing Irish as the national language of Ireland was achieved, many of these organizations disappeared.

> The shame and insecurity traditionally associated with Irish may also have been a factor in distancing people from the revival. However, the fact that emigrants continued to use Irish in their homes and neighbourhoods would seem to contradict this. Thus, while emigrants were not hostile to Irish, they did not universally embrace the revival. Emigrants could have supported the revival movement while adopting English for everyday use, as indeed some did. However, the revival ultimately failed because emigrants chose not to pass on Irish to their children. (Ní Ghabhann 1998)

An Gaodhal/The Gael, started in Brooklyn in 1881, was a monthly journal devoted primarily to the Irish language. Editor Mícheál Ó Lócháin (Michael Logan) had founded the Brooklyn branch of the Philo-Celtic Society in the 1870s. The monthly bilingual journal remained under his direction until the end of 1898 and continued to be published until 1904. It enjoyed about 3,000 subscribers at the height of its popularity and typically contained between six and eight pages of Irish material, including language lessons, linguistic notes, correspondence, traditional narratives, speeches, sermons, proverbs, toasts, announcements, editorials, history, biographies, material copied from Irish language columns of other newspapers, folklore transcribed from oral tradition and texts from manuscripts (Uí Fhlannagáin 1990: 22-23, 126). *An Gaodhal* served the supporters of the Irish revival movement by informing them of news and publications in Ireland, especially those related to language revitalization. The literary expressions contained in *An Gaodhal* attempted to bridge the rich literary past with the future possibilities for publishing in the language. After the passing of Mícheál Ó Lócháin in 1899, *The Gael* was publishing primarily in English.

Several other Irish-American newspapers, such as *The Irish-American*, *The Irish People* and *The Irish Echo*, continued to publish either Irish-language columns or the occasional Irish text during this period. Short-lived Irish columns even appeared in some mainstream anglophone newspapers in the 1880s, such as the *Chicago Citizen* and the San Francisco *Monitor*. One of the most prolific, sophisticated and radical of Irish-American poets was Patrick O'Byrne, a native of Donegal who immigrated to New York ca. 1880. He also composed the words for *An Bard agus an Fó* (The Poet and the Knight), probably the first Irish-language musical (contata) ever performed on stage anywhere (Nilsen 2002b: 207-213).

Books with Irish-language focus and content were published in New York in the early 1870s and soon thereafter in Boston. They were often printed on the same presses as the aforementioned Irish newspapers. Most were for Irish language learners, but of course this would include both English-dominant learners of the language and native Irish speakers learning to read and write. Parts two and three of Rev. Eugene O'Growney's *Simple Lessons in Irish* indicate that they were written in 1894 in California and Arizona respectively (Ihde 2005: 147).

Some Irish Americans made significant contributions to Irish scholarship in the late 19th century. James Mooney, better known for his work among Native Americans as a member of the Bureau of American Ethnology, was the son of Irish emigrants. In the years 1886-1889 he published three extensive articles on Irish folklore, drawing largely upon his family and other Irish immigrants in the U.S., including Irish-language speakers. Jeremiah Curtain, also the son of Irish parents and a member of the B.A.E., was educated at Harvard and published two volumes of folktales that he collected in Ireland, *Myths and Folk-Lore of Ireland* (1889) and *Hero-Tales of Ireland* (1894). Both men made frequent comparisons with Native American materials in their research (Ó Siadhail 2010). Folklore transcribed from Irish immigrants in the 1880s and 1890s also appeared in *The Irish Echo* and *The Irish-American* (Nilsen 2002b: 214).

1940s-Present

Irish immigrants from the Gaeltachtaí have continued to immigrate to North America. As the Gaeltachtaí shrink, so too would one expect those percentages to decline of overall Irish immigration. Space here does not permit looking at each wave of immigrants and its percentage of Irish speakers. However, in a 1990 article concerning Irish speakers in Portland, Maine, Kenneth Nilsen stated, "they have always formed a substantial percentage of Irish immigrants to the United States. I estimate that they represent at least ten to fifteen percent of Irish-born in the United States as late as the early 1980s" (1990: 7). As one would expect, the proportion of one out of ten immigrants in a given community dictates that Irish-speaking immigrants assimilate not only into their cohort of predominantly English-speaking fellow immigrants but also into the greater English-speaking Irish America and mainstream America. However, in some areas such as Boston, numbers have been large enough for the language to have "community" status in certain gathering venues. Groups such as *Cumann na Gaeilge i mBoston* could hold dances and sporting events advertised exclusively in Irish with large turnouts (O'Carroll 1988: 16). Bob Quinn directed a series of television programs entitled *Pobal i mBoston* which documented Irish speakers in Boston by letting them tell their own stories. The programs produced by Cinegael were aired on RTÉ television in 1990. Similar documentation has taken place of Irish speakers in Chicago, Minnesota and New York.

Despite this vitality, recent immigrants rarely pass the language on to their children, with the result that the language dies out in a generation. When immigration ceases, the language will slowly fade. For as long as Irish-language learners and the rich revival campaign in North America will keep the language at the forefront, the loss of the native speaker will be mourned. Kenneth Nilsen reported after visiting Irish speakers in Portland, Maine, that "several informants mentioned that some of their American-born children picked up Irish at home and, during at least one interview, it was clear that an elderly couple's daughter understood what they were saying and even ventured to say a few words in Irish" (1990: 10).

Changes in modes of transportation and employment trends have enabled Irish-language authors to move more easily from Europe to the diaspora and back again. As in the exceptional case of Rev. O'Growney in the late 19th century, Irish-language writers ply their trade in North America as well as in Ireland and many of the traditions of the past have continued into the present. We see Irish immigrant newspapers with columns in Irish, books in Irish from Ireland being republished in North

America, and even a collection of recent *The Irish Echo* newspaper columns being published in book form (Mhic Suibhne and Zurell 2008). Both newspaper articles and books written in North America are now regularly published in Ireland. Pádraig Ó Siadhail in Canada and Muiris Ó Bric in the United States are just among the many writers of Irish whose work regularly appears in print in Ireland.

Future Research

Researching the topic of native Irish speakers in the Americas is a challenging task. Immigration extends over several centuries and is scattered throughout the New World. In the past, most researchers have limited themselves to the history of the Irish language revival in the United States. That history has been well documented and current activities include the Irish government's recent support of Irish language courses at universities in Canada and the United States, the history of the immersion weekends affiliated with the student organization Daltaí na Gaeilge, the establishment of NAACLT (North American Association for Celtic Language Teachers), the acquisition of land near Erinsville, Ontario, for language teaching (Permanent North American Gaeltacht), and the list could go on. However, the task at hand is to sift through reams of raw data and identify who the first-language speakers were and are and tell their unique story.

The researcher today has several tools available that did not exist when many of the researchers cited above were at work on their projects. The 1901 and 1911 censuses from Ireland with detailed information are now available and await researchers on both sides of the Atlantic. These returns can be researched electronically, enabling a more complete sampling of the data. Similarly, many of the newspapers of the day have been digitized. While access to these digital archives may be limited in many cases, if scholars throughout the Americas join in researching Irish speakers locally, the community of researchers should soon be able to draw a more detailed picture of native Irish speakers and their communities in the history of the Americas. The legacy of the Irish in Canada—especially those who were Irish speakers—is only beginning to be explored. Recent research has uncovered multigenerational Irish-speaking communities in the Maritimes and the Ottawa Valley, some of them Protestant (McMonagle 2012: 145-47).

Lastly, the important work by Kenneth Nilsen on Irish-language manuscripts needs to be expanded beyond Boston and New York to create a more comprehensive view of literary activity in the Americas in the 19th century.

References

Burke, Joseph P. 1912. Farewell Letter to the People of the Church of St. Columba. *Historical Records and Studies* 6 (2): 212-15. Reprinted from the *New York Herald*, 26 June 1846.

Byrne, Cyril. 1988. Irish Language in Newfoundland. In *Proceedings of the First North American Congress of Celtic Studies held at Ottawa from 26th-30th March, 1986*, ed. Gordon W. MacLennan, 1-8. Ottawa: Chair of Celtic Studies, University of Ottawa.

Callahan, Joseph. 1994. The Irish Language in Pennsylvania. In *The Irish Language in the United States*, ed. Thomas W. Ihde, 18-26. Westport, CT: Bergin & Garvey.

The Celtic Race. 1857. *Corning Journal* (NY). 8 January, 1.

Doyle, David Noel. 1981. *Ireland, Irishmen and Revolutionary America 1760-1820*. Dublin: The Mercier Press.

German, Richard U. and Edwin R. Colston, eds. 1847. Spirit of the Irish Press. *Oneida Morning Herald*. 23 November, 1.

Government of Ireland. 1926. *Gaeltacht commission: report*. Dublin: Stationery Office.

———. 1956. *Gaeltacht Areas Order*. Dublin: House of the Oireachtas. http://www.irishstatutebook.ie/1956/en/si/0245.html (accessed 22 July 2012).

Ihde, Thomas. 2005. Irish Language Learning Textbooks Published in the United States: 1873-1904. *New Hibernia Review* 9:137-51.

———. 2008. Irish American Identity and the Irish Language. In *Affecting Irishness*, ed. James P. Byrne, Padraig Kirwan and Michael O'Sullivan, 219-30. New York: Peter Lang.

Johnson, H. N., ed. 1848. Horrible Scene at an Irish Execution abridged from the Cork Examiner. *Mohawk Courier* (Little Falls, NY). 20 April, 1.

Johnson, William, ed. 1857. News Items. *Geneva Courier* (Geneva, NY). 17 June, 1.

Kallen, Jeffery L. 1994. Irish as an American Ethnic Language. In *The Irish Language in the United States*, ed. Thomas W. Ihde, 27-40. Westport, CT: Bergin & Garvey.

Keating, Geoffrey. 1866. *Foras Feasa ar Eirinn do réir an Athar Seathrun Céiting, Ollamh Ré Diadhachta/ The History of Ireland from the earliest period to the English Invasion*. Trans. John O'Mahony. New York: James B. Kirker.

Laura Keene's Theatre (advertisement). 1862. *New York Herald*. 22 March, 7.

Local Intelligence: Services in Trinity Church. 1860. *Evening Express* (New York, NY). 12 November, 2.

Mac Aonghusa, Proinsias. 1979. An Ghaeilge i Meiriceá. In *Go Meiriceá Siar*, ed. Stiofán Ó hAnnracháin, 13-30. Baile Átha Cliath: Cumann Merriman.

Mather, Cotton. 1914. Memorable Providences, relating to Witchcrafts and Possessions by Cotton Mather, 1689. In *Narratives of Witchcraft Cases, 1648-1706*, ed. George Lincoln Burr, 89-144. New York: Barnes & Noble.

McGowan, Lynn. 1994. The Irish Language in America. In *The Irish Language in the United States*, ed. Thomas W. Ihde, 3-8. Westport, CT: Bergin & Garvey.

McMonagle, Sarah. 2012. Finding the Irish language in Canada. *New Hibernia Review* 16 (1): 134-49.

Meeting for the Irish Society. 1859. *Evening Express* (NY). 20 September, 2.

Mhic Suibhne, Hilary and Eibhlín Zurell, eds. 2008. *Súil Siar Barra Ó Donnabháin*. New Jersey: Daltaí na Gaeilge.

Miller, Kerby A. 1985. *Emigrants and Exiles*. New York: Oxford University Press.

Morley, Vincent. 2007. Irish Political Verse and the American Revolutionary War. *Journal of Irish and Scottish Studies* 1 (1): 45-59.

Ní Ghabhann, Gillian. 1998. The Gaelic Revival in the U.S. in the Nineteenth Century. *Chronicon: An Electronic History Journal* 2. http://www.ucc.ie/chronicon/nigh2fra.htm (accessed 1 August 2012).

Nilsen, Kenneth E. 1990. Thinking of Monday: Irish Speakers of Portland, Maine. *Éire-Ireland* 25 (1): 6-19.

———. 1996. The Irish Language in New York, 1850-1900. In *The New York Irish*, ed. Ronald H. Bayor and Timothy J. Meagher, 252-74. Baltimore: The John Hopkins University Press.

———. 2002a. Irish in nineteenth century [sic] New York. In *The Multilingual Apple: Languages in New York City*, ed. Ofelia García and Joshua A. Fishman, 53-69. 2nd ed. New York: Mouton de Gruyter.

———. 2002b. Irish Gaelic Literature in the United States. In *American Babel: Literatures of the United States from Abnaki to Zuni*, ed. Marc Shell, 188-218. Cambridge, MA: Harvard University Press.

Ó Buachalla, Breandán. 1979. Litreacha Phádraig Phiarais Cúndún. In *Go Meiriceá Siar*, ed. Stiofán Ó hAnnracháin, 31-37. Baile Átha Cliath: Cumann Merriman.

O'Carroll, I. 1988. The Boston Gaeltacht. *Irish Voice* (New York). 16 July, 16.

Ó Diollúin, Séamus. 2009. Lámhscríbhinní Gaeilge i Meiriceá. *An Gael* (New York) Geimhreadh: 12-15.

Ó Dúill, Gréagóir. 1994. Emigrant Letters from the Donegal *Gaeltacht*. In *The Irish Language in the United States*, ed. Thomas W. Ihde, 57-66. Westport, CT: Bergin & Garvey.

Ó Foghludha, Risteárd. 1932. *Pádraig Phiarais Cúndún 1777-1856*. Baile Átha Cliath: Oifig Díolta Foillseacháin Rialtais.

Ó Giollagáin, Conchúr, Seosamh Mac Donnacha, Fiona Ní Chualáin, Aoife Ní Shéaghdha and Mary O'Brien. 2007. *Comprehensive Linguistic Study of the Use of Irish in the Gaeltacht: Principal Findings and Recommendations*. Dublin: The Department of Community, Rural and Gaeltacht Affairs.

Ó hEadhra, Aodhán. 1997. *Na Gaeil i dTalamh an* Éisc. Baile Átha Cliath: Coiscéim.

Ó Laoire, Lillis. 2009. Is mé go déanach i mBaile Sheáin: Donnchadh Rua Mac Conmara agus Talamh an Éisc. *Léann* 2: 105-128.

Ó Liatháin, Pádraig. 2011. An Ghaeilge agus Talamh an Éisc: Taighde agus Taithí Phearsanta. In *An Ghaeilge i gCéin: Pobal agus Féiniúlacht Idirnáisiúnta*, ed. Siún Ní Dhuinn, 39-49. Baile Átha Cliath: Leabhair Comhar.

Ó Lócháin, Mícheál, ed. 1883. Philo-Celts. *An Gaodhal/The Gael* (Brooklyn, NY) 2 (5): 189.

Ó Siadhail, Pádraig. 2010. "The Indian Man" and the Irishman: James Mooney and Irish Folklore. *New Hibernia Review* 14 (2): 17-42.

Preparation for the Fenian Trials at Sweetsburg. 1866. *The World* (New York). 14 December, 1.

The Redlegs. 2012. http://www.moondance.tv/broadcast-barbados.htm (accessed 22 July 2012).

Roinn Oideachais, An. 1978. *Atlas a dó do scoileanna na hÉireann*. Baile Átha Cliath: Oifig an tSoláthair.

Society Notices: A Lecture in the Irish Language. 1865. *New York Sun*. 3 February, 1.

Sweeny, James M. 1864. City Government [official] Board of Councilmen. *New York Evening Express*. 28 October, 1.

Sweetsburgh, C.E. 1866. The Fenian Trials. *New York Times*. 13 December.

Uí Fhlannagáin, Fionnuala. 1990. *Mícheál Ó Lócháin agus An Gaodhal*. Baile Átha Cliath: An Clóchomhar.

Wall, Maureen. 1969. The Decline of the Irish Language. In *A View of the Irish Language*, ed. Brian Ó Cuív, 81-90. Dublin: The Stationery Office.

Michael Newton

Bards of the Forests, Prairies and Skyscrapers: Scottish Gaels in the Americas

Understanding the legacy of Scottish Highlanders in the Americas—past and present—requires keeping in mind four fundamental considerations that are often overlooked in standard accounts of Scottish immigrant history.

The first is that Scotland is not one nation, in the older sense of "a people united by common descent, culture and language," but two. Highlanders—or *Gàidheil* (Gaels), as they called themselves—considered themselves to be the indigenous people of Scotland who were relegated to the islands and rougher, higher regions of the north and west after anglophones usurped the better agricultural lands of the Lowlands and national institutions. The opposition between Highlander and Lowlander is a fundamental one which coloured Gaels' perceptions of ethnicity and historical experience, in both "Old" and "New" worlds (MacInnes 2006: 34-47; Newton 2011b).

Secondly, Gaelic literature—prose and poetry, written and oral—has a very long history as old as any in western Europe. Gaelic is popularly misrepresented as lacking a written literary tradition, but in fact centuries of professional literati enriched the verbal arts greatly. Gaelic poetry in particular has been the primary vehicle of individual and communal expression, and even the lowest social ranks have been influenced by the literary conventions of the professional élite. Due to the hostility of educational institutions controlled by the anglophone world toward the language and its adherents, however, literacy has been uncommon and the development of Gaelocentric education and scholarship has been inhibited until very recently. Regardless, copious oral and written Gaelic sources exist and provide key insights into Highland experiences.

Furthermore, Gaels commonly interpreted large-scale emigration as the culmination of cultural disasters which signified their growing subordination to the anglophone world and the lack of control over their own futures. Although the process of disenfranchisement started early—the 12th century—it was not complete until the mid-18th century. While many historians will dismiss the Battle of Culloden (1746, the last battle in a series of Jacobite Risings) as an overblown farce, it was seen by many Gaels as the last major action taken independently by them as a people—and a crushing military, political and emotional blow when it failed (Newton 2009: 34-39, 70-72). Centuries of alienation from and marginalization by the central government fostered what has been deemed a Gaelic "siege mentality" (MacInnes 2006: 27, 317).

Finally, since being effectively defused and subjugated within the British polity, many of Gaeldom's cultural assets

Figure 1. *The poet Iain MacGilleain's gravestone, in Glenbard, Antigonish County, Nova Scotia. (Michael Newton)*

have been appropriated by various groups and organizations, extracted from their previous owners and contexts and modified to suit new purposes (but accruing little if any benefits to Gaelic communities). This has not only been detrimental to the integrity of Gaelic culture but has caused widespread confusion as popular activities bearing the name of Highlanders are no longer representative of their origins (Newton 2011b).

Migration Patterns

Even before the Battle of Culloden, top-down pressure from landlords, who were accumulating debt and increasingly anglicized, made emigration an increasingly attractive option for families and communities. As early as 1729, one of the Duke of Argyll's agents observed that tenants in Kintyre were being inspired by Irish neighbours to leave for America. Colonial schemes attempting to occupy and defend British territories encouraged emigration: during the 1730s, planned settlements of Scottish Gaels were established in Darien (Georgia) and the Cape Fear Valley of the Carolinas, and one failed attempt in New York province stranded some 450 Highlanders (Newton 2001: 69-71; Murdoch 2010: 41-49).

The Board of Annexed Estates took control of forfeited Jacobite lands from 1749 onwards, imposing social and economic "improvement" on Gaelic society. This often forced people to change their mode of production to fit the needs of the wider British economy and to resettle in barren, peripheral lands, breaking Gaelic attachment to place and making Highlanders more likely to undertake larger-scale migration. By ca. 1760 landlords were starting to replace cattle with sheep as the basis of the Highland economy, often accompanied by Lowland shepherds (Newton 2001: 73-79; 2009: 37-39).

An estimated 12,000 Highlanders were recruited to fight in North America during the Seven Years' War (1755-1763), and many were rewarded with land grants upon which they settled relations from home. With rapidly rising rents in the Highlands and diminishing economic prospects, many saw emigration as the best means of avoiding financial ruin and securing their cultural and linguistic freedoms. Chain migration to established bases became common, highlighting the Highland preference to remain in family and community units. Those with the most to lose were usually the first to leave, with the middle-class tacksmen taking a leading role in instigating and organizing migrations. Emigration from the Highlands peaked just as the American Revolutionary War started, with settlement beginning in the Atlantic Maritimes. Religious persecution was a factor in the sizable Catholic exodus (Newton 2001: 37, 71-83, 93, 103; Kennedy 2002: 18-19; Nilsen 2010: 91).

Some 21,000-24,000 Highlanders were recruited to fight for the British Crown in eighteen regiments during the American Revolutionary War. When the new United States required citizens to pledge their allegiance, many Highlanders relocated to Glengarry, Ontario. Loyalist veterans were rewarded with land grants in Ontario,

Figure 2. Culloden Cairn at Knoydart, Nova Scotia, where three survivors of the Battle of Culloden are buried. (Michael Newton)

Québec, New Brunswick and Nova Scotia. Although some migration to the United States continued, such as small bursts to the Carolinas in the late 18th century, most Scots were redirected to Canada (Gibson 1995: 21; Newton 2001: 112, 163-66; Murdoch 2010: 57-58).

Gaels resorted increasingly to emigration as a protest against the economic, cultural and religious policies of landlords, with substantial numbers leaving for Ontario and the Maritimes. Fearing the departure of servile labourers who made them a tidy profit producing kelp, landlords lobbied Parliament to pass the *Passenger Act* of 1803, which made emigration too expensive for most. Regardless, Lord Selkirk (Thomas Douglas) made relief of Highlanders via emigration a very public cause, supervising settlement in Prince Edward Island (1803-1808) and the Red River Valley of Manitoba (1813-1815).

After the hostilities between Britain and France ceased in 1815, kelp, cattle, wool, fish and grain prices collapsed and landlords quickly changed their tune: tenants, no longer able to turn financial profits, were unwanted. This accelerated the era of Clearances, when landlords expelled tenants (often already relocated to marginal lands) and loaded them on ships for the colonies. Deprived of traditional modes of production and access to productive land while the population simultaneously swelled, those Highlanders who remained became dependent upon the potato. The potato blight of the 1840s precipitated a crisis for survival. Emigration was the obvious solution, as it did not require addressing the economic and political monopoly of the landed classes (Newton 2001: 60-61, 76-80; Harper 2004: 44-61).

By this time, the Maritimes were crowded. The border between the U.S. and Canada was porous, and Canadian-born Gaels were drawn to the booming economies of the northern United States and western frontier. In 1846 the first Gaelic-medium church was founded in Boston, and Gaels were mining for gold in California by the 1850s. Large Gaelic-speaking communities also formed in Chicago, New York, Detroit, Toronto, Vancouver, Duluth and Montréal. Emigration agents were drawing Highlanders to the prairies by the 1870s, but some found conditions so harsh that they drifted elsewhere. Recruitment to the prairies continued into the 1920s (Newton 2001: 167-71, 189, 212; Campey 2008: 110-18). In the 1930s, 10,000 Gaelic speakers were estimated in Vancouver and 20,000 in Toronto (MacKinnon 1935).

Highlanders referred to the entire continent (regardless of political boundaries) as "America," or by the kenning *Dùthaich nan Craobh* (Land of Trees) or variants thereof. There were other smaller and lesser-known Gaelic settlements in the Americas outside of Canada and the U.S.: small numbers of Gaels (particularly single men from Lewis) went to Argentina between the 1860s and 1939 (James 2010); a trickle of Gaels, mostly men, went to the Caribbean as early as the 1650s as prisoners of war and then in various capacities on plantations from the mid-1700s into the early 1800s (Newton 2001: 67-68, 205-206; Kidd 2010).

Gaelic Voices

The discourse of Highland communities—reflections on their values, experiences and concerns—is accessible best in the Gaelic oral traditions that have operated "below the radar" of formal institutions. Folklorist John Shaw has summarized the use of informal native institutions (especially the *céilidh*) to construct, transmit and discuss tradition, allowing in turn for an integrated sense of history and identity meaningful to those within the community:

> Storytelling, in its varied settings, has also functioned in a more practical way, serving as an effective means of affirming and maintaining distinctive cultural values, promoting social cohesion, situating the community and each individual within a larger Gaelic interior oral historical record, socialising children and teaching them about the world of adults, and maintaining the Gaelic intellectual life that had continued even after the aristocracy stopped supporting professional performers, some three centuries ago. In a culture that had only rarely received any support from formal institutions—and where physical punishment for speaking Gaelic in the schoolhouse is still recalled—oral performance in the language in an intensively supportive social context functioned as an effective antidote to cultural pressures from the English-speaking world and as a means of regularly affirming group identity while avoiding direct confrontation. (2007b: xvii)

Gaelic texts open windows into the community and mindset of individuals, but they pose their own challenges: handling them requires fluency in the Gaelic language, knowledge of the conventions of the Gaelic literary tradition and its specific genres, familiarity with the larger corpus so as to recognize intertextual allusions, sensitivity to variations, omissions and elaborations of the standard conventions, and an awareness of how the context and agenda of the author has conditioned the text. Gaelic texts are refracted through the lenses of literary tradition and historical experience and may be pressed into service for particular purposes. Continuing to neglect them, however, would be to continue to deny Gaels' own role in the creation of and participation in their own history.

The Gaelic poetic tradition was a conservative one that derived directly from medieval practice. Continuity from the professional literati is evident in numerous immigrant poets: Iain MacGilleain, "the Bard MacLean"

(1787-1848), one of the last professional poets to enjoy patronage from a clan chieftain (Dunbar 2010); Iain "am Pìobaire Mór" MacGilleBhràth (1784-1860), who was official piper to MacDonald of Glenaladale (Dunbar 2004-2006: 27-8); Ailean "the Ridge" MacDhomhnaill (1794-1868), a scion of the Keppoch MacDonalds (Rankin 2004); poets Iain and Lachlann MacMhuirich of Cape Breton (fl. 1890-1920), descended from Clanranald historians. Not only did such poets bring an "oral canon" and set of literary conventions with them, a few also brought Gaelic manuscripts (and other cultural relics).

One of the first tasks of Gaelic poets, as spokespeople of the immigrant community, was to make sense of the experience of migration.

> Gaelic poetry was used by the poets of the emigrant generation in much the same fashion as it had traditionally been used in the Old World—to define and reinforce the values of their society, particularly at times of crisis—and for the poets of the emigrant generation, there was no greater crisis than that brought on by the departure from the Old World and the challenge of rebuilding Gaelic communities in the New. (Dunbar 2004-2006: 25)

Some poets entered versified debates about the merits or failings of emigration. A close examination of the range of emigrant poetry reveals a diversity of opinions about leaving Scotland: the most upbeat tended to be those who were young, had come with their family or community, belonged to the lower socio-economic rank, or settled in well-resourced regions; those most despondent tended to be those who were older, were lacking a social support network, belonged to the higher socio-economic rank or who arrived in harsh conditions (Dunbar 2004-2006: 39-76). Some must have felt it necessary to put a positive spin on the experience: rather than recounting emigration as the result of cultural subjugation by despised enemies, it was sometimes recast as an heroic adventure and the overcoming of hardships.

As in Scotland, Gaelic songs served a variety of purposes: social commentary, personal reflection, sheer entertainment and so on. Songs could be pressed into promoting solidarity, such as those composed to mobilize Gaels in political campaigns to vote for particular people or parties, or to join (or abandon) the temperance movement (Dunbar 2004-2006: 79-82, 106-11). Songs also promoted pride in Gaelic cultural values and achievements, and the language itself. This is particularly clear in songs composed for and printed in Gaelic-medium periodicals, and those composed for and performed at social organizations (77-79, 101-102; Newton forthcoming). Songs, almost constantly present in people's lives, cannot but have had a pivotal role in their cultural makeup and perceptions of history and identity. There are records of hundreds of Gaelic poets across North America, active in both rural and urban settings.

Gaelic literary tradition consists of many other genres as well: international wonder tales, Fenian tales, clan sagas, fairy legends, etc. Some fictional oral narratives, a few surviving to the present, are directly derived from medieval literature, having entered oral tradition after being read aloud from manuscripts centuries ago in the courts of chieftains (Shaw 1988: 80-81). Some idea of the richness of these narratives and the propagation of their variants across Gaelic communities is suggested in the chapters by MacDonald and Sumner in this volume.

Shaw has recently suggested a classification of Gaelic legends in Nova Scotia, grouping them according to the degree to which they are rooted in Scotland or the immigrant setting. There are many legends chronicling noteworthy beliefs, characters and events, including the experiences of emigration, settlement and the interactions between various groups. Amongst those analyzed by Shaw is a group of legends, which he terms the Dòmhnall Gorm Cycle, centred on "a specific ruthless soldier from Scotland during the war between the French and the British for the control of North America from 1756 to 1763" (2007a: 52). The implicit message of these tales is that Dòmhnall Gorm is an agent of the Devil and of the British Empire who inflicted brutality upon Native and French peoples:

> In spite of his impeccable Gaelic pedigree and central role in the Eastern Theatre of the war, Gaelic legend is consistent in emphasising his demonic aspects rather than the qualities of bravery and military valour recorded by his British masters. Storytellers convey a grudging respect for his cunning and effectiveness as a soldier, but the most striking characteristic of the oral accounts is the unbridled savagery that he loosed upon the French-speaking Acadian population of the island. (54)

Nor is Dòmhnall Gorm represented as beneficent to his own people. Such narratives convey viewpoints and opinions not readily available in official documentation, and alert us that the commonly designated role of Highlanders as "imperial shock troops" was not relished or endorsed by all. Similarly revealing is an analysis of Gaelic first-encounter narratives in Nova Scotia which display guilt about occupying Native territory and the desire to reconcile with indigenous neighbours (Newton 2011a).

Education, Literacy and Print Culture

The Reformation (and Counter-Reformation) fostered a strong correlation between religion, education and literacy: religious denominations used education as a means of indoctrinating and securing the loyalty of congregations against the lure of competing faiths, with vernacular literacy providing direct access to tracts. Scottish central government rejected the vernacular provision of this premise by espousing a formal policy in 1616 to use English-medium education to "abolish and remove" Gaelic as part of a wider effort of cultural and religious assimilation (Newton 2009: 31).

The Society in Scotland for Propagating Christian Knowledge (SSPCK) was established in Edinburgh in 1709. Its first mission was to eradicate Catholicism and Gaelic from the Highlands. In 1729 it extended its mandate to converting Indigenous Americans and seems to have sponsored one minister in the colonies who served both Gaelic settlers and Native peoples. He was to preach to the older generation in their native tongue but "teach and catechise the children in English" (Meek 1989: 387). By the mid-1700s the SSPCK moderated their goal of imposing English, acknowledging that native languages expedited conversion on the road to assimilation (Meek 1989).

By the late 18th century, religious schools were raising rates of Gaelic literacy. This was concentrated at the higher ranks of Gaelic society, so the greater rate of migration among the upper and skilled classes may have skewed education toward colonists (Nilsen 2002: 127; Meek 2007b: 107; 2007a: 154, 166). Rev. James MacGregor's letter to the British and Foreign Bible Society in 1807 implies that literacy was widespread:

> Many of the younger generation, and numbers of the old, can read the Gaelic, for though we have but three or four full copies of the Bible and a few odd volumes, yet we have plenty of Psalters, Catechisms, and some religious tracts. It would certainly be a great mercy to have Gaelic Bibles somewhat plenty among them. (Nilsen 2002: 139)

MacGregor may have been overstating literacy to boost his campaign for texts, but, in any case, increased migration of poorer people reduced the averages (Kennedy 2002: 42-44, 125).

The connection between literacy and its spiritual applications remained strong for generations. The first Gaelic publications in North America were sermons delivered at the Raft Swamp church of North Carolina in 1791. The Gaelic Bible, printed in its entirety in 1807, spurred the drive towards universal literacy. Religious titles account for 75 per cent of all Gaelic publications in the 19th century (Meek 2007a: 154-61). By the 1830s religious texts—mostly Protestant, but Catholic as well—were being composed and printed in the Maritimes. Of 353 Bibles sent to Pictou in 1836, 119 were in Gaelic (Nilsen 2002: 127-31). Even immigrants who left Scotland in the 18th century must have maintained contract with the Highlands, for many copies of Gaelic Bibles, psalters and catechisms can still be found in the Carolinas, upper New York, Mississippi and elsewhere.

Secular publications (and manuscripts) also attest to wide interests in Gaelic culture and history. The *Prince Edward Island Times* became the first

North American newspaper to carry a Gaelic column in 1836, although most material was recycled from Scottish sources. The Gaelic newspaper *An Cuairtear Gaelach*, printed in Scotland 1840-1843, reached the Bard MacLean, whose ode to it set a precedent followed by Gaelic poets at the outset of practically every other Gaelic newspaper to appear. John Boyd of Antigonish printed a short-lived (and largely derivative) newspaper, *An Cuairtear Òg Gaelach*, in 1851. This was followed by the enduring *Casket* in 1852 which began as a half-English, half-Gaelic weekly but quickly diminished its Gaelic content (Nilsen 2002: 130-33; Dunbar 2004-2006: 101; Newton forthcoming).

After generations of attack and marginalization by anglophones in Scotland, Gaelic immigrants found themselves confronting essentially the same prejudices and demands. These experiences contributed to an inferiority complex, a lack of social cohesion (e.g., higher-than-average rates of out-migration), and lowered resistance against hegemonic pressures (Kennedy 2002: 71-75; Bennett 2003: 277-315).

> In one important social aspect Gaelic is different from many other non-English languages in America, such as the French of Quebec and the German of Pennsylvania: the parent language in its old country had, until recently, a status no better than that it enjoys in the new land.... The Highlanders who emigrated to Canada were free, for a time, from these repressive influences; but they carried with them the idea that education was coincident with a knowledge of English, and when state schools were founded in Nova Scotia in 1864, no provision for the teaching of Gaelic was made.... In general the level of Gaelic scholarship and literacy appears to be lower amongst Canadian Gaelic speakers than it is in Scotland. (Campbell 1936: 130)

Gaels recognized that the lack of formal education in Gaelic weakened intergenerational transmission of the language, enfeebled its ability to keep pace with modern life, and contributed to a negative perception of the value and prestige of the language. More attempts were made to establish Gaelic-medium schools in immigrant communities than is generally recognized, but these efforts were inevitably short-lived because of the lack of Gaelic teaching materials, the lack of training for teachers in the language, and an unyielding anglocentric hegemony (Dunbar in this volume). One such anecdote, from Mississippi, exemplifies the difficulties:

> The first school was established about 1812. The Gaelic language was spoken exclusively among the settlers, and was also taught in their school. This language remained the vernacular until the early [18]20s, when other settlers arrived, some of whose children

knew English alone. For the sake of the English-speaking children
the teacher then forbade the further use of Gaelic in the school
room. Having been discarded in the school, the Gaelic language
soon fell into disuse except to a limited extent among the older
people. (Wilkins 1902: 266)

Other fragmentary 19th-century evidence attests to limited efforts to provide Gaelic-medium education to children in Glengarry, Ontario (1824), St. Ann's, Cape Breton (1820s-1840s), Arisaig, Nova Scotia (1836), and Megantic, Québec (1836) (Kennedy 2002: 42-53; Fairney 2010: 72-73; Nilsen 2010: 97-98).

Despite formidable pressures, some North American Gaels were determined enough to continue their struggles to perpetuate their language, even to the present day. There was a renewed sense of purpose in the 1870s, when Gaels had created enough intellectual resources to assert "a sense of the collective worth of Gaelic literature" (Meek 2007a: 168). This was ultimately undermined, however, by the *Scottish Education Act* of 1872 (and equivalent education policies in North America), which prompted further defensive responses.

The first issue of the newspaper *An Gàidheal*, published in Toronto, opened with an editorial about the stigmatization of Gaelic and the need to protect and develop it. Although the paper soon relocated to Glasgow, it retained readers throughout North America who contributed to this revitalization (Newton 2003: 68). Gaelic columns appeared in Nova Scotian newspapers in the 1880s, but the most significant achievement was the all-Gaelic newspaper *Mac-Talla* printed in Cape Breton 1892-1904 with readers all over North America and Britain (Dunn 1991 [1968]: 84-88). Further Gaelic newspapers followed, as well as columns in English newspapers which have flourished and faded to the present (Nilsen 2010: 101).

Two Canadian Gaelic scholars active at the turn of the 20th century merit special note. Alexander Maclean Sinclair (1840-1924) of Nova Scotia was the product of a very literate Gaelic family (his grandfather being the Bard Maclean). He published fifteen volumes of Gaelic poetry, conducted fieldwork recording oral tradition and contributed many items to newspapers (Linkletter 2010). Alexander Fraser (1860-1936), a native of Inverness-shire, Scotland, immigrated to Toronto in 1886. Fraser also recorded Gaelic oral tradition in Canada, edited several Gaelic books and newspapers and became the first archivist of Ontario in 1903 (Fraser 1998-2007).

The loosening of anglocentric hegemony and extension of multiculturalism has improved the ideological climate for minoritized groups, but only after the Gaelic speech community has dwindled. Important folklore collections and literary anthologies from Nova Scotia have been published, especially since the 1990s, and hundreds of recordings are now available online (Nilsen 2010: 101-103). In 1997, the Nova Scotia Department of Education initiated a Gaelic Studies Curriculum for High School; it is currently offered at fifteen schools (Office of Gaelic Affairs). In 2011 the Royal National Mòd in Scotland awarded Lewis MacKinnon, a native of Antigonish and currently CEO of the Office of Gaelic Affairs, the Bardic Crown for his poetry collection *Famhair*. This was the first time the honour was conferred on someone born outside of Scotland and indicates renewed links between Scotland and Canada.

Language, Ethnicity and Identity

Language has always been a central defining feature of Gaelic/Highland identity (Newton 2009: 52-55) and this remained so after emigration. When Gaelic texts composed in North America self-consciously define who "we" are, the ethnonym *Gàidheil* is almost invariably used, not *Albannaich* (Scots); there is no Highland-Lowland synthesis in Gaelic tradition (with the exception of song-poetry commemorating military engagements and for organizations with strong loyalty to the British Empire).

Many materials demonstrate the desire to maintain some degree of communal cohesion by reference to past unity, despite increasing fragmentation and assimilation. The rhetorical conventions, literary devices and historical landmarks used to express these aspirations across a wide expanse of space and time—from medieval Scotland into 20th-century North America—illustrate that Gaels had stable and rich cultural resources which afforded them a sense of continuity as a distinctive ethnic group, and that study of the Highland immigrant experience must begin in Gaelic Scotland. The ethnonyms for identifying self and the many others encountered are very important aspects of ethnic consciousness lost in translation into English (Newton 2011b, forthcoming).

In the aftermath of the last Jacobite Rising (1745-1746), an oppositional culture in Gaeldom was effectively eliminated and deference to the British Crown was reinforced. The Gaelic world was circumscribed by anglocentric institutions that monopolized all means of social and economic advancement at a crucial point in its development. Rather than being able to foster social, educational, political and economic institutions from their own norms and precedents, a disjuncture was imposed between the Gaelic past (rural, kin-based, subsistence-level) and the process of "modernization" introduced by an anglocentric regime. Kinship networks and informal social practices remained, but they lacked élite leadership and were not sufficiently resilient to withstand assimilationist policies. Participation in and rewards from wars in North America cemented loyalties and realigned cultural focuses toward the British Crown (Newton 2001: 103-62; Dziennik 2012).

Early Gaelic immigrant communities in the United States were interdependent with anglophone communities that did not value cultural diversity and may have been tainted by the stain of loyalism during the American Revolution. Despite failing to designate an official national language, Gaelic immigrants stood to lose their citizenship and property because of being unable to interact with governmental apparatus through the medium of English, even before the end of the 18th century (Gibson 1995: 42-45).

In British North America, Gaelic élite who occupied key positions of power were subservient to anglophone norms, even when it compromised their mother tongue and culture (Kennedy 2002). Prominent Gaelic poets and scholars were generally advocates of British imperialism who attempted to reserve a special niche for the Gaels (especially as soldiers) within its order but were seldom willing to question its moral authority or cultural framework. Some were, in fact, quite vocal in distancing themselves from any allegations of allegiance to Gaelic. This left Gaeldom without effective leadership, especially as the élite ranks were quicker to assimilate than the lower (Newton 2003: 84-85; 2010b, 2011b).

Much ink has been spilt over the origins of tartanism and Highlandism, but very little from a Gaelic perspective. The rise of these iconographic cults coincided with Gaeldom's unparalleled crises for survival and reflects its subordinate status in the British polity and corresponding inability to maintain its own cultural resources or participate equitably in its own self-representation. Like other subaltern peoples, the conquered Gaels were turned into "noble savages" whose cultural assets were stripped and repurposed by the élite, resulting in new symbols, arts and activities derived from tradition but no longer controlled by Gaels nor representative of their culture (Newton 2010b).

Although it is commonly assumed that the Highland Games were established to preserve aspects of Scottish Highland culture, for example, these events

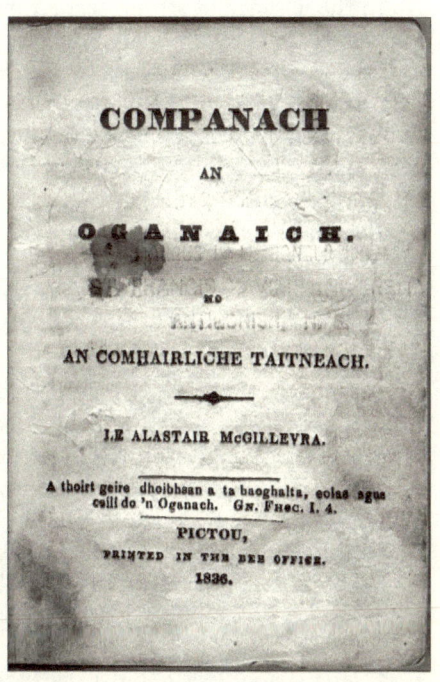

Figure 3. Title page for Scottish Gaelic book Companach an Òganaich, *published in Nova Scotia, 1836. (St. Francis Xavier University Library Archives)*

were orchestrated by the landed gentry. The Games enabled them to enhance their own image as the natural leaders of Highland society, to project a romantic image of themselves and their estates and to underscore their commitment to the British Empire by promoting a narrow role for Highlanders as loyal soldiers. The actual functions and competitions at the Games were crafted to highlight Highlanders as brawny, macho and militaristic rustics eager to win the approval of their superiors, to the exclusion of their other cultural achievements or traditions. Had the Games been run by Highlanders for the purposes of maintaining Highland culture, they would have featured the many aspects of Gaelic oral and literary tradition; commitment to such internal touchstones was instead compromised to provide entertainment for anglophones. In other words, the Highland Games were part of a series of measures designed to transform selected elements of Highland tradition into palatable commodities agreeable to the tastes and fantasies of the "respectable" classes of British society, and to orient Gaels toward meeting the demands made of them by the British State and away from their own development as a separate and independent culture. Similar problems surround Highland Dancing, tartan, bagpipe bands and so on.

In the absence of strong secular institutions, religion took on greater importance in Gaelic society, especially as Church establishments tightened their grip over followers in the 19th century. While some ministers and priests did support Gaelic, the ultimate focus of religion is God rather than language development, and institutional support for "minority interests" was always tentative (Kennedy 2002: 123-30; Bennett 2003: 139-42, 285; Newton 2003: 74-78).

Recent research on Canadian census statistics reveals the wide distribution of the language in the 19th century—"the largest non-official language at the time of Confederation" (1867)—but also how rapidly it retreated in the face of the above factors:

> A comparison of the 1901 and 1931 figures illustrates the extent to which Gaelic was truly a *Canadian* language at the turn of the century, with robust communities across the country. Conversely, it also shows how rapidly the language went into decline in the intervening three decades. Whereas Nova Scotia lost about half of its Gaelic speaking population, Ontario's Gàidhealtachd fell by almost 90%. Quebec and PEI fared little better, losing 80% and 85% of its speakers respectively. (Dembling 2006: 207)

Gaelic stereotypes about Lowlanders (*Goill*) conditioned perceptions of and expectations about non-Gaelic peoples, whether fellow European immigrants or First Nations. Despite this, race was not always as strong a determinant in defining identity as we might assume today: there are many anecdotes in Gaelic oral tradition about people of non-European ancestry becoming fluent in Gaelic and accepted as members of the wider Gaelic community. Such anecdotes served not only to discuss the disparities between racial and linguistic definitions of identity, but to criticize Gaels who abandoned their mother tongue (Newton 2010a). The Reverend Tormad Domhnullach provides typical remarks:

> Thachair gu leòir oirnn ann an Canada anns nach eil boinne de fhuil a' Ghàidheil, a thàinig nan cloinn a-nall á Sasainn agus a thog a' Ghàidhlig gun saothair anns na taighean 'san deach an togail agus a labhras an-diugh i cho fileanta ciatach ri Gàidheal sam bith nach dh'fhàg Alba riamh. Chan e sin a-mhàin, ach chunnaic sinn daoine de gach dath agus cinneadh ann an Canada a labhras i gu eireachdail. (Domhnullach 1933: 2)

> (We have encountered plenty [of people] in Canada who don't have a drop of Highland blood, who immigrated as children from England and picked up Gaelic without any effort in their own homes and who speak it as fluently and winsomely as any Highlander who never left Scotland. Not only that, but we ourselves have seen people of every colour and ethnic group in Canada who speak it eloquently.)

Languages were exchanged in all directions. Coming from a multilingual environment, often fluent in Gaelic, English and French, Highland fur traders were noted for being open to and adept at learning Indigenous American languages. Some of their "mixed-race" children were just as multilingual, as this account from the North-West Territories of Canada attests:

> He states that many of the half-breeds talk splendid Gaelic, and if asked where they came from they name some place in Lewis, though they have never seen Scotland. The explanation of this is that their fathers, who were Hudson Bay Company's servants, and had married squaws, hailed from Lewis. The half-breed is proud of his Gaelic, as he thinks it connects him with his father's country, of which he is also very proud. (*The Scottish-American Journal*, 9 April 1902)

In the late 19th century, a number of Gaelic organizations emerged where there were large Gaelic-speaking communities, such as New York; Chicago; Boston; Detroit; Toledo; Washington, DC; Seattle; Toronto; Guelph; Montréal; Vancouver; Hamilton; Winnipeg; Antigonish and Sydney (Cape Breton). They mostly restricted themselves to social activities, but some supported literacy instruction, new literary composition and celebrations of traditional culture. Some were inspired by Welsh and Irish neighbours, but their effectiveness at enabling the next generation to become Gaelic speakers was often compromised by the factors outlined above (Newton 2003).

Individual learners of Gaelic and societies supporting them can be found throughout North America, with surprising amounts of activity beyond traditional speech communities (Newton 2005). The Office of Gaelic Affairs in Nova Scotia was established in 2006, the first official organ supporting Gaelic language initiatives in Canada. This has facilitated the development of materials for education and other official institutions, as well as funded grassroots initiatives in local communities.

Future Research

Given the lack of attention to Scottish Gaelic in North American academia, much fundamental groundwork is yet to be done, even before localized studies and macro-scale analyses (such as those ventured in this chapter) can be written conclusively.

Arguably the most important tasks yet to be done are identifying and editing Gaelic texts from books, manuscripts, periodicals (especially local newspapers), records from Gaelic organizations, posters and other ephemera. There are also many audio recordings of Gaelic tradition bearers and social gatherings (such as *céilidh*s) in private collections. Sustained research on such materials could reveal how tradition and cultural patterns adapt to local contexts and conditions, move along social networks, are harnessed selectively for particular reasons and contribute to ethnic cohesion, division and/or assimilation.

As MacDonald's chapter in this volume demonstrates, place names in many Gaelic immigrant communities

Figure 4. Program for Evan MacColl Memorial Concert in Toronto, 1930. (Michael Newton)

(especially Nova Scotia, eastern Québec [Bennett 2003: 43-45, 243] and Ontario) might still be recovered from oral tradition but are quickly passing out of memory. Place names are of many varieties and reflect a range of attitudes. Place names may be coined in Gaelic, transliterated into Gaelic (such as *Glasbaidh* for "Glace Bay," Cape Breton), translated into Gaelic, transliterated from Gaelic to English, etc. Some are new coinages describing the actual location or people thereof (such as *Muileann an t-Sagairt* for Alexandria, Ontario or *Inverhuron*, Tiverton, Ontario); some reflect a direct transference from the locale of the original immigrants (such as Glengarry); and others reflect aspirations corresponding to the wider homeland but not the original locale of the immigrant community itself (such as Aberdeen, North Carolina or New Glasgow, Nova Scotia). Taking such nuances into consideration can inform us about the survival of cultural memory, the relationship to land in the immigrant context, language shift and the trajectories of assimilation.

Notes

1. At the minimum. The largely Norse-derived peoples of Orkney and Shetland would constitute another.

References

Bennett, Margaret. 2003. *Oatmeal and the Catechism: Scottish Gaelic Settlers in Quebec.* Montréal and Kingston: McGill-Queen's University Press.

Campbell, John L. 1936. Scottish Gaelic in Canada. *American Speech* 11 (2): 128-36.

Campey, Lucille. 2008. *An Unstoppable Force: The Scottish Exodus to Canada.* Toronto: Natural Heritage Books.

Dembling, Jonathan. 2006. Gaelic in Canada: new evidence from an old census. In *Cànan & Cultur / Language & Culture: Rannsachadh na Gàidhlig 3*, ed. Wilson McLeod, James Fraser and Anja Gunderloch, 203-214. Edinburgh, Scotland: Dunedin Academic Press.

Domhnullach, Tormad. 1933. An Iomlaid Amaideach: Sgeul airson Luchd Àicheadh na Gàidhlig. *Teachdaire nan Gaidheal* 5 (8): 1-2.

Dunbar, Robert. 2004-2006. Poetry of the Emigrant Generation. *Transactions of the Gaelic Society of Inverness* 64:22-125.

———. 2010. Am Bàrd MacGilleuin: Am Bàrd agus Alba Nuadh. In *Rannsachadh na Gàidhlig 5 / Fifth Scottish Gaelic Research Conference*, ed. Kenneth Nilsen, 42-66. Sydney, NS: Cape Breton University Press.

Dunn, Charles. 1991 [1968]. *Highland Settler: A Portrait of the Scottish Gael in Cape Breton and Eastern Nova Scotia.* Wreck Cove, NS: Breton Books.

Dziennik, Matthew. 2012. "Cutting Heads from Shoulders": The Conquest of Canada in Gaelic thought, 1759-1791. In *1759 Revisited: The Conquest of Canada*, ed. Phillip K. Buckner and John Reid, 241-66. Toronto: University of Toronto Press.

Fairney, Janice. 2010. The Branch Societies of the Highland Society of London. In *Rannsachadh na Gàidhlig 5 / Fifth Scottish Gaelic Research Conference*, ed. Kenneth Nilsen, 67-77. Sydney, NS: Cape Breton University Press.

Fraser, Marie. 1998-2007. Alexander Fraser [1860-1936]. *Clan Fraser Society of Canada*. http://www.clanfraser.ca/alexande.htm (accessed 5 June 2012).

Gibson, Joyce. 1995. *Scotland County Emerging: 1750-1900*. Laurel Hill, NC: Gibson.

Harper, Marjory. 2004. *Adventurers and Exiles: The Great Scottish Exodus*. London: Profile Books.

James, Clive. 2010. Gàidhlig ann an Argentina/Scottish Gaelic in Argentina. In *Rannsachadh na Gàidhlig 5 / Fifth Scottish Gaelic Research Conference*, ed. Kenneth Nilsen, 108-115. Sydney, NS: Cape Breton University Press.

Kennedy, Michael. 2002. *Gaelic Nova Scotia: An Economic, Cultural, and Social Impact Study*. Halifax, NS: Nova Scotia Museum.

Kidd, Sheila. 2010. Turtaran is faclairean: Ceanglaichean eadar Gàidheil na h-Alba agus Gàidheil nan Innseachan an Iar. *Aiste* 3:19-48.

Linkletter, Michael. 2010. Gaelic at St. Francis Xavier University and the Rev. Alexander Maclean Sinclair. In *Rannsachadh na Gàidhlig 5 / Fifth Scottish Gaelic Research Conference*, ed. Kenneth Nilsen, 134-48. Sydney, NS: Cape Breton University Press.

MacInnes, John. 2006. *Dùthchas nan Gàidheal: Selected Essays of John MacInnes*. Edinburgh: Birlinn.

MacKinnon, Jonathan. 1935. Gaelic Speech in Canada. *Sydney Post-Record*. 7 May, 7.

Meek, Donald. 1989. Scottish Highlanders, North American Indians and the SSPCK: Some Cultural Perspectives. *Records of the Scottish Church History Society* 23:378-96.

———. 2007a. Gaelic Communities and the Use of Texts. In *Ambition and Industry, 1800-1880*. Vol. 3 of *The Edinburgh History of the Book in Scotland*, ed. Bill Bell, 153-72. Edinburgh: Edinburgh University Press.

———. 2007b. Gaelic Printing and Publishing. In *Ambition and Industry, 1800-1880*. Vol. 3 of *The Edinburgh History of the Book in Scotland*, ed. Bill Bell, 107-22. Edinburgh: Edinburgh University Press.

Murdoch, Alexander. 2010. *Scotland and America, c.1600–c.1800*. New York: Palgrave Macmillan.

Newton, Michael. 2001. *We're Indians Sure Enough: The Legacy of the Scottish Highlanders in the United States*. Richmond, VA: Saorsa Media.

———. 2003. "Becoming Cold-Hearted Like the Gentiles Around Them": Scottish Gaelic in the United States 1872-1912. *eKeltoi* 2:63-131.

———. 2005. "This Could Have Been Mine": Scottish Gaelic Learners in North America. *eKeltoi* 1:1-37.

———. 2009. *Warriors of the Word: The World of the Scottish Highlanders*. Edinburgh: Birlinn.

———. 2010a. "Have you heard about the Gaelic-Speaking African?": Gaelic Folklore about Race. *Comparative American Studies* 8:88-106.

———. 2010b. "Paying for the Plaid": Scottish Gaelic Identity Politics in Nineteenth-Century North America. In *New Perspectives on Tartan*, ed. Ian Brown, 63-81. Edinburgh: Edinburgh University Press.

———. 2011a. The Macs meet the "Mic-macs": First Encounter Narratives in Scottish Gaelic from Nova Scotia. *Journal of Irish and Scottish Studies* 5(1): 67-96.

———. 2011b. Scotland's Two Solitudes Abroad: Scottish Gaelic Immigrant Identity and Culture in North America. In *The Shaping of Scottish Identities: Sex, Nation, and the Worlds Beyond*, ed. Jodi A. Campbell, Elizabeth Ewan and Heather Parker, 215-33. Guelph, ON: Guelph Series in Scottish Studies.

———. forthcoming. *Seanchaidh na Coille: Litreachas Gàidhlig an Canada*. Sydney, NS: Cape Breton University Press.

Nilsen, Kenneth. 2002. Some Notes on pre-Mac-Talla Gaelic Publishing in Nova Scotia. In *Rannsachadh na Gàidhlig 2000*, ed. Colm Ó Baoill and Nancy McGuire, 127-40. Aberdeen: An Clò Gaidhealach.

———. 2010. A' Ghàidhlig an Canada: Scottish Gaelic in Canada. In *The Edinburgh Companion to the Gaelic Language*, ed. Moray Watson and Michelle Macleod, 90-107. Edinburgh: Edinburgh University Press.

Office of Gaelic Affairs. Gaelic in Nova Scotia. http://www.gov.ns.ca/oga/aboutgaelic.asp (accessed 5 May 2012).

Rankin, Effie. 2004. *Às a' Bhràighe / Beyond the Braes: The Gaelic Songs of Allan the Ridge MacDonald, 1794-1868*. Sydney, NS: Cape Breton University Press.

Shaw, John, 1988. Observations on the Cape Breton Gàidhealtachd and its relevance to Present-Day Celtic Studies. In *Proceedings of the First North American Congress of Celtic Studies*, ed. Gordon MacLennan, 75-87. Ottawa: University of Ottawa.

———. 2007a. (E)migrating Legends and Sea Change. *Folklore: Electronic Journal of Folklore* 37:43-58.

———. ed. 2007b. *Na Beanntaichean Gorma agus Sgeulachdan Eile à Ceap Breatainn / The Blue Mountains and Other Gaelic Stories from Cape Breton*. Montréal and Kingston: McGill-Queen's University Press.

Wilkins, Jesse. 1902. Early Times in Wayne County. *The Mississippi Historical Society* 6:265-72.

Gethin Matthews

Miners, Methodists and Minstrels: The Welsh in the Americas and their Legacy

The relationship between the immigrant Welsh and the home country is fascinating because it is multi-faceted and complex, making it challenging to summarize concisely. Naturally, individuals left Wales in greatly varying circumstances for a wide range of destinations and looked back upon their home country and its culture in a host of different ways. Even the Wales that these individuals left was "a plural experience" (Smith 1999: 36), with a wide spectrum of subcultures, each of which evolved with time. Although this overview will focus primarily on the middle and latter decades of the 19th century—the period with the highest rates of emigration to the Americas and the greatest vitality of Welsh-speaking communities in North America—there were important movements from the late 17th century, and the echoes of Welsh trans-Atlantic migration still resounded through the 20th century.

There were a variety of motivations to leave Wales in the first place, although economic opportunities in the destination were almost always a key factor. Some individuals ventured across the Atlantic alone, some in small family groups, others in more organized migrations. Most headed toward places where other Welsh had already gathered; sometimes there was an element of strategic direction in the emigration movement, forming part of a plan to set up a new Welsh homeland overseas. The venture about which most has been written is Y Wladfa, the Welsh settlement in Patagonia (see Johnson and Birt in this volume), but, despite its fame and longevity, this community is not representative of the general Welsh migrant experience in the Americas. Many more Welsh ventured to putative Welsh homelands in the U.S. than went to Argentina; the numbers of Welsh entering Canada in the years 1911-1914 was double the number that emigrated to Y Wladfa in 1865-1912 (David Williams 1935: 411; Glyn Williams 1991: 41).

In short, one cannot make any sweeping statements about "the Welsh in the Americas" without listing a number of caveats and exceptions. Even the defining aspect of these migrants—their Welshness—can be a slippery feature. There were plenty of migrants who seemingly escaped from Wales and welcomed their rapid assimilation into the host culture, never to cast a backward glance at their homeland.

When, Where, Why and How Many

The history of Welsh emigration lacks complete and accurate statistical data (W. D. Jones 1992: xvii). The majority of Welsh emigrants departed from an English port (Liverpool) at a time when no records were kept of who was leaving the United Kingdom. Those who landed in the United States did have their details recorded, and U.S. immigration officials were supposed to differentiate between the Welsh and English. However, the statistics clearly demonstrate that the Welsh were under-recorded. According to U.S. immigration records, 6,319 Welsh migrants entered the country during the 1850s, yet Van Vugt estimates a total of 3,250 Welsh newcomers in 1851 alone (1991: 547). The aggregated U.S. immigration statistics record 89,603 Welsh migrants between 1820 and 1950; however, the 1890 census lists 100,079 individuals who were born in Wales. One estimate puts the number of Welsh that emigrated across the Atlantic at up to three times that figure (Glanmor Williams 1976: 4).

The paucity and unreliability of the statistical evidence means that researchers are often obliged to consider a variety of evidence to gain an accurate impression of the scale of emigration. Statistics are particularly lacking for the early centuries of emigration to the Americas; yet, even for this period, studies have shown the qualitative impact of emigration on the Welsh nation.

From the beginnings of Welsh emigration to the New World, movements were localized, with certain parts of Wales witnessing substantial outflows, and selective to certain types of individuals. Thus the departures changed the makeup of communities in Wales. One clear example of this can be seen in the first large-scale organized emigration from Wales to America in the late 17th century, when the Quakers were seeking to escape persecution by establishing a colony under the leadership of William Penn. The numbers that departed Wales for Pennsylvania from 1682 to the end of that century may not seem inordinately large (nearly three hundred families, or about two thousand individuals), but their departure did have a major impact upon the areas that they left (particularly Merionethshire) and certainly acted to weaken substantially the Quaker cause in Wales, as many of the denomination's leaders left *en bloc* (Dodd 1958: 112).

The emigration from Wales to America spearheaded by Quakers and Baptists in the late 17th and early 18th centuries was followed by a lull for a few decades. Although individual migration did occur (including Nonconformist chain migration along pathways which had been laid by chapel members) (H. M. Davies 1995: 56-57), the reduced emigration rate can be explained by factors such as the diminution of religious persecution, the relative strength of the British economy and the disruption caused by numerous wars (David Williams 1942: 102). When emigration picked up again at the end of the 18th century, circumstances had changed, both in the receiving destinations and, most particularly, in Wales itself, where society was undergoing sustained and rapid change. The economy was being transformed by industrialization; the religious outlook had been reconfigured by the Methodist Revival and was being influenced by the growth of nonconformity; not unconnected to both these factors was the development of radical political ideas (marginal at first, but then subsumed into the Welsh psyche).

It is not easy to identify continuities between Welsh migration to America prior to and following the Revolutionary War. For example, although the radical Baptist preacher Morgan John Rhys was to a great extent obliged to emigrate across the Atlantic in 1794 to escape religious and political persecution, one is struck by how his venture was more the precursor of what was to come than the continuation of an old tradition of emigration. Rhys's ambition was to found a new homeland for the Welsh in the United States: a "Beulah" founded on democratic principles where they could start anew. Whereas earlier Welsh Baptist immigrants had concurred with, and profited from, slave-holding, Rhys fervently campaigned against the practice. Hundreds of families braved the treacherous ocean crossing and tried their luck in the New World, only to find that the opportunities did not live up to Rhys's rhetoric (Gwyn Williams 1980). This venture can be seen as the forerunner of numerous attempts to set up new Welsh settlements, which continued for generations as the American frontier moved westward, depositing numbers of Welsh families in states such as Tennessee, Missouri, Texas and Washington (Knowles 1999: 300-303; Conway 1961: 94-96, 118-19, 157; 1973: 212-16). The fate of so many of these, like Rhys's Beulahland, was to leave little tangible legacy behind, as the migrants dispersed or dissolved into the Anglo-American mainstream.

Although the urge to set up a new Welsh homeland remained a factor for a minority of emigrants through the 19th century, the principal consideration for most was the relative level of economic opportunities available for them in the target destination. A rough (but, as we shall see, problematic) distinction can be made between those who sought agricultural opportunities and those who sought their rewards in industry. Numerous case studies have shown that particular migration movements from rural Wales were premised on the availability of relatively cheap land to own outright, far beyond what a tenant farmer could dream of obtaining in Wales (Knowles 1997a: 114-16, 135-38; Carter 2011: 115-18). It is clear that in the half-century after 1790, migration from Wales was dominated by those who remained in agriculture; it is also now beyond doubt (contrary to what some scholars had previously argued) (M. Jones 1975-1976: 87) that by the mid-19th century emigration from industrial areas was dominant (Van Vugt 1991: 560-61).

Whatever the true total figure of Welsh migrants to America, it is much smaller than the numbers of Irish, Scottish and English migrants, and, in terms of proportion, the impact was substantially less than that on Ireland and Scotland. This is most readily explained by the momentous and rapid growth of industry in Wales in the 19th century: at a time when other parts of the United Kingdom were suffering economic downturns, social dislocations and (*pace* Ireland) occasional catastrophic tragedies, the Welsh economy kept growing. This was all fuelled by the demand for coal, and in particular the high quality steam-coal of the mid-Glamorgan valleys. The culmination was seen in the early years of the 20th century: in the decade leading up to the 1911 census, the Welsh population rose by 408,045 (20.3 per cent); the increases in the southeastern counties of Glamorgan and Monmouthshire were 30.3 per cent and 32.8 per cent, respectively (John Williams 1985: 7, 17, 20). Thus, there was little economic imperative for the Welsh to emigrate: footloose young men in rural Wales could better their lot by moving to one of the booming coal towns in the valleys.

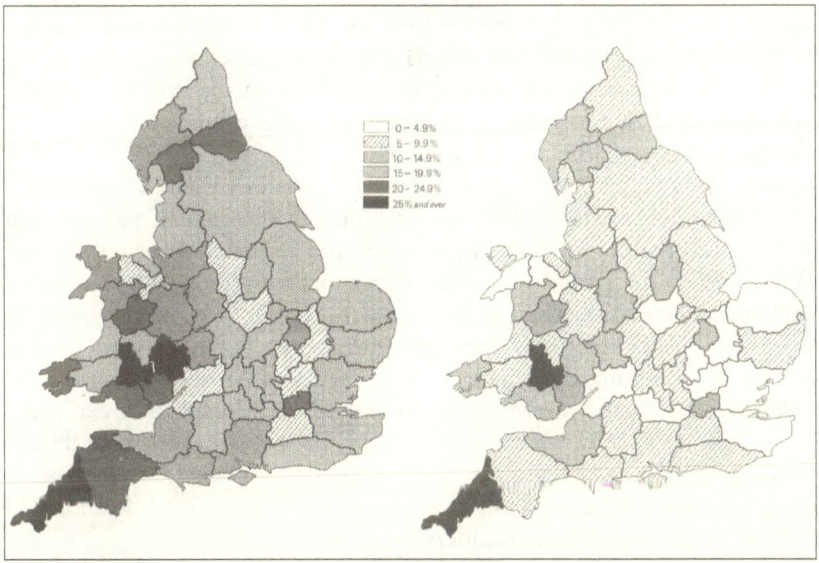

Figure 1. Emigration by natives of English and Welsh counties (net of returns), 1861-1900, as a percentage of those aged 15-24: males on the left and females on the right. Source: Baines 1985, by courtesy of the author.

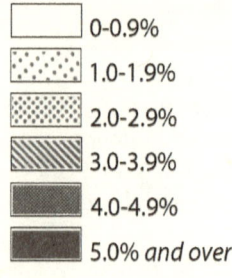

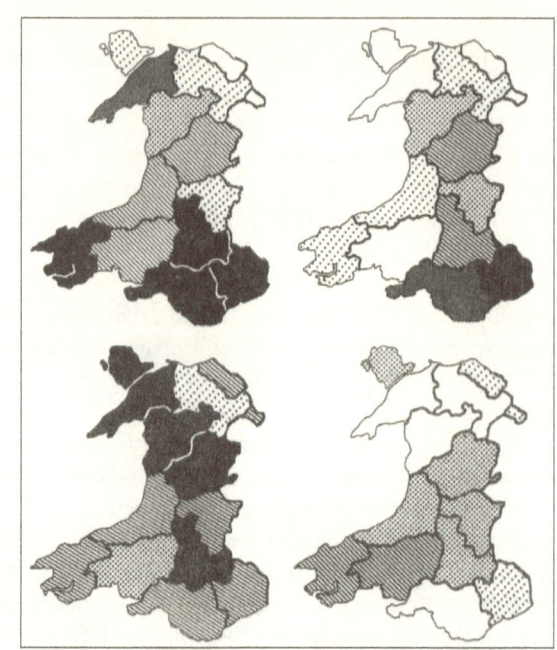

Figure 2. Native emigration from Welsh counties (net of returns) by decade, as a percentage of total native population (mid-range estimates). Clockwise from top left: 1861-1870; 1871-1880; 1891-1900; 1881-1890. Source: Baines 1985, by courtesy of the author.

Despite this, there were times and places in Wales even during the industrial heyday when emigration to America was a live issue. This can clearly be seen in the painstaking census research undertaken by Dudley Baines to establish overseas migration rates by county. In the "league table" showing emigration rates between 1861 and 1901 of the fifty-two counties of Wales and England (1985: 150-51), Welsh counties occupy five of the top ten places, for both males and females. Nine of the thirteen counties of Wales show an emigration rate greater than the average for Wales and England. Studying the maps decade by decade (1985: 188-91), a number of interesting patterns emerge: emigration is generally limited from northeast Wales, where the emigration rate mirrors the general pattern seen in England (rising to a peak in the 1880s and 1890s); however, southeast Wales begins the period with very high emigration rates, which steadily declines to a trickle by the 1890s (corresponding to the economic boom in the South Wales valleys and the fact that many migrants returned). The emigration rate from Caernarfonshire in northwest Wales was high in the 1860s and 1880s and low in the 1870s and 1890s, which can be explained by the relative fortunes of the slate industry in Wales and the U.S. during the period (P. Jones 1989: 614-15, 619-20). Thus the analysis emphasizes the importance of regional and local factors in the emigration decision and the influence of economic considerations.

One caveat with the statistics generated by Baines is that they are skewed by return migration.[1] He estimated that between the 1870s and 1914, 40 per cent of the emigrants from Wales and England eventually returned home (1985: 128), but it is highly likely that the Welsh figure is actually higher. The phenomenon of Welsh coal miners returning across the Atlantic in the 1890s from the depressed coal fields of Pennsylvania to the booming valleys of South Wales has been noted (Berthoff 1953: 52-55; R. L. Lewis 2011: 45). It is possible to find numerous families in the late 19th- and early 20th-century census in places like the Rhondda valley where some of the children were born in the U.S. (Matthews 2011: 127). Recent work by Carter has demonstrated that many of the Welsh in industrial parts of the U.S. could best be described as sojourners rather than migrants: of the male Welsh-born population in 1870 Pittsburgh, 39 per cent could be found living in Wales a decade later (Carter 2012: 291-92).[2]

A further facet of the data generated by Baines from the census returns is that 37 per cent of emigrants from Wales and England in the second half of the 19th century were female (151). For every county, the emigration rate for males exceeded that of females, but in general the gap is smaller in counties that were predominantly rural, where the emigrants were more likely to depart as a family group. In contrast, in those counties where the migration was heavily influenced by the employment opportunities for industrial workers, a greater discrepancy in the emigration rate for males and females indicates that a higher proportion of single men left to exploit their skills in the American job market. Yet, the discrepancies in the emigration rate between sexes in some counties is not easily explained: whereas 5.4 per cent of Breconshire-born females left compared to 5.9 per cent of Breconshire-born males, the corresponding figures for Caernarfonshire are 0.6 per cent and 3.3 per cent (150-51).

One corollary of Baines's study is that the county is actually too large a unit of study, and that there is a variety of patterns to be seen within certain counties. The high overall emigration rate from Breconshire, Glamorgan and Monmouthshire, for example, hides the fact that there were some areas in these counties where the flow of emigrants was minor and others where emigration was seen as one of the accepted life choices (Matthews 2011: 124-25). In this context, one of the key Welsh towns where emigration was woven into the fabric of community life was Merthyr Tydfil (W. D. Jones 2001, 2005; Strange 2005: 168-79). Having been at the forefront of the Industrial Revolution, the town's skilled iron-workers had developed an international reputation, and consequently a taste for departing for pastures new to maximize their earnings. The area developed a culture of emigration, nurtured by some of its newspapers, which meant that young men (in particular) accepted the idea that moving abroad to seek a better life was an option to be considered. When the newspapers of Merthyr and Aberdare refer to "*y dwymyn ymfudol*" (emigration fever), the scale of the contemporary impact is clear (W. D. Jones 2004: 33).

The map in Figure 3, which is the product of Knowles's researches into the period 1791 to 1853, shows how uneven the pattern of emigration was across Wales.[3] Even this detailed map *hides* some patterns, for each of the four main areas of emigration identified had different dynamics within this 60-year period. Emigration from the Llanbrynmair area began early and was steadily high throughout this period; emigration from Pen Llŷn (the Llŷn peninsula of Caernarfonshire) also began early but peaked earlier than from the other areas identified; emigration from Cardiganshire peaked between 1837 and 1847; the emigration from the iron district only took off in the 1830s, and kept on growing for the next few decades (Knowles 1995: 251).

The latter emigration was ostensibly different in quality from the other three, which outwardly seem to be migrations *from* rural areas *to* rural areas, yet as both Knowles (1997a: 35-36) and Van Vugt (1991: 560-61) have pointed out, one has to be careful about characterizing emigration as either "agricultural" or "industrial." Knowles's research highlights the fluidity of the situation, detailing examples of individuals who moved from Cardiganshire to industrial South Wales and thence to southern Ohio; others who moved from Cardiganshire to industrial Pennsylvania, and then on to Ohio; and some who moved from Cardiganshire to industrial South Wales to industrial Pennsylvania and finally to Ohio (1995: 259-62; 1997a: 35-41).

Thus many may have emigrated with a long-term goal of owning their own farm in America, but to get there they had the short-term option of working in industry to raise the necessary funds. As many of them al-

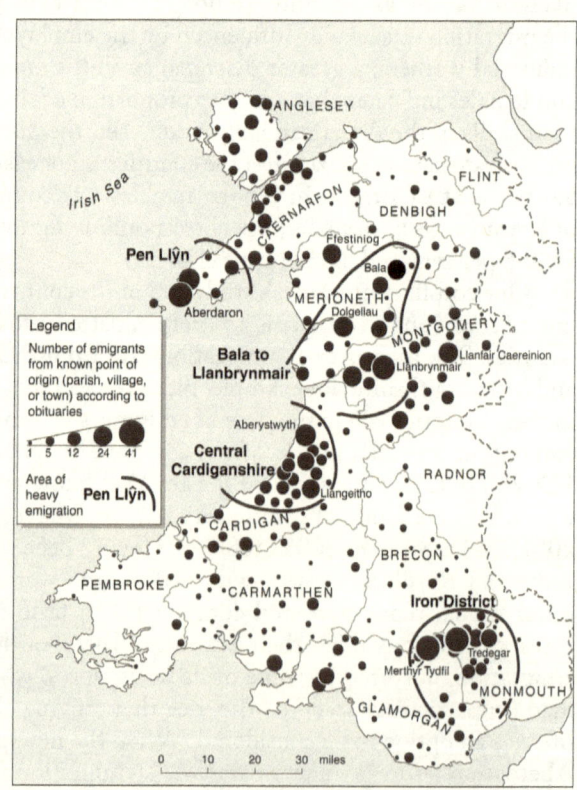

Figure 3. Welsh emigrant origins and emigration regions, 1791-1853. Source: Knowles 1997a, by courtesy of the author.

ready had experience of industry in Wales, and could move along pathways well-trodden by previous Welsh emigrants, there was no obstacle. This strategy was characterized by Conway as being a "knight's move" (1973: 226).

Knowles has explored how the differing local patterns of emigration from Wales created a number of Welsh settlements in the United States with distinct identities related to a particular part of Wales, particularly so for those established earlier (1997a: 25-27). Sometimes the connection was highly localized. For example, J. Glyn Davies characterized the settlement of Cambria, Wisconsin as "an outpost of Dolwyddelan" (1958: 128). Other agricultural settlements away from the eastern seaboard were more heterogeneous, being the product of step-migration from older Welsh American communities (where the availability of relatively cheap land had been exhausted) as well as migration direct from Wales (Knowles 1997a: 28, 197-98; E. Davies 2003a: 51).

Most Welsh communities in industrial settlements gathered together individuals from all over Wales. Exceptions to this would be the slate-quarrying areas, which were dominated by North Wales emigrants, and sometimes had very local patterns fed by chain-migration (G. Roberts 1998: 15-19). Similarly, some towns with a flourishing iron industry might have a concentration of individuals from Merthyr or Tredegar, but in general, the newer urban settlements contained immigrants from a variety of Welsh origins. Overall, the pattern is one of a series of discrete rivulets running from particular parts of Wales to particular parts of America, rather than one cohesive and easily described migration stream. The strength of flow observed with each rivulet would vary with time and the situation within America itself was fluid, so that the initial destination would not prove to be the permanent home, but rather only the first step on the journey.

North America was always more of a draw than South America and, from the turn of the 20th century, Canada became a more significant destination than the U.S. for Welsh migrants. This is partially because there was still cheap land available on the Canadian prairies, and indeed some initiatives specifically to attract Welsh farmers to these (W. Davies 1999), as well as other ventures to promote migration from Wales to Canada (2001). In addition, Welsh emigration to traditional industrial destinations lessened, and in particular the state of the U.S. economy as the troubled decade of the 1920s wore on meant that there were fewer opportunities and less of a welcome for migrants seeking jobs. This would have clear implications for the continuation of Welsh culture in North America.

Language and Cultural Institutions: Adaptation, Survival and Loss

The Welsh chapel was undoubtedly the most distinctive marker of Welshness in America (Taylor 1983: 315; Knowles 1997b: 282-83). The building of thousands of chapels was one of the unique features of Welsh society during the industrial period (John Davies 1993: 420-27) and the Welsh overseas adhered to this tradition wherever they settled in sufficient numbers. Hartmann's list of 555 chapels in eighteen states of the U.S. is incomplete (1967: 170-91), yet it shows the diversity of destinations for Welsh emigrants (and can also be used to plot their progress west across the continent).[4] Some offer striking examples of longevity: for example, Horeb chapel (in Jackson County, southeast Ohio) established in 1838 kept its proceedings entirely in "the language of heaven" until 1901, and the last Welsh-language sermon was preached there after the First World War (Knowles 1997a: 221-22). Emrys Jones found that two chapels in Utica continued Welsh-language services after the Second World War, even if the majority of the congregations had made the switch to English (1954: 22-24, 34). The Welsh Presbyterian Church of Los Angeles existed from 1888 to 2012.

Despite this latter example, Knowles's research illustrates qualitative differences between rural/agricultural Welsh settlements and urban settlements. Whereas the Welsh community in New York City in 1851 may have been numerically the largest in America, the population was scattered, "with little cohesion or sense of ethnic identity" and only one Welsh-language chapel to cater to their needs. At the same time the Welsh community in southeast Ohio had built itself seventeen chapels (1997a: 28, 136). These chapels were much more than just religious centres: they also operated as social and cultural centres, sometimes as places where business deals could be done or information about employment opportunities disseminated, and always as tangible links with the land left behind. Just as in Wales, the buildings were most often given Biblical names, often replicating the name of the "mother chapel" back across the Atlantic.

Assuming a simplified agricultural/industrial dichotomy among the Welsh American communities, one clear pattern that emerges is that the rural-agricultural communities held onto the Welsh language and customs for longer than the urban-industrial communities. The places where the Welsh language lasted longest were settled rural communities such as that in Utica, where a strong connection endured with a part of Wales that remained strongly Welsh-speaking (Pen Llŷn), including a steady supply of new immigrants up until the First World War (E. Jones 1954: 15). Similarly, southeast Ohio's Welsh community was replenished by newcomers from Cardiganshire long after the peak in emigration in the 1830s and 1840s: some families in Jackson County were bringing up their children solely in Welsh up to school age in the 1920s (Knowles 1997a: 224).

The places where the Welsh language disappeared the quickest were settlements where the population was mobile and heterogeneous, with the Welsh forming a small minority, such as the western gold fields. The relative shortage of Welsh-speaking women decreased the likelihood of raising a family in a Welsh environment (Matthews 2010: 164-65). The Welsh language also disappeared relatively quickly from coal-mining districts (although the rate of language-loss was not uniform across settlements): Welsh miners, particularly the single men, were free to follow the news of where the best economic opportunities were to be found. The Welsh-American media (such as *Y Drych*) were instrumental in this process, and indeed Aled and Bill Jones go so far as to call the newspaper an "employment agency" (2001a: 58). As Lewis has observed, Welsh coal miners in America made "decisions about when and where to go based on knowledge passed along through networks of personal and professional relationships that bound Welsh occupational communities together" (R. L. Lewis 2005: 192). There is plenty of evidence that the Welsh miners gravitated to coal towns where Welsh owners and superintendents were in charge. This accounts for the Welsh communities near Birmingham, Alabama, where the Welshman George A. Davis managed a mine owned by David Roberts, another Welshman, and in Black Diamond, Washington, where Morgan Morgan was the boss (R. L. Lewis 2008: 85, 68). Thus the influence of the Welsh mine managers in attracting Welsh labour could work both to weaken the Welsh community in established settlements and to gather the Welsh together in new mining towns.

Figure 4. Gravestone of Evan Lewis in Camptonville, California, bearing an engraving of Luke 2:29-32 in Welsh. (Gethin Matthews)

Even in the large and settled Welsh American mining communities, circumstances militated against the long-term survival of the language. The archetypical example of this comes from the anthracite coal field of Pennsylvania, where in the 1860s and 1870s the towns of Scranton and Wilkes-Barre were home to the largest Welsh community in America. Bill Jones found that in the 1860s and 1870s the Welsh community was "overwhelmingly Welsh-speaking," with seven Welsh chapels operating in Scranton alone in 1870, including America's largest Welsh Baptist chapel, which attracted congregations of 800 (1992: 90-92). However, soon afterward, the process began of English-language churches seceding from the Welsh mother-churches, followed inexorably by the Welsh churches switching to English. Although some Welsh-language provision continued into the 1920s, Jones found little evidence of Welsh being publicly spoken in Scranton at the turn of the 20th century (106, 108, 113).

In the aftermath of the First World War, global economic problems led to a notable decline in migration between Wales and the U.S. (although emigration to Canada remained an option). The lack of new blood reaching the old-established Welsh-American communities led inexorably to their increased assimilation into the anglophone mainstream, and a declining relationship with Wales. As the 20th century wore on, the principal Welsh-American organizations had to evolve or decline.

A pattern of rapid growth followed by gradual decline, similar to that seen in the Welsh chapels, can be observed in the history of the *eisteddfodau* held in America. The *eisteddfod* (plural *eisteddfodau*) is a literary and musical competitive festival: the long organic tradition of such events became formalized in Wales during the 19th century, culminating in the early 1860s with the establishment of the National Eisteddfod. The growth of the eisteddfodic tradition in America mirrors both the development of the tradition in Wales and the increasing numbers in the Welsh communities in America. Although evidence of Welsh American eisteddfodau is patchy in the 1840s, the tradition began to gain a foothold in the 1850s (Hartmann 1967: 146). The role of enthusiastic individual bards in propagating the eisteddfodic tradition needs to be taken into account: when the energetic Thomas Gwallter Price (known in bardic circles as "Cuhelyn") followed the trail of gold to North San Juan, California, he gathered the numerous Welshmen in the locality together and organized the first eisteddfod in the state, held on July 4, 1860 (Fourth at North San Juan 1860).

Next to the chapels, the eisteddfod was the most potent symbol of Welsh exceptionalism in the Americas. As such, the success of each locality's eisteddfod became a status symbol within the diaspora: something to boast about in the pages of *Y Drych*, or one of the other periodicals. The declaration by the Welsh Philosophical Society of Scranton in 1875 that the eisteddfod they organized was the National Eisteddfod of America (W. D. Jones 1992: 101-105) was a way of claiming pre-eminence. The fate of this eisteddfod ably demonstrates the pressures to assimilate. A description of the event in 1893 noted that crowds of 3,000 to 4,000 attended the festival and that it was "fast becoming a recognised Scranton institution" (Darlington 1894: 351). However, its Welshness had been diluted, with the Welsh language being marginalized as the organizers sought to include other nationalities, such as the Irish and the Germans, in the festivities (351). Over time, as the Welsh community in Scranton became more Americanized, their expressions of Welshness became more superficial. Instead of holding a two-day eisteddfod with poetry and singing in Welsh, from 1907 the community organized a "Welsh Day" at the local amusement park. The first one attracted a crowd of 23,000, and although there were still some cultural competitions at these festivities, the emphasis was on fun and less challenging events, such as the competition to find the tallest and shortest Welshmen in the audience. These "Welsh Days" continued well into the 20th century, but they became a celebration of something the community had lost, rather than something that was still an important, vibrant component in their daily lives (W. D. Jones 1992: 122-24).

Attempts to transplant the key ceremonial aspects of the Welsh eisteddfod tradition across the Atlantic were not a success. The American Gorsedd (mimicking the quasi-druidic tradition invented in the late 18th century) failed to flourish, never attracting a membership of more than 303 (Hartmann 1967: 149-51; W. D. Jones 1992: 178-92). One tradition that did catch on in America, indeed becoming more prominent than in the home country, was the Gymanfa Ganu (hymn-singing festival). Even if the audience did not understand the words they were singing, they could still pronounce them phonetically and appreciate the majesty of the tunes and choral arrangements (Hartmann 1967: 152-54). The National Gymanfa Ganu began in 1929 when the leaders of the St. David's Society of Youngstown, Ohio, organized an event at Niagara Falls which attracted 2,400 participants; in 1933, the event was expanded to become a two-day festival; in 1949, a three-day and, from 1955, a four-day event (Reese 2004: 5, 15, 29, 39). Although the organizing body was renamed from the "Welsh National Gymanfa Ganu Association" to the "Welsh North American Association" in 2011 (B. M. Jones 2011), the Gymanfa Ganu remains the focal point of the North American Festival of Wales, which visits a different venue every year. Despite some unseemly bickering between committee members from the U.S. and Canada in the 1970s (Reese 2004: 79), the event promotes harmony between Canadians, Americans and guests from Wales, with all three national anthems given pride of place. A greater proportion of the Canadian participants at recent events are first-generation immigrants, with a high proportion of them being Welsh-speaking. One of the very few Welsh chapels where religious services are still regularly held in Welsh in the second decade of the 21st century is *Eglwys Dewi Sant*, Toronto.

Writing in 1958, Emrys Jones characterized the demise of the Welsh-language chapel tradition in America as inevitable. The process of Welsh chapels switching to worship in English had been on-going since the earliest days of migration to America. Those congregations that refused to compromise (such as in Chicago) were doomed to disappear as the last Welsh speakers died off, whereas those that did face the linguistic reality of the situation held onto their separate identity, even if the services were now held in English (1958: 248-49).

The fate of the eisteddfodau was strongly linked to the Welsh language, although some survived by accommodating the shift to English. Emrys Jones's investigations into the Utica eisteddfod noted that the percentage of English-language competitions rose from under 10 per cent prior to 1910 to nearly 30 per cent in 1930 and 100 per cent in 1948 (245).

There were exceptional cases of individuals in some of the older-established U.S. communities continuing to speak Welsh into the 21st century. For example, Hunter found some elderly American-born Welsh speakers in Utica and the Slate Valley in 2001 (2003b: 43); the couple Richard and Bronwen Pritchard of Lehigh Valley, Pennsylvania, were interviewed for the Welsh-language television program *America 08: Dewi Llwyd ar Daith* in the summer of 2008. As the last remnants of this old guard fade away, this same documentary showed that a different version of Welsh-language culture will continue to be alive in the U.S. for the foreseeable future, driven both by new immigrants and Americans of Welsh descent who wish to reconnect with their roots, facilitated by the ease of modern telecommunications.

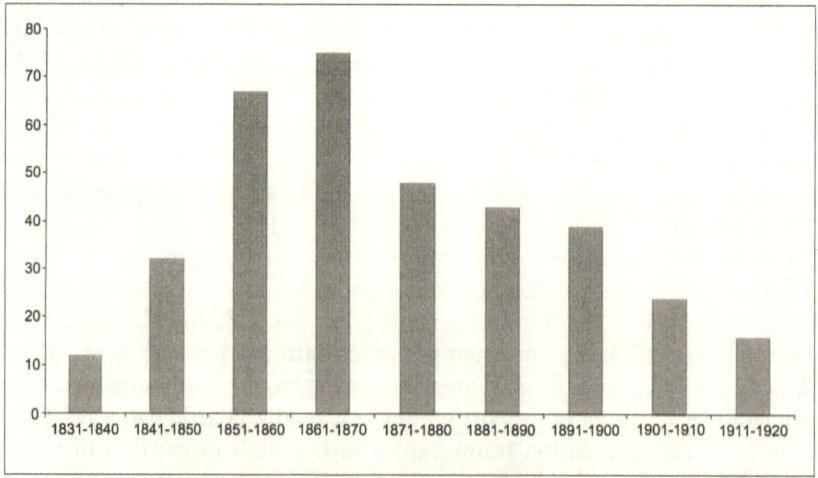

Figure 5. Welsh-language books and pamphlets published in the U.S. by decade, 1831-1920. Source: E. Davies 2003b, by courtesy of the author.

Literary Remains

The history of publishing in the Welsh language in the Americas extends back to 1721, when *Annerch i'r Cymru* (An Address to the Welsh), a treatise that sought to spread the Quaker message among the Welsh, was published in Philadelphia. This religious tone was continued in the next three books to be published in Welsh in America, *Cyd-gordiad Egwyddorawl o'r Scrythurau* (A Principled Concordance to the Scriptures, 1730), *Y Dull o Fedyddio a Dwfr* (The Way to Baptise with Water, 1730) and *Myfyrdodau Bucheddol* (Meditations on Life, 1735) (W. Williams 1942, 1943; D. H. E. Roberts 1983-1984: 4-5). After this early flurry of activity there passed almost a century before there arose a lively Welsh-language press in the United States: one clear continuity was that the viewpoint and mores of Welsh chapel culture dominated the content of the books. Eirug Davies illustrates these connections with the four expositions of the Book of Revelations published between 1846 and 1911 (the first a re-print of a work published in Wales, the others the fruit of American-based Welshmen). Almost forty of the works are biographies of preachers, mainly Welsh-Americans (2003b: 107-108).

There is also a strong link between the eisteddfod tradition and the printed word, with thirty-three publications (from 8 to 464 pages in length) being the fruit of such festivals. Although most of these were published in Utica (which became the hub of the Welsh-American publishing business), they represent the output of eisteddfodau in a wide range of locations, including settlements far from the eastern seaboard such as Racine, Denver and San Francisco (2003b: 113-15).

The Welsh-American periodical press also had a symbiotic relationship with the religious institutions established to service the Welsh diaspora in the United States. Although there had been previous attempts to publish a Welsh-language periodical in America, the first to leave its mark was *Y Cyfaill o'r Hen Wlad yn America* (The Friend from the Old Country in America), whose history is explored by Rhiannon Williams in this volume. Initially published as an inter-denominational journal in 1838, this became the organ of the Calvinistic Methodists as the other denominations launched their own monthly journals. After its birth in New York City, publication of *Y Cyfaill* alternated between the metropolis and Oneida County before it settled in Utica in 1858, where the journal lasted until 1933. Other long-lived denominational journals were *Y Cenhadwr Americanaidd* (The American Missionary), published by Congregationalists in Steuben/Utica, 1840-1901, *Y Seren Orllewinol* (The Western Star), published by Baptists in Utica, 1844-1867, and *Y Glorian* (The Scales), published by Baptists in Youngstown, Ohio, 1872-1894 (I. Lewis 1942).

Beyond the denominational press there appeared through the later 19th century an interesting variety of Welsh-language newspapers and journals in America (Owen 1950). Although these were not in hock to the nonconformist denominations, even a cursory glance reveals that most of them sang from identical hymn-sheets: chapel activities are at the heart of the reports of many correspondents. The majority of these publications were short-lived with only a few lasting a decade, so the longevity of *Y Drych* (The Mirror) is exceptional. First published in New York City in 1851, the newspaper relocated to Utica in 1860, where it continued to be published for over a century. *Y Drych* was so pivotal to Welsh American life for such a long period of time that the definitive study of the paper's history is not just a "biography of a newspaper" (A. Jones and B. Jones 2001a: xi) but also an exploration of how the disparate Welsh American communities evolved, saw themselves and communicated with one another. In addition to reflecting the culture of the Welsh in America, the newspaper sought to shape it: its pages reveal "a series of concerted attempts by its editors and main correspondents to define a Welsh identity, an ideology, if you like, for the Welsh in America" (A. Jones and B. Jones 2001b: 44). It was certainly a patriotic publication, both in terms of Wales and of the United States, and at times of tension between the respective governments in London and Washington, there were examples aplenty of correspondents forcefully siding with the U.S.

Daniel Williams has emphasized that Welsh-American culture evolved in parallel with Welsh culture back in the old country, and that the pace of development was rapid in the mid- to late 19th century, when "'Welshness' was being invented simultaneously on both sides of the Atlantic" (2002: 344). Thus some developments moved in tandem (such as the central role of the chapel, the blooming of eisteddfod culture, and even concerns about the decline of the Welsh language) while in other cases there were divergences, as evidenced by the Welsh-Americans' incomprehension and bemusement at the growing obsession with rugby in Wales (Smith 1984: 29-33). Baseball was the sport played at Scranton's "Welsh Days" (W. D. Jones 1993: 192-93).

The Canadian contribution to the Welsh-language print culture was generally limited to contributions to U.S.-based periodicals. The only exception to this rule was the short-lived *Welsh Pioneer*, based in Winnipeg, which included Welsh columns among the English-language reports of the activities of Welsh individuals and societies. Only a few issues of this publication appeared in 1910; in contrast, *Y Drych* contained a steady (if minor) flow of reports from Welsh individuals in Canada from the 1860s through the paper's incorporation with its rival *Ninnau* in 2003.

Despite remaining committed to the Welsh language for as long as was reasonably possible (and indeed, beyond), *Y Drych* became an English-language newspaper during the years of the Second World War, with the Welsh language reserved for occasional articles and poetry (A. Jones and B. Jones 2001a: 114-16).

Rather than the published books, it is probably the newspapers and journals that hold the most diverse and interesting store of Welsh-language material generated in the Americas (Hunter 2003b: 32). Their pages contain a wealth of material on a vast range of contemporary topics, which have as yet barely been tapped by academic researchers. The detailed work of Jerry Hunter (2003a, 2007) in reconstructing Welsh American attitudes toward, and experiences during, the American Civil War has rightly been applauded, but there remains an enormous potential for further groundbreaking research.

Writing the History of the Welsh in the Americas

All immigrant groups display a tendency to filiopietism when writing the history of their contribution to the host country. The Welsh have not been exceptions to this rule. The relative paucity of Welsh emigrants—memorably described by Conway as "little more than a corporal's guard" (1973: 178) in comparison with the "battalions" that went over from other European countries—has meant that those who wished to "boost" the credentials of the Welsh communities overseas have had to stress the quality of the Welsh contribution rather than its quantity. There are copious examples of Welsh Americans making unsustainable claims about the number of Welshmen who signed the Declaration of Independence, or the number of U.S. presidents whose ancestors hailed from Wales (David Williams 1942: 97, 102-103; Conway 1961: 6; Hartmann 1967: 55-57). Patriotic authors find it necessary to overstate the remarkable qualities of their fellow countrymen. Henry Blackwell (a bibliographer and biographer of Welsh-Americans) declared that the Welsh were the "pioneers who prepared the way for civilization and progress" in America (Glanmor Williams 1976: 23). As Carter has wryly observed, "the Welsh in America are therefore the strictest of teetotallers and the hardest of drinkers, the most conservative of Republicans and the most ardent of unionists" (2011: 23).

One consequence of the writing of Welsh American history by those with a patriotic agenda is that some uncomfortable truths can be glossed over (a failing which can indeed be seen in much historical writing about the Welsh in Wales). The role of the Welsh as abolitionists, campaigning vigorously against the slave trade (James 2007; Hunter 2010), is a more popular subject for study than the role of the Welsh as slaveholders (Breeze 2011). Historians are only now beginning to examine the ways in which Welsh culture constructed images of Native Americans (Hunter 2012; Matthews 2009; Brooks in this volume).

It is taken for granted that the Welsh made "good" Americans, and it is an oft-quoted statistic that the Welsh were the most eager of all immigrant nationalities to take up U.S. citizenship (David Williams 1942:

108). This has been a useful starting-point for numerous investigations into the Welsh Americans' sense of identity, whether by studying the literature they generated (e.g., the work of Daniel Williams and Jerry Hunter), their working lives (e.g., Ron Lewis's investigations) or the institutions they established (e.g., Anne Kelly Knowles's research). Yet despite this growing body of scholarly works, there are still gaps to be filled, in part because the experience of the Welsh in the Americas *was* so diverse, with different patterns developing according to localized conditions.

Since William D. Jones's pioneering exploration of the Welsh community in Scranton (1992), the detailed study of individual Welsh American communities that grew up in different circumstances across the North American continent has garnered greater attention. Recent examples include Eirug Davies's books on the Welsh in Colorado (2001) and Tennessee (2012) and Walley's book on Iowa (2009). This trend is best viewed as a deepening rather than a fragmentation of Welsh-American studies.

Another outcome of trans-Atlantic Welsh migration, which is receiving a growing share of attention, is the impact that constructions of "America" and American ideals had in Wales. Those communities that supplied a disproportionate number of emigrants were also affected by the flow of ideas back across the Atlantic. This can be clearly seen during the American Civil War, when the issues were vigorously debated in Wales, and the progress of the war tracked in locations such as the Stag Inn in Aberdare (Hunter 2003a: 64). The connection can also be seen in more creative contexts, such as the enhancement of the rich Welsh musical tradition by trans-Atlantic practitioners such as Joseph Parry and Daniel Protheroe (Rhys 1998; W. D. Jones 1991: 31). The flow of Welsh individuals with experience of living in the United States back to the South Wales valleys influenced the culture and outlook of those communities: indeed this part of the country was dubbed "American Wales" because of its self-confidence and its outward-looking, cosmopolitan nature (Smith 1993: ix). This "American" outlook was influenced by individuals who had experience of living across the Atlantic, and thus the American dimension to Welsh history is seen to be influential *before* Anglo-American culture achieved its more recent global currency.

One of the interesting strands of the trans-Atlantic migration in the early 20th century was the flow of Welsh boxers, eager to make their names and their fortunes. Champions such as Jim Driscoll, Freddie Welsh and Jimmy Wilde certainly succeeded in both of these ambitions in the years on either side of the First World War (O'Leary 2008; Smith 2008; Gareth Williams 2008). Numerous commentators have noted how apt it was that when the two great lightweights Welsh and Driscoll fought in December 1910, the venue was Cardiff's American Roller Rink.

If the story of Welsh emigration in general is under-researched, the story of Welsh women emigrants is doubly so because so much of the qualitative evidence privileges the actions and viewpoints of male emigrants. For example, in a list of over 350 letters from America published in the Aberdare-based newspaper *Y Gwladgarwr* between 1861 and 1882, only one was penned by a woman, and five co-written by a husband and wife.[5] It is no surprise, therefore, that many otherwise laudable histories are dominated by details of what the men did.

There is enormous scope for research that examines the activities of Welsh American communities through the lens of gender. One pioneering study is that by B. Jones and Lewis, which analyzes the case of Hattie Williams who caused a "storm of controversy" when she began working at the Monongohela tinplate works, Pittsburgh, particularly among the Welsh American community who regarded Hattie as bringing shame upon the Welsh nation by her actions (2007: 183-84). Further research is needed to examine the expectations and limitations put upon both male and female Welsh migrants.

Although historians have worked hard to improve the situation since Van Vugt declared that Welsh emigration was in need of more basic historical research than that of other nationalities (1991: 545), there are still fundamental issues to be addressed and new approaches to be taken. One needs to work hard to escape from the shadow of the filiopietists, and their endeavours to highlight the contribution of the Welsh to the development and culture of North America. One also needs to work hard against the fundamental fact that the Welsh were a minority in almost all the destinations where they settled; thus the evidence of their activities is not always easy to find, nor interpret, nor always representative of the experiences of the Welsh community as a whole.

Perhaps Muriel Chamberlain's summary of the Welsh influence on Canada could summarize the situation in the Americas: "The Welsh in Canada are rather like the Cheshire cat in *Alice in Wonderland*, continually disappearing except for the smile left behind" (1998: 265). At least the legacy is a smile, rather than a frown.

Notes

1. For example, migrants who left during the 1880s but returned to Britain during the 1890s and were still around to be counted in the 1901 census will reduce the net figure of migration recorded for the 1890s.

2. Carter was able to locate 74 per cent of the Welshmen resident in Pittsburgh in 1870 in the U.S. Census of 1880 and the U.K. Census of 1881: thus the true figure for returnees is likely to be higher than 39 per cent, given that 26 per cent of the population are unaccounted for.

3. The map was constructed from information in obituaries in Welsh-language American journals, and thus will under-represent emigration from those parts of Wales that were English-speaking in the early 19th century.

4. Although Hartmann's list is the best that has been compiled, one can point to numerous omissions and potential errors. For instance, the single Welsh chapel in Alabama is missing, and the list of Californian chapels omits the one established in North San Juan.

5. I am grateful to Dr. Huw Walters for allowing me access to the list he compiled. Around a tenth of the letters were signed by authors using initials only, or a pseudonym, but there is no reason to suppose that a high proportion of these were written by women.

References

Baines, Dudley. 1985. *Migration in a Mature Economy: emigration and internal migration in England and Wales, 1861-1900*. Cambridge: Cambridge University Press

Berthoff, Rowland. 1953. *British Immigrants in Industrial America, 1790-1950*. Cambridge, MA: Harvard University Press.

Breeze, Andrew. 2011. Review of *Wales and the Wider World: Welsh History in an International Context*. *English Historical Review* 126 (520): 628-30.

Carter, Matthew. 2011. Industrial, Industrious, and Diverse: Comparative Case Studies of the Welsh in Urban and Rural America During the Late Nineteenth Century. PhD diss., Cardiff University.

———. 2012. *Sustainability Accounting and Migration Choice: Late 19th Century Welsh Migration to Pittsburgh*. Richmond, VA: Gardner Institute Press.

Chamberlain. Muriel. 1998. The Welsh in Canada: Historical Sources. *Welsh History Review* 19 (2): 265-88.

Conway, Alan, ed. 1961. *The Welsh in America: Letters from the Immigrants*. Minneapolis: University of Minnesota Press, 1961.

———. 1973. Welsh emigration to the United States. *Perspectives in American History* 7:177-271.

Darlington, Thomas. 1894. The Welsh in America. *Wales* 1 (8): 349-52.

Davies, Eirug. 2001. *Y Cymry ac Aur Colorado*. Llanrwst: Gwasg Carreg Gwalch.

———. 2003a. *Gwladychu'r Cymry yn yr American West*. Llanrwst: Gwasg Carreg Gwalch.

———. 2003b. Llyfrau a Phamffledi Cymraeg a gyhoeddwyd yn yr Unol Daleithiau. *Llên Cymru* 26:106-36.

———. 2012. *The Welsh of Tennessee*. Talybont: Y Lolfa.

Davies, John. 1993. *A History of Wales*. London: Penguin.

Davies, J. Glyn. 1958. Cambria, Wisconsin in 1898. *Transactions of the Honourable Society of Cymmrodorion* (session 1957): 128-59.

Davies, Hywel M. 1995. *Transatlantic brethren: Rev. Samuel Jones (1735-1814) and his friends; Baptists in Wales, Pennsylvania, and beyond.* Bethlehem: Lehigh University Press.

Davies, Wayne K. D. 1999. "Falling on deaf ears?": Canadian Promotion and Welsh Emigration to the Prairies. *Welsh History Review* 19 (4): 679-712.

———. 2001. "Send a thousand Welsh farm labourers to Canada!": The Crow's Nest Pass Work Scheme and Damage Control. *Welsh History Review* 20 (3): 466-94.

Dodd, A. H. 1958. The background of the Welsh Quaker migration to Pennsylvania. *Journal of the Merionethshire Historical and Record Society* 3 (2): 111-27.

Fourth at North San Juan. 1860. *Sacramento Daily Union.* 11 July, 2. *California Digital Newspaper Collection.* http://cdnc.ucr.edu/cdnc/cgi-bin/cdnc?a=d&d=SDU18600711.2.13&cl=CL2%2e1860%2e07&srpos=0&e=-------en--20--1--txt-IN-----# (accessed 1 September 2010).

Hartmann, Edward G. 1967. *Americans from Wales.* Boston: Christopher Publishing.

Hunter, Jerry. 2003a. *Llwch Cenhedloedd: Y Cymry a Rhyfel Cartref America.* Llanrwst: Gwasg Carreg Gwalch.

———. 2003b. Y Traddodiad Llenyddol Coll. *Taliesin* 118:13-44.

———. 2007. *Welsh Writing from the American Civil War: Sons of Arthur, Children of Lincoln.* Cardiff: University of Wales Press.

———. 2010. "What can the Welsh do?" : Robert Everett and the Welsh-American abolition movement, 1840-4. In *Wales and the wider world : Welsh history in an international context,* ed. T.M. Charles-Edwards and R. J. W. Evans, 157-83. Donington: Shaun Tyas.

———. 2012. *Llwybrau Cenhedloedd: Cyd-destunoli'r Genhadaeth Gymreig i'r Tsalagi.* Cardiff: University of Wales Press.

James, E. Wyn. 2007. Welsh Ballads and American Slavery. *The Welsh Journal of Religious History* 2:59-86.

Jones, Aled and Bill Jones. 2001a. *Welsh Reflections:* Y Drych *and America, 1851-2001.* Llandysul: Gomer Press.

———. 2001b. Y Drych and American Welsh Identities, 1851-1951. *North American Journal of Welsh Studies* 1 (1): 42-58.

Jones, Barbara M. 2011. New Name for WNGGA. *Ninnau* 36 (6) (November-December): 1.

Jones, Bill and Ron Lewis. 2007. Gender and Transnationality Among Welsh Tinplate Workers in Pittsburgh: the Hattie Williams Affair, 1895. *Labor History* 48 (2): 175-94.

Jones, Emrys. 1954. Some aspects of cultural change in an American Welsh community. *Transactions of the Honourable Society of Cymmrodorion* (Session 1952): 15-41.

———. 1958. Welsh-Speaking in the New World: I. The United States. *Lochlann* 1:241-50.

Jones, Maldwyn. 1975-1976. From the Old Country to the New: The Welsh in Nineteenth-Century America. *Flintshire Historical Society Publications* 27:85-100.

Jones, Peter E. 1989. Migration and the Slate Belt of Caernarfonshire in the Nineteenth Century. *Welsh History Review* 14 (4): 610-29.

Jones, William D. (Bill). 1991. Daniel Protheroe, Haydn Evans and Welsh choral rivalry in late-nineteenth century Scranton. *Welsh Music* 9 (3): 25-34.

———. 1992. *Wales in America: Scranton and the Welsh, 1860-1920*. Cardiff: University of Wales Press.

———. 1993. "Y Gymuned Fwyaf Gymreig yn y Byd": Y Cymry yn Scranton, Pennsylvania c.1850-1920. In *Cof Cenedl VIII*, ed. Geraint H. Jenkins, 165-96. Llandysul: Gwasg Gomer.

———. 2001. "We Will Give You Wings To Fly": Emigration Societies in Merthyr Tydfil in 1868. *Merthyr Historian* 13: 27-47.

———. 2004. "Raising the Wind": Emigrating from Wales to the USA in the late nineteenth and early twentieth centuries. *The Cardiff Centre for Welsh American Studies, Cardiff University*. http://www.cf.ac.uk/cymraeg/resources/RaisingTheWind.pdf (accessed 1 August 2012).

———. 2005. Inspecting the "extraordinary drain": emigration and the urban experience in Merthyr Tydfil in the 1860s. *Urban History* 32:100-13.

Knowles, Anne Kelly. 1995. Immigrant Trajectories through the Rural-Industrial Transition in Wales and the United States 1759-1850. *Annals of the Association of American Geographers* 85 (2): 244-66.

———. 1997a. *Calvinists Incorporated: Welsh Immigrants on Ohio's Industrial Frontier*. Chicago: University of Chicago Press.

———. 1997b. Religious Identity as Ethnic Identity: the Welsh in Waukesha County. In *Wisconsin Land and Life*, ed. R. C. Ostergren and T.R. Vale, 282-99. Madison: University of Wisconsin Press.

———. 1999. Migration, Nationalism, and the Construction of Welsh Identity. In *Nested Identities: Nationalism, Territory, and Scale*, ed. Guntram H. Herb and David H. Kaplan, 289-315. New York: Rowman & Littlefield.

Lewis, Idwal. 1942. Welsh Newspapers and Journals in the United States. *National Library of Wales Journal* 2 (3/4): 124-30.

Lewis, Ronald L. 2005. Networking among Welsh Coal Miners in nineteenth century [*sic*] America. In *Towards a Comparative History of Coalfield Societies*, ed. Stefan Berger, Andy Croll and Norman LaPorte. Burlington, VT: Ashgate.

———. 2008. *Welsh Americans: A History of Assimilation in the Coalfields*. Chapel Hill, NC: University of North Carolina Press.

———. 2011. Reconstructing Welsh Identity in the American Coalfields. *North American Journal of Welsh Studies* 6 (1): 32-52.

Matthews, Gethin. 2009. "Y Dynion Mwyaf Diniwed ar Wyneb y Greadigaeth": Y Cymry a Brodorion Columbia Brydeinig. *Y Traethodydd* 164 (690): 147-56.

———. 2010. "Addoli'r Dduwies Aur" ("Worshipping the Goddess Gold"): The Patterns and Processes of Nineteenth Century Welsh Migration to the British Columbia Gold-fields. PhD diss., Cardiff University.

———. 2011. The Irish are everywhere. Where are the Welsh? In *A New History of Wales: Myths and Realities in Welsh History*, ed. Huw Bowen, 121-27. Llandysul: Gomer Press.

O'Leary, Paul. 2008. "Peerless": The Life and Legend of Jim Driscoll. In *Wales and its Boxers: The Fighting Tradition*, ed. Peter Stead and Gareth Williams, 17-31. Cardiff: University of Wales Press.

Owen, Bob. 1950. Welsh American Newspapers and Periodicals. *National Library of Wales Journal* 6 (4): 373-84.

Reese, Alfred J. 2004. *History of the Welsh National Gymanfa Ganu Association, 1929-2003*. Hartland, MI: Welsh National Gymanfa Ganu Association.

Rhys, Dulais. 1998. *Joseph Parry : bachgen bach o Ferthyr*. Cardiff: University of Wales Press.

Roberts, D. Hywel E. 1983-1984. The Printing of Welsh Books in the United States – An Introductory Survey. *Journal of the Welsh Bibliographical Society* 12 (1): 3-25.

Roberts, Gwilym R. 1998. *New Lives in the Valley: Slate Quarries and Quarry Villages in North Wales, New York, and Vermont, 1850-1920*. Somersworth: New Hampshire Printers.

Smith, Dai. 1984. *Wales! Wales?* London: George Allen & Unwin.

———. 1993. *Aneurin Bevan and the world of South Wales*. Cardiff: University of Wales Press.

———. 1999. *Wales: A Question for History*. Bridgend: Seren.

———. 2008. Freddie Welsh: Welsh American. In *Wales and its Boxers: The Fighting Tradition*, ed. Peter Stead and Gareth Williams, 33-53. Cardiff: University of Wales Press.

Strange, Keith. 2005. *Merthyr Tydfil Iron Metropolis: Life in Merthyr in the Nineteenth Century*. Stroud: Tempus Publishing.

Taylor, Clare. 1983. Paddy's Run: A Welsh Community in Ohio. *Welsh History Review* 11 (3): 302-16.

Van Vugt, William E. 1991. Welsh Emigration to the U.S.A. During the Mid-Nineteenth Century. *Welsh History Review* 15 (1991): 545-61.

Walley, Cherilyn A. 2009. *The Welsh in Iowa*. Cardiff: University of Wales Press.

Williams, Daniel. 2002. The Welsh Atlantic: Mapping the Contexts of Welsh-American Literature. In *American Babel: Literatures of the United States from Abnaki to Zuni*, ed. Marc Shell, 343-68. Cambridge, MA: Harvard University Press.

Williams, David. 1935. Some Figures Relating to Emigration from Wales. *Bulletin of Celtic Studies* 7:396-415.

———. 1942. The Contribution of Wales to the Development of the United States. *National Library of Wales Journal* 2 (3/4): 97-108.

Williams, Gareth. 2008. Jimmy Wilde, the "Tylorstown Terror." In *Wales and its Boxers: The Fighting Tradition*, ed. Peter Stead and Gareth Williams, 55-70. Cardiff: University of Wales Press.

Williams, Glanmor. 1976. *A Prospect of Paradise*. Cardiff: BBC Wales.

Williams, Glyn. 1991. *Welsh in Patagonia: the State and Ethnic Community*. Cardiff: University of Wales Press.

Williams, Gwyn A. 1980. *The search for Beulah Land: the Welsh and the Atlantic Revolution*. London: Croom Helm.

Williams, John. 1985. *Digest of Welsh Historical Statistics*. Vol. 1. Cardiff: Welsh Office.

Williams, William. 1942. The first three Welsh books printed in America. *National Library of Wales Journal* 2 (3/4): 109-19.

———. 1943. More about the first three Welsh books printed in America. *National Library of Wales Journal* 3 (1/2): 19-22.

Part II: Language

Robert Dunbar

Understanding Canadian Multiculturalism Policies and Cultural Diversity in a 21st-Century Context from a "Celtic" Perspective

Canadian multiculturalism can be understood in many different ways: "descriptively," as a sociological fact; "prescriptively," as an ideology; from a "political perspective," as a public policy; and as "a set of intergroup dynamics," a process (Dewing 2009: 1). In this chapter, Canadian multiculturalism will be considered primarily as a set of public policies.

Pollsters have found that, in Canada, there tend to be higher levels of support for multiculturalism as a social reality than as an official policy, although such support also tends to dip during periods of economic recession. In terms of multiculturalism as an official policy, "many Canadians are unsure of what [it] is, what it is trying to do and why, and what it can realistically accomplish in a liberal-democratic society such as ours" (10).

It may be this very policy that led to the well-known stereotype of Canada as a mosaic, but such a stereotype needs to be examined. It is not at all clear, for example, to what extent official Canadian multiculturalism policies have themselves fostered diversity. As a sociological fact, Canada is undoubtedly an ethnically diverse country, but this diversity is more a result of Canada's relatively generous immigration policies, especially those of the last two generations or so, than of any official policy of multiculturalism. Furthermore, it is far from clear that levels of ethnic identification and of adherence to ethnic cultural practices and to ethnic languages are in fact more durable in Canada than in the United States or, for that matter, in other societies having similarly high levels of immigration.[1]

Language is a particularly good case in point. Arguably, language loyalty is somewhat easier to measure, based, for example, on census results rather than other less measurable cultural practices. Language is a particularly important marker of identity, and many aspects of culture are embedded in language and tend to be lost once the language ceases to be spoken. Studies of language maintenance among immigrants to Canada have shown, however, that both knowledge and use of the immigrant language decline dramatically from the first to the second, and then the second to the third generation, although there are variations between different ethnic groups (Weinfeld 1994: 240-41; see also Chow 2001).

The experience of Scottish Gaelic in eastern Nova Scotia and particularly in Cape Breton is somewhat unusual in this respect, as surviving native speakers are often fourth-, fifth- and occasionally even sixth-generation Canadians. Undoubtedly, physical isolation in rural areas, high intra-group marriage among those who remained in such areas and the relatively late arrival of good transport links and modern telecommunications technology have played a part. While more research needs to be done on the survival of Gaelic outside Cape Breton, the experience of speakers of Celtic languages, including speakers of Gaelic in other areas of heavy Gaelic settlement, are not markedly different from the general pattern of intergenerational language loss just described. What is also relatively clear is that the general pattern of intergenerational loss of language is not markedly different from the experience of Gaelic groups in the United States or, for that matter, in other countries that have high levels of immigration.

It may not be surprising, then, that Canada's multiculturalism policy has generated considerable criticism. Some have suggested, cynically, that it was simply an attempt by the Liberal Party of Canada to effectively buy the loyalty of burgeoning new immigrant communities that were emerging as a result of the more open immigration policies of the 1960s and 1970s (Edwards 1995: 28-31). There may be an element of truth to this charge; however, in the 1980s, the Conservative government of Brian Mulroney also embraced the policy, perhaps for similar reasons. As we shall see, since the 1990s in particular, there has been a significant change in emphasis in federal multicultural policy, and it is now probably more difficult to sustain an argument that the policy is simply ethnic pork-barrelling.

Another concern is that a multicultural policy promotes diversity at the expense of integration. This view was most forcefully expressed by the Canadian novelist and broadcaster Neil Bissoondath in his 1994 book *Selling Illusions: The Cult of Multiculturalism in Canada*. Bissoondath argued that multiculturalism isolated ethnic groups from each other, fostering an inward-looking and isolationist perspective. This ostracization might serve the interests of ethnic elites who benefited from federal and provincial funding, but was not in the interests of the members of the communities themselves, who deserved the benefits of full economic, social and political participation in Canadian society. Furthermore, Bissoondath argued that the policy tends to pit one ethnic group against another in competition for recognition and, with it, funding and influence.

These concerns have been echoed by other commentators, and have certainly gained traction in Canada and other jurisdictions that have followed a policy of multiculturalism, including the U.K., in the wake of 9/11 and of more recent terrorist incidents that have been perpetrated by "home-grown" extremists. Once again, though, the criticisms of the multiculturalism policy seem rather overwrought. The federal policy has never been particularly well resourced, and it is doubtful that ethnic "laagers" are traceable to the federal policy. Furthermore, research does not support the idea that the adoption of a policy of multiculturalism has had a negative impact on the rate of integration of immigrants (Kymlicka 1998; Vigdor 2011).[2] Indeed, as we shall see, the Canadian policy of multiculturalism was always firmly based on the goal of integration, and changes of emphasis in the policy in the last twenty years or so have pushed it in a more strongly integrationist direction. Those aspects aimed at maintaining ethnic cultures and languages seem to have weakened.

In short, it is not clear what impact official multiculturalism has had, beyond the rhetorical, the symbolic and the mythological. As shall be argued in this chapter, it is certainly difficult to demonstrate that the federal policy has made much difference to Canadians of a Celtic heritage. However, rhetoric, symbols and myths are important, and can be useful. Combined with the generally positive experience, at least as reflected in opinion polling on the matter, that Canadians have of multiculturalism, it may be that the mix of day-to-day experiences and rhetoric, symbols and mythology has in fact encouraged Canadians of a Celtic heritage to explore aspects of that heritage; indeed, this is an issue that deserves in-depth exploration and further research. It would be interesting to see, for example, the extent to which multiculturalist attitudes and policies have played a part in the decision to enrol in courses in Celtic languages at Canadian universities, or at institutions such as the Gaelic College in St. Ann's, Cape Breton, or at night school or in other courses such as those based on the Gàidhlig aig Baile methodology in Nova Scotia.

Just as importantly, the term "multiculturalism" can be a useful rhetorical tool to those wishing to make the case for greater institutional support for the acquisition and maintenance of Celtic languages, for more research and teaching on Celtic languages and cultures and for other forms of support for Celtic cultures in Canada. As shall be seen, international institutions of relevance to Canada and international law more generally have embraced multiculturalism as the preferred policy option for the management of diversity within states. While such international standards do not always produce dramatic changes in state policies, they can also have an impact when drawn upon by non-governmental organizations and the constituencies which such organizations represent, in support of arguments for more favourable domestic policies.

Before turning to current Canadian multiculturalism policies, it would be useful to briefly consider previous Canadian approaches to the management of diversity, and to consider how such policies have impacted people of Celtic heritage in Canada, and particularly those of Scottish Gaelic heritage in Nova Scotia. It should be noted that, like multiculturalism, "Celtic" is a rather slippery term, and that the focus here will be on peoples who actually spoke or still speak a Celtic language.

Historical Approach to Cultural Diversity: Anglo-Conformity

Until well into the 20th century, the dominant approach to the existence of cultural and linguistic diversity in almost all of those territories that now form the Canadian federation was one which has been described as "anglo-conformity" (Day 2000: 122-25). This approach to diversity was essentially assimilationist: cultural and linguistic difference should be replaced by a common identity based on a shared language—English—and shared cultural values—"British" ones, broadly speaking. This approach to diversity was based on assumptions about the supposed superiority of anglophone British culture, and the belief that "lesser" peoples would benefit from participation in a supposedly "higher" civilization—a highly chauvinist approach. It was the dominant approach in the British Empire, and was reflected in, and drew strength from, the thinking of the leading British intellectuals of the Victorian period. Take, for example, the following, from John Stuart Mill's *Considerations on Representative Government*:

> Experience proves that it is possible for one nationality to merge and be absorbed in another: and when it was originally an inferior and more backward portion of the human race the absorption is greatly to its advantage. Nobody can suppose that it is not more beneficial to a Breton, or a Basque of French Navarre, to be brought into the current of the ideas and feelings of a highly civilised and cultivated people—to be a member of the French nationality, admitted on equal terms to all the privileges of French citizenship, sharing the advantages of French protection, and the dignity and prestige of French power—than to sulk on his own rocks, the half-savage relic of past times, revolving in his own little mental orbit, without participation or interest in the general movement of the world. The same remark applies to the Welshman or the Scottish Highlander as members of the British nation. (Mill 1865: 122)

Such an approach was certainly applied to Celtic peoples, both within Britain and in the colonies, including the colonies of British North America. Take, for example, this passage, from the 1850 Education Report of John William Dawson, the Nova Scotia Superintendent of Education:

> English reading is the most important branch of intellectual school education. Beginning with the earliest attempts of school instruction; when developed to its full extent, it places within reach of the pupil all the rich treasures of English literature, making the wisest and best of men his daily companions, and giving him, in his ordinary avocations, in all his difficulties, duties and aspirations, the counsel and aid of all human wisdom and of Divine revelation. (Qtd. in Kennedy 2002: 48)

The territory that is now Québec escaped the worst effects of this approach, largely due to the demands of geopolitics. After the conquest of New France, British colonial officials had the intention of assimilating their new francophone subjects. The increasingly precarious political situation in the American colonies in the early 1770s forced a reconsideration of policy. Fearful that republicanism might infect Québec as well, the British sought to appease these new francophone subjects. The *Québec Act* of 1774 resulted. It sought to guarantee position of the Roman Catholic Church in the colony: still proscribed in the U.K. itself, Mass could be openly celebrated in Québec, and, unlike their co-religionists in the U.K., Catholic inhabitants of the Colony of Québec could hold public office. It also sought to guarantee the continuation of French law and, by implication, the position of the French language in Québec in public life and in public institutions.

The *Québec Act* was an exceptional response, though, and the goal of assimilation was certainly lurking in the wings in the 19th century. It reared its head in Lord Durham's report, undertaken in response to the rebellions in Upper and Lower Canada of 1837. The recommendation, subsequently implemented, of a union of predominantly francophone Lower Canada and predominantly anglophone Upper Canada was in part motivated by the desire to promote the assimilation of the francophone population (Bothwell 2006: 184-86). Only with Canadian Confederation in 1867—brought about in no small part as an attempt to deal with the tension that the union of the two colonies had produced—was the bilingual nature of British North America recognized and institutionalized, and the goal of assimilation of the francophone population of Québec abandoned.

British policy in relation to the Celtic languages in the Celtic homelands in the 18th and 19th century was clearly one of anglo-conformity. The experience of the Scottish Gaels is broadly typical. The predominant view among the elite in Scottish and British society was that the Gaelic language was a source of "barbaritie and incivilitie,"[3] and religious charities such as the Society in Scotland for the Propagation of Christian Knowledge (SSPCK) sought, through the establishment of schools in Highland and Island parishes, to assimilate Gaels to the English tongue. SSPCK schools only began using Gaelic as a medium of instruction once they found that teaching monolingual Gaels through the medium of English was not producing scholars with sufficient levels of fluency in English (MacKinnon 1991: 54-56, 63-64). Rather than an early example of enlightened multiculturalism, these methods aimed at transitional "subtractive" bilingualism (Baker 2011: 207-10, 215-17). With the introduction of state-supported education in Scotland in 1872, though, even transitional "subtractive" bilingualism was abandoned: no provision was made for the use of Gaelic in Highland and Island schools. Indeed, the state made no attempt to accommodate Gaelic speakers, including the sizeable monolingual Gaelic-speaking population that existed in the 19th and into the early 20h century: the extension of the British state into Gaelic-speaking areas through institutions such as county councils, created near the end of the 19th century, was done through the medium of English.

A very similar approach was taken in Nova Scotia (Kennedy 2002). Once again, anglo-conformity was the prevailing policy, and one could argue that this policy continued until quite recently, at least at the provincial level. Over the last ten years, thanks first to the efforts of Nova Scotia Premier (2006-2009) Rodney MacDonald and some supportive civil servants, things have begun to change in the province, and the policy changes he ushered in, first as minister then as Premier, have generally been adopted by the present New Democrat government. The position under federal multiculturalism will be considered below. As in Scotland, education policy was the area in which anglo-conformity has been pursued most aggressively. While the *Nova Scotia School Act* of 1840 authorized the payment of public grants to local schools using German or Scottish Gaelic as the language of instruction, the possibility of Gaelic as a language of instruction created by the legislation was never pursued, in no small part due to administrative indifference and even opposition. The attitudes of the anglophone, colonial elite in Halifax toward the Nova Scotia Gaels were generally similar to those of the Edinburgh- and London-based political and administrative elites to Gaels in the homeland (Kennedy 2002: 42-53).

Gaelic oral tradition provides a good picture of the reality of the cultural politics, and indeed the cultural and linguistic hierarchies of the colony, and subsequently of the Province of Nova Scotia. Take, for example, the song "Don Phàrlamaid Ùir" (To the New Parliament), composed by the Bard MacLean (Dunbar 2006). During the 1830 election campaign in the colony, the poet was told that one of the Liberal candidates had made disparaging remarks about the Gaels. The candidates were all members of the small, anglophone elite based in Halifax. The poet was infuriated by this insult to his people, and responded by composing a poem which he himself sang at an election rally. One gets a sense of his anger, and of the nature of the insult, from these lines:

> Gur mòr an t-adhbhar nàire dhuibh,
> Ma ghèilleas sibh do Làsonach,
> Do Dheòrsa na do dh'Àrchibald,
> 'S an tàir a thug na h-uaislean.
>
> 'S e 'thuirt iad gu mi-chiatach,
> Gur pronnasg a bha 'dhith orra,
> 'S gun glanadh iad a' sgrìobach
> Do na Gàidheil mhiothair shuarach.
>
> (Great is the cause of shame [to the Gaels]
> if you submit to Lawson,
> George or Archibald,
> and the offence these nobles caused.
>
> What they said most improperly
> was that they needed sulphur
> so that they could clean out the mange
> of the beggarly, worthless Gaels.)

Lawson, George and Archibald were the Liberal candidates. The bard went on to recount the martial virtues of the Gaels' ancestors. He emphasized that such Gaels would never have put up with an insult of the sort proffered by the Liberal candidates. MacLean had experienced similar attitudes to the Gaels in Scotland prior to his emigration in 1819, and his keen awareness of the ethnic distinctiveness of the Scottish Gaels and his suspicion of the Lowlander is evident in several of his early poems (Dunbar 2008).

The same sense of cultural and linguistic hierarchies is evident in other Gaelic sources in Nova Scotia. One of the best examples is the well-known song "An Tè a Chaill a' Ghàidhlig" (Creighton and MacLeod 1979: 26-30; The Girl who Lost her Gaelic), in which a young Cape Breton Gael meets a local woman who, like many Gaels of eastern Nova Scotia, had emigrated to New England for work. Dressed in the high style of the city, he barely recognizes her, thereby emphasizing the economic gap which existed between the rural Gaels and the growing population of urban centres. He speaks to her in Gaelic, but she answers contemptuously—in English—illustrating the social gap that existed between the two languages and, by implication, their speakers, a product of the ideology of anglo-conformity.

A final illustration of the impact of anglo-conformity on Canadian Gaels is evident in the attempt by Thomas MacInnes in 1891 to gain recognition for Gaelic in the Canadian Parliament (Kennedy 2002: 35-39). MacInnes was a native of Inverness County and a Gaelic speaker. He had trained as a medical doctor at Harvard, had gone to British Columbia, and was ultimately appointed to the Canadian Senate. He was aware of the widespread use of Celtic languages in Canada and particularly of Gaelic. As a result, MacInnes tabled a bill in the Canadian Senate to make Gaelic an official language of the Canadian Parliament. Not surprisingly, the Bill was handily rejected. Francophone senators generally opposed it, mainly on the grounds that any recognition of another language would compromise the privileged status of French as one of the languages of Canada's two "founding peoples." Anglophone senators were generally equally opposed, but on the basis that Gaelic was not a suitable language for such purposes. Section 133 of the *British North America Act*, the Canadian Constitution, guaranteed the position of French, but that was as far as the policy of anglo-conformity would allow.

Canada as a "Mosaic"

Almost immediately after Confederation in 1867, Canadian politicians and policy-makers recognized the need to populate the Canadian west. They were motivated by the fear that if they did not do so, settlers drifting north from the United States would fill the territory, and that this might ultimately lead to its annexation by the Americans. The construction of the Canadian National Railway was in large part driven by such concerns. It quickly became apparent, though, that internal migration from other parts of Canada and immigration from Britain and Ireland would be insufficient to meet the needs of this expansionist policy. For this reason, immigration policy was changed to allow greater numbers of migrants from other parts of Europe, first from northwest Europe, and then from southern and eastern Europe. The large-scale immigration which followed, and which continued largely unabated throughout the 20th and into the 21st century (albeit for evolving policy purposes), irrevocably changed Canada's ethnic composition.

While the policy of anglo-conformity continued, scholars and other observers began to speak in different terms about the nature of Canadian society. The metaphor that began to be used was that of a mosaic. Richard Day notes that perhaps the first use of the metaphor of the mosaic appeared "not with a self-conscious attempt to provide a name for a particularly Canadian form of nation-building, but with a passing reference in a traveller's journal" (Day 2000: 149). The traveller's journal was Victoria Hayward's 1922 book *Romantic Canada*, and the reference was in a passage in which she commented on the diverse forms of church architecture, music and worship that she encountered on the Canadian prairie: "it is, indeed, a mosaic of vast dimensions and great breadth" (Hayward 1922: 187). As Day notes, though, this diversity was not perceived to be a problem, as it was for the purveyors of anglo-conformity, but "a positive and precious opportunity for a roving spirit with a collector's gleam in her eye" (Day 2000: 150).

It is a delicious irony that Hayward was an American. Her metaphor stuck, and it seemed to capture the social reality in many parts of rural and urban Canada of significant cultural and linguistic diversity, even if such diversity was not being consciously fostered by public policy (other than immigration policy).

The reality of the Canadian mosaic was not, however, without its critics. Writing in the 1960s, before the federal policy of multiculturalism had been adopted, John Porter, in his classic book *The Vertical Mosaic* (1965), traced the inequities of opportunity and power that existed in Canada among various racial and ethnic groups, with anglophone Canadians of British stock disproportionately occupying the positions of privilege. He writes, "Segregation in social structure, to which the concept of the mosaic or multiculturalism must ultimately lead, can become an important aspect of social control by the charter group" (qtd. in Day 2000: 30), that is, the British "founding race." Like Bissoondath, Porter's concern was not the perpetuation of the social dominance that anglo-conformism tended to produce, but to create the conditions for full and equal participation in Canadian society, irrespective of ethnic origin or social class. Here we have the classic problem with which Canadian multiculturalism has had to deal: how to promote the possibility of maintenance of ethnic and cultural identity while ensuring full equality of opportunity and full participation in wider Canadian society for all, regardless of identity.

Bilingualism and Biculturalism: The Multicultural Response

In 1963, the Canadian federal government of Prime Minister Lester Pearson established a Royal Commission on Bilingualism and Biculturalism. Its creation was motivated by the concern about growing frictions over language in the province of Québec (Bothwell 2006: 439). However, in attempting to respond to the linguistic crisis, the creation of the Royal Commission exposed other fissures. As a result of the massive increase in non-British and non-French immigration during the 20th century, by the 1960s more than a quarter of the population was of neither British nor French ancestry, and some of these Canadians argued that the emphasis on a French-English duality ignored their experience and effectively made them into second-class citizens. Groups representing Ukrainian-Canadians were particularly active in lobbying for an expansion in the remit of the

Commission (Kallen 2010: 178-79). In response, Prime Minister Pearson added two representatives of such groups to the Royal Commission to "safeguard" the contribution of "other ethnic groups" (English 2009: 143). The idea of Canada as a country with two founding peoples, the British and the French, also resulted in the complete exclusion of Canada's Aboriginal peoples, and by the 1960s this exclusion was increasingly being challenged; significantly, however, questions relating to aboriginal peoples continued to be excluded from the remit of the Commission.

The terms of reference instructed the Royal Commission

> to recommend what steps should be taken to develop the Canadian Confederation on the basis of an equal partnership between the two founding races, *taking into account the contribution made by the other ethnic groups to the cultural enrichment of Canada and the measures that should be taken to safeguard that contribution.* (Royal Commission 1970: 3; emphasis added)[4]

Volume 4 of the Commission's final report deals with the cultural contribution of these "other ethnic groups," defined as "those whose ethnic origin is neither French nor *British*" (xxv; emphasis added). In volume 4, the Commissioners state that they would look at the contribution of these groups to Canadian life, "and especially to the enrichment that results from the meeting of a number of languages and cultures," noting that this contribution is seen "in the active participation of those *whose mother tongue is neither French nor English* in various facets of community life" (3-4; emphasis added). They added the following:

> Our analysis will examine the following questions: to what degree have Canadians whose origin is neither French nor British integrated with Francophone or Anglophone society? To what degree do they remain attached to their original cultures and languages? (12)

Note the conflation of "British" origin and "English" mother tongue, a conflation that pervades the volume. The Commission seems generally to have overlooked the fact that very many persons of British origin in Canada were persons whose mother tongue was not English. Celtic peoples speaking Celtic languages were therefore effectively written out of the Royal Commission's narrative.

For example, in all of volume 4, the word "Scottish" appears only rarely, and almost all such references are in relation to census tables from the 1961 Canadian census, in which "Scottish" is recognized as a possible ethnic origin, as is Irish and Welsh. Indeed, these are the only references at all to Irish or Welsh in volume 4, and there are no references at all to Breton.

There are, however, a couple of specific references to Scottish Gaelic. One is in a section on "Social Patterns," in a passage on the language of instruction in schools. The Commissioners note that in the *Nova Scotia School Act* of 1840, the payment of public grants to local schools using German or Scottish Gaelic as the language of instruction was authorized (102). In part 3 of volume 4, in a section on the maintenance of language and culture, it is noted that in the 1961 census, only 14 per cent of the population of the Atlantic provinces reported mother tongues other than English and French (126). The Commissioners note specifically that Gaelic was one of these languages, and indicate in a footnote the following:

> Among those of British origin in Nova Scotia in 1961, there were almost 3,700 persons who gave Gaelic as their mother tongue, almost half of the Canadian total of 7,500 persons who reported Gaelic as their mother tongue. Presumably, many of these were native born. However, the number of persons of Gaelic mother tongue is declining rapidly. (126n2)

Finally, in chapter 6 of part 3, on education, in the section on higher education, reference is made to the Celtic Studies department at St. Francis Xavier University, which had four courses in the Gaelic language and literature and two in history (166).

The treatment of Celtic peoples stood in sharp contrast to that of other groups. The historical narrative is relatively simple. Canada was "a vast territory inhabited in the beginning by Indians and Eskimos"(4). In the early 17th century it was first colonized by the French, then by the British. The first Germans "arrived towards the end of the 17th century" (4). Jews had arrived by the middle of the 18th century, and Poles in the second half of that century. "After 1870, the Danes, Dutch, Icelanders and others made their way to the prairies in ever increasing numbers" (4). In 1891 Ukrainians began arriving. And so on. The detailed narrative concentrates on the 20th century, and on those groups, all of which were of non-British and non-French origin, associated most closely with successive waves of 20th-century migration. Specific attention was given to aspects of the experience of a wide range of groups, including Doukhobors, Ukrainians, Germans, the Dutch and Scandinavians, Japanese, Italians, Hungarians and Jews, as well as broader groupings, such as Asians and "Negroes" (Royal Commission 1970: 17-32).

One or two of the recommendations (228-34) in volume 4 focused on issues of integration. For example, the commissioners recommended that provinces that had not yet enacted legislation on fair employment practices, fair accommodation practices and prohibitions on discrimination should do so (Recommendation 1). An important aspect of integration into a bilingual society is instruction in the two official languages. The commissioners therefore recommended that special instruction in the appropriate official language be provided for children who enter the public school system, and that the federal government provide assistance to the provinces, which under the constitution have responsibility for education, with any additional costs associated with such instruction (Recommendation 4).

However, the bulk of the recommendations focused on fostering the languages and cultures of Canada's ethnic communities. For example, they recommended that the teaching of languages other than English and French, and cultural subjects related to them, be incorporated as options in the public elementary school program, where there was sufficient demand (Recommendation 3). They also recommended that more advanced instruction and a wider range of options in languages other than English and French and in cultural subjects related to them be provided in public high schools, also subject to the condition that there be sufficient demand (Recommendation 5). At the tertiary level, the commissioners recommended that universities broaden their practices in giving standing or credits for studies in modern languages other than French and English, both for the purposes of admissions and for degrees (Recommendation 6), and that universities expand their studies in the fields of the humanities and social sciences relating to areas other than those related to the English and French languages (Recommendation 7). A practical difficulty here, though, was that education is a provincial responsibility under the Canadian constitution, and the federal government, to whom the Commission reported, ultimately had little influence with respect to the implementation of any of these recommendations.

With regard to the media, the commissioners also recommended that the CRTC, the communications regulator, remove all restrictions on private broadcasting in languages other than French or English (Recommendation 8), and that the CBC both recognize the place of languages other than English and French in Canadian life and remove its proscription on the use of such languages in broadcasting (Recommendation 9). They also recommended that the CRTC should undertake studies in the field of broadcasting in other languages to determine the best means by which radio and television "can contribution to *the maintenance of languages and cultures*" (emphasis added) and that the CBC should participate in such studies, perhaps with pilot projects in Montréal or Toronto (Recommendation 10), and that research should be undertaken through the CRTC concerning the nature and effects of the portrayal of other cultural groups on all English- and French-language radio and television stations (Recommendation 13).

Finally, the commissioners had a number of recommendations relating to other cultural institutions. They recommended that the National Film Board "undertake to publicize the fact that it produces prints of many of its films in languages other than English and French" (Recommendation 12), and that it continue to develop the production of films that inform Canadians about one another, "including films about the contribution and problems of both individuals and groups of ethnic origin other than British and French" (Recommendation 13). They recommended that government agencies should receive "the financial means they require" to support cultural and research organizations whose objectives were "to foster the arts and letters of cultural groups other than the British and French" (Recommendation 14). Finally, they recommended public funding for the administrative costs of the Canadian Folk Arts Council (Recommendation 15), and that the National Museum of Man be given adequate space and facilities and sufficient funding to carry out its projects regarding the history, social organizations and folk arts of cultural groups other than the British and French (Recommendation 16).

Three things are particularly notable about the recommendations. First, a large majority of the recommendations focused on matters relating to the maintenance of the cultures and languages of ethnic communities. As we shall see, the federal policy on multiculturalism which emerged from the report was somewhat ambivalent about this aspect of the recommendations, and the Prime Minister himself appears to have been rather reluctant to foster linguistic diversity, believing that maintenance of non-official languages and, to a certain extent, other aspects of culture were private matters. As we shall also see, the maintenance of linguistic identities has in recent years receded even further in the federal policy. Second, the references in the Commission recommendations tend to be to languages and cultures, rather than groups themselves. Third, these references are to languages and cultures other than French and English. As a result, although the prevailing treatment in the Commission report itself of "British" as an undifferentiated group had the tendency to write Celtic peoples out of the story of Canadian multiculturalism, reference in many of the key recommendations to languages other than French and English opened the door to the Celtic languages and cultures.

Multiculturalism as an Official Policy

The federal government's response to the recommendations in book 4 of the Royal Commission's report came in 1971. On October 8 of that year, Canada became the first state in the world to announce an official state policy of multiculturalism. In his statement to the House of Commons on that day, Prime Minister Trudeau made the following comments:

> It was the view of the royal commission ... that there cannot be one cultural policy for Canadians of British and French origin,

another for the original peoples and yet a third for all others. *For although there are two official languages, there is no official culture, nor does any ethnic group take precedence over any other. No citizen or group of citizens is other than Canadian, and all should be treated fairly.* (Trudeau 1971; emphasis added)

Trudeau's statement announced the government's response to volume 4 of the Report of the Royal Commission on Bilingualism and Biculturalism, and it was accompanied by a written statement. As John English, Trudeau's biographer, has pointed out, far from recognizing any sort of group rights, the statement to Parliament announcing the new policy made clear Trudeau's suspicion of such rights. Arguing that one's adherence to one's ethnic group is influenced most by "one's sense of belonging to the group, and by what the commission calls the group's 'collective will to exist'" Trudeau also noted that

> The individual's freedom would be hampered if he were locked for life within a particular cultural compartment by the accident of birth or language. It is vital, therefore, that every Canadian, whatever his ethnic origin, be given a chance to learn at least one of the two languages in which his country conducts its official business and its politics.

> A policy of multiculturalism within a bilingual framework commends itself to the government as the most suitable means of assuring the cultural freedom of Canadians. *Such a policy should help to break down discriminatory attitudes and cultural jealousies.* National unity, if it is to mean anything in the deeply personal sense, *must be founded on confidence in one's own individual identity; out of this can grow respect for that of others and a willingness to share ideas, attitudes and assumptions.* A vigorous policy of multiculturalism will help create this initial confidence. (English 2009: 145-46; emphasis added)

For Trudeau, then, multiculturalism was a means of fostering integration of an increasingly diverse Canadian population. Trudeau went on to say that the government would "support and encourage the various cultures and ethnic groups that give structure and vitality" to the country, and laid out four ways in which the government would apply such support:

> First, resources permitting, the government will seek to assist all Canadian cultural groups that have demonstrated a desire and effort to continue to develop a capacity to grow and contribute to Canada, and a clear need for assistance, the small and weak groups no less than the strong and highly organized.

Second, the government will assist members of all cultural groups to overcome cultural barriers to full participation in Canadian society.

Third, the government will promote creative encounters and interchange among all Canadian cultural groups in the interest of national unity.

Fourth, the government will continue to assist immigrants to acquire at least one of Canada's official languages in order to become full participants in Canadian society. (Trudeau 1971)

In the accompanying written statement, the government noted that cultural diversity was being eroded by "the impact of industrial technology, mass communications and urbanization" (Trudeau 1971), and the concern of many contemporary writers was that mass-produced culture and entertainment threatened to "denature and depersonalize man." The government noted that a basic human need was "a sense of belonging" and that while ethnic groups were "certainly not the only way in which this need for belonging can be met," "they have been an important one in Canadian society." Furthermore,

> ethnic pluralism can help us overcome or prevent the homogenization and depersonalization of mass society. Vibrant ethnic groups can give Canadians of the second, third, and subsequent generations a feeling that they are connected with tradition and with human experience in various parts of the world and different periods of time. (Trudeau 1971).

The government noted that multiculturalism was not a threat to one's allegiance to Canada. The following passage is particularly interesting in the context of this paper:

> There is no reason to suppose that a citizen who identifies himself with pride as a Chinese-Canadian, who is deeply involved in the cultural activities of the Chinese community in Canada, will be less loyal or concerned with Canadian matters *than a citizen of Scottish origin who takes part in a bagpipe band or highland dancing group.* Cultural identity is not the same thing as allegiance to a country. (Trudeau 1971; emphasis added)

On this point, the government concluded that ethnic loyalties need not, and usually do not, detract from wider loyalties to community and country, and that Canadian identity would not be undermined by multiculturalism. Indeed, the government believed that "cultural pluralism is the very essence of Canadian identity. Every ethnic group has the right to preserve and develop its own culture and values within the Canadian context." The emphasis on culture and on certain forms of cultural expression—in the Scottish context, rather stereotypical ones that are removed from the cultural forms that are more strongly represented in the living Gaelic culture of eastern Nova Scotia (and other parts of Canada) at the time—and the omission of language is notable.

With regard to the first of the ways mentioned above in the Prime Minister's statement, that the government would support ethnic communities, the written statement noted that English and French cultures in Canada both have the resources "to be self-supporting," that "general cultural activities tend to be supportive of them," and that they are already supported under official languages programs. As a result, new programs were being proposed "to give support to minority cultural groups in keeping with their needs and particular situations." However, they also noted the following:

> The government cannot and should not take upon itself the responsibility for the continued viability of all ethnic groups. The objective of our policy is *the cultural survival and development* of ethnic groups to the degree that a given group exhibits a desire for this. Government aid to cultural groups must proceed on the basis of aid to self-effort. And in our concern for *the preservation of ethnic group identity*, we should not forget that individuals in a democracy may choose not to be concerned about maintaining a strong sense of their ethnic identity. (Trudeau 1971; emphasis added)

Maintenance of the cultural and linguistic identity of ethnic groups was a central aspect of the recommendations of the Royal Commission's volume 4. This was, however, only one of four key objectives of the government's policy, and the commitment was conditional and made no direct reference to languages.

The announcement of the policy was followed by the appointment of a federal minister of state with responsibility for multiculturalism in 1972, the creation, also in 1972, of a Multiculturalism Directorate within the Department of the Secretary of State to assist in the implementation of the policy and related programs, the establishment in 1973 of a Canadian Consultative Council on Multiculturalism (later renamed the Canadian Ethnocultural Council) to establish formal links between ethnic organizations and the government and to advise the minister, and the creation of a Ministry of Multiculturalism, also in 1973, to monitor implementation within government. Critics of the policy argued that it "nourished stereotypes of minority ethnic groups as strange upholders of quaint customs"

(Kallen 2010: 181), that it fostered a conception of Canada as a kind of "ethnic zoo" where "the function of the zookeeper was to accumulate ethnic exotica and to exhibit them publicly once a year" (Brotz 1980, qtd. in Kallen 2010: 180), and, simply, that it was nothing more than the provision of money for "folk dances, songfests and parties" (English 2009: 146). Certainly, money did become available for such purposes, but the thrust of the policy, and of its implementation, was toward broader aspects of integration which tended not to focus on the cultural. Nonetheless, in the first stage of the implementation of the new policy, initiatives relating to maintenance of ethnic communities' languages and cultures received considerable support, including almost $200 million during the first decade of the policy (Dewing 2009: 4).

It is notable that, despite the ambiguous position of the Celtic languages and cultures in the Royal Commission Report, those interested in such languages and cultures immediately saw the opportunities that the new federal policy presented. Comunn Gaidhlig Cheap Breatunn, or the Cape Breton Gaelic Society, grew out of a non-credit Gaelic class conducted in 1968-1969 at Xavier College, Sydney, by the Rev. Sr. Margaret Beaton and Hugh F. MacKenzie. It developed the aims of providing "a social and cultural medium for Gaelic speakers, the majority of whom have reached an age when mobility has been reduced and, therefore, communication interrupted," and of persuading "authorities at all levels to create formal opportunities in the education system for young people who have missed the oral transmission of the language to acquire it as part of the learning and development process" (Comunn Gaidhlig Cheap Breatuinn 1972).

The Society recognized the significance of Prime Minister Pierre Trudeau's 1971 policy statement on multiculturalism, but noted that within the statement the federal government was unclear about the role of minority languages in the development of a strong multicultural framework, a perceptive and important point upon which some critics of the policy had focused (Kallen 2010: 181). The Society stated the following:

> The Gaelic Society would simply emphasize that its assessment of cultural development suggests language is essential to any true culture. Without its own language, a culture evolves into a caricature. Its soul and distinctiveness vanish leaving behind only a loose collection of superficial trappings. It becomes as mute as a violin without strings and the only value remaining lies in the commercial distribution of ornaments.
>
> . . .
>
> Without a strong language orientation Canada's multicultural policy will buy us, for many millions of dollars, nothing more than

a short term illumination of a variety of cultural groups. It will be of great entertainment value to everybody and it could even lead to creative exchanges between the various groups. But the light will wane steadily as Canada's third-languages decline and eventually will be extinguished as the last of our real tradition bearers passes away—the kilted figures will continue to dance to the bagpipes, but when the language is gone it will be the dancing and music of ghosts. (Comunn Gaidhlig Cheap Breatuinn 1972: 5)

Nonetheless, the Society also recognized the possibilities that the new policy created:

Here was an opportunity for members of the Society to organize a project that would directly advance society objectives, and also provide a valuable testing ground to demonstrate just how serious Society members are about sustaining a real cultural development program. (6)

The executive of the Society was keen to advance this, and asked two members, Linden MacIntyre, now a senior CBC journalist and an award-winning author, and John Campbell, to investigate ways in which the Society could participate in new programs that might emerge.[5] In February 1972, MacIntyre and Campbell met with a regional officer for The Department of the Secretary of State, Citizenship Branch, who explained the general terms of the new multiculturalism policy and "made several useful suggestions for steps the Gaelic Society should take if it hoped to participate." The Society submitted its proposal for financial support in March, 1972. The application was successful, and a three-week event, called Caidreabh nan Gàidheal (Gaelic Companionship) was held that summer. The event involved the following elements:

daily seminars and cultural workshops dealing with: historical, musical, oral aesthetic aspects of Gaelic culture; mechanics of communication; practical demonstrations of Cape Breton violin technique and music, step and Highland dancing; Gaelic folklore and songs; tartan weaving; pioneer crafts; interdenominational religious service in Gaelic. Public seminars in conjunction with the workshops, will lead up to a festival of Gaelic folk arts and crafts for Gaels and non-Gaels everywhere. (Comunn Gaidhlig Cheap Breatuinn 1972: 7)

The purposes were described in the following terms:

To develop a greater awareness among Gaels of their culture and traditions; to share the culture and tradition with the community at large; and to demonstrate to Gaels and the community at large the importance of Canadian Gaelic culture and tradition to Canada's past and future development. To reopen channels of communication between the older generation of Canadian Gaels which is still rooted in the culture and tradition of the past and the younger generations which have lost direct contact with their roots, but which represent Canada's potential for the future.

By all accounts, the event was a success. However, while it showed that the new multicultural policy could be of relevance to Celtic ethnic communities, it also illustrated some of the limitations of the policy. While it was clearly much more than simply an occasion for "folk dances, songfests and parties," Caidreabh nan Gàidheal was a one-off event; funding did not extend to the creation of any ongoing programming to support Gaelic language acquisition or the development of Gaelic cultural skills, something that the Cape Breton Gaelic Society clearly had in mind.

Two other initiatives from the first period of the multiculturalism policy's life did, however, show that the policy could have a longer-term impact for the benefit of Celtic languages and cultures. The first was the Nova Scotia Gaelic Folklore Project, which ran from 1977 to 1982. The project involved the collection of Gaelic oral tradition, mainly on Cape Breton Island. In total, about two thousand folklore items were collected, including a large number of songs and traditional folk narrative, housed on over 300 tapes. The project was developed at St. Francis Xavier University under the leadership of Dr. Margaret MacDonell, with Dr. John Shaw acting as field collector. It was funded by way of grants from the Multiculturalism Directorate of the Government of Canada. In addition to leading to the publication of four important collections of folklore and songs (MacDonell 1981; Shaw and MacNeil 1987; Shaw and MacLellan 2000; Shaw 2007), most of the collection has now been digitized, and is available online to researchers, learners and others interested in the material, at the excellent St. Francis Xavier "Sruth nan Gàidheal/Gael Stream" website (www.gaelstream.stfx.ca). The University received about $18,000 in funding from Heritage Canada for the digitization project, but through the Canadian Culture Online Program, Library and Archives Canada and the Canadian Council of Archives, rather than through any multiculturalism funding streams (Kathleen MacKenzie, personal communication, 28 November 2011; Gael Stream).

The other initiative was the creation of Celtic chairs at Canadian Universities. There are now three such chairs: the Sister St. Veronica Chair of Gaelic Studies, established at St. Francis Xavier University in 1984, the D'Arcy McGee Chair of Irish Studies, established at St. Mary's University in Halifax in 1986, and the Chair of Celtic Studies, also established in 1986, at the University of Ottawa. The chairs were funded in part by the

Chair Endowment Assistance Program, itself a product of the Canadian Ethnic Studies Program, which had been created by the Multiculturalism Directorate and which operated between 1973 and 1997. The first of these so-called "ethnic chairs" was created in 1978. Under the program, any Canadian university, or any voluntary organization in collaboration with a Canadian university, could propose a chair of ethnic studies, if the organization or university matched or surpassed the government offer of $300,000 to endow the chair and satisfied a number other conditions. By 1987, twelve such chairs had been created. Thereafter, however, in keeping with changes of emphasis within the multiculturalism policy which will be discussed shortly, the funding of ethnic chairs came to an end. The program moved beyond chairs for single ethnic groups toward a greater emphasis on chairs to promote cross-cultural, cross-disciplinary study of general issues of ethnicity, cultural identity, immigration, history, racism, intergroup relations and so forth (Cameron 2002). In total, thirty uni-ethnic and thematic chairs were created between 1978 and 1995; the Celtic chairs represent 10 per cent of the total.

In the 1980s, the Canadian policy of multiculturalism was given a firm legal basis. First, there were important provisions of relevance in the *Canadian Charter of Rights and Freedoms*, which formed part of the *Constitution Act* 1982. Section 15(1) guaranteed that every individual is equal before and under the law and has the right to equal protection and equal benefit of the law without discrimination on a variety of grounds, including race, national or ethnic origin, and so forth. As we have seen, non-discrimination has always been a key aspect of the developing policy of multiculturalism. The *Charter* included another provision of relevance, section 27. It states that the *Charter* "shall be interpreted in a manner consistent with the preservation and enhancement of the multicultural heritage of Canadians." It is important to note that, unlike section 15 and most other provisions of the *Charter*, section 27 does not create any new legal right; rather, it is an interpretative provision, which needs to be considered when interpreting other provisions in the *Charter*. It has been applied mostly in the context of a balancing of different and competing rights, such as the balancing of the right to freedom of expression with the goal of protecting individuals or groups against special threatening forms of speech. It has not, however, led to the evolution of significant new cultural or linguist rights for ethnic minorities.

The election of a majority Conservative government in 1984 did not result in any weakening of support for the policy of multiculturalism. Indeed, in 1988, the Mulroney government passed the *Canadian Multiculturalism Act* (R.S.C., 1985, c. 24 [4th Supp.]). Section 3 sets out a range of things that would form part of the policy of the Government of Canada. One set of principles involved the maintenance of ethnic identities. For example, there was an acknowledgement of the freedom of all members of Canadian society "to preserve, enhance and share their cultural heritage" (section 3(1)(a)). There was also reference to the enhancement of the development of communities whose members share a common origin (section 3(1)(d)) and to the preservation and enhancement of the use of languages other than English and French—subject, however, to the qualification that these were to be done while also strengthening the status and use of the official languages (section 3(1)(i)). Similarly, the goal of advancing multiculturalism throughout Canada was to be accomplished "in harmony with the national commitment to the official languages of Canada" (section 3(1)(j)).

Another set of principles related to non-discrimination includes the promotion of full and equitable participation of individuals and communities of all origins in the continuing evolution of all aspects of Canadian society and the assistance in the elimination of any barrier to that participation (section 3(1)(c)). There was also reference to ensuring that all individuals receive equal treatment and protection under the law (section 3(1)(e)). Finally, yet another set of principles emphasized interculturalism: promoting the understanding and creativity that arise from the interaction between individuals and communities of different origins (section 3(1)(g)), fostering the recognition and appreciation of the diverse cultures of Canadian society and promoting the reflection and the evolving expressions of those cultures (section 3(1)(h)).

The provisions on maintenance of ethnic identities are of obvious relevance to people interested in maintaining Celtic languages and cultures in Canada. Also pertinent are certain provisions in section 5, which requires the Minister of State to take such measures as the Minister considers necessary to implement the multiculturalism policy, which may include encouraging the preservation, enhancement, sharing and evolving expression of the multicultural heritage of Canada (section 5(1)(e)); facilitating the acquisition, retention and use of all languages that contribute to the multicultural heritage of Canada (section 5(1)(f)); and providing support to individuals, groups or organizations for the purpose of preserving, enhancing and promoting multiculturalism in Canada (section 5(1)(h)).

The promotion of non-official languages seemed to take another step ahead in 1991 with the passage of the *Canadian Heritage Languages Institute Act* (S.C. 1991, c. 7). It defined a heritage language as a language, other than an official language, "that contributes to the linguistic heritage of Canada" (section 2). As its name suggests, the *Act* was meant to create an institute, and the purposes of that institute (set out in section 4) included:

(a) promoting, through public education and discussion, the learning of heritage languages and their benefit to Canada;
(b) providing the public with information about heritage language resources;
(c) developing programs to improve the quality of heritage language instruction;

(d) assisting in the production and dissemination of Canadian-oriented materials related to the study of heritage languages;
(e) assisting in the development of standards for the learning of heritage languages;
(f) conducting research into all aspects of heritage languages; and
(g) establishing scholarly and professional links between the Institute and universities, colleges and other organizations and persons interested in the Institute's work.

This legislation never came into force, and was eventually repealed in 2008 (c. 20, s. 3.), so the Institute does not exist. This is symptomatic of a change in emphasis in multicultural policy from the early 1990s which began under the Progressive Conservatives and has continued under successive Liberal and Conservative governments. Where policy had previously concentrated on cultural preservation and intercultural sharing, the new approach emphasizes cross-cultural understanding and the attainment of social and economic integration through institutional change, affirmative action to equalized opportunity where necessary, and the removal of discriminatory barriers (Dewing 2009: 7).

This change of emphasis is reflected in changes in funding decisions under the Canadian multiculturalism policy. Recent research on projects funded by the Canadian multiculturalism program between 1983 and 2002 identified three major phases in the multicultural policy (McAndrew et al. 2008). The first, from 1971 until the early 1980s, saw an emphasis on the reproduction of heritage languages and "cultures of origin" and was associated with the longer-standing communities, in which Celtic peoples would generally be included. The second, from the 1980s to the early 1990s, saw a greater emphasis on issues such as participation, dealing with racism, institutional adaptation and awareness raising. This change in emphasis was undoubtedly in response to the much larger presence of visible minorities in Canada, due to changes in immigration policy that resulted in much larger immigration from places outside Europe. In the third phase, from the mid-1990s to the present, the promotion of a sense of belonging to Canada and of social cohesion took on more importance.

In assessing the funding decisions, the researchers identified several trends. One was a notable percentage increase in initiatives focused on the fight against racism. A second was an increase, in percentage terms at least, in support for projects involving intercultural understanding and institutional adaptation. A third was a major decrease, in both real and percentage terms, in support for minority languages and cultures. Above and beyond that, the researchers noted that the funding allocated to the multiculturalism policy had been stagnant for the ten years leading up to 2002.

From the foregoing discussion, the following conclusions can be made. Despite its inauspicious beginnings, at least from the perspective of Celtic peoples in Canada, the Canadian federal multiculturalism policy did nonetheless present an opportunity to advance a variety of projects based in and designed to be for the benefit of the maintenance of Celtic languages.

The case of Scottish Gaelic is illustrative of both the opportunities and the limitations inherent in them. The nature of the available programs and the relatively limited amounts of funding to support them imposed limitations on the ability of multicultural programs to support longer-term and systematic initiatives aimed at language and cultural maintenance for languages such as Gaelic. However, some of the projects that multicultural policies enabled, such as the Nova Scotia Gaelic Folklore Project and the Chairs of Gaelic, Irish and Celtic Studies, created an infrastructure that is still serving as the basis for linguistic and cultural maintenance. The Canadian multicultural policy was, and remains, fundamentally a policy of integration, and has had four key elements: cultural preservation for those ethnic groups who desired to maintain their cultures, and, as we have seen, their languages; the promotion of interculturalism, through cultural sharing between ethnic groups; the promotion of equality of opportunity and non-discrimination in order to facilitate full participation by members of ethnic groups in Canadian society; and the promotion of the acquisition by all members of ethnic groups of at least one of the two official languages, French or English, something that is also meant to facilitate full participation by members of minorities in Canadian society.

From about 1990, the emphasis of federal multicultural policy has shifted fairly dramatically away from cultural preservation, and increasingly toward measures that facilitate full participation. This is partly in response to the fundamental change in the nature of immigration to Canada over the last forty years or so, which has been characterized by much higher levels of non-European immigration. However, a consequence has been the reduced relevance of multicultural policy for more established ethnic groups, including those of Celtic origins, who have never faced racial barriers to full participation in Canadian society. From the point of view of those who identify themselves with Celtic ethnic communities, therefore, the shifts in emphasis in the federal policy of multiculturalism in recent years have not been favourable.

Present Context

Canadian multiculturalism does not exist in isolation. Many other countries that have an ethnically diverse population have been moving toward the adoption of policies of multiculturalism, sometimes, as in Canada, supported by legislation (Kymlicka 2006). In international institutions and in international law more generally, multiculturalism has become the preferred policy option for dealing with the management of diversity in ethnically complex societies. As in Canada, multiculturalism in the international context is aimed at integration of ethnic groups, and, as in Canada, it is based on the facilitation of full participation by members of all ethnic groups through policies of promotion of equality of opportunity, non-discrimination and the promotion of the acquisition of the official language or languages by all. Also, the sort of multiculturalism that has been adopted by Canadian and international institutions and in Canadian and international law has sought to facilitate cultural and linguistic maintenance and even revitalization.

International organizations of which Canada is a member, such as the United Nations, UNESCO (the United Nations Educational, Social and Cultural Organisation) and the Organisation for Security and Cooperation in Europe (OSCE) have all developed standards that promote the maintenance and promotion of languages of ethnic minorities, for example through the teaching and use of such languages in schools, in broadcasting, in public administration and so forth, as well as standards aimed at the strengthening of the infrastructure that supports both languages and cultural expression of ethnic minorities (Henrard and Dunbar 2008). These standards have been developed largely in the last twenty years, and have been prompted by two concerns: the need to respond to the sort of ethnic violence that broke out in the early 1990s in the wake of the collapse of communism in central and eastern Europe; and the need to respond to the perceived threat to cultural diversity of the homogenizing impact of globalization.

Although these policies were, in the first instance, conceived in the context of so-called "old minorities"—minorities that have existed on the territory of modern nation-states for centuries, such as the Scottish and Irish Gaels and the Welsh in their homelands—it is increasingly accepted that policies of multiculturalism should also be applied to so-called "new minorities," those groups whose presence on the territory of modern nation-states has resulted from immigration, such as the Scottish and Irish Gaels and Welsh and other Celtic peoples of Canada and of other parts of the Americas. Given the highly developed nature and relatively long history of Canadian policies with respect to multiculturalism, language rights, aboriginal rights and other related matters, there is perhaps a tendency to pay less attention to relevant international standards than is the case in many countries in Europe and elsewhere. Ironically, however, given the shifts in the application of Canadian multiculturalism, shifts that have not been to the advantage of Canadians interested in the maintenance of Celtic languages and cultures in Canada, it may be useful for such Canadians, and the federal and provincial institutions of relevance to them, to look more carefully at these international standards for inspiration.

Notes

1. A very large amount of research has been done in both the United States and Canada on patterns of intergenerational language attrition among different immigrant groups. While there is variation, generally speaking, linguistic assimilation in the United States tends to follow a three generation model: the first generation is dominant in their native tongue; the second generation is bilingual; and the third speaks English only (Veltman 1983; Fishman 1972; Glenn and DeJong 1996). It appears that this pattern continues to be the norm (Waters and Jiménez 2005: 110). The pattern in English Canada is very similar, where the three generation model is generally the norm (Castonguay 1998: 48, 58-59; Houle 2011).

2. In a comparative study of rates of assimilation—by which I mean integration of immigrants into society along various dimensions, including economic indicators such as educational attainment, earnings, occupational prestige, employment status and labour-market participation; civic factors such as citizenship; and cultural factors such as the ability to speak the dominant language of the state, marital status and number of children—Canada exhibited the highest rates of assimilation of nine developed countries in Europe and North America (Vigdor 2011).

3. This reference is from the 1616 *Statutes of Iona*, which sought, among other things, to anglicize the elites of Gaeldom (see MacKinnon 1991: 47, 40-52).

4. Some of the terminology used by the Commission is by today's standards both archaic and inappropriate, such as references to "founding races," although the use of the term was clarified somewhat in the preface to the first volume of the report, where the authors pointed out that the word "race" "is used in an older meaning as referring to a national group, and carries no biological significance" (1: xxii).

5. For some insights on the activities of the Cape Breton Gaelic Society in the early 1970s, see John Alick Macpherson's entertaining and insightful autobiography (Mac a' Phearsain 2011: 282-86).

References

Baker, Colin. 2011. *Foundations of Bilingual Education and Bilingualism*. 5th ed. Bristol: Multilingual Matters.

Bissoondath, Neil. 1994. *Selling Illusions: The Cult of Multiculturalism in Canada*. Toronto: Penguin.

Bothwell, Robert. 2006. *The Penguin History of Canada*. Toronto: Penguin.

Brotz, H. 1980. Multiculturalism in Canada: A Muddle. *Canadian Public Policy* 6 (1): 41-46.

Cameron, James D. 2002. Ethnicizing Atlantic Canadian Universities: The Regional Impact of the Canadian Ethnic Studies Program, 1973-1997. Canadian Ethnic Studies 34 (2): 1-24.

Castonguay, Charles. 1998. The fading Canadian duality. In *Language in Canada*, ed. John Edwards, 36-60. Cambridge: Cambridge University Press.

Chow, Henry. 2001. *The Challenge of Diversity: Ethnic Identity Maintenance and Heritage Language Retention in the Canadian Mosaic*. Report commissioned by the Department of Canadian Heritage for the Ethnocultural, Racial, Religious and Linguistic Diversity and Identity Seminar, Halifax, Nova Scotia, November 1-2, 2001. http://www.canada.metropolis.net/events/ethnocultural/publications/chall_diver_e.pdf (accessed 24 June 2011).

Comunn Gaidhlig Cheap Breatuinn. 1972. *Caidreabh '72*. New Waterford, NS.

Creighton, Helen, and Calum MacLeod. 1979. *Gaelic Songs in Nova Scotia*. Ottawa: National Museums of Canada.

Day, Richard J. F. 2000. *Multiculturalism and the History of Canadian Diversity*. Toronto: University of Toronto Press.

Dewing, Michael. 2009. "Canadian Multiculturalism," Parliamentary Information and Research Service, PRB 09-20E, revised 15 September 2009. http://www.parl.gc.ca/Content/LOP/ResearchPublications/prb0920-e.htm (accessed 9 August 2012).

Dunbar, Robert. 2006. The Secular Poetry of John MacLean, "Bàrd Thighearna Chola," "Am Bàrd MacGilleain." Ph.D. diss., University of Edinburgh.

———. 2008. Iain MacGilleain, "Bàrd Thighearna Chola," agus Tiriodh. *Scottish Gaelic Studies* 24:181-206.

Edwards, John. 1995. Monolingualism, Bilingualism, Multiculturalism and Identity: Some Lessons and Insights from Recent Canadian Experience. *Current Issues in Language and Society* 2 (1): 5-37.

English, John. 2009. *Just Watch Me: The Life of Pierre Trudeau 1968-2000*. Toronto: Knopf.

Fishman, Joshua A. 1972. *The Sociology of Language*. Rowley, MA: Newbury.

Gael Stream. *St. Francis Xavier University*. http://gaelstream.stfx.ca/greenstone/cgi-bin/library.cgi?a=p&p=home&l=en&w=utf-8 (accessed 24 June 2011).

Glenn, Charles L. and Ester J. De Jong. 1996. *Language Minority Children in School: A Comparative Study of Twelve Nations*. New York: Garland.

Hayward, Victoria. 1922. *Romantic Canada*. Toronto: Macmillan.

Henrard, Kristin and Robert Dunbar, eds. 2008. *Synergies in Minority Protection: European and International Law Perspectives*. Cambridge: Cambridge University Press.

Houle, René. 2011. Recent evolution of immigrant-language transmission in Canada. Component of Statistics Canada Catalogue no. 11-008-X, Canadian Social Trends. Ottawa: Statistics Canada.

Kallen, Evelyn. 2010. *Ethnicity and Human Rights in Canada*. Toronto: Oxford University Press.

Kennedy, Michael. 2002. *Gaelic Nova Scotia: An Economic, Cultural, and Social Impact Study*. Halifax: Nova Scotia Museum. http://museum.gov.ns.ca/site museum/media/museum/Gaelic-Report(1).pdf (accessed 10 August 2012).

Kymlicka, Will. 1998. *Finding Our Way: Rethinking Ethnocultural Relations in Canada*. Toronto: Oxford University Press.

———. 2006. The Global Diffusion of Multiculturalism: Trends, Causes, Consequences. In *Accommodating Cultural Diversity*, ed. Stephen Tierney, 17-34. Aldershot: Ashgate.

Mac a' Phearsain, Seonaidh Ailig. 2011. *Steall à Iomadh Lòn*. Inbhir Nis: Clàr.

MacDonell, Margaret. 1981. *Luirgean Eachainn Nìll: a collection of folktales told by Hector Campbell*. Stornoway: Acair.

MacKinnon, Kenneth. 1991. *Gaelic: A Past and Future Prospect*. Edinburgh: The Saltire Society.

McAndrew, Marie, Denise Helly, Caroline Tessier and Judy Young. 2008. From Heritage Languages to Institutional Change: An Analysis of Projects Funded by the Canadian Multiculturalism Program (1983-2002). *Canadian Ethnic Studies* 40 (3): 149-69.

Mill, John Stuart. 1865. *Considerations on Representative Government*. London: Longman, Green, Longman, Roberts and Green.

Porter, John. 1965. *The Vertical Mosaic: an analysis of social class and power in Canada*. Toronto: University of Toronto Press.

Royal Commission on Bilingualism and Biculturalism. 1970. *Report of the Royal Commission on Bilingualism and Biculturalism*. Volume IV: The Cultural Contribution of Other Ethnic Groups. Ottawa: Queen's Printer for Canada.

Shaw John, ed. 2007. *Na Beanntaichean Gorma agus sgeulachdan eile à Ceap Breatainn*. Montréal and Kingston: McGill-Queen's University Press.

Shaw, John, ed., with Lauchie MacLellan. 2000. *Brìgh an Òrain/A Story in Every Song: the songs and tales of Lauchie MacLellan*. Montréal and Kingston: McGill-Queen's University Press.

Shaw, John, ed., with Joe Neil MacNeil. 1987. *Sgeul gu Latha/Tales until Dawn: the world of a Cape Breton Gaelic story-teller*. Montréal and Kingston: McGill-Queen's University Press.

Trudeau, Pierre. 1971. Pierre Trudeau, on Multiculturalism. *The History of Canada Online*. 8 October. http://canadachannel.ca/HCO/index.php/Pierre_Trudeau,_on_Multiculturalism (accessed 24 June 2011).

Veltman, Calvin J. 1983. *Language Shift in the United States*. Berlin: Mouton.

Vigdor, Jacob L. 2011. *Comparing Immigrant Assimilation in North America and Europe*. Civic Report No. 64, Centre for State and Local Leadership at the Manhattan Institute. New York: Manhattan Institute.

Waters, Mary C. and Tomás R. Jiménez. 2005. Assessing Immigrant Assimilation: New Empirical and Theoretical Challenges. *Annual Review of Sociology* 31:105-25.

Weinfeld, Morton. 1994. Ethnic Assimilation and the Retention of Ethnic Cultures. In *Ethnicity and Culture in Canada: The Research Landscape*, ed. J. W. Berry and J. A. Laponce, 238-66. Toronto: University of Toronto Press.

Ian Johnson

Revitalizing Welsh in the Chubut Province, Argentina: The Role of the Welsh Language Project

This paper examines the impact of the Welsh Language Teaching Project upon the revitalization of Welsh in the Chubut Province, Argentina. Welsh was the primary language of the Chubut Province from the colony's founding in 1865 until the early 20th century when it was eclipsed by Spanish, the national language. A formal language-teaching project, sponsored by the British Council and Welsh Office and then Welsh government, began in 1997, building on previous work by voluntary teachers to re-establish Welsh as a language of communication. Thousands of students have followed courses in the past fifteen years but progress in the socialization of Welsh outside the classroom has been slow. The majority of learners are following beginners' level classes and are young people doing so within formal educational settings. There has been a noticeable slump in voluntary adult participation in classes. While the project has been a success in raising awareness of the Welsh language and the levels of Welsh ability in the community, it has failed in its own aims of reversing language shift. Welsh learning in the Chubut Province is an additive bilingualism in addition to, rather than a replacement for, Spanish, and the project should show more regard for the motivations of Welsh learners.

Context of the Welsh in Patagonia

The mid-19th century was a period of unprecedented emigration from Wales, most commonly to North America (A. Jones and B. Jones 2001). However, there were concerns in Wales that this emigration ultimately led to the loss of the Welsh language among emigrants, replaced by English due to the need to integrate, and to the loss of religious and cultural values. The suggested solution to this loss of language, religion and culture was the founding of a colony distant from any other settlements, thereby obviating the need to integrate with other ethnic groups and allowing the Welsh language and Welsh values to flourish unhindered. A number of suitable locations were considered (I. Jones 1934), but those organizing the venture eventually decided upon the River Chubut region of Argentina where they were promised land by the Argentine government in return for accepting Argentine sovereignty over the region (Owen 1977). There was no permanent settled population in this region of Argentina, although nomadic tribes used the Chubut region on a seasonal basis.

The first colonists left from Liverpool in May 1865, arriving at the modern-day Porth Madryn (Puerto Madryn in Spanish) on July 28. The colonists had been poorly prepared for the situation they faced in Patagonia, but after better farming methods were introduced, the colony survived initial difficulties and allowed the integration of more immigrants from Wales (Owen 1977). However, despite these increases the total immigration into the Chubut region from Wales was no more than 3,000 people in the period from 1865 to 1912 (G. Williams 1991: 41). In this period, towns were founded at Porth Madryn on the coast and at Rawson, Trelew and Gaiman along the course of the River Chubut. In the Cordillera de los Andes area six hundred kilometres to the west of the Atlantic Coast, the towns of Trevelin and Esquel were founded. The town of Dolavon was later founded in the Chubut Valley.

Although receiving economic and political support from the Argentine government, the Welsh settlement in the Chubut Valley was largely independent and self-sufficient. The Welsh developed their own education system, forms of local government, religious buildings and an economic company to organize their business interests. A local Welsh-language newspaper, *Y Dravod*, was published on a regular basis. At this time, the population of the region was predominantly Welsh, but in-migration from Wales itself ended and there was significant and consistent in-migration from Spanish speakers who began to make up a greater percentage of the local population and held a higher status as speakers of the national language (G. Williams 1991: 252).

For much of the period between the turn of the century and the 1920s, Welsh and Spanish held similar economic positions in Chubut social life and vitality, but this was to change during the following decades. Welsh began to visibly lose its status in the region, under pressure from immigration of Spanish speakers and inter-group marriages that gave priority to Spanish as the national language, as well as economic changes that pushed the Welsh ethnic group to the margins. As a result of these changes, the Welsh community lost a great deal of their economic and political influence and this loss hastened an already clear shift toward Spanish in place of Welsh in the Chubut (G. Williams 1991: 252-56).

After the Second World War, and with Argentina under military control, the Welsh language in the Chubut did not appear strong. The closure, in 1947, of Coleg Camwy, a trilingual secondary school that taught in Spanish, Welsh and English, meant that Welsh was no longer being taught as a written language in the province. The language was therefore only supported through the domains of the family and the Welsh churches, although the *Y Dravod* newspaper continued to be published at irregular intervals. Spanish had become the lingua franca of the Chubut communities, with Welsh used only among Welsh-speaking families and in religious circles (G. Williams 1991; R. O. Jones 1996; Virkel 1999; Brooks 2004). However, the centenary celebrations of the founding of the colony in 1965 saw a shift towards recognition of the importance of the Welsh role in the region as the people who colonized the Chubut (Brooks 2005). This re-assessment of the importance of the Welsh led to an improvement in status for the Welsh ethnic group and maintenance of Welsh culture in the region.

Use of the Welsh language in the Chubut rose during the first half of the 1990s (R. O. Jones 1996, 2004b; Birt 2005). There was a growing interest in the language and Welsh culture among the inhabitants of the region, reflective of curiosity regarding the origins of the original settlers, greater freedoms allowed since the restoration of democracy to Argentina and devolution of powers to individual provinces.

The Modern Chubut Province

The modern-day Chubut Province has a varied population of many different ethnic groups. Although the Welsh were the first ethnic group to permanently settle in the region, there were indigenous tribes, such as the Tehuelche and the Mapuche, who visited the region on a seasonal basis, with the Mapuche still resident (Virkel 1999). Since the arrival of the Welsh colonists, there has been immigration into the region from various ethnic groups, including Spaniards, Italians, Germans, Portuguese, Basques and Poles, among others. There are no monolingual Welsh speakers and, with the exception of recent emigrants from Wales, all members of the Welsh ethnic group hold a dual ethnicity as Argentineans of Welsh extraction. Most members of the Welsh community can lay claim to a number of ethnic identities as a result of mixed marriages that have taken place in the past century (Brooks 2004). This inter-relationship between communities makes it difficult to distinguish in- and out-groups as the majority of residents in the region hold sometimes competing and sometime complementary group memberships.

Spanish is the common language of everyday usage in the Chubut Valley and Cordillera regions and it is assumed that with the few exceptions of recent immigrants from Wales, all permanent residents have communicative fluency in Spanish. There are no available statistics to indicate the number of Welsh speakers in the region, but it is believed that as a percentage of the Chubut province's population of 400,000 it is probably no more than 1-2 per cent. There has been a clear failure in the intergenerational transmission of the Welsh language in the Chubut Valley and Cordillera (Virkel 1999). The number of Welsh speakers is difficult to estimate because some informants may deliberately inflate their claimed knowledge of the language to gain acceptance as a Welsh speaker while others may conceal their ability to speak Welsh in order to "pass" more easily as a native Spanish-speaking resident (Piller 2002). There are no accurate census records of language ability.

It is easier to trace the genealogy of the Welsh ethnic group but there are again no confirmed figures of the modern-day residents of the Chubut Province descended from the Welsh settlers. At its highest, the Welsh ethnic group is estimated at not being more than between 5-10 per cent of the total regional population of around 220,000 in the north of the Chubut Province. The number of people claiming a Welsh ethnic identity through genealogy is therefore a linguistic and ethnic minority of no great number.

Welsh-language ability or identity is not a constant across the Chubut Province, and depends largely upon local factors. Gaiman is generally considered to be the urban area in the Chubut that has most attachment to Welsh language and culture (R. O. Jones 1976; Glanzmann and Virkel de Sandler 1981; Plwm 1992). It has a population of approximately 6,000, including the farms that surround the town. Gaiman is a tourist location, with many visitors arriving in the town for "Welsh tea," a service of tea, savoury items and cakes (Lublin 2006) and has a visible Welsh presence with the language used on business signage around the town (Coupland and Garrett 2010).

Trelew (Lewis Town or El Pueblo de Luis), with around 90,000 people, is the most highly populated city in the Chubut Valley, acting as an economic and cultural magnet for the smaller centres of population nearby (Rawson, Gaiman and Dolavon). There are two Welsh chapels in the city, both of which are in use. The Tabernacl (Tabernacle) in the centre of the city features fortnightly services in Welsh which alternate with Spanish language services. Moriah, further to the south, alongside the River Chubut, holds a symbolic importance as the burial place of many of the original colonists and for that reason was chosen as one of the first Welsh chapels to be restored under the provincial government's Welsh Chapel Restoration Project. Alongside the chapel, the Asociación San David (Cymdeithas Dewi Sant, Saint David's Association) also acts as a centre for Welsh community life in Trelew. A Welsh-Spanish bilingual school, Ysgol yr Hendre, was opened in 2006 and in 2011 moved to new, larger premises with support from the municipal educational authority.

Esquel is the most populated urban area in the Andes Cordillera in the Chubut Province with a population of 28,000 people. It is the home of Canolfan Gymraeg yr Andes (Andes' Welsh Centre), a community centre used by the Welsh for social functions, meetings and teaching purposes, and which acts as a focal point for all Welsh activities in the town (Novella and Oriola 2004).

Trevelin (El Pueblo del Molino, Milltown) is located twenty-five kilometres to the south of Esquel, near the border with Chile, with a population of around 6,000. This area was settled prior to Esquel after being discovered by Europeans in 1888 and given the title Cwm Hyfryd (Lovely Valley) by the Welsh who moved there. As the first colonists, the Welsh took much of the land in the region, and remain farmers and landowners with significantly larger homesteads than those in the Chubut Valley (Fiori and de Vera 2002a, 2002b). More than a third of the total population of Trevelin live outside of the town itself, including a large number of the Welsh community.

The Welsh cultural festival, the Eisteddfod, remains at the heart of Welsh-language life in the Chubut. The main Eisteddfod del Chubut (Chubut Eisteddfod) is held on an annual basis in Trelew at the end of October, while there is also an Eisteddfod de la Juventud (Youth Eisteddfod) held in Gaiman in September and regional Eisteddfod in Trevelin and in Porth Madryn (Neumann 2004; Johnson 2007).

The Welsh Language Teaching Project

The Welsh Language Teaching Project came into existence in 1997 following a period of several years from 1991 in which volunteers and retired teachers spent time in the Chubut assisting in teaching Welsh. A 1996 report by Robert Owen Jones argued for financial support from the British Council and the Welsh Office to send three teachers annually to the province, concentrating their efforts in three different regions—Trelew/Rawson/Porth Madryn and Gaiman/Bryn Gwyn/Dolavon in the Chubut Valley area and a further teacher to Esquel and Trevelin in the Cordillera de los Andes region. Further funding was recommended to be given to re-establishing the *Y Dravod* newspaper (R. O. Jones 1996). The scheme, which was initially for three years, has been continuously funded on a rolling three-year program, and has now been in existence for fifteen years. It is jointly funded by the British Council and the Welsh government, who took over funding from the Welsh Office after political devolution in Wales in 1999.

As project coordinator, Robert Owen Jones carries out an annual report on the status of the project, providing data upon the numbers attending classes, the age range of participants and standard of classes. He also provides commentary upon the scheme's progress and events outside the project within the Welsh community in Patagonia, not least the developments regarding Menter Patagonia—a related project whose aim is to stimulate the use of Welsh outside of the classroom. Table 1 provides a very helpful series of longitudinal statistics and comments regarding the project.

Table 1: Participants in the Welsh Language Teaching Project (R.O. Jones 2002, 2004a, 2006, 2011)

	Gaiman	Trelew	The Andes	Total
1997	348		225	573
1998	428		212	640
1999	443		220	663
2000	501		241	742
2001	509		157	666
2002	405	108	149	662
2003	314	104	162	580
2004	372	108	102	581
2005	364	104	150	618
2006	425	117	118	660
2007	407	86	88	581
2008	378	97	112	587
2009	474	76	153	703
2010	527	85	150	762
2011	582	133	131	846

As Table 1 illustrates, the number of students registering on the scheme has remained relatively stable since its inception in 1997, varying within a relatively limited frame between a low point of 573 students in 1997 and a registration of 846 in 2011, a new high point in terms of numbers. Indeed, the past three years have shown a significant increase in numbers from around 580 people in 2007 and 2008 to above 700 in 2009 and 2010 to the present figure. School teaching years in Argentina run from March to December so the references made are to both calendar and academic years.

However, minority language revitalization is not a question of quantity but also of quality. Therefore the raw number of registrations must be qualified according to the level of course which they are following and their subsequent progress, motivation for language learning and use of Welsh outside the classroom. The location of language learners is also important given the aims of language revitalization within small-scale community groups as recommended by Fishman (1991), with interaction differences between individuals located within loose urban networks and those who are within tightly bound communities (Johnson 2007, 2009).

Table 2 shows that the profile of language teaching is geared primarily toward those at beginner levels. More than two-thirds of classes have consistently been aimed at those in early stages of language learning, reaching a high point of 78 per cent in 2010. Under some circumstances this profile of language learning, especially in the early years of a language teaching project, could indicate a high level of enthusiasm among the wider community for language learning. However, after fifteen years of formal language teaching in the Chubut, this suggests that the overwhelming majority of students do not progress from beginner levels to advanced levels of fluency—and that those who do are the exceptions to the rule.

Table 2: Level of classes being taught (R.O. Jones 2000, 2001, 2002, 2004a, 2006, 2007, 2008, 2009, 2010, 2011)

	BEGINNERS		ADVANCED			
	Level 1	Level 2/3	Level 4	Level 5/6	Level 7	Total
2000	31	19	17	9	4	80
2001	38	17	12	9	4	80
2002	40	12	13	13	6	84
2003	28	11	11	5	5	60
2004	16	15	17	3	6	57
2005	20	21	9	7	5	62
2006	29	20	15	6	3	73
2007	49			19		68
2008	17	29	13	5	3	67
2009	29	26	5	2	3	65
2010	30	31	9	4	4	78
2011	27	30	10	8	7	82

In part the high number of students at the beginner level can be explained from the age profile of language learners and the institutional settings in which Welsh is taught. Table 3 shows that the profile is very clearly slanted toward young people who learn Welsh in an educational setting. This shows that the aims of Welsh revitalization, or at least awareness of Welsh language and culture, have been understood by those developing the curriculum and that there are attempts to teach Welsh to young people. However, despite the popularity of teaching Welsh as a second language in educational settings at primary and secondary educational level, Robert Owen Jones (2011) warns against expectations of language attainment as the input level is low—often just one hour of classroom work per academic week.

Table 3: Age of Welsh learners in the Welsh Language Teaching Project (R.O. Jones 2006, 2008, 2009, 2011)

	ADULTS	YOUTH	CHILDREN	POST NURSERY	NURSERY
1997	279	131	120	12	31
1998	239	109	205	36	51
1999	210	145	239	39	30
2000	234	223	211	29	45
2001	148	120	320	30	48
2002	202	161	182	37	80
2003	149	140	169	43	78
2004	150	216	118	30	67
2005	208	228	71	26	85
2006	167	290	85	35	83
2007	122	293		166	
2008	91	311		185	
2009	79	307	209	46	69
2010	83	296	241	84	58
2011	114	293	262	110	67

Institutional teaching of Welsh can therefore be separated into two groups: the appropriation of Welsh as a second or foreign language into the ordinary curriculum and the integration of Welsh as a core language for teaching the curriculum as seen, for example, at Ysgol yr Hendre in Trelew. Welsh language achievement levels of children attending the school are significantly better than those who receive only limited Welsh language input and consequently have little knowledge beyond basic phrases, songs and understanding of the history of the Welsh as pioneers of the Chubut.

Differences in attainment between children can be explained through input and the institutional settings in which they learn Welsh, including, of course, the limited number of school hours in which Welsh is available as a second/foreign language.

More crucial, though, for the revitalization of Welsh, is the steep fall in the number of adults who are learning the language. The numbers have fallen quite consistently from 279 of the original learners in 1997—around half of the total number of learners—to as low as 72 in 2009—a little more than 10 per cent. The number of adult learners rallied slightly in 2011 but remains low. Concerns regarding this have been noted in the annual report and ideas put forward to re-engage with adult audiences—particularly with those who have previously participated in Welsh-learning activities.

These numbers are particularly concerning in terms of adult socialization in the language and because almost all adults up until those in their mid-thirties (which includes the new parent generation) would have had language-learning opportunities through school but have opted not to continue further. Willingness to participate in Welsh cultural activities and to use their language skills, and support for their children in such activities, suggest that this is not a rejection of Welsh but, possibly, as Robert Owen Jones suggests (2011), a satisfaction with this (relatively low) level of language ability, perhaps mixed with extra-curricular concerns such as employment commitments and uncertainties in an unstable economic environment.

The initial purpose of sending teachers from Wales was to stimulate local interest in teaching Welsh and to impart knowledge to local communities who would then take on the organization and development. This task has proven to be more enduring than was predicted and annual reports are consistently critical of the failure of local committees to take on greater responsibility for teaching, leaving the project as a crutch for Welsh-language teaching. Consequently, whenever there have been difficulties with teacher recruitment from Wales, there has been a continuous change in teaching staff who are usually employed for just one year in Patagonia. It is intuitive that most progress has been made when there has been continuity in teachers from one academic year to the next. The focus of the project is therefore now on providing stable institutions for language teaching. There are four local committees who take responsibility for the organization of Welsh classes alongside tutors who come from Wales. Two of these local committees are in the Chubut Valley in Trelew and Gaiman, where most language teaching takes place. There are apparently no classes in Rawson, which is not mentioned in the latest report, and limited teaching in Porth Madryn and in Dolavon. The other two committees are in Esquel and Trevelin in the Andes. To all intents and purposes the project is largely confined to these four locations where local interest has been maintained, and is in line with vitality assessments (Johnson 2009).

Location therefore plays an important role in the socialization of Welsh in the Chubut Province. The small towns of Gaiman and Trevelin both act as heartlands of Welsh in their respective parts of the province with the larger urban areas of Trelew and Esquel containing Welsh centres that act as a hub to activities. Gaiman is perceived as the town with traditionally the greatest Welsh-speaking population and identity and it is no surprise that Welsh is taught extensively through the formal educational system in order to provide a civic identity as well as promoting its wider linguistic value, as explained by informants (Johnson 2010). This means that children and their parents see value in Welsh-language learning, even at its most basic level. In Trelew, the majority of teaching is for children inside the Welsh language education system at Ysgol yr Hendre, while in the Andes communities the majority of teaching is for adults—the figures are not separated according to Trevelin and Esquel. The teaching profile can be explained thus: that teaching in Gaiman is geared toward integration into the wider community in which the Welsh play a significant cultural role, that teaching in Trelew is geared toward improving Welsh language skills among young people at Ysgol yr Hendre and that in the Andes it is geared toward adult learning and communication within the traditional Welsh ethnic community.

The annual reports on the Welsh Language Teaching Project are a valuable source of material to analyze the progress of the scheme. However, there are gaps in the data presented. The clearest difficulty is that no data are given on the individuals' progress through the project, for example the number who begin at level 1 and then follow a level 2 course in subsequent years. There are also no data collated about those who complete courses or the number of courses that run throughout the allotted period, rather than collapse early due to lack of numbers or teachers. Accordingly, no accurate figure can be given of the number of people who have attempted to learn Welsh or those who completed the study schedule. While it is relatively easy to assume completion of classes in formal educational settings, the number of completions in the adult or voluntary settings is perhaps more indicative of successful teaching schemes. It is also difficult to assess the success of the project as a whole as outcomes appear not to be tested save for a handful of individuals who complete Welsh examinations (nine students sat Welsh Joint Education Committee examinations in 2011, eight passing and four receiving distinctions). Information is not always broken down to sufficient detail for longitudinal analysis. For example, the collapsing of the numbers in the Chubut Valley were for many years treated together as one group rather than according to the Gaiman or Trelew coordinated areas, something that is also true of Esquel and Trevelin in the Andes, which remain listed as one group.

Discussion

Annual reports of the Welsh Language Teaching Project in the Chubut Province show an understandably narrow frame of society in the province as they are examining the specific progress of a government-funded program, even ignoring the fact that this opinion is one from outside the community. However, any critique of the program's success must be placed within the context of Patagonian and Argentine society. As previously noted, the modern-day Chubut Province is a multi-ethnic society in which inhabitants can access multiple ethnic identities within their own personal history and can also opt-in to other cultures, should they so wish. They do this against the background of an overwhelmingly Spanish-language society. Argentina is a country with a population of around 40 million people and Spanish is the fourth most spoken language in the world. Welsh, in contrast, has around 700,000 speakers worldwide and remains a minoritized language even within its own home territory (H. Jones 2012).

There are therefore a number of clear problems in developing the socialization of Welsh within the Chubut Province in the form assumed by the annual reports.

In an environment where high-level Welsh-language skills are rarely necessary on a daily communicative basis, the principal motivations regarding Welshness appear to be related to identity. However, Welsh identity is more easily practised through participation in non-linguistic events, such as folk dancing or wearing of recognizable Welsh symbols, than in language learning which is difficult and involves significant effort and time investment to reach fluency. Other language motivations include speaking with people from Wales, winning scholarships to Wales, speaking with family members and learning the family heritage language (Johnson 2010).

As noted in the annual reports, there is a low participation in Welsh-language learning from adult learners, possibly because their language-learning motivations have already been met by basic level classes and were often of a symbolic nature: the ability to greet or to participate in cultural events such as singing in choirs.

There are, however, committed sectors of society, notably in education, and individuals who are highly motivated to teach Welsh and ensure that their children are fluent in the language. However, with the possible exception of Gaiman, where Welsh identity is a central part of the town's civic identity, this level of commitment does not reach across the wider community.

There is a fundamental failure to ensure a dedication to this linguistic ideology from the wider Welsh community, illustrated by the annual reports' continued concerns about the role of the local committees in developing and organizing Welsh-language courses. The interest in developing Welsh-language skills and maintenance comes from Wales as much as it does from Argentina, if not more.

Even where members of the Welsh ethnic community note the personal egocentric importance of Welsh-language skills to their identity (Johnson 2007, 2010; Glanzmann and Virkle de Sandler 1981), they express them as an additive bilingualism (Baker 2006) where their Welsh-language skills are an addition to their Spanish, and not a replacement of it.

The expressed aims and motivations of learners are therefore different from the socialization of Welsh as envisaged by Robert Owen Jones in the project's annual reports. There, he argues that the goal of Welsh-language teaching in the Chubut is to reclaim domains previously used by Welsh, a theory known in sociolinguistic literature as "reversing language shift" (Fishman 1991). What Fishman argues as being the crucial stage of home-neighbourhood-family as the nexus for language transmission has long been broken for Welsh in the Chubut Province (Glanzmann and Virkel de Sandler 1981; G. Williams 1991; R. O. Jones 1996; Brooks 2004; Johnson 2007) and is, understandably, not being replaced on a community-wide level and only rarely at the level of the individual family—and even then most often with families that include a Welsh-born, native Welsh-speaking parent.

Conclusions

As individuals, and as a group, Welsh community members have hybrid identities, changing "face" according to need. Their ethnic Welsh identity exists in addition to their civic Argentine identity and other possible ethnic identities that are part of their repertoire and can be used whenever necessary (Birt 2004).

Research confirms the generally positive attitude toward the Welsh language, especially among the Welsh community in the Chubut Province (Johnson 2009), but that such an attitude does not necessarily lead to language usage. This is especially clear when compared to the frequent participation in Welsh cultural events, including choirs or folk dancing wearing Welsh-identifying clothes. These language and cultural practices can be more symbolic and are generally easier than language learning.

Living within a community where Spanish is an unmarked majority language, Welsh learners in the Chubut are generally happy to be semi-speakers and their language aims and practices reflect this. They are not necessarily looking to become fluent in Welsh, never mind have Welsh replace Spanish as their dominant language. As a result of this, initial Welsh Language Teaching Project aims for the socialization of Welsh within new domains are unlikely to be achieved, either in the present circumstances or without an additional commitment from significant sections of the community.

However, that is not to argue that the Welsh Language Teaching Project has been a failure in any sense other than its own over-ambitious aims for Welsh in the Chubut Province. Where, a generation ago, the language was in danger of falling out of usage, there are now thousands of semi-speakers of Welsh and perhaps a few hundred new speakers with higher-level skills. The language has a noticeable profile, particularly so in Gaiman where it has a significant presence in the town's linguistic landscape (Coupland and Garrett 2010) and the history and relevance of the Welsh to the Chubut Province is taught to thousands of children in the next generation. Among this, the relative success of Ysgol yr Hendre will ensure a new generation of bilingual children who can participate and hopefully excel in language-based activities. The continued generation of innovative language uses in Welsh stems from the Welsh Language Teaching Project and the spin-off activities from Menter Patagonia are therefore direct results of the investment from the British Council and the Welsh government.

In the same way that the British Council's investment in the promotion of English elsewhere is not directly intended to create monolingual English speakers, so the Welsh Language Teaching Project's aims should be modified to recognize the reality of the situation in the Chubut Province. Such modifications include accepting that the promotion of Wales and Welsh identity and language skills as a central aim, not a replacement of Spanish in particular domains. The Project should better aim to reflect the motivations of the community it seeks to empower rather than assert a language ideology that clashes with the community's own aims.

Of course, further success will depend in part upon consistent and well-resourced programs. At present the British Council receives £190m in grants from the U.K. government (2011: 6-7) and presents itself as the premier international organization for teaching English, with more than 1.3 million hours of English-language classroom teaching in 2010-2011. If only a fraction more of that money could be used to resource the promotion of Welsh in the Chubut Province, then the Welsh Language Teaching Project may produce markedly better results in language acquisition, in addition to the status of the language in the province. Given continued disputes between the governments of the United Kingdom and Argentina, the introduction of a more effectively resourced Welsh language scheme may reap dividends for all involved and, most importantly, for language learners within the community in the Chubut Province.

References

Baker, Colin. 2006. *Foundations of Bilingual Education and Bilingualism*. Clevedon, U.K.: Multilingual Matters.

Birt, Paul. 2004. La comunidad galesa en la argentina: Construcción o desconstrucción de la identidad? In *Los Galeses en la Patagonia*, 11-34. Puerto Madryn, Argentina: Fundación Ameghino CENHYS.

———. 2005. The Welsh language in Chubut Province, Argentina. In *Rebuilding the Celtic Languages – Reversing Language Shift in the Celtic Countries*, ed. Diarmuid O'Neill, 115-51. Talybont, U.K.: Y Lolfa.

British Council. 2011. *Annual Report 2010-11*. http://www.britishcouncil.org/new/PageFiles/13001/2010-11%20AnnualReport.pdf (accessed 16 January 2012).

Brooks, Walter Ariel. 2004. Algunas consideraciones sobre los patrones de casamientos en el valle del Chubut 1900-1960. Paper Presented at Segundo Foro Internacional Sobre Los Galeses en la Patagonia, Puerto Madryn, 24 October.

———. 2005. 1965 – A Welsh-Patagonian milestone. The celebrations of the centenary of the Welsh landing in the Chubut. Paper presented at Language and Global Communication Conference, Cardiff, 7 July.

Coupland, Nikolas and Peter Garrett. 2010. Linguistic landscapes, discursive frames and metacultural performance: The case of Welsh Patagonia. *International Journal of the Sociology of Language* 205:7-36

Fiori, Jorge and Gustavo de Vera. 2002a. *1902: El protagonismo de los colonos galesas en la frontera argentino-chileno.* Trevelin, Argentina: Municipalidad de Trevelin.

———. 2002b. *Trevelin: Un pueblo en los tiempos del molino.* Trevelin, Argentina: Municipalidad de Trevelin.

Fishman, Joshua. 1991. *Reversing Language Shift.* Clevedon, U.K.: Multilingual Matters.

Glanzmann, Cecilia Gonzalez de and Ana Virkel de Sandler. 1981. *Aspectos Bilingüismos Español-Galés en el Valle del Chubut.* Trelew, Argentina: IUT

Johnson, Ian. 2007. Subjective ethnolinguistic vitality of Welsh in the Chubut Province, Argentina. PhD diss., Cardiff University / Prifysgol Caerdydd.

———. 2009. How green is their valley? Subjective vitality of Welsh language and culture in the Chubut Province, Argentina. *International Journal of the Sociology of Language* 195:141-71.

———. 2010. Tourism, transnationality and ethnolinguistic vitality: the Welsh in the Chubut Province, Argentina. *Journal of Multilingual and Multicultural Development* 31 (6): 553-68.

Jones, Aled and Bill Jones. 2001. *Welsh Reflections: Y Drych and America 1851-2001.* Llandysul: Gomer.

Jones, Hywel. 2012. *Darlun ystadegol o'r iaith Gymraeg* (Statistical Picture of the Welsh Language). http://www.byig-wlb.org.uk/Cymraeg/cyhoeddiadau/Cyhoeddiadau/Darlun%20ystadegol%20o%20sefyllfa%20y%20Gymraegf2.pdf (accessed 24 February 2012).

Jones, Idris. 1934. *Modern Welsh History: From 1485 to the Present Day.* London: G Bell and Sons.

Jones, Robert Owen. 1974. Amrywiaeth tafodiaethol a phatrwm newid ieithyddol yng Nghymraeg y Wladfa. *Studia Celtica* 18-19:253-67.

———. 1976. Cydberthynas amrywiadau iaith a nodweddion cymdeithasol yn y Gaiman, Chubut. *Bulletin of the Board of Celtic Studies* 27:51-64.

———.1996. *A report on the Welsh language in Argentina's Chubut province 1996: Adroddiad ar yr iaith Gymraeg yn nhalaith Chubut, yr Ariannin 1996.* Cardiff: British Council.

———. 2000. The Welsh Language In Chubut Project. 2000 Monitoring Report. Cardiff: British Council.

———. 2001. The Welsh Language In Chubut Project. 2001 Monitoring Report. Cardiff: British Council.

———. 2002. The Welsh Language In Chubut Project. 2002 Monitoring Report. Cardiff: British Council.

———. 2004a. The Welsh Language In Chubut Project. 2004 Monitoring Report. Cardiff: British Council.

———. 2004b. Sociología del idioma galés, con énfasis en el Proyecto de Enseñanza del Idioma, o sea, el nuevo interés en el galés desde los '90. Paper presened at Segundo Foro Internacional Sobre los Galeses en la Patagonia, Puerto Madryn, 25 October.

———. 2006. The Welsh Language In Chubut Project. 2006 Monitoring Report. Cardiff: British Council.

———. 2007. The Welsh Language In Chubut Project. 2007 Monitoring Report. Cardiff: British Council.

———. 2008. The Welsh Language In Chubut Project. 2008 Monitoring Report. Cardiff: British Council.

———. 2009. The Welsh Language In Chubut Project. 2009 Monitoring Report. Cardiff: British Council.

———. 2010. The Welsh Language In Chubut Project. 2010 Monitoring Report. Cardiff: British Council.

———. 2011. The Welsh Language In Chubut Project. 2011 Monitoring Report. Cardiff: British Council.

Lublin, Geraldine. 2006. The War of the Tea Houses, or How Welsh Heritage in Patagonia Became a Valuable Commodity. *Journal of Interdisciplinary Celtic Studies* 1:69-92

Neumann, Dora Beatriz. 2004. Eisteddfod del Chubut: Cultura galesa e identidad regional. In *Los Galeses en la Patagonia*, 183-94. Puerto Madryn, Argentina: Fundación Ameghino CENHYS

Novella, Maria Marta and Jorge Oriolla. 2004. *Historia de la Capilla Seion*. Esquel: Asociación Galesa Esquel.

Owen, Geraint Dyfnallt. 1977. *Crisis in Chubut*. Swansea: Christopher Davies Publishers.

Piller, Ingrid. 2002. Passing for a native speaker: Identity and success in second language learning. *Journal of Sociolinguistics* 6 (2): 179-206.

Plwm, Mici. 1992. Patagonia: Disney dosbarth canol Cymraeg. *Golwg* 4 (32): 6.

Virkel, Ana. 1999. El Español Hablado en el Chubut. PhD diss., Universidad de Alicante. http://descargas.cervantesvirtual.com/servlet/Sirve Obras/12702744225695940543435/008133_8.pdf (accessed 6 February 2005).

Williams, Glyn. 1991. *Welsh in Patagonia: the State and Ethnic Community*. Cardiff: University of Wales Press.

Emily McEwan-Fujita

Gaelic Revitalization Efforts in Nova Scotia: Reversing Language Shift in the 21st Century

Scottish immigrants and their descendants have been speaking Gaelic in Nova Scotia since the last quarter of the 18th century. Gaelic users and supporters are working to revitalize the language in the province in the early 21st century. This chapter demonstrates how academic studies of endangered languages apply to the situation of Nova Scotia Gaelic. The level of endangerment of Nova Scotia Gaelic is determined by using original and expanded versions of Joshua Fishman's Graded Intergenerational Disruption Scale (GIDS). After reviewing some critiques of the scale in light of linguistic anthropology, a new expanded GIDS tailored specifically to Nova Scotia Gaelic is presented which lists the situation, priorities, recommended actions and challenges of each stage of revitalization. The scale can help clarify and guide efforts to reconstruct Gaelic as a spoken language of daily community-based use. Finally, previous 20th-century revitalization efforts are assessed and recommendations are made for goal-setting and coordination between all institutions and voluntary groups involved with Gaelic.

Current Situation and Demographics

Scottish Gaelic speakers began emigrating from Scotland to Nova Scotia in the last quarter of the 18th century; the main period of emigration lasted 1770-1840. They came over largely in chain migrations of entire families and communities, adapting to the New World while maintaining and developing their Gaelic language, culture and oral traditions through to the 20th century (Kennedy 2002: 18-19).

The intergenerational transmission of Gaelic from parents to children in homes ceased on a community-wide basis in the 1930s and 1940s in Cape Breton. The timing of this shift was identified through linguistic anthropology field research in Cape Breton, including interviews and Gaelic-language proficiency tests conducted with Gaelic speakers in the communities of Mabou and the North Shore in 1978-1979 (Mertz 1982). The actual intergenerational language shift from Gaelic to English as the language of child-rearing most likely occurred in the previous generation, when the Gaelic-English bilingual parents of children born in the 1930s and 1940s were raised themselves in both Gaelic and English by parents who had been extensively exposed to English in their schooling and employment-related emigration. This conclusion was reached through historical research and the results of a door-to-door survey conducted in Christmas Island and the North Shore in 1990 (Dembling 1991).

A 5 per cent sample produced from the 1901 census results reports Gaelic as the fourth most commonly spoken language in Canada after English, French and German. The sample indicates that the total Gaelic-speaking population of Canada was approximately 90,000 out of 5.37 million, with about 50,000 living in Nova Scotia. In the 1931 census, the number of Gaelic speakers living in Nova Scotia was about 24,000 (Dembling 2006: 207). Twentieth-century Canadian census figures reported by Cosper (1998) show the decline of Gaelic in Nova Scotia since this time, although since 1941 the reported number of "Gaelic" speakers has included both Scottish and Irish Gaelic (Dembling, personal communication, 27 May 2012). The 1941 Canadian census reported 12,065 people with Gaelic as a mother tongue in the province; the 1961 census reported 3,702 people with Gaelic as a mother tongue and the 1981 census reported 1,270 people in Nova Scotia with a "Celtic language" as a mother tongue.

Just as in the 20th-century census, speakers of Scottish Gaelic were not enumerated separately in the 2006 Canadian census statistics (Statistics Canada 2007). Instead, the statistics reported numbers of Gaelic speakers in the two unclear and potentially overlapping categories already mentioned. The first is "Gaelic languages," which could include speakers of both Scottish Gaelic and Irish.[1] The second is "Celtic languages," which could include speakers of Scottish Gaelic, Irish and Welsh. The total reported population of Nova Scotia in 2006 was 913,462. Based on a 20 per cent sample of respondents (those who completed the long census form), the census results reported 890 speakers of "Gaelic languages" in the Province of Nova Scotia, of whom 245 were reported in Cape Breton Island and 200 in the provincial capital of Halifax, with the rest elsewhere in the province. Of these 890 speakers of "Gaelic languages" in the province as a whole, 460 reported "Gaelic languages" as a mother tongue, whether Irish or Scottish Gaelic.[2]

Reversing Language Shift (RLS) and the Graded Intergenerational Disruption Scale (GIDS)

Gaelic in Nova Scotia may be classified as a language that is undergoing a shift and which is the subject of revitalization efforts. In this section I define these terms, and then describe and critique a model that assesses just how "endangered" or "vital" a given language may be. The model also includes recommended actions to take in order to reverse language shift at each stage of the process, and, in the following section, I apply the model to analyze the particular situation of Nova Scotia Gaelic.

"Language shift" can be defined as a process in which "the habitual use of one language is being replaced by the habitual use of another" in "bilingual towns, villages, or neighborhoods" (Gal 1979: 1). In such contexts, it is possible for an individual to abandon speaking a language in his or her own lifetime, but more often the way language shift works is that people maintain the use of that language with members of a particular social network throughout their lifetime, and speak a different language to children and others outside that network (McEwan-Fujita 2010a: 30; Kulick 1992; Gal 1978).

Users of the language undergoing a shift, or their descendants, may engage in "language revitalization" to try to change this situation. Joshua Fishman, a sociologist of language, has defined language revitalization in a specialized way as "reversing language shift" (RLS): "the theory and practice of assistance to speech communities whose native languages are threatened because their intergenerational continuity is proceeding negatively, with fewer and fewer users ... or uses every generation" (Fishman 1991: 1). More generally, language revitalization can be defined as "the attempt to add new forms or new functions to a language which is threatened with language loss or death, with the aim of increasing its uses and users" (King 2001: 4).

Fishman has proposed the Graded Intergenerational Disruption Scale (GIDS) as a tool to determine a language's relative vitality or endangerment on a scale "from full use by many users to no use by any users" (Lewis and Simons 2010: 105). The greater a language's level of endangerment, the further along it is in the process of shift, with the ultimate outcome of shift being language "death" or obsolescence. The scale also suggests the actions that are most important to take in order to ensure the continuation of a language at any given level or stage of endangerment (Fishman 1991: 81). Fishman originally described the GIDS in narrative form, but he later restated it in the form of a table which is adapted here as Table 1.

Table 1: A summary of Fishman's Graded Intergenerational Disruption Scale (GIDS) adapted from Fishman (2001: 466) and Lewis and Simons (2010: 3). The chart should be read from the bottom up, starting at Stage 8.

STAGE	SITUATION	GOAL
1	The language is used for local and regional mass media and government services	Using the language in education, work sphere, mass media and governmental operations at higher and nationwide levels
2	The language is used in the local or regional work sphere	Using the language in local and regional mass media and government services
3	Children attend schools providing some or all education through the medium of the language	Using the language in the local/regional (i.e. non-neighbourhood) work sphere, both among in-group members and out-group members
4	The language is used orally by all generations and is effectively used in written form throughout the community	Setting up schools that offer some or all instruction in the minority language, either public or private, and either substantially under majority curricular and staffing control or substantially under in-group curricular and staffing control
5	A new generation of children are learning to speak the language as a first language	Setting up schools for literacy acquisition in the language, for the old and young, outside of and supplementary to their compulsory education
6	A cohort including teenagers, younger adults and parents of young children use the language in daily life	Restarting intergenerational mother tongue transmission of the language in an intergenerational and demographically concentrated home-family-neighbourhood-community context
7	Cultural interaction in the language primarily involving the community-based older generation(s)	Creating a cohort including teenagers, younger adults, and parents of young children who speak the language comfortably with one another and with older people
8	The only remaining speakers of the language are members of the grandparent generation	Reconstructing the language as it was actually used, and adult second language acquisition of the language

The name of the scale, "Graded Intergenerational Disruption," indicates that its main concern is the degree to which transmission of the language from one generation to the next has been disrupted or maintained. This disruption occurs because when speakers stop transmitting a language from one generation to the next, they lose the main way of creating new fluent speakers in a culturally acceptable context, and hence of reproducing their language community. Therefore, Fishman insists that GIDS stage 6, "intergenerational [language] usage within the confines of the home, family, neighbourhood and face-to-face community" (1991: xii), should be encouraged and stabilized first and foremost in RLS efforts. Although efforts to achieve stages 5 through 1 on the scale are often attempted, and may even seem more urgent and feasible, they will not contribute to reversing language shift unless they also support transmission of the spoken language in homes, families, neighbourhoods and communities.

The GIDS is a powerful tool; it "remains the foundational conceptual model for assessing the status of language vitality" (Lewis and Simons 2010: 104). It has also been criticized for shortcomings, both conceptual and technical. The conceptual points will be dealt with in the following section. To address some of the technical shortcomings, linguists from SIL International have proposed a new version called the Expanded Graded Intergenerational Disruption Scale or EGIDS (Table 2), which incorporates the endangerment evaluation scale developed by linguists for UNESCO in 2003, and the language vitality categories developed for SIL International's *Ethnologue*, which aspires to list, describe and categorize all of the world's known languages.[3]

Table 2: EGIDS – Expanded Graded Intergenerational Disruption Scale adapted from Fishman 1991 (reproduced from Lewis and Simons 2010: 8).

Level	Label	Description	UNESCO
0	International	The language is used internationally for a broad range of functions.	Safe
1	National	The language is used in education, work, mass media, government at the nationwide level.	Safe
2	Regional	The language is used for local and regional mass media and governmental services.	Safe
3	Trade	The language is used for local and regional work by both insiders and outsiders.	Safe
4	Educational	Literacy in the language is being transmitted through a system of public education.	Safe
5	Written	The language is used orally by all generations and is effectively used in written form in parts of the community.	Safe
6a	Vigorous	The language is used orally by all generations and is being learned by children as their first language.	Safe
6b	Threatened	The language is used orally by all generations but only some of the child-bearing generation are transmitting it to their children.	Vulnerable

7	Shifting	The child-bearing generation knows the language well enough to use it among themselves but none are transmitting it to their children	Definitely Endangered
8a	Moribund	The only remaining active speakers of the language are members of the grandparent generation.	Severely Endangered
8b	Nearly Extinct	The only remaining speakers of the language are members of the grandparent generation or older who have little opportunity to use the language.	Critically Endangered
9	Dormant	The language serves as a reminder of heritage identity for an ethnic community. No one has more than symbolic proficiency.	Extinct
10	Extinct	No one retains a sense of ethnic identity associated with the language, even for symbolic purposes.	Extinct

The original GIDS in Table 1 has eight stages, while the EGIDS in Table 2 has 13 levels, although the new levels are still numbered to correspond clearly to Fishman's GIDS stages. The column marked "UNESCO" correlates the UNESCO Atlas designations of degree of endangerment with the numbered levels. The column marked "Label" incorporates the SIL *Ethnologue* vitality categories and characterizes the overall level of use (Lewis and Simons 2010: 110).

Most of the new levels have been added at the threatened end of the scale, where the authors felt that the most clarification was needed in order to use the scale as a tool to classify the state of endangerment and assist revitalization efforts. For example, the EGIDS subdivides the goal of GIDS Stage 6, "The language is used orally by all generations and is being learned by children as their first language" into Level 6a "Vigorous/Safe" and Level 6b "Threatened/Vulnerable," with the difference between them being that at Level 6a, "The language is used orally by all generations and is being learned by children as their first language" for *all* children of the child-bearing generation, while at Level 6b this is only the case for *some* children of the child-bearing generation. These designations are problematic, but they represent an attempt to capture the complexities of language shift in a diagnostic tool.[4]

Levels 0, 9 and 10 are totally new, with level 0 corresponding to international use of the language for many functions—a new ultimate "Safe" category—and levels 9 and 10 further adding to the endangerment end of the scale. Level 9, "Dormant," was incorporated from the 16th edition of the *Ethnologue*, to which it had been added in response to "editorial correspondence from members of ethnic groups who objected to the label of 'extinct' even though no remaining first-language speakers could be identified" (Lewis and Simons 2010: 109).

The authors acknowledged that the general direction of language shift (metaphorically "upward" toward revitalization or "downward" toward obsolescence or death) is as important to consider as the individual stages, and here we see a disjuncture between Fishman's original narrative formulation of the GIDS and its EGIDS adaptation. The original, described as "a typology of disadvantaged languages and ameliorative priorities," is written in an "upward" direction, with recommendations and encouragement for revitalization proponents (Fishman 1991: 81-121). However, the reformulated EGIDS (Table 2) keeps the typology and omits the "ameliorative priorities," resulting in a scale that is based on language shift in a "downward" direction. This does not accord well with the perspective of those engaged in language revitalization efforts.

Therefore, Lewis and Simons also produced an alternate version of the EGIDS (Table 3), with levels 6b through 9 reframed as moving toward revitalization rather than extinction. For example, the EGIDS Stage 6b "Threatened"—"The language is used orally by all generations but only some of the child-bearing generation are transmitting to their children"—is re-conceptualized as the Revitalization EGIDS Stage 6b, "Re-established": "Some members of a third generation of children are acquiring the language in the home with the result that an unbroken chain of intergenerational transmission has been re-established among all living generations" (Lewis and Simons 2010: 117).

Table 3: Revitalization EGIDS Levels (reproduced from Lewis and Simons 2010: 117).

Level	Label	Description
6a	Vigorous	The language is used orally by all generations and is being learned by all children as their first language.
6b	Re-established	Some members of a third generation of children are acquiring the language in the home with the result that an unbroken chain of intergenerational transmission has been re-established among all living generations.
7	Revitalized	A second generation of children are acquiring the language from their parents who also acquired the language in the home. Language transmission takes place in home and community.
8a	Reawakened	Children are acquiring the language in community and some home settings and are increasingly able to use the language orally for some day-to-day communicative needs.
8b	Reintroduced	Adults of the parent generation are reconstructing and reintroducing their language for everyday social interaction.
9	Dormant	Adults are rediscovering their language for symbolic and identificational purposes.

Sociolinguistic and Cultural Factors Impacting Assessment of Endangerment

The GIDS and EGIDS are tools for comparative and macro-level analysis. Yet anthropological studies of language shift at the micro-level, the local or community level, show us that much of what is salient and important to understand about each situation of language shift actually happens at the level of cultural ideologies, affective experiences, and face-to-face interaction, in the context of particular historical experiences (Gal 1978; King 2001:17-21; Kulick 1992; McEwan-Fujita 2010a; Mertz 1982). Linguistic anthropological analyses also contribute several points about the nature of communities and language use that must be incorporated into any assessment of language endangerment and priorities for revitalization. Three of these points are described here.

1. Language shift and revitalization efforts are uneven, both demographically and ideologically. The stages of language shift represented in the GIDS and EGIDS are not always sequential or mutually exclusive, and revitalization efforts never proceed smoothly or without contestation. As will be discussed in the following section, multiple stages of both shift and revitalization can be occurring simultaneously in different areas of any given geographical region. Multiple stages can even be occurring in the same time frame within a given family, a point that follows on from the observation that families are not homogeneous sites of language transmission (see point 2 below). Moreover, as can be in Table 4, column V, "Main Challenges," cultural and ideological factors play key roles in processes of language shift and revitalization efforts (Dauenhauer and Dauenhauer 1998). Revitalization efforts are subject to the multiple and conflicting ideologies of participants, and can engender encounters laden with both positive and negative affect (McEwan-Fujita 2010a, 2010b).

2. Children are socialized not only in families, but also in communities. Assumptions about how children are socialized to speak a native language must be expanded. A "mother tongue" is not only or necessarily learned from a child's mother. Families and homes are not necessarily institutions where parents reproduce biologically or linguistically. Siblings in the same family can develop very different levels of competence in the first language of the parent(s) (Spolsky 2009), and can also develop different ideologies and affective orientations toward the minority language depending on birth order, education experiences, emigration and other factors (e.g., Dorian 1980).

Many supporters and detractors of Fishman's GIDS overlook his point that the *entire* home-family-neighbourhood-community nexus is included in the support of intergenerational transmission, including neighbourhood institutions (1991: 92-93). This nexus encompasses not only parent-child and grandparent-grandchild relationships, but also many other kinds of language socialization relationships (see Ochs 1990: 302-303). Adults can socialize other adults and can socialize children of all ages in many capacities (extended family member, family friend, teacher, coach, lunchroom supervisor, religious leader, store clerk, etc.). Children can socialize each other and can socialize adults, as well. In fact, any "expert" can socialize any "novice," as long as the people involved take the roles of expert and novice in interaction. Canadian education researcher Mark Fettes (1997) expands on the idea that multiple kinds of social relationships besides home-based and parentally provided immersion can help to reverse language shift: "any meaningful long-term relationship conducted in the language helps to establish an intergenerational network of relationships."

3. *"Community" can be defined in many different ways.* There are multiple ways of conceptualizing minority-language speakers as a community or communities, and these impact the assessment of a language's level of endangerment. In Nova Scotia, a "Gaelic community" can be defined in two different ways: (1) as a traditional geographically defined locale where people speak Gaelic to one another in face-to-face settings in daily life (a town, village, district, island, etc.), or (2) as "communities of practice" which are defined as "groups of people who share a concern or a passion for something they do and learn how to do it better as they interact regularly" (Wenger 2006). A Nova Scotia-wide[5] Gaelic community of practice is composed not of Gaelic-speaking localities where individuals encounter one another in daily life, but rather of Gaelic-speaking individuals who gather and work together in smaller communities of practice at multiple levels (Wenger 1998; McEwan-Fujita 2010c). Gaelic communities of practice include social networks of friends and acquaintances (including digitally mediated networks), voluntary organizations, Gaelic language classes, cultural and recreational events and part-time and full-time employment. Although a sense of geographical place is culturally significant and important to community members, and travel times and fuel costs constrain their mobility, 21st-century Gaelic communities of practice are built more fundamentally around members' shared concern and passion for Gaelic, their shared learning experiences and regular interaction at planned events than around chance daily encounters and shared residence in a locale.

Nova Scotia Gaelic: Level of Endangerment and RLS Priorities

How endangered is Nova Scotia Gaelic, and where is it currently positioned on the EGIDS? I have created the Nova Scotia Gaelic EGIDS (Table 4) to help answer this question. The table adapts the numbering and wording of Fishman's original GIDS stages (Table 1), the terminology and some expanded numbering of the Lewis and Simons EGIDS shift and revitalization scales (Tables 2 and 3) and the points made above. For each stage, separate columns describe the starting point (II), the recommended goal (III), specific actions to achieve the goal (IV), and the major challenges, both ideological-emotional and technical-practical (V). The GIDS framework is not often presented in a table form tailored to one particular language situation, but this format (inspired by Dauenhauer and Dauenhauer 1998) allows for greater inclusion of relevant local and cultural factors in the scale. Separating the starting point from the goal helps to clarify the difference between these two for each stage, and to highlight the key role of the goals in the scale; these points are not as clear in previous summary versions of the GIDS (Fishman 2001: 466; Lewis and Simons 2010: 3).

Assessing the situation from the perspective of a Nova Scotia-wide community of practice, Gaelic is at GIDS Stage 8. I shall discuss this in greater detail but first must make the point that although revitalization efforts are ongoing in a community of practice, language shift is also still advancing or already completed in most traditional geographically bounded communities that were formerly Gaelic speaking. In most areas of its former heartland, Cape Breton Island, Gaelic is at EGIDS Stage 8b "Nearly Extinct": "The only remaining speakers of the language are members of the grandparent generation or older who have little opportunity to use the language" (Table 3; also see Table 4, stage 8, column II). For most other geographical areas in eastern Nova Scotia where Gaelic was spoken in the 18th through 20th centuries, for example in Pictou and Antigonish Counties, it is currently at EGIDS Stage 9 "Dormant": "The language serves as a reminder of heritage identity for an ethnic community. No one has more than symbolic proficiency." Gaelic is also "Dormant" in the Halifax area: families and individuals migrated from Cape Breton to the Halifax area, and many know that they had Gaelic-speaking parents, grandparents, great-grandparents or ancestors. Therefore, when these areas are considered as *traditional geographically based communities*, Gaelic is in the end stages of language shift, although in these areas there is also a great deal of goodwill toward Gaelic which could still be mobilized to help both people themselves and the language. It is only within intentional *communities of practice*, composed mainly of active groups of adult Gaelic learners, that we can assess Gaelic as in the process of being at Stage 8 of revitalization.

The twin goals of GIDS Stage 8, the reconstruction of spoken Nova Scotia Gaelic for multiple social uses and the creation of a core group of fluent middle-aged Gaelic users, are currently being pursued by individuals, a range of voluntary groups and institutions, and the Gaelic Affairs division of the Nova Scotia Department of Communities, Culture and Heritage. Adults are learning Nova Scotia Gaelic by teaching and taking language courses and participating in various cultural events and organizational activities. The introduction of "Total Immersion Plus" Gàidhlig aig Baile classes in Nova Scotia in the past decade appears to have strengthened this

Table 4: The Nova Scotia Gaelic EGIDS. Selected stages of Fishman's Graded Intergenerational Disruption Scale or GIDS (1991: 81-111) and Lewis and Simons' Expanded GIDS or EGIDS (2010), adapted to the situation of Gaelic in Nova Scotia. NOTE: Read scale from the top down.

I. STAGE	II. STARTING POINT	III. GOAL	IV. HOW TO ACHIEVE	V. MAIN CHALLENGES
10	*Extinct:* In many formerly Gaelic-speaking areas, no one retains a sense of ethnic identity associated with Gaelic, even for symbolic purposes	*Rediscovered:* Make people, particularly those of Scottish ancestry, aware that one-third of people in Nova Scotia have Gaelic-speaking ancestors and that Gaelic is still spoken in Nova Scotia	Public, voluntary and personal awareness efforts, consciousness-raising, advertising, marketing, encouraging the use of written, spoken and sung Gaelic in public	People's lack of knowledge about provincial and family history; Gaelic is written out of history books, and knowledge of its existence suppressed Logistical and financial limitations of advertising and marketing
9	*Dormant:* Gaelic serves as a reminder of heritage identity for some members of the Gaelic and Scottish ethnic communities in Nova Scotia, but no one has more than symbolic proficiency (e.g., using the phrases *"Ciad mìle fàilte"* and *"Ciamar a tha sibh?"*)	*Rediscovered:* Adults rediscover their language for symbolic and identificational purposes (including symbolic displays of written Gaelic, memorization and performance of song texts, and casual participation in social events and language courses)	Public, voluntary and personal awareness efforts, consciousness-raising, advertising, marketing, encouraging the use of written, spoken and sung Gaelic in public Make people aware that the Gaelic language is a unique aspect of Nova Scotian culture and a preferred vehicle of Gaelic culture, and that there are opportunities to learn and speak Gaelic in present-day Nova Scotia	Joking, animosity, willful ignorance and lack of interest from non-speakers, including people claiming Scottish ethnicity Logistical and financial limitations of advertising and marketing Many adults' satisfaction with remaining at this level or lack of resources (time and money) to take their Gaelic-learning efforts further

| 8 | *Rediscovered yet Moribund:* Some adults use Gaelic for symbolic purposes, but the language is only spoken natively by elderly people, some of whom are socially active (EGIDS 8a, Moribund), but most of whom have few opportunities for social interaction (EGIDS 8b, Nearly Extinct) | *Reintroduced:* Reconstruct spoken Nova Scotia Gaelic for multiple social uses

Build a core group of middle-aged adult Gaelic learners and users (who may be geographically scattered) | Locate as many Gaelic-speaking elders as possible and socially re-integrate them into Gaelic-medium interaction

Documentation: record everyday spoken-language, expressions, oral traditions from native speakers

Create courses and programs in which adults acquire Gaelic as a second language

Bring native Gaelic-speaking elders into contact with interested adults through the medium of Gaelic | Possible social isolation or poor health of elderly people; possible refusal to identify themselves as speakers of a formerly stigmatized language

Setting documentation goals: dialects, words, expressions, discourse genres (conversation, childcare, storytelling, etc.)

Coordinating community-level and academic documentation efforts

Archiving documented language and utilizing it in teaching materials so that it is accessible to learners

Designing Gaelic language curricula and teaching methods that are both effective and culturally acceptable

Adults obtaining language instruction of sufficient duration and intensity to attain fluency in Gaelic—more than a few hours per week

Selecting a target Gaelic variety to acquire—which dialect, which teachers

Difficulty of acquiring accurate pronunciation of Gaelic as a second language

Possibility that Internet-based interaction and Gaelic cultural events (singing, instrumental music, dance, storytelling) may not lead to acquisition of daily spoken language |

| 7 | _Reintroduced_: Gaelic is used for cultural interaction primarily by adults who are middle-aged and older ("beyond child-bearing age"), with one another and with elders | _Reawakened_: Build a cohort including teenagers, younger adults and parents of young children who comfortably and regularly speak Gaelic as a second language with one another and with older people. Create "communities of practice" where young people witness adults speaking Gaelic (based on geographical proximity, social networks and regular, enjoyable gatherings and events). | Generate interest in Gaelic among teenagers and young adults and parents of younger children. Provide effective instruction in spoken Gaelic for teenagers, young people and parents. Create youth groups, parenting groups and family-friendly multi-generational events | Competing with majority culture and English-medium jobs to attract interest and time commitment of young people. Parents' inability to attend Gaelic classes and events without childcare. Insufficient level of Gaelic instruction in public education and universities for bringing students to spoken fluency. Universities' not being allowed to release contact information of Gaelic students/alumni to facilitate network building. Traditional geographical communities no longer the basis for daily Gaelic use; must plan for "communities of practice" based on shared orientations to Gaelic. Different needs and characteristics of different Gaelic communities of practice (e.g., rural vs. urban). Competition with, rather than medium of, family and leisure activities. Gaelic cultural activities (e.g. singing, music and dance) not necessarily supporting acquisition of daily spoken Gaelic by parents, young adults, adolescents and children |

| 6 | *Reawakened*: A cohort that includes teenagers, younger adults and parents of young children is using Gaelic as a second language with each other and older people | *Re-established and Revitalized*: Children are raised in Gaelic in the home and/or daycare, by parents, grandparents and/or other caregivers. In this way, a new cohort of first-language Gaelic speakers is created

Gaelic speakers are demographically concentrated in multigenerational communities, or at least gather regularly face-to-face

Gaelic-speaking communities are reinforced by the support of local institutions | Encourage and support Gaelic speakers who become parents to use Gaelic in the home when raising children

Train young adults and older adults to be Gaelic-medium childcare providers

Create Gaelic-medium daycare and preschools to support families

Develop other "family-friendly" Gaelic institutions and events | Most new Gaelic users' lack of language skills, registers and confidence to speak Gaelic to children

Some new Gaelic users' possible transmission of a hybridized, anglicized Gaelic to children

Children raised speaking Gaelic become socially isolated from other Gaelic speakers

Support of Gaelic by one parent only

Other challenges continue as at Stage 7 |

I. STAGE	II. STARTING POINT	III. GOAL	IV. HOW TO ACHIEVE	V. MAIN CHALLENGES
5	*Revitalized and Vigorous*: Children are learning Gaelic as a native language, starting at age 0-3. Gaelic is spoken by people of all generations with one another informally in daily life (child-parent-grandparent, older-younger, expert-novice)	*Written*: Children acquire "guided" Gaelic literacy to support their speaking abilities All Gaelic-speaking community members acquire literacy which can indirectly and directly support Stage 6 RLS goals (indirectly in terms of symbolic identity and status; directly in terms of intergenerational social interaction)	Provide Gaelic literacy instruction to children and adults at the local or community level, under Gaelic community control (for example, incorporate basic Gaelic literacy instruction into children's Gaelic-medium programs such as summer camps and extracurricular activities) Develop goals, a curriculum and lessons for providing basic Gaelic literacy instruction	Lack of fluent adult Gaelic speakers who are also literate in Gaelic Some speakers' cultural preference for orality and oral cultural forms Gaelic orthography challenging for literate English speakers Possibility that Gaelic literacy activities may substitute for, not support, intergenerational transmission of spoken Gaelic Possibility that community-based literacy instruction be seen as competing with the schools

| 4 | *Written*: There is a Gaelic community of children and adults who understand and speak conversational Gaelic and can read and write basic Gaelic | *Educational*: Children attend schools providing some or all education in Gaelic

The schools represent Gaelic cultural space, and are not just agencies for the transmission of "neutral" (majority) knowledge, skills and attitudes. Ideally, they are publicly funded (like Fishman's type 4b schools) but substantially controlled by Gaelic speakers (like Fishman's type 4a schools, e.g., *Conseil Scolaire Acadien Provincial* in NS). | Obtain the legal right and funding to set up Gaelic-medium public schools. (Depends on parental demand, lobbying by Gaelic voluntary groups, political goodwill, political patronage and federal or provincial official status legislation.)

Build schools, create an administrative framework

Develop a Gaelic-medium curriculum following NS provincial guidelines

Develop new Gaelic teaching materials for the curriculum (books, activities, lesson plans)

Train fluent Gaelic-speaking teachers

Ensure that schools are "indigenized" in their operations, personnel, program revision and control, budgets, etc. | Possibility of conflict between culturally appropriate Gaelic-medium subject matter and teaching methods and majority anglophone federal and provincial guidelines for a literacy-based school curriculum

Possibility that adult Gaelic users will view Gaelic-medium schools for children as the saviour of Gaelic, and feel that they have no personal responsibility to socialize children in Gaelic outside of formal education

Necessity of a written standard or norm for the development of written educational materials

Possibility that education activities, most of which are literacy-related, will be based on a standardized form of Gaelic that is not accessible or acceptable to traditional native speakers

Parents' view that their children's future employment prospects are linked to English-medium schooling

Public opposition to use of public funding for Gaelic-medium schools |

3	*Educational:* People educated in Gaelic seek work, but also wish to maintain ethnolinguistic identity and revitalize their communities in economic terms	*Trade:* Gaelic is used by adults in the work sphere outside of the Gaelic community, beyond the sphere of education already implied in Levels 5 and 4	Discussion omitted here	Discussion omitted here
2	*Trade:* Gaelic is transmitted in home and community, taught in schools and used in some work situations	*Regional:* The beginning of the "Big League": Gaelic is used in "lower" governmental services and mass media	Gaelic Affairs provincial government office is in place Further discussion omitted here	Discussed omitted here
1	*Regional:* Gaelic is used in "lower" governmental services and mass media.	*National:* Gaelic is used in some higher level educational, occupational, governmental and media efforts	Discussion omitted here	Discussion omitted here

stage, as has the development in recent years of the Bun is Barr program based on the California Master-Apprentice program developed by Hinton et al. for aboriginal languages (Hinton 1997; Hinton, Vera and Steele 2002).

The essential measure of success at this stage is whether a "core group" of adult speakers has yet been created. However, "core group" is a fundamentally ideological concept, and its existence cannot be assessed in purely quantitative terms. Future research may be able to quantify how many adults are currently involved in Gaelic-language learning, how much time they spend learning and their levels of fluency and use. A documented increase in the number of fluent speakers would indeed be a very helpful point of reference, but in itself does not guarantee the formation of a core community of practice that can work together to reverse language shift.

However, an evaluation of whether this core group exists can still be made with reference to progress through the GIDS stages. On the basis of recent participant observation and experience, it is clear to the author that members of the adult Gaelic-speaking community of practice in Nova Scotia do strongly wish to sustain the language, but the community cannot yet support the attainment of GIDS Stages 7 and 6.

How close is the Nova Scotia Gaelic community of practice to the starting point of Stage 7, where Gaelic is being used for regular social interaction primarily by adults who are middle-aged and older? As already mentioned, this is a question not only of how many middle-aged and older users there are (enough to sustain regular interaction and a variety of voluntary activities), but also a question of the proficiency level of those users (how many are fluent) and the frequency of their Gaelic-medium interactions (which is partly though by no means wholly a function of their physical proximity). My assessment is that currently there are not enough fluent middle-aged Gaelic users who interact with each other frequently enough in Gaelic to form a solid social network base for sustaining progress toward the goal of Stage 7: to create a "younger cohort of [Gaelic]-as-a-second-language-users" (Fishman 1991: 90), a cohort including teenagers, younger adults and parents of young children who regularly speak Gaelic as a second language with one another and older people.[6] As was the case throughout the 20th century, the people who are currently working for and in Gaelic are spread too thinly on tasks both central and peripheral to RLS, and risk burning out. Other Gaelic speakers have been "brain drained" away from the province.

Even if the community were considered to have already advanced to the starting point of Stage 7, the challenges of achieving the Stage 7 goal of creating a cohort of fluent Gaelic-speaking young adults and parents of young children are still very great. Devoting time to Gaelic learning is difficult for parents of young children. Participation in adult Gaelic evening classes and many Gaelic events in the province requires leaving one's young child(ren) with a non-Gaelic speaking caregiver. This creates a situation in which Gaelic learning tends to be an activity for retirement-age adults. Attracting parents and young adults is also difficult because Gaelic also has to compete with other highly valued family and leisure activities, such as hockey, rather than serving as a medium for such activities. Gaelic RLS supporters are competing with the majority English-medium culture and its employment opportunities to attract the interest and time commitment of young people. When Gaelic does capture their interest in public education and universities, the courses do not bring students to fluency, and most students of Gaelic melt back into the general populace after graduation rather than integrate into a Gaelic community of practice.

There is some progress toward the Stage 7 goal: approximately ten to fifteen young adults in their twenties have become fluent in Gaelic during the past five years or so through a combination of university courses, courses at the Gaelic college Sabhal Mòr Ostaig in Scotland, Gàidhlig aig Baile classes, and the Bun is Barr master-apprentice program. They are actively involved in a Nova Scotia Gaelic community of practice; for example, periodically over the past two years, one person has held a Gaelic immersion week for young adults on the North Shore. However, we do not know how the number of young adults involved now compares to the number of young adults involved in Gaelic in the 1970s, or the 1990s.

Where is Nova Scotia Gaelic with respect to achieving the all-important RLS goal of Stage 6, intergenerational transmission of Gaelic in the home-family-neighbourhood-community context? This goal is highlighted in bold type in Tables 1 and 4 to indicate its importance as the foundation or keystone of RLS. Some individuals in eastern Nova Scotia are making efforts to transmit Gaelic to children in the home. I have identified fewer than twenty families in eastern Nova Scotia with one or more children aged 0-18 in which one parent can speak Gaelic, and two families in which both parents can speak Gaelic, in which one or both parents are making, or have recently made or plan to make attempts to speak Gaelic to the children. There is enormous diversity among these families both in terms of their geographical areas of residence (scattered across eastern Nova Scotia) and the type of family (two-parent or single-parent, "original" or blended, biological or adopted children). Gaelic usage patterns are similarly diverse among the parents in these families, with a Gaelic-speaking parent attempting to use all Gaelic, some Gaelic, or a few words and phrases. Some parents working on Stage 6 goals experienced the interruption of intergenerational transmission in their own lifetime, or married into a family that did, and others are introducing Gaelic into their families for the first time ever or for the first time within living memory.

These parents are dedicated, but what is still missing to achieve the goal of Stage 6 is not only greater numbers but also the "neighbourhood-community" element of the "home-family-neighbourhood-community" nexus which can be built up when the goal of Stage 7 is achieved. As described already the third section of this chapter, children are socialized not only in families, but also in communities, and the entire home-family-neighbourhood-community nexus is included in the support of intergenerational transmission, including neighbourhood institutions (Fishman 1991: 92-93) such as voluntary organizations. This nexus encompasses many kinds of language socialization relationships, as already mentioned (Ochs 1990: 302-303).

When new efforts to revitalize Nova Scotia Gaelic are placed on the EGIDS, one can see more clearly how they relate to the priority of achieving the goal of intergenerational transmission at Stage 6. Some efforts support the goals of Stages 8, 7 and 6 directly, some indirectly and some perhaps not at all. For this reason, Fishman's original GIDS description advocates treating "higher-order" RLS efforts with caution until intergenerational transmission has been achieved, lest resources and efforts be diverted inappropriately. This does not mean that no higher-order efforts should be attempted; sometimes they seem essential to overcoming centuries of oppression and denigration of the language (Fishman 2001). For example, the 2006 establishment of the Office of Gaelic Affairs, now a division of the Department of Communities, Culture and Heritage in the Nova Scotia provincial government, is a highly significant recent achievement at GIDS Stage 2 and 3, bringing Gaelic into governmental services and the (non-education-related) work sphere. Gaelic Affairs supports the goals of Stages 8, 7 and 6 directly: it produces publicity materials which may bring more adults from Stage 9 into Stage 8, runs its own Stage 8 project (Bun is Barr), materially supports another Stage 8 effort (the teaching of Gàidhlig aig Baile courses to adults) and provides grants to community groups whose projects may work toward the goals of Stages 8, 7 and 6.

On the other hand, Gaelic is also taught in some public primary schools, which might initially be considered an example of GIDS Stage 4. However, Gaelic can only be taught as a subject to some children in selected public primary schools in Antigonish County and Cape Breton Island, which is very different from the Stage 4 goal of a Gaelic-medium school with a culturally Gaelic curriculum under the control of Gaelic-speaking administrators (see Table 1 and Table 4). A place for Gaelic in Nova Scotian public schools has only been achieved through strenuous effort, and is maintained and developed through many hours of hard work, both paid and voluntary, by dedicated and talented individuals. But the level of "foreign" language instruction that is allowed to be provided in Nova Scotia public schools has never supported pupils to attain fluency in Gaelic, or even in French (which is not only one of Canada's federal official languages, but also a living and heritage language of many Nova Scotians). Thus, the limited way in which Gaelic is currently allowed to be taught in the schools draws some of the most concentrated efforts to assist Gaelic, but it does not appear to directly support the attainment of Stage 6, intergenerational transmission. It supports Stages 10 and 9: it may make more parents and students aware of Gaelic as a "real" language with a history in the province, and may awaken an interest in some parents and students to learn their heritage language after the "critical period" for children's language acquisition is past.

A Historical Perspective on RLS: 20th-Century Revitalization Efforts

The Nova Scotia Gaelic EGIDS presents the recommended way forward if a community of practice wishes to revitalize Gaelic as a spoken language of daily use. However, the scale cannot account for all relevant factors, and a brief review of previous revitalization efforts produces a more sobering assessment of the obstacles to attaining GIDS Stage 6 and reversing Gaelic language shift in Nova Scotia.

In looking at accounts of "Gaelic revival" in 20th-century Nova Scotia, we find that while language *shift* progressed gradually from EGIDS Level 6a, through 6b and 7, to 8a, 8b and 9 (Table 2), concurrent Gaelic *revitalization* efforts did not successfully move beyond the goal of GIDS Stage 8, creating a significant group of fluent adult speakers who are middle-aged and older (Table 4). Mertz summarized efforts to revitalize Gaelic in eastern Nova Scotia from the 1920s through 1980 (1982: 187-227) and noted that

> There have been revival attempts emanating from [Sydney, Antigonish and St. Ann's] at sporadic intervals throughout much of the twentieth century. Yet these separate attempts have generally failed to unite the disparate groups supporting Gaelic in Cape Breton – or in Nova Scotia as a whole. Aside from [these three centres], there have also been many individual attempts by members of rural communities in Cape Breton, and by residents of communities elsewhere in Nova Scotia, to teach Gaelic. (208-209)

These efforts helped to cast Gaelic in a new light for Cape Bretoners, as something of value, in contrast to the many years of denigration and neglect it had received. In this sense, they were extremely positive (Dorian 1987). However, in many of these efforts, "a precise examination of the message conveyed reveals that it involved a revival of *interest* in Gaelic more than a revival of language use" (Mertz 1982: 219).

Mertz found four factors common to the efforts from 1920s-1980: 1) the revival attempts were made by educational elites or professionals; 2) people who initiated revival attempts were either from "away" or were Cape Bretoners who had spent considerable time away from the island; 3) the division between predominantly Catholic and Protestant areas played out as a mutual avoidance and lack of interaction between people in these areas with respect to Gaelic revitalization efforts; and 4) a divide between the urban centre of Sydney and the rural areas of Cape Breton also manifested itself in the lack of coordination of revitalization efforts (209-11).

Dembling assessed journalistic accounts of the 1990s "Gaelic revival" in Cape Breton and found that while one article referenced an increase in the number of Gaelic students at St. Francis Xavier University, almost everything else referred to as "Gaelic revival" in the media related to the prominence of professional recording artists, most of whom were not actually learning Gaelic. Census statistics notwithstanding, it was not possible to say how many Gaelic speakers or learners there were in the province, and that is still the case today. Dembling did find that the counter-culture, "bottom-up" trend of the 1970s brought by the hippies and folklorists was still positively influencing revitalization efforts to focus more on ordinary people's experiences (1997: 67-68). Tartanism was downplayed, while community-organized efforts such as Feis an Eilein were initiated and the *Am Bràighe* newspaper was launched.

Dembling also found that the influences of the 1970s carried through to the 1990s in the classroom. Gaelic classes featured increased local cultural content, immersion, role-playing and visits from native speakers (77). These gains may or may not have necessarily translated into greater numbers of learners becoming fluent, but there is no way to know without having counted. Dembling did carry out a survey of sixty-six adult Gaelic learners in 1996 and found that respondents were enthusiastic, but "the trend from the sample would indicate that only a few learners persist to the higher levels of fluency" (106).[7] Most of the survey respondents also indicated that they did not feel they had enough opportunities to speak Gaelic (113). At the same time, a handful of Gaelic learners who had achieved fluency and some recent native-Gaelic-speaking immigrants from Scotland were raising their children in Gaelic (64-65).

Across the 19th and 20th centuries, dedication, energy and talent were poured into Gaelic revitalization activities: teaching, writing, publishing, musical events, folklore collection, raising children in Gaelic. Many people have strongly wished to revitalize the language. For example, Malcolm MacDonald, a Gaelic instructor at the Gaelic College, wrote in the College's short-lived newspaper *The Canadian-American Gael* (which was published 1943-1948):

> Feumaidh sinn an dìleab phrìseal so ionnsachadh do'n oigridh le
> bhi 'ga bruidhinn anns na dachaidhean... agus ma nì sinn an nì so,
> cha'n eil teagamh nach dean iadsan an nì ceudna ri'n gineal. (*CAG* 1
> [14], qtd. and trans. in Dembling 1997: 56).

> (We need to impart this precious legacy to the younger generation
> by speaking it in the homes ... and if we do this, no doubt they will
> do the same with their children.)

But thus far, despite a very strong desire for revitalization among Gaelic users, and strenuous efforts among some, the shift from Gaelic to English has not yet been reversed. In 2012 all remaining geographically based communities where Gaelic was a language of daily use have shifted to EGIDS Stage 8a, "Severely Endangered," or 8b, "Critically Endangered," (Table 2). Revitalization efforts have not moved beyond GIDS Stage 8. Stage 7 has not yet been achieved, let alone Stage 6 (Table 4).

Conclusion

The GIDS and EGIDS are useful tools, but they are limited and static. They do not take account of unique local conditions, and they do not predict or describe the events of the past or the future. They can be used to help formulate a set of goals and define the intermediate steps that are needed to reach those goals. In this way, the scales are useful tools for language revitalization goal-setting and planning. This assessment is presented in order to identify some of the ideological-emotional and technical-practical barriers to Gaelic revitalization.

As is often noted in situations of language shift, nothing can substitute for the positive will of Gaelic users themselves to change the current situation. But as the 20th century shows, positive will alone has not been enough to move from GIDS Stage 8 to Stage 7 and eventually to Stage 6. What is still missing? Coordination and cooperation.

The Gaelic community of practice must work together in several related areas:

(1) Agreement by voluntary groups and public institutions on clearly-defined RLS goals for Nova Scotia Gaelic—are most participants content at Stage 8, or do enough people want to work toward Stage 6 to make it worthwhile? (See Table 1).

(2) Improving the design, implementation and funding of Gaelic-language acquisition beyond current levels in order to significantly increase the numbers of adults being brought to fluency.

(3) Coordinating efforts of voluntary groups and public institutions so that all resources support agreed RLS goals as effectively and efficiently as possible, and pooling ideas to identify new funding sources and create innovative forms of cross-institutional support.

(4) Positive acknowledgement of a diverse Nova Scotia Gaelic community of practice encompassing the passions and practices of rural and urban, young and old, conservative and innovative, oral and literate, Cape Breton-oriented and Nova Scotia Scottish-oriented, Canadian and non-Canadian, novice and old-timer and heritage and new Gaelic users.

Notes

1. In theory it could also include Welsh, since anglophone folk understandings of the Celtic language family sometimes mistakenly identify Welsh as a "Gaelic language" rather than a Celtic language, even referring to it as "Welsh Gaelic."

2. The 2011 census results on language were not available at the time of writing, but they were scheduled to be released in October 2012.

3. SIL International (www.sil.org), formerly known as Summer Institute of Linguistics, is an evangelical Christian linguistics organization. Some linguists and indigenous peoples find their missionary activities and orientation offensive, although SIL has also made major contributions to language documentation and community language revitalization worldwide. SIL's *Ethnologue* publication is available online at www.ethnologue.com.

4. The designations "all" and "some" are based on the concept of ethnic groups as bounded and internally homogeneous, a point for which Fishman's RLS theory has been criticized. "All" users of a language will never be doing the same thing in a situation of language shift (or indeed in any other situation). Thus "all" and "some" should be interpreted not as quantifiable percentages of a population, but as the cultural-ideological positions "normatively" ("all" meaning either taken-for-grantedness or the explicit position that "all members of our group do this, or all members should") and "selectively, no-longer-normatively" ("some"). At the heart of language shift is this shift from the "old norm" of socializing children in one language, to the "new norm" of socializing children in another language. The question of what percentage of residents in a geographically bounded community or region makes this shift before it becomes the "new norm"—in other words, the demographic point of "tip"—is still open to investigation (Ó Giollagáin 2011). The point of tip is more likely located in the realm of ideological changes and accompanying shifts in behaviour by key individuals in various social networks (Mertz 1989).

5. Or more accurately, eastern Nova Scotia-wide.

6. I base this assessment on the efforts of a voluntary organization in 2011-2012 to run a weekly family-oriented Gaelic event in the Halifax area, and observation of other Gaelic events taking place 2010-2012 in different areas of Nova Scotia.

7. This was a non-random sample carried out in 1996 of individual Gaelic learners in Halifax and elsewhere, students in Gaelic courses at St. Francis Xavier University in Antigonish and University College of Cape Breton in Sydney, a Gaelic Day at St. Francis Xavier, a weekend immersion event in Margaree and the Gaelic festival Feis an Eilein in Christmas Island. Dembling was not allowed to survey adult summer students at the Gaelic College because the leadership at the time refused; they objected to the inclusion of questions about the Gaelic College on the survey (1997: 79).

References

Cosper, Ronald. 1998. Language in Nova Scotia. In *Language in Canada*, ed. John Edwards, 355-71. Cambridge: Cambridge University Press.

Dauenhauer, Nora Marks and Richard Dauenhauer. 1998. Technical, emotional, and ideological issues in reversing language shift: Examples from southeast Alaska. In *Endangered languages: Current issues and future prospects*, ed. Lenore A. Grenoble and Lindsey J. Whaley, 57-116. Cambridge: Cambridge University Press.

Dembling, Jonathan. 1991. Ged a Tha Mo Ghàidhlig Gann: Cape Breton's Vanishing Gàidhealtachd. BA thesis, Hampshire College.

———. 1997. Joe Jimmy Alec Visits the Gaelic Mod and Escapes Unscathed: The Nova Scotia Gaelic Revivals. MA thesis, Atlantic Canada Studies, Saint Mary's University.

———. 2006. Gaelic in Canada: new evidence from an old census. In *Cànan & Cultar/Language & Culture: Rannsachadh na Gàidhlig 3*, ed. Wilson McLeod, James Fraser and Anja Gunderloch, 203-14. Edinburgh: Dunedin Academic Press.

Dorian, Nancy C. 1980. Language Shift in Community and Individual: The Phenomenon of the Laggard Semi-Speaker. *International Journal of the Sociology of Language* 25:85-94.

———.1987. The value of language-maintenance efforts which are unlikely to succeed. International *Journal of the Sociology of Language* 1987 (68): 57-68.

Fettes, Mark. 1997. Stabilizing What? An Ecological Approach to Language Renewal. In *Teaching Indigenous Languages*, ed. Jon Reyhner, 301-18. Flagstaff, AZ: Northern Arizona University. http://jan.ucc.nau.edu/~jar/TIL_25.html (accessed 2 February 2012).

Fishman, Joshua A. 1991. *Reversing language shift: Theoretical and empirical foundations of assistance to threatened languages*. Clevedon: Multilingual Matters.

———. 2001. *Can Threatened Languages Be Saved? Reversing Language Shift Revisited: A 21st Century [sic] Perspective*. Clevedon: Multilingual Matters.

Gal, Susan. 1978. Peasant men can't get wives: Language change and sex roles in a bilingual community. *Language in Society* 7 (1): 1-16.

———. 1979. *Language shift: Social determinants of linguistic change in bilingual Austria*. New York: Academic Press.

Hinton, Leanne. 1997. Survival of Endangered Languages: The California Master-Apprentice Program. *The International Journal of the Sociology of Language* 123:177-91.

Hinton, Leanne, Matt Vera and Nancy Steele. 2002. *How to Keep Your Language Alive: A Commonsense Approach to One-on-One Language Learning*. Berkeley: Heyday.

Kennedy, Michael. 2002. *Gaelic Nova Scotia: An Economic, Cultural, and Social Impact Study*. Halifax: Nova Scotia Museum. http://museum.gov.ns.ca/site-museum/media/museum/Gaelic-Report(1).pdf (accessed 29 September 2012).

King, Kendall A. 2001. *Language Revitalization Processes and Prospects: Quichua in the Ecuadorian Andes*. Clevedon, U.K.: Multilingual Matters.

Kulick, Don. 1992. *Language shift and cultural reproduction: Socialization, self, and syncretism in a Papua New Guinean village*. London: Cambridge University Press.

Lewis, M. Paul and Gary F. Simons. 2010. Assessing Endangerment: Expanding Fishman's GIDS. *Revue Roumaine de Linguistique* 55 (2): 103-20. http://www.lingv.ro/resources/scm_images/RRL-02-2010-Lewis.pdf (accessed 5 June 2011).

McEwan-Fujita, Emily. 2010a. Ideologies and Experiences of Literacy in Interactions between Adult Gaelic Learners and First-Language Gaelic Speakers in Scotland. *Scottish Gaelic Studies* 26:87-114

———. 2010b. Ideology, Affect and Socialization in Language Shift and Revitalization: The Experiences of Adults Learning Gaelic in the Western Isles of Scotland. *Language in Society* 39 (1): 27–64.

———. 2010c. Sociolinguistic Ethnography of Gaelic Communities. In *The Edinburgh Companion to the Gaelic Language*, ed. Moray Watson and Michelle Macleod, 172-217. Edinburgh: Edinburgh University Press.

Mertz, Elizabeth. 1982. "No burden to carry": Cape Breton pragmatics and metapragmatics (Nova Scotia). PhD diss., Duke University.

———. 1989. Sociolinguistic creativity: Cape Breton Gaelic's linguistic "tip." In *Investigating obsolescence: Studies in language contraction and death*, ed. Nancy C. Dorian, 103-16. Cambridge: Cambridge University Press.

Ochs, Elinor. 1990. Indexicality and socialization. In *Cultural Psychology*, ed. James W. Stigler, Richard A. Shweder and Gilbert Herdt, 287-308. Cambridge: Cambridge University Press.

Ó Giollagáin, Conchúr. 2011. Irish in the Gaeltacht: Problems and Prospects. Keynote address at Maintaining and Revitalising Minority Languages in their "Heartlands" conference, Sabhal Mòr Ostaig, Scotland, September.

Spolsky, Bernard. 2009. Language beliefs and the management of endangered languages. Paper presented in the ELAP Workshop on Beliefs and Ideology in Endangered Languages, The Hans Rausing Endangered Languages Project, School for Oriental and African Studies, London, February.

Statistics Canada. 2007. Population by mother tongue, by province and territory (2006 Census): (Newfoundland and Labrador, Nova Scotia, Prince Edward Island). http://www.statcan.gc.ca/tables-tableaux/sum-som/l01/cst01/demo11a-eng.htm (accessed 1 June 2011).

Wenger, Etienne. 1998. *Communities of Practice: Learning, Meaning, and Identity*. Cambridge: Cambridge University Press.

———. 2006. Communities of Practice: A Brief Introduction. http://www.ewenger.com/theory/index.htm (accessed 11 November 2011).

Part III: Cultural Expression

Gearóid Ó hAllmhuráin

The Stranger's Land: Historical Traditions and Postmodern Temptations in the Celtic Soundscapes of North America

The academic study of Celtic music has come rather late to the ivy citadels of Celtic studies. Long consigned "below the salt" to the world of collectors, performers and dilettantes, inherited understandings of Celtic music have been epistemologically narrow, ontologically selective and generally divorced from mainstream historiographical research. It has barely registered a perfunctory blip on the raging radars of post-colonialism, post-structuralism and postmodernism of recent times. At academic conferences, it is deployed to create *atmosphere* when, to quote historian Martin Dowling, "the serious business of demythologizing, revision and deconstruction is done, [and] academics gather to gossip at receptions and dinners, buoyed by cheap wine and the reassuring ambience of Ireland's timeless music" (Dowling 2010: 146).

In a quirky stroke of wisdom, the English conductor, Thomas Beecham (1879-1961), once quipped that "the function of music is to release us from the tyranny of conscious thought" (Atkins and Newman 1978: 80). It seems to me that this is an appropriate point of departure for any critique of Celtic music, for any theoretical foray that might take us beyond Enya's synthetic keening, Loreena MacKennitt's perambulations through the mists of Avalon or, indeed, Celtic Woman touting their syrupy charms on public television. In removing us from the tyranny of conscious thought,

Beecham's paradigm has found an ideal specimen in Celtic music, a genre for which there are no clear definitions, no precise territorial markers, no detailed chronologies and few musicological taxonomies.

In a manner of speaking, Celtic music is an ethnomusicological chameleon, a sonic ragbag that contains everything from New Age mysticism to saccharine pop music (Quinn 2005: 23; Porter 1998: 205-24). The kaleidoscopic proliferation of Celtic music ensembles in all corners of the globe in recent years features born-again Celts, Anglo-Celts, Afro-Celts, Cuban Celts, Serbian Orthodox Celts, Elvis Celts, Russian-Celts, Sino-Celts and a more recent mobilization of Iberian Celts from Galicia and Asturia who have no linguistic connection to "real" Celts, although they share the same Y-chromosome as the Irish male (Sykes 2006: 162). In music, however, aesthetics are seldom curtailed by ethnic binaries, imagined or otherwise. Celtic music makers today are less interested in minding their Ps and Qs than expanding their own creative portfolios—hanging out with all sorts of contemporary musicians from rock and jazz to techno and trance (Mathieson 2001: 4). Our challenge, therefore, is to unravel the sonic palimpsest that is Celtic music, not least, the role played in this soundscape by Irish and Scottish music makers in North America. This unravelling requires that we first question some pre-existing assumptions about Celtic music in the Old World.

The prevailing wisdom that the six Celtic "nations"—Scotland, Ireland, Man, Cornwall, Brittany and Wales—contain the sonic residue of centuries of overland migration from a mysterious Indo-European or Bohemian homeland appears very much at odds with the prevailing body of musical evidence. Despite a sprinkle of archaeological artifacts (Halstatt lyres found in Hungary and bronze figures depicting naked Celtic dancers in Gallo-Roman France) and a few cursory observations by classical writers like Diodorus Siculus and Polybius, we know nothing about the sound of the music played by ancient Celts, its modes, transmission patterns or tonal features (Megaw 1991).

The historical record was all of 1,100 years into the Common Era before it yielded a single written account about the sound of Irish music, namely, from the pen of the Cambro-Norman cleric, Giraldus Cambrensis in the late 12th century. Given the oral-based maritime histories shared by insular Irish, Scots and other Oceanic Europeans for a millennium prior to arrival of ethnomusicologist Cambrensis, it is likely that the music they shared had as much in common with the music of Scandinavia and North Africa as it had with a select club of Iron Age Celts who fought a rear guard action from the Alps to the Atlantic in the centuries before the birth of Christ. The supposition that each of the Celtic nations shared a common soundscape seems equally spurious. Despite the romantic teleologies and imaginings of musicologists and music journalists, there is still very little common ground between the P-Celtic musics of Wales and Brittany and their Q-Celtic "cousins" in Scotland and Ireland. While recent pan-Celtic musical exchanges have opened up some melodic portals, vocal and linguistic barriers are still largely intact between the majority of P-Celtic and Q-Celtic performers. Yet, their diffuse worlds are shrouded in a romantic illusion of a single archaic Celtic soundscape.

Defining the Undefinable: The Musical Celt

The origin of this illusion is embedded in the ideological morphology of Celticism that first found its voice in the work of the Welsh polymath Edward Lluyd (1660-1709). Lluyd's *Archaeologia Britannica*, published in 1707, is regarded as the founding charter of Celtic studies (Davies 1999: 90). Inspired by Breton writer Paul-Yves Pezron (who sought to distinguish his countrymen from the French), Lluyd's *opus* was written in reaction to the British government's neglect of traditional Welsh culture and, more broadly, in response to new ideas spawned by the Enlightenment. He was succeeded by other Celtophiles in Scotland and Ireland throughout the 18th century: the former disturbed by the repression that followed the Jacobite Risings, the latter dismayed by the injustices of English rule in Penal Ireland (Davies 1999: 91). As the British imperial plan unfurled at home and abroad in the 18th century, it sparked various strains of cultural and political nationalism, most of which subscribed in some form or other to the radical heuristics of the Romantic movement.

Far from morphing into a simple *them* and *us* binary of colonialism and its dialectic opponent, nationalism, Irish Celticism and cultural nationalism developed into a murky ideological battleground in the 19th century, as Anglo-Irish Protestants (some of them evangelists in lamb's clothing), Presbyterian dissenters and Gaelic-speaking Catholics jostled each other to harvest Ireland's Celtic artifacts (if not convert their keepers) for nation and empire alike (Whelan 1998; Colley 1992; Chatterjee 1986). This enterprise was not just confined to the remote Celtic fringe. As the British Empire matured into the modern world's first information society, its insatiable thirst for data was served by legions of map makers, statisticians, linguists and clerks scattered across the globe from Bangor to Bombay, from Inverness to Invercargill (Richards 1993). Some of the most celebrated Celtic scholars of the 19th century (hagiography specialist, Whitley Stokes, for example) acquired their first taste of antiquarian fieldwork as colonial servants of the queen. Reappraising the chemistry of Celtic revivalism in Ireland and Scotland during this period, Dutch historian Joep Leerssen noted that

> The period 1760-1845 witnesses a crucial transformation in Irish culture in that the native Gaelic tradition, with pre-modern

attitudes, with its historical vision leading back to Ireland's primal Milesian settlement, with its catastrophic interpretation of history and its Messianic hopes for a deliverance from English rule, is interiorized by a modernizing, urban-centered, English-speaking and essentially Victorian Ireland. A similar process took place in Scotland, with the establishment of Highland Societies and the canonization of kilt, clans and bagpipes; but what in Scotland remained a cultural *couleur locale* within the imperial context was in Ireland a total political reinvention, a collective psychological de-anglicization. (2002: 24)

Music harvesting too became a key feature of Celtic revivalism. The Welsh harper Edward Jones published his *Musical and Poetical Relicks of the Welsh Bards* in 1784. His example was followed in Ireland by Joseph Cooper Walker whose *Historical Memoirs of the Irish Bards* appeared in 1786, and Charlotte Brooke who published her *Reliques of Irish Poetry* in 1789. They were followed by nineteen-year-old Edward Bunting who transcribed the last remnants of the "ancient music of Ireland" at the Belfast Harp Festival in July 1792. Other music collectors and antiquarians came to the fore in the years leading up the Great Irish Famine in the 1840s, most notably George Petrie, James Goodman and James Hardiman. By then, the published collections from Scotland's "Golden Age of Fiddling"—especially those of Neil and Nathaniel Gow and William Marshall—had reached new audiences far beyond the Highlands of Scotland.

While music makers continued to perform and composers continued to publish, ideologues embroiled in the colonial debate continued to make tactical use of musical discourse, not least, in their romantic safaris in search of the Celt. For the English cultural critic Matthew Arnold, the Celt was "always ready to react against the despotism of fact" (Arnold 1900: 82). The Celt supposedly had an advanced cultural sensibility but was quite incapable of functioning in the real world. Yet, Arnold's self-appointed task was to co-opt Britain's marginal Celts into a peaceful political arrangement with the archipelago's dominant power. In a series of lectures delivered in 1867 and 1891, he attempted to "flatter the Scots, Welsh and Irish into acquiescence, proposing that they were delightful people possessed of qualities without which the British imperial project could not advance" (Smyth 2009: 85). One of the most enduring ideas to emerge from Arnold's stereotypical schema was that of the musical Celt, whose function was to provide light relief from the rigours of the real world, or, as historian Gerry Smyth has suggested, "to entertain the English after a hard day at the empire" (Smyth 2009: 86).

The obsession of defining the music of the Celts triggered a cacophony of romantic dross throughout the 19th century. French philosopher Ernest

Renan penned this requiem in 1859. Clearly, there was no sadness like the dour musical sadness of the Celt:

> Its history is itself only one long lament.... Its songs of joy end as elegies; there is nothing to equal the delicious sadness of its national melodies. Never have men feasted so long upon these solitary delights of the spirit, these poetic memories, which simultaneously intercross all the sensations of life, so vague, so deep, so penetrative, that one might die from them, without being able to say whether it was from bitterness or sweetness. (Storey 1988: 57)

A century and a half later, the enigma of Celtic music still defies the tyranny of conscious thought, or so it seems. Posing the question: "What is Celtic Music?" in her *Complete Guide to Celtic Music: From the Highland Bagpipe and Riverdance to U2 and Enya*, June Skinner Sawyers proffers the following *je ne sais pas quoi*:

> When all the techniques are checked off, the element that the music of the Celtic lands most commonly shares is something a lot more intangible and certainly less quantifiable – a feeling or quality that evokes emotions of sadness or joy, sorrow or delight. Some of Celtic music's qualities, it is true, derive from the modal scales of traditional music, but others are hard to pin down. All share, for want of a better word, a Celtic spirit, a unique bond with one another that transcends time, distance, and political units. (2000: 5)

While not exactly removed from the rose-coloured spectacles of Arnold and Renan, Sawyers's mysterious "something" animates an entire world view of Celtic music, in the Celtic outposts of the Old World, as much as in Celtic diasporic communities in North America and, indeed, among millions of want-to-be, vicarious and virtual Celts, who embellish their candlelight dinners, voicemail and jacuzzis with Celtic music. Much as it grates against the grain of academic criticism, Celtic music appears to be defined by the undefinable, by a transhistorical "something," a "feeling," a "spirit," which has arbitrarily infused an entire soundscape. This oblique therapeutic synergy is the calling card of the Celtic music industry today. Just as Matthew Arnold recruited the Celt "to consolidate late Victorian British identity, so the modern phenomenon of Celtic music performs specific ideological tasks within a global popular market" (Smyth 2009: 87). As Smyth suggests,

> "Celtic music" represents a lucrative niche market in which certain unique experiences are offered to those willing to invest—emotion-

ally, certainly, but also financially—in the notion of some inherent Celtic spirituality which is supposedly non-compliant towards the modern world. (2009: 87)

Where then do we place the music makers—the enablers and tradition bearers—and, in particular, Celtic music makers in North America, in this process? A perusal of Irish and Scottish history would undoubtedly shed light on the diaspora that brought this music to the "New World" and, in the process, underline the importance of sanctuaries like Cape Breton, San Francisco, Glengarry and South Boston. Uncovering these inner worlds, or *gameinschaften*, in isolation, however, will not explain the complex chemistry of Irish and Scottish music in North America. They need to be contextualized within the mainframe of a much broader musical *gessellschaft*, to use Tönnies's term, with its legions of media moguls, music industry handlers, festival brokers and overlords who have a direct stake in the health and longevity of these communities. Any consideration of Irish and Scottish music in North America must critique the brittle interface between these two worlds, and the confluence of global currents that bring them together and keep them apart.

Unwrapping the Diasporic Celt: Irish and Scottish Music in the "New World"

The distillation of Irish, Scottish, Welsh and indeed Breton, Manx and Cornish diasporas into one Celtic master narrative in the Americas is, in many respects, a futile exercise in historiographical teleology. The Celtic diaspora is intensely diffuse and is characterized by multiple layers of cultural hybridity and transculturation. Above all, the experiences of its so-called source nations in exile differ radically from each other. The diasporic experience of Welsh-speaking Patagonians in the 20th century was very different from Irish-speaking slaves sent to the Caribbean in the 17th century. Scots-Irish Presbyterians who settled in the foothills of the Appalachians in the late 1700s lived in a very different cultural milieu from the yuppie cyber world inhabited by Irish software engineers in Silicon Valley in the 1990s. The Lowland Scot Andrew Carnegie ate from a very different table than fiddler Dan R. MacDonald in Mabou, Cape Breton. Yet, they all lay claim to a piece of Celtic tartan in exile. Long before Celtic scholars, genealogists and marketing gurus ushered them all into a universal church of latter-day Celts, Highlanders fleeing the Clearances and famine and Irish fleeing hunger saw themselves first as *Mùideartaich* (Moidart men), *muintir Chonamara* (people of Conamara) or exiles from whatever townland or *clachán* dispatched them to the emigrant ship. That they might be Celts from a long lost Shangri-La of warrior ancestors and obscure pronouns mattered less than their ability to survive in the New

World. What is significant, however, is that these disparate Highland and Lowland Scots, Gaelic and Anglophone Irish, and Scots-Irish spawned several heteroglossic soundscapes that contributed to virtually every genre of mainstream music in North America during the past two centuries (Mathieson 2001: 5).

While sharing some ethnic traits, these soundscapes had no exclusive genesis before coming to the New World. That said, it should be remembered that music is a nomadic art that spans time and space easily. Prior to crossing the Atlantic in the mid-18th century, for example, both Irish and Scottish soundscapes showed signs of "other" musical residue. By then, Italian violins and cellos had made their way to both countries, augmenting indigenous instruments like pipes and harps. Discarded French flutes and German concertinas would flow into Ireland a century later and would, in turn, be transported by emigrants to the New World. If Gaelic songs, *pìobaireachd* and fiddle tunes were the mainstay of Scottish music and *sean nós* and piping the sonic stables in Ireland, these "core" elements were augmented by a *bricolage* of Baroque tunes, English hornpipes and ballads, Bohemian polkas, French galops and Polish mazurkas that were "indigenized" by Irish and Scottish performers throughout the 18th century. Vernacular dances from the high art salons and courts of Europe were also grafted onto Irish and Scottish repertoires, especially in the *sattelzeit* period from 1760-1840, which saw the demise of the *ancien régime* and the emergence of the post-Napoleonic nation-state. Both Ireland and Scotland had nations-in-waiting on the European mainland in the 18th century, which explains, to some degree, the intense traffic of Irish and Scottish dancing masters travelling back and forth to the mainland before the 1840s. The transition from minuet to quadrille dancing, for example, had a profound impact on dance music in both countries during this intense period of cultural transformation (Raviart 1990: 53-70; Szwed and Marks 1988: 29-36; De Garmo 1875).[1]

How then can we unwrap these soundscapes and track their diffusion in the New World? For an ethnomusicologist, it would seem convenient to adapt an ethnomusicological approach. After all, there is a century of fieldwork and theoretical riches to draw on, from evolutionism and functionalism to phenomenology and postmodernism. The rhizomorphic girth of Scottish and Irish music in North America, however, calls for something more comprehensive, a periodic table of elements that embodies the historical past and the contemporary present, the traditional *gameinschaft* and the global *gessellschaft*, in short, a framework that interrogates the local, translocal and transnational in a soundscape that oscillates across a broad spectrum of living traditions.

To do this, I will refer to a model developed by Indian anthropologist, Arjun Appadurai, whose research on global cultural flows offers a vista of new perspectives on historical as well as contemporary cultural change. Eschewing oppositional tropes like *centres* and *peripheries*, *tradition* and *modernity*, Appadurai critiques the lives that people live in the context of a world that is becoming increasingly deterritorialized. Rationalizing the breakdown of old master narratives fuelled by the Enlightenment (rationalism, evolution, the nation-state), his thesis challenges the simplistic binary between homogenization and heterogenization (Appadurai 1996: 33). To explore these disjunctures, he devised five conceptual lenses to explore cultural flows: *ethnoscapes, ideoscapes, mediascapes, technoscapes* and *financescapes*. These are not objectively weighted concepts as much as constructs inflected by historical, linguistic and political scenarios orchestrated by different actors: nation-states, transnational companies, diasporic communities, subnational groups and movements (Appadurai 1996: 33). Given the global cultural flows that impact Irish and Scottish soundscapes in North America today, it is instructive to view them through Appadurai's panoptic model. As well as bringing multiple perspectives to bear on a subject that is often critiqued in contextual isolation, it will also allow sufficient latitude to peruse the complex transatlantic relationship between these diasporic soundscapes and their former homelands in Ireland and Scotland.

(i) Ethnoscapes

Appadurai defines an ethnoscape as a shifting cartography of farmers, industrial workers, immigrants, refugees, civil servants, teachers, tourists, etc., who people the world in which we live. He underlines the importance of movement and stability as prime factors in all ethnoscapes, opposite sides of the same coin, so to speak. The dual paradigm of movement and stability is particularly evident in the diasporic histories of Ireland and Scotland. Perched on the edge of the "Old World" in the 17th century, both countries were on the edge of the "New World" a century after. The globalization of cod, tobacco, cotton and spice combined with the scramble for New World colonies by Old World powers had radically altered the older alchemies of the Atlantic.

Among the masses of soldiers, crofters, servants and missionaries dispatched across the Atlantic by war, colonization and new markets were Highland and Lowland Scots, Gaelic Irish, Scots-Irish and a cohort of Anglo-Irish. Settling in an arc from Newfoundland to the Carolinas and inland along the Appalachian spine, these diasporic communities were marked by a constant interplay of mobility and stability after settling in the New World. In so far as one can make broad delineations in settlement history, it seems that the Irish who fled to America in the wake of the Great Famine were unique in abandoning their rural lifestyles to live in cities along the industrial corridor from Boston to Baltimore and, later, in the upper midwest. In contrast, Highland Scots dispatched to the New World by the Clearances generally settled in rural communities in Atlantic Canada, Québec and Ontario. Similar rural-urban contrasts do not mark the histories of the Scots-Irish in Kentucky and Tennessee, nor the Irish who settled in the outports of Newfoundland in the 18th century. What does distinguish all of these communities, however, is a history of out-migration to other parts of the U.S. and Canada, a practice that has continued in varying degrees to the present day, resulting in hybridity, transculturation and ethnic fade across the entire Celtic spectrum in the continent.

In contrast to the macro effects of ethnic fade, geographic isolation has often been a key factor in preserving older musical traditions—assuming geographically isolated communities are capable of sustaining viable economies. Situated in a liminal space between two former colonial projects, Cape Breton has had a perplexed sense of its own isolation, animated by a volatile industrial culture and a history of out-migration from the island. Yet, this "isolated" place has maintained one of the most enduring Scottish soundscapes in North America. There are multiple reasons for this, some of which will become clear in Appadurai's other parameters. From the perspective of Cape Breton's indigenous ethnoscape, its music, song and dance were embedded in an unbroken Highland world that was transported across the Atlantic and buttressed until recent times by a Gaelic-speaking *gameinschaft*. Its music makers were also willing to share their traditions with neighbouring communities of Mi'kmaw, Acadian, Irish, English, American and African descent. Despite the decline of Gaelic and the deracination that comes with language loss, the island's web of extended musical families indigenized a lot of musical change that came from without and compensated for the effects of out-migration by passing on its dance music to successor generations of younger performers. Similarly, local folk composers continue to flourish in Cape Breton.

Ironically, Irish Gaelic song in the U.S. has not fared as well as its Gàidhlig cohort north of the border. Although Irish-speaking immigrants from Conamara huddle together in south Boston and north Chicago to listen to *sean nós* songs sung by their ancestors, the language of their music is seldom sustained by their American-born offspring. Irish Gaelic, in word or song, has not been a survivor in the New World, at least, in urban America where the Irish have had a history of rapid integration. Short of being a classroom curiosity, or an academic commodity, Irish continues to die with the immigrants who bring it to America. With the exception of isolated communities in the Beauce and in Pontiac counties in rural Québec, where Irish survived as a vernacular until the 1950s, its longevity as a carrier of music in Canada has not been impressive either.

Irish dance music in America has had a radically different destiny, as has Irish step dancing. The success and longevity of Irish dance music in America are largely attributed to the ability of its hereditary keepers to adapt quickly to changing circumstances in their new urban world and their capacity to reach out to new audiences and performers. In its history of perpetual motion since the mid-19th century, Irish dance music burst its ethnic banks very quickly in America and climbed the ladder from the shanty and the street corner to fandango houses, minstrel shows, vaudeville and, eventually, Hollywood. Many Irish musicians left Ireland as anonymous "musicianers" and finished their lives as professional celebrities in America, even those who followed their bedraggled patrons after the famine of the 1840s. *Uilleann* piper William Connolly was a classic case in point. Born in Miltown, Co. Galway in 1839, Connolly played the professional circuit in the U.S. in the 1850s before crossing the Canadian border to play on steam packets playing the St. Lawrence. At one stage before the end of his life, he paid a visit back home to Ireland. On arriving at the edge of the village of Miltown where he was born, he hailed a young lad and paid him to walk in front of him through the village carrying his pipes. He wanted his old neighbours to see how well he had done for himself in America (O'Neill 1913: 226).

While isolated enclaves of Scots-Irish music in the Appalachians, the Ozarks and Texas spawned the high lonesome sound of bluegrass, old-time and Texas swing, equally isolated enclaves of Irish music in Newfoundland, New Brunswick, the Ottawa Valley and Québec have sustained and renewed themselves for two centuries after arriving in the New World. The rhizomorphic nature of these soundscapes dispersed music, song and dance across multiple social, sectarian and ethnic milieux and, in the process, exposed repertoires that were once isolated and exclusive to new music makers, performance settings and modes of transmission. A similar disposition marks Irish music scenes in modern urban settings in the U.S. and Canada. Even since German-American John J. Kimmel (1866-1942) recorded the first Irish dance music to be put on disc in America in the 1920s, non-Irish performers have been a vibrant, if unacknowledged, part of the Irish American musical ethnoscape. This transcultural milieu has an eclectic caste of global villagers: Asian American fiddlers like Dana Lyn and Tina Leck, Jewish American bodhrán player Myron Bretholz, Greek American and Mexican American dancers Miriam Adrianowich and Samuel Satuyo, African American bassist John Goodman, Canadian Austrian guitarist Reinhard Goerner, Canadian Polish dancer Nathan Polanski, as well as Franco Ontarian, Athapaskan, Cree and Métis fiddlers, Québécois *gigeurs* and Irish exiles who apparently speak with an accent.

(ii) Ideoscapes

Appadurai defines ideoscapes as "concatenations of images" (1996: 36). Frequently political, they can relate to the ideologies of states and the counter-ideologies of movements "explicitly oriented to capturing state power or a piece of it" (1996: 36). Euro-American master narratives derived from the Enlightenment yielded a formidable crop of these ideas, terms and images—popular concepts of freedom, civil rights, social welfare, sovereignty, representation and that most controversial ideoscape: democracy. Music has acted on behalf of ideologies for centuries, especially nationalism that manifests itself across a vast geopolitical spectrum from legal patriotism to illegal terrorism. Couched beneath the rambling contours of cultural nationalism, for example, are sacrosanct codes about musical identity and authenticity, rights and ownership and that most troubling of sins to cultural nationalists: musical change and how to broker it.

Irish and Scottish music in North America have not been spared these forces. Thomas Moore, for example, brought Irish romantic nationalism to America with his airs and songs in the early 1800s. Described as a "musical snuff box" by the poet William Hazlitt, Moore's melodies still occupy pride of place on the piano stand in thousands of Irish American homes today (Ó hAllmhuráin 1999). Throughout the 19th and 20th centuries, formal ideas of Irishness and Scottish were reinforced all over North America by the Gaelic League, Highland Societies, Comhaltas Ceoltóirí Éireann, An Comunn Gàidhealach, The Royal National Mòd and An Coimisiún le Rincí Gaelacha. In marking out their musical turf in exile, they copper fastened notions of what was "authentic" Irish or "authentic" Scottish music with a great deal of nationalist pride and an occasional relapse into nationalist xenophobia. Irish tunes played in Scottish competitions, or Scottish tunes played in Irish competitions can still ruffle the feathers of official game-keepers today.[2]

While the communal prosaic of the marketplace determines the external aesthetics of Celtic music, much of the internal aesthetics of Irish and Scottish music and dance in North America is driven by competitive norms prescribed in the Old World and exported across the Atlantic. These are based on a pyramid system of set standards that are designed to weed out the majority of players (who fail to measure up) and make Grand Masters and World Champions of a small cohort. Nowhere is this exercise in skewed cultural preservation more evident than in competitive Irish step dancing, which underwent major globalization in the wake of *Riverdance*. This expensive cultural "sport" is governed in the U.S. and Canada by the powerful North American Feis Commission who dispatch thousands of kids to the World Irish Dancing Championship every year where they compete against children from Europe and Australasia. Decked out like little divas, children compete in an arena where every single detail of their performance is rigidly codified, from their triple batter down to the cosmetic minutiae of wigs, eye shadow and fake tans. The transformation from old quadrille sets danced in the kitchens of rural Ireland to the glitter of a Vegas-style extravaganza has added much more than mere colour to the ideoscape of Irish dancing.

Informal hierarchies of instruments also prevail in Irish and Scottish music scenes. Ask any bodhrán player found guilty of breaking and entering a "quiet session" of Irish music without an invitation. Guitar players too are suspect. Once decried as purveyors of "jungle music" by diehard nationalists, they are still "barred" from Irish *céilí* band competitions, be it in New York or Rosmuc. Ironically, the buzouki, which arrived in Ireland from the Balkans in the 1960s, has fared much better in the ideoscape of Irish music, its seedy Arabesque origins in the brothels of Istanbul having managed to elude the gatekeepers of Irish musical purity (Stokes 1992).

After enduring jazz in the 1930s, and the British and American folk revivals in the 1950s and 1960s, Irish traditional music experienced a series of recurring identity crises in the 1970s and 1980s, as new genres stormed the battlements and the alchemy of globalization focused new attention on the dischord between culture and economics. In the 1990s, Irish musicians on both sides of the Atlantic underwent a musical inquisition in which the binary aesthetics of tradition and innovation were pitted against each other in an effort to make sense of the cultural challenges thrown up by the Celtic Tiger (Vallely et al. 1999). Now that the said beast has been deprived of its claws, Irish social discourse is focusing on the tribulations of a fiscally tattered nation whose music makers are again taking flight to foreign shores.

(iii) Mediascapes

In Appadurai's coda, mediascapes refer to the capacities of private and public interests to select, produce and disseminate information and the resulting images of the world created by these media. Mediascapes are elementary forces in all music environments in that they influence internal transmission and preservation, as well as external dissemination. Like other ethnic genres in the Old World, Irish and Scottish music were oral arts sourced historically in a common Gaelic culture that stretched from Cape Clear in the southwest of Ireland to the northern tip of Lewis. Both soundscapes arrived in the New World carrying their oral repertoires with them. Their engagement with New World mediascapes, however, shifted their music into a radically new matrix. Sedentary Scottish and Irish communities in rural Canada and in rural parts of the U.S. maintained oral traditions much longer than their homologues who settled in rapidly changing urban environments. Both soundscapes were also marked by different degrees of musical literacy. Scotland's Golden Age of published fiddle music coincided with the early Clearances from the Highlands. Hence, many immigrants arrived bearing the published collections of Neil and Nathaniel Gow and William Marshall with them. Others arrived having learned the rudiments of musical literacy as pipers and drummers with Highland regiments in the British army. The Scots continued to nurture a tradition of musical literacy in exile. In Atlantic Canada, for example, local folk composers showed a formidable grasp of musical literacy, composing tunes in a range of keys, styles and tempos. Their compositions continue to find their way into print media today.

The Irish and Scots-Irish, on the other hand, brought very little musical literacy with them. Marginalized by what Benedict Anderson termed "the age of print capitalism," in particular, by commercial music publishers in metropolitan hubs like New York and Chicago, the majority of Irish musicians in the New World had no means of recording or preserving their own music in print (Anderson 1983). What little we know of their early dance music and song is gleaned from popular lyrics and music scores issued by Tin Pan Alley and consumed by piano-playing upper and middle classes in urban America (Williams 1996). In 1882, however, New England collector, William Bradbury Ryan and his mentor, Elias Howe, published *Ryan's Mammoth Collection* in Boston. This single volume is one of the most important repositories of 19th-century American music (Sky 1995: 14). It contains music created by singers, dancers and blackface minstrels, much of which would develop into country music, blues and ragtime by the early 20th century. It also contains instructions for contemporary social dances like the lancers, gallops and walk-arounds, many of which were cognates of quadrille sets taught by dancing masters in Ireland and Scotland. Much of Ryan's work was liberally incorporated into Captain Francis O'Neill's *Music of Ireland*, published in Chicago in 1903. This latter volume was so highly regarded by Irish performers that it was referred to as "the bible," or "the book" until recently, thus excluding all other collections before or since.

This print mediascape changed radically, however, after Thomas Edison invented sound recording in 1877 and the first ethnographic recordings of music were made at the World's Columbian Exposition in Chicago in 1893. Music now entered what Nicholas Carolan has termed its Second Age, during which

> the link between performance and the old lived reality was broken. Now it became possible to put a musician in a box, to listen to the dead, to make the piper on the record play the tune over and over and over, quickly or slowly – and now, he played it exactly the same every time. Space had been abolished along with death, time and human interaction. (Carolan 2006: 138; Bohlman 2002: 148)

By the end of the 1890s, Irish musicians in the U.S. had joined the technology nexus and were recording their own music on wax cylinders, among them, celebrated vaudevillian piper, Patsy Touhey (Carolan 1997: 37). It was only a matter of time before Scottish performers followed suit, first, in industrial hubs like Detroit and the "Boston states" that had vibrant enclaves of Cape Breton fiddlers and, later, in settings closer to the source of their tradition in Atlantic Canada.

Irish and Scottish soundscapes underwent other pivotal swings with the arrival of radio in the 1930s and television in the 1950s. While propagating new stars and styles (particularly along the Appalachian chain in the U.S. and Canada, where Nashville became the new mecca), these new mediascapes led to an increased privatization of leisure, as families gathered around radios and TVs to enjoy the passive modern entertainment of Don Messer and Ed Sullivan. Adaptations of these media continued to impact Irish and Scottish performers in North America until cyberspace and the Internet projected them into a brave new virtual world in the 1990s. During the past two decades, musical borders have continued to collapse and the lines between fictional and realistic landscapes have been blurred irrevocably by a hyper chemistry of print, celluloid and electronic media. In the resulting fetish of Hollywood emporiums, Irish and Scottish music have aided and abated a fantasy world of tartan superheroes, Celtic dance lords and leprechaun ninjas, just as much as they have functioned as portals into diasporic worlds in the past.

(iv) Technoscapes

Appadurai's technoscapes are ever-changing global networks of mechanical and informational technologies. From musical instruments to iPods, humanly generated tunes to iTunes, technoscapes are breaching all kinds of previously impervious musical boundaries (Appadurai 1996: 34). The history of Irish and Scottish musical technoscapes in the New World runs the gamut from the most rudimentary instruments like Jews' harps, fiddles and tin whistles to the most sophisticated audio-visual studio equipment today. While Highland and uilleann pipe makers flourished in the New World, their instruments were often pitched to a very select clientele. In the U.S., uilleann pipes (especially, concert pitch sets developed in Philadelphia by the Taylor brothers in the 1890s) were expensive and, hence, beyond the means of the vast majority of performers. Fiddles, flutes, accordions and even pianos were far more accessible, especially in the Irish soundscape. In the Scottish milieu, the fiddle enjoyed major prominence, followed by Highland pipes, small pipes, church harmoniums and, later, by guitars and pianos that were distributed across North America via ubiquitous Sears-Roebuck mail order networks.

With the age of recorded sound came wax cylinders, Victrola gramophones, 78 rpm flat discs, 45 rpms, LPs, magnetic tape recorders, cassette machines and the Walkman, the quintessential music accessory of the 1980s. The transition from analog to digital code radically altered the range of recording and editing possibilities and brought an unprecedented level of pristine quality to music that previously languished beneath the hiss of crackling needles and ruffled tape. Digital recording also created an obsession with mechanical correction (the sonic "cut and paste") that Celtic musicians and engineers have become so adept at, with the result that modern Celtic recordings, like those of other contemporary genres, have became sterile and "dirtless."

The availability of cutting-edge technology, however, has not made for easy coexistence between music makers, technology owners and market moguls. Accessing a marketplace where 650 million CDs a year were sold (in the period 2000-2005 before MP3s and iTunes caused another seismic swing in the market pendulum) has been a herculean challenge for Irish and Scottish musicians. As Irish sociologist Kieran Allen remarked:

> Music has become an industry dominated by a handful of corporations who hamper access to new forms of creativity. Five companies – Warner Music, EMI Group, Universal Music Group, Bertelsmann Music Group and Sony – have taken over vertical and horizontal control of almost every aspect of the industry. They control virtually every known label, 80 percent of all titles produced in the US and comparable percentages elsewhere, most of the major distribution companies, and much of copyrighted music. Real existing capitalism – as distinct from the propagandistic fantasies about a "free" market – leads to the creation of great oligopolies. (2005: 4)

While a tiny minority of Irish and Scottish musicians have been fortunate to make it through one of the five pearly gates, others circumnavigate the road block by creating independent labels. This trend became widespread in the U.S. and Canada in the 1990s, especially in Cape Breton, Newfoundland, Québec and California.

(v) Financescapes

Financescapes, the final concept in Appadurai's coda, are fiscal flows that pass through a vast nexus of currency markets and trading forums around the world. Financescapes have cast a long shadow on the history of Irish music in America. The journey across the Atlantic for many Irish musicians marked a fiscal crossing of the Rubicon, from a traditional rural world of free communal house dances to the cash economy of variety theatre, vaudeville circuits and the "take it or leave it" world of record companies, where every man took care of himself. Few, if any, of the Irish-born players who recorded during the Golden Age of Irish Music in America in the 1920s were equipped to deal legally or fiscally with the bevy of companies who put them on disc. Lump sums "paid up front" were generally chosen over royalties by most musicians who recorded—even stars like Michael Coleman, James Morrison and Paddy Killoran, all three immigrants from Co. Sligo on the northwest coast of Ireland. In New York, they were glad to find work recording music and seldom considered the long-term royalties they might accrue from their records that are still selling today, almost a century after they were first recorded.

Royalty and copyright ethics continue to raise eyebrows among Irish and Scottish music makers. Mired in a limbo between a "free-for-all" public domain and a legally-protected private domain, most Irish and Scottish musicians in North America are men and women of no musical property, at least no musical property in the eyes of the law. Apart from sporadic compositional or mechanical rights, they have little or no legal control over the common musical heritage, or *patrimoine*, they share with thousands of their cohorts. In the absence of adequate folk copyright law, virtually no royalty or copyright returns are paid to collective music communities whose heritage is expropriated by "big name" stars, or music industry moguls. Warnings about cultural property violations raised by international forums like UNESCO and the World Intellectual Property Organization are consistently ignored by big business. Hence, musical plunder continues unhindered, not least in the vast viscous world of Celtic music.

After numerous folk revivals, media swings and bouts of pan-Celtic resuscitation, the financescape of Irish and Scottish musicians in North America today looks very different from that of their predecessors two centuries ago. Despite the monopolies and oligopolies of the recording industry, Irish and Scottish super stars and groups working professionally in the U.S. and Canada have access to a menagerie of competing music festivals, from Cape Breton's Celtic Colours that showcases music in small community halls to Milwaukee's mammoth green circus where kitsch knows no shame. Their portfolios also brim with Grammy, Academy and Juno awards, all of which add to their competitive edge in the marketplace. Their professional circuits are also governed by the whims of the tourist industry, as "trad music" is now a key asset in the promotion of roots tourism—from tartanism to shamroguery—at both ends of the diasporic curve (Kaul 2009; Basu 2007). While financescapes impact all sorts of Celtic performers from stars whose careers "max out" after ten years to anonymous session players who are nonchalant about making big fortunes, its synergy reached epic heights in recent years in the dance extravaganza and the global surge of Irish pubs that are now new temples of the Celtic soundscape.

The *crème de la crème* of success in the Celtic music industry in North America is the dance extravaganza *Riverdance* and its spinoffs, Michael Flatley's *Lord of the Dance*, *Feet of Flames* and *Celtic Tiger*. Since it began touring in 1995, *Riverdance* has grossed over £1 billion, (€1.25 billion, or $1.94 billion Canadian). With three shows touring, by 2008 it had been staged on four continents, in 32 countries, at 280 venues; performed more than 9,000 times; and seen by almost twenty million people (Ó Cinnéide 2000, 2002; Yoshida 2008).[3] While shows like *Riverdance* and *Lord of the Dance* create a synthesis between tradition and innovation and enable dancers to foster creativity, there is also a school of thought among traditional performers that is perturbed by the ideological impact of chief priests like

Michael Flatley who rationalize their success with invidious quips like "nothing exceeds like excess" (O'Connor 2003: 122-41). Such ostentatious individualism fits poorly within the philosophy of a soundscape that has traditionally been communal and inclusive.

Celtic music is also central to the commercial invention known as "the Irish pub," where it functions largely as sonic wallpaper, or "aural carpet," as musician and producer Tony MacMahon more cuttingly describes it (MacMahon 1999: 112-20). Modelling their products on architectural styles drawn from Ireland's eight thousand old-style pubs, several companies are now exporting Irish pubs all over the world. The Irish theme bar, or "pub-in-a-box" is a thriving global industry. In the past decade, more than 1,600 have opened for business in cities from Berlin to Beijing. Working in tandem with Guinness, the Dublin-based Irish Pub Company describes itself as the largest supplier of Irish pubs in the world. Its catalogue includes options to suit every nostalgic taste, from small country cottage pubs to the classic wood and glass pubs of Victorian Dublin. These boxed sets come complete with Irish-born bar staff with real "brogues," kitsch furniture, Irish musicians (of various pedigrees and degrees of proficiency) and tailor-made training courses in "the craic" (the Irish art of fun and conviviality) that act as an introduction to Ireland for drinkers unfamiliar with the island, or its social idiosyncrasies. Hence, music has become a form of what Fintan Vallely calls "Gucci-Paddy kitsch," highlighting the Irish pub as a magnet for tourists and a major source of revenue for Irish drink companies throughout the world (McGovern 2003: 83-103).

Conclusion

Before closing, I should like to stress again that this paper was intended as a panoptic critique of two Celtic music diasporas in North America, rather than a detailed travelogue through them. In drawing on cultural flow theory, I have attempted to chart the complex coordinates of the Irish and Scottish soundscapes in North America within a macro historical and contemporary global context. What is abundantly clear in this transdisciplinary synthesis is that both soundscapes shaped and were shaped by vast flows of musical currents in and out of the New World for centuries: from the initial expulsion of unwanted Celts from the Old World to the recent co-option of Celtic music by neo-liberal myth makers and "world music" industry moguls.

Despite this ubiquitous profile, the academic role of Celtic music in the New World still remains dubious and selective. While independent schools and institutions from Cape Breton to California undertake exemplary work teaching and preserving Celtic music, it is untenable that this soundscape receives so little attention from the upper echelons of Celtic scholarship in North America. Buried beneath a hubris of staid text-based epistemologies, Celtic studies in the U.S. and Canada has taken its research and pedagogical cues largely from its Old World homologues. This genre of old school research has already felt the ire of forward-looking scholars in Europe and North America. In his 1977 exegesis of text-based historiography, French historian Jacques Attali, for example, noted that "for twenty-five centuries, Western knowledge has tried to look upon the world. It has failed to understand that the world is not for the beholding. It is for the hearing. It is not legible but audible" (Attali 1985 [1977]: 1).[4] For Attali, music is not simply a unidimensional reflection of any given culture, but a harbinger of change, a metaphor for a broad historical and cultural vanguardism. Anthropologists, cultural geographers and ethnomusicologists like Keith Basso, Yi-Fu Tuan and Martin Stokes have echoed Attali in their criticism of vision-based scholarship and have called for consideration of the other senses in exploring the cultural patterning of perception.

Regrettably, as a crucible of cultural memory (real, imagined or forgotten), Celtic music in the New World has been consigned to what Jacques Le Goff termed an "indefinable residue of historical analysis" (Le Goff 1974: 77-79). This is hardly surprising given the stark statistics of formal Celtic scholarship in North America. In a continent that boasts over seventy million people of Celtic ancestry , there are fewer than twenty-five chairs of Irish, Scottish and Celtic studies in the U.S. and Canada. Of these, fewer than ten offer courses in Celtic music or ethnomusicology. In the quest to educate the Celts of North America, it is clear that the "score" between Harvard and Hollywood is a very uneven one indeed. Today, most North American Celts learn more about themselves, their history and their music from Mel Gibson, Sting, *Riverdance* and the Irish pub-in-a-box than they do from Celtic scholars labouring away over the annals of the past. The Irish proverb *An t-iomárd ná feictear, is é is mó a ghoilleann* (the affliction that is unseen is the one that hurts most) seems to add disturbing weight to the truth of this paradox.

As a nomadic and polysemic art that has consistently travelled ahead of written perceptions of the past, Irish and Scottish music is inscribed in what Pierre Nora terms *lieux de mémoire* (places of memory) on both sides of the Atlantic (Nora 1989: 7-24). In excavating these sonic footprints, it is time to re-centre the trajectory of Celtic music diaspora to North America within the mainframe of broader cultural flows that changed the ethno-histories of the Atlantic since 1492. A critical point of departure in this remit requires scholars to emerge from the cocoon of a unidirectional music diaspora. This antiquated binary has blinded scholars to the abundance of the cultural traffic that has crossed the Atlantic in reverse to the Old World in the past two centuries: from Dan Emmet's *Virginia Minstrels* who brought the banjo to Ireland in 1844 to the Cree fiddlers from James Bay who brought forgotten music back to Orkney in 1978, from Buddy MacMaster's trip to Lochaber in 1993 to Seán McKiernan's return to Carna as a child in the 1950s, not just as a future piper but as a native speaker of Irish born in Boston. It is imperative to treat the Celtic music diaspora to North America as an all-encompassing rhizomorphic phenomenon with multidirectional roots and routes that have spanned the Atlantic and its bordering landmasses for centuries. Not to do so is to fail to comprehend the synchronic and diachronic processes of tradition making, musical hybridity and transculturation that continue to mark the abundant soundscape of the Celts in the Americas.

Notes

1. By the time the Irish and Scots began to arrive in North America in large numbers in the late 18th century, the quadrille had ensconced itself along the eastern seaboard from Newfoundland to the Caribbean and was being indigenized by multiple hybrid soundscapes.

2. As an adjudicator at the All Ireland Fleadh Cheoil (Ireland's World Championship forum) in 1998, I was quietly tapped on the shoulder and told by a rules "guru" to disqualify a young musician because he had played a "Scottish strathspey in an Irish competition." Rather than undermine his confidence after a long summer of qualifying competitions, I invited him back to play a reel instead of the strathspey. Our game-keeper didn't seem to mind that he came back and played "Lucy Campbell," a Scottish reel that, like scores of other sinful Scottish tunes, has enjoyed currency in Ireland for over two hundred years.

3. One thousand four hundred dancers have taken part in this show to date, its Grammy-winning CD has sold over 2.5 million copies and its video sales exceed $9 million.

4. Attali notes that music is "prophesy. Its styles and economic organization are ahead of the rest of society because it explores, much faster than material reality can, the entire range of possibilities in a given code" (1985 [1977]: 3).

References

Allen, Kieran. 2005. An Appeal to Musicians to Rise Up against the Neo-Liberal Order. *The Journal of Music in Ireland* 5 (2): 4-7.

Anderson, Benedict. 1983. *Imagined Communities: Reflections on the Origins and Spread of Nationalism*. London: Verso.

Appadurai, Arjun. 1996. *Modernity at Large: Cultural Dimensions of Globalization*. Minneapolis: University of Minnesota Press.

Arnold, Matthew. 1900. *On the Study of Celtic Literature*. London: Smith, Elder & Co.

Atkins, Harold and Archie Newman. 1978. *Beecham Stories: Anecdotes, sayings and impressions of Sir Thomas Beecham*. London: Robson.

Attali, Jacques. 1985 [1977]. *Noise: The Political Economy of Music*. Trans. Brian Massumi. Manchester: Manchester University Press.

Basu, Paul. 2007. *Highland Homecomings: Genealogy and Heritage Tourism in the Scottish Diaspora*. London: Routledge.

Bohlman, Philip V. 2002. *World Music: A Very Short Introduction*. Oxford: Oxford University Press.

Carolan, Nicholas. 1997. *A Harvest Saved: Francis O'Neill and Irish Music in Chicago*. Cork: Ossian Publications.

———. 2006. Voices: Rhythmic Reflections - Re-Imagining Irish Traditional Music. In *Re-Imagining Ireland: How a storied island is transforming its politics, economy, religious life, and culture for the twentieth-first century*, ed. Andrew Higgins Wyndham, 137-39. Charlottesville: University of Virginia Press.

Chatterjee, Partha. 1986. *Nationalist Thought and the Colonial World: A Derivative Discourse*. London: Zed Books.

Colley, Linda. 1992. *Britons: Forging the Nation 1707-1837*. New Haven: Yale University Press.

Davies, Norman. 1999. *The Isles: A History*. Oxford: Oxford University Press.

De Garmo, William B. 1875. *The Dance of Society: A Critical Analysis*. New York: W. A. Pond.

Dowling, Martin. 2010. From Vernacular to "Traditional": Music in Post-Famine Ireland. In *Power and Popular Culture in Modern Ireland: Essays in Honour of James S. Donnelly, Jr.*, ed. Michael De Nie and Seán Farrell, 145-71. Dublin: Irish Academic Press.

Kaul, Adam. 2009. *Turning the Tune: Traditional Music, Tourism and Social Change in an Irish Village*. New York: Berghahn Books.

Leerssen, Joep. 2002. *Hidden Ireland, Public Sphere: Research Papers in Irish Studies*. Galway: Arlen House for the Centre for Irish Studies.

Le Goff, Jacques. 1974. Les Mentalités: une histoire ambiguë. In *Faire de l'histoire*, ed. Jacques Le Goff and Pierre Nora, 77-79. Paris: Gallimard.

MacMahon, Tony. 1999. Music of the Powerful and Majestic Past. In *Crosshealach an Cheoil - The Crossroads Conference 1996*, ed. Fintan Vallely, Hammy Hamilton, Eithne Vallely and Liz Doherty, 112-20. Dublin: Whinstone Music.

Mathieson, Kenny. 2001. *Celtic Music*. San Francisco: Backbeat Books.

McGovern, Mark. 2003. The Cracked Pint Glass of the Servant: The Irish Pub, Irish Identity and the Tourist Eye. In *Irish Tourism: Image, Culture and Identity*, ed. Michael Cronin and Barbara O'Connor, 83-103. Clevedon, U.K.: Channel View Publications.

Megaw, J. V. S. 1991. Music Archaeology and the Ancient Celts. In *The Celts*, ed. V. Kruta, O. H. Frey, B. Raftery and M. Szabó, 643-48. New York: Rizzoli International.

Nora, Pierre. 1989. Between Memory and History: Les Lieux de Mémoire. *Representations* 26:7-24.

Ó Cinnéide, Barra. 2000. Riverdance Dispute Settled on Steps. *Sunday Business Post*. 16 June.

———. 2002. *Riverdance: The Phenomenon*. Dublin: Blackhall.

O'Connor, Barbara. 2003. Come Dance with Me in Irlande: Tourism, Dance and Globalization. In *Irish Tourism: Image, Culture and Identity*, ed. Michael Cronin and Barbara O'Connor, 122-41. Clevedon: Channel View Publications.

Ó hAllmhuráin, Gearóid. 1999. The Great Famine: A Catalyst in Irish Traditional Music. In *The Great Famine and the Irish Diaspora to North America*, ed. Arthur Gribben, 104-32. Boston: University of Massachusetts Press.

O'Neill, Captain Francis. 1913. *Irish Minstrels and Musicians*. Chicago: Regan Printing House.

Porter, James. 1998. Introduction: Locating Celtic Music (and Song). *Western Folklore* 57 (4): 205-24.

Quinn, Bob. 2005. *The Atlantean Irish: Ireland's Oriental and Maritime Heritage*. Dublin: Lilliput Press.

Raviart, Naïk. 1990. Danse irlandaise traditionnelle et dance française ancienne: histoire en deçà, ethnologie au delà. In *Tradition et histoire dans la culture populaire: recontres autour de l'oeuvre de Jean-Marie Guilcher*, 53-70. Doc. d'Ethn. Rég. 11, C.A.R.E. (Centre alpin et rhodanien d'ethnologie).

Richards, Thomas. 1993. *The Imperial Archive: Knowledge and the Fantasy of Empire*. London: Verso.

Sawyers, June Skinner. 2000. *Complete Guide to Celtic Music: From the Highland Bagpipe and Riverdance to U2 and Enya*. London: Aurum Press.

Sky, Patrick. 1995. *Ryan's Mammoth Collection: 1050 Reels and Jigs, Hornpipes, Clogs, Walk-Arounds, Essences, Strathspeys, Highland Flings and Contra Dances with Figures and How to Play Them*. Pacific, MO: Mel Bay.

Smyth, Gerry. 2009. *Music in Irish Cultural History*. Dublin: Irish Academic Press.

Stokes, Martin. 1992. *The Arabesque Debate*. Oxford: Oxford University Press.

Storey, Mark, ed. 1988. *Poetry and Ireland since 1800: A Source Book*. London: Routledge.

Sykes, Bryan. 2006. *Saxons, Vikings, and Celts: The Generic Roots of Britain and Ireland*. New York: W. W. Norton.

Szwed, John F. and Morton Marks. 1988. The Afro-American Transformation of European Set Dances and Dance Suites. *Dance Research Journal* 20 (1): 29-36.

Vallely, Fintan, Hammy Hamilton, Eithne Vallely and Liz Doherty, eds. 1999. *Crossbhealach an Cheoil - The Crossroads Conference 1996*. Dublin: Whinstone Music.

Whelan, Irene. 1998. *The Bible War in Ireland*. Dublin: Lilliput Press.

Williams, William H. A. 1996. *"Twas Only an Irishman's Dream": The Image of Ireland and the Irish in American Popular Song Lyrics, 1800-1920*. Urbana and Chicago: University of Illinois Press.

Yoshida, Momoko. 2008. Riverdance to shake a leg in Japan. *Asahi Weekly*. 2 May. www.asahi.com/english/Herald-asahi/TKY200805020049.html (accessed 15 May 2011).

Shamus Y. MacDonald

Micro-Toponymy in Gaelic Nova Scotia: Some Examples from Central Cape Breton

Gaelic speakers named much of the natural and built landscape they encountered during their daily lives in Nova Scotia, including small features like brooks, hills, hollows and bridges. Larger aspects of the local environment, such as mountains and lakes, were also named as part of this process. Employed for generations but relevant only within a limited geographic area, such place names were common but rarely made official.

In recent years, bilingual highway signs featuring traditional Gaelic place names have been erected at a number of key locations in eastern Nova Scotia and Cape Breton Island. In many ways, they represent a welcome, and tangible, reminder of the extent of Highland settlement in the province. For obvious reasons, however, such signs are usually restricted to marking major geographical sites, such as towns, villages and county boundaries. In this chapter, I will focus on the larger, but more localized, Gaelic place name tradition in Nova Scotia.

As we might expect, historical publications and modern fieldwork have preserved many Gaelic place names in Nova Scotia. Often, however, they are embedded within stories or songs and their inclusion in the historical record is incidental and peripheral to the fieldworker's initial research goals. Such is not always the case, however. Kenneth Nilsen, for example, published a list of more than fifty place names collected from the last generation of native Gaelic speakers on the mainland of the province. Approximately 20 per cent of these are the highly localized variety on which this paper is based: Tobar nam Bòcan (Well of the Ghosts) and Drochaid na Cailleachag (The Bridge of the Little Old Woman) are two examples (Nilsen 1991). Jeff MacDonald, in his undergraduate thesis, also provides a list of minor place names. Collected from native speakers in southern Inverness County, these names include Loch nan Gillean Ruadh (Lake of the Red Boys), Tobar Nill (Neil's Well) and Drochaid a' Chlachair (The Mason's Bridge) (MacDonald 1992). Extensive fieldwork, conducted over many years by Jim Watson, has also resulted in the collection of local place names in Cape Breton. Many of these are now on a website hosted by the Office of Gaelic Affairs (2010).

Although minor place names enjoy limited currency outside their home communities, they often contain important information about settlement patterns, commemorate traditional activities and occupations, and perpetuate local oral traditions. In an article focused on how Bòcan Brook, Inverness County, was named, Gordon MacLennan makes clear the value of working with place names to unlock oral traditions by highlighting three local variants of this etiological legend (MacLennan 1984).

As a result of ongoing collaboration with local tradition bearers, I have been able to collect more than a hundred Gaelic place names from central Cape Breton. This fieldwork, based in Iona and Christmas Island, includes outlying settlements traditionally considered part of the informal parish boundaries of these communities. In this way, a regional sense of identity rather than formal borders guides this research.

Immigrants from the Island of Barra, Scotland, settled this region during the early years of the 19th century. Over the next several decades, friends and family from the island, enticed to emigrate by a variety of economic, social and religious factors, joined them. The first settlers were quick to claim ownership of the prime lands situated along the shoreline. This land was often more fertile and the close proximity to the water was especially desirable for people accustomed to the sea. Subsequent waves of settlers were forced to take up residence on the less desirable lands located away from the water. Eventually, many of these backland settlements were abandoned as residents sought work prospects elsewhere—a process that continues today.

Spending an afternoon driving around the community with tradition bearers and asking them about the places we passed proved an especially effective and enjoyable way of encouraging place names and associated oral traditions to surface.[1] By using a video camera mounted to the dash of the car, an audio-visual record was also produced of the places discussed. This facilitated the later production of a map which, in turn, made it easier for multiple informants to confirm place names and locations. The continuing contributions of these tradition bearers make clear the vital ways in which minor place names can underpin major elements of the regional oral narratives corpus.

Preliminary evidence suggests that many of the place names that early immigrants gave to expansive parts of their surroundings were generic. An Gleann Mór (The Big Glen), An Caolas (The Strait) and An Cùl (The Rear) are typical examples. As travel between communities became easier, however, and post offices were established throughout the region, more specific names were required to differentiate these communities from others with the same name. Several settlements in this region, including Barra Glen, Castle Bay and St. Columba, carry names that resulted from this process. Indeed, Iona is itself a place name that only appeared generations after settlement (Fergusson 1967: 309).[2]

In general, minor place names in this region are divided into two primary categories: those connected to natural landscape features, such as hills, brooks and ponds, and those linked to man-made ones, including roads, properties and bridges. As we might expect, many examples are related to ownership. Of course, such a way of looking at the world, and naming it, is not universal. Mi'kmaw place names, for instance, typically describe the physical characteristics and natural resources of a location. While names like these are not absent in the Gaelic tradition—Gob an Rubha (Tip of the Point), Beul a' Phòin (Mouth of the Pond) and An Cnoc Ruadh (The Red Hill) are good examples—they remain notably scarce.[3]

Instead, place names collected by this research often recall the presence of former community residents. For example, Beinn Ceitaidh Thòmais (Katie Thomas's Mountain) commemorates the presence of a woman who lived on its slopes and Fuaran Bean Eachainn Dhòmhnaill Ruairidh (Hector Donald Rory's Wife's Spring) brings to mind a woman whose spring was once a welcome landmark for thirsty travelers. According to oral tradition, the graveyard in Christmas Island, Cladh Nìll Bhàin (Fair Neil's Graveyard), is named after the person who donated the land to the parish upon the death of the first settlers. Overlooking the mouth of Benacadie Pond, Beinn Phàdraig (Patrick's Mountain) recalls the man who first cleared its slopes. According to local legend, Patrick Mulligan, an Irish immigrant, settled on the property in the early 19th century. Soon thereafter, he married a local girl. Several years later, a woman arrived in the area asking about Mulligan. It soon became clear the stranger was his wife from Ireland whom he had promised to send for years earlier. Mulligan left the area shortly thereafter, but his name and story remain (D. MacNeil 2004).

The act of naming a place is a powerful human force. It brings our surroundings into the human realm and provides parts of an anonymous, and potentially intimidating, landscape with an individual identity. Since land ownership was such a critical force in the settlement of central Cape Breton, we should not be surprised that so many place names in this community are associated with former residents. Naming a place, after all, can be a clear and effective way of laying claim to it. Indeed, the relative paucity of Mi'kmaw place names adopted by early settlers may be attributed, at least partly, to this motivation.

For the interested observer, place names can shed light on settlement patterns and family ties. In the following interview, Catherine MacNeil provides evidence of the manner in which properties, divided over generations, allowed multiple members of the same family, identified through their patronymic, to live in close proximity to each other and give their names to nearby landscape features:

> CM: Àite Ruairidh Mhurchaidh a bha seo. Àite Eairdsidh Mhurchaidh a bha seo. Àite Rod Mhurchaidh a bha seo. Àite Eòs Nìll an uair sin. Uell, bha iad uileadh càirdeach. Àite Ruairidh Iain. Ruairidh Iain. Cha chreid mi nach e, am pìos seo, Àite Sheumais Dhòmhnaill Eòin.
> SM: Tha an t-allt ann.
> CM: Allt Sheumais Dhòmhnaill Eòin. (C. MacNeil 2009)

> (CM: Rory Murdock's place was here. Archie Murdock's place was here. That was Rod Murdock's place there. Then Joe Neil's place. Well, they were all related. Rory John's place. Rory John. I believe this is, this piece, is James Donald Hugh's place.
> SM: The brook's there.
> CM: James Donald Hugh's Brook.)

Central Cape Breton is home to a rich folklore and folktale tradition. Perhaps as a result, several of its place names are associated with the supernatural. In the following anecdote, Maxie MacNeil describes the lasting interest people had in a tree stump in Barra Glen where a variety of supernatural phenomena have been observed.

> MM: I would say Stumpa nam Bòcan (Stump of the Spooks) was one of the spots that never lost its name at all. Other things came, well, you know, you forgot about, but Stumpa nam Bòcan was well remembered. Even as of today. It was right here. I guess there was a big pine tree and it fell down and there was a stump that was kind of renowned there for a while and I guess in the stories if a person was going to see anything it would be around the stump.
> SM: And what was it? Lights?
> MM: It wasn't too much lights I don't think. Well, the one I remember quite a bit was *Frans Mhurachaidh* (Francis Murdock) in Barra Glen. When he used to work in at the convent at Iona. It was nothing for him to come home and when he'd be passing there, there'd be a lady come and sit in the wagon with him. Now I don't know, did he talk to her, but he got a little bit bolder as the years went by, I think, and when she'd get to about the crossings, she'd disappear. (Maxie MacNeil 2010)

As with many other communities in Gaelic Nova Scotia, Christmas Island was also home to a mound in which the fairies were reputed to live. Before it was largely leveled by road construction, Cnoc nan Sìthichean (The Fairy Knoll) overlooked Benacadie Pond. In fact, according to the late Jimmy Mick Sandy MacNeil, a local traveller is said to have seen upwards of a hundred fairies gathered together on the frozen pond below the knoll one crisp winter evening long ago (J. MacNeil 2006).[4] Even places without names directly connected to the supernatural can elicit stories of this nature. In the following, Cathee MacKinnon begins by describing a now-abandoned road, Rathad nan Làibeanan (Road of the Puddles), when she sees the location of a former bridge:

> CM: 'Nisd, Rathad nan Làibeannan, tha i às an turn a tha ann a' sin, a' dol a-staigh mar siod. 'S bha rathad ann, 's bhiodh poidhle de thraffic air. Bhiodh iad a' dol sios dhan Bhìte Mhór, 's a' dol mar sin, 's gheobh iad a-staigh seachad aig—seo Drochaid Eòghainn! Drochaid Eòghainn. Eòghainn: the Gillises.
> SM: Bhiodh iad a' faicinn solus a' seo. Tha mi creidsinn gu robh iad a' faicinn solus.
> CM: O, bha iad a' faicinn poidhle de bhòcain. Ach, seann Father MacDonald, Angus R., chur e run air an deamhainn mas e a bh'ann. Chan fhaca iad cus tuilleadh dheth. (MacKinnon 2009)

> (CM: Now, the Puddle Road, it's in that turn that's there, going in like that. And it was a road, and there would be a pile of traffic on it. They would be going down to Big Beach, going like that, and they would pass—there's Hugh's Bridge! Hugh's Bridge. Hugh: the Gillises.
> SM: They would be seeing a light there. I believe they were seeing a light.
> CM: Oh, they were seeing a lot of ghosts! But, old Father MacDonald, Angus R., he put a run on the devil, if that's what it was. They never saw any more of it.)

According to local legend, Father Angus R. MacDonald stopped at the brook on the way to a sick call so his horse could take a drink. Almost immediately, the horse was spooked and refused to drink. Aware the bridge was reputedly haunted, MacDonald cursed aloud any spirit that would delay his mission. With that, a whistling noise was heard that grew in intensity so greatly the priest had to cover his ears. As quickly as it started, however, the noise stopped. The horse proceeded to drink freely and MacDonald continued on his way. No more spirits ever delayed travellers at the bridge.[5]

Although the accuracy of legends should not be privileged, their potential contribution to the historical record should be recognized. In communities where such a record is lacking, oral narratives can prove especially valuable. In the following, for example, Roddie John Dan MacNeil relates the historical importance of an area near Iona:

RM: Uell, seo Bruthach Ruairidh Eachainn. Uell, bha Pòl Ruairidh Eachainn, bha esan a' fuireach an uair sin. Tha cuimhne agamsa air Pòl Ruairidh Eachainn. Agus bha, uell, ma dh'fhaodte gu robh sia taighean ann aig aon àm. Agus bha cidhe ann far am biodh am bàta a' deanamh acarsaid, agus a' faighinn uiste, 's a leithid sin, air an taobh eile.
SM: Robh fuaran ann no tobar?
RM: Bha. Bha i furasda a' faighinn uiste. (R. MacNeil 2010)

(RM: Well, this is Rory Hector's Hill. Well, Paul Rory Hector was, he was living then. I myself remember Paul Rory Hector. And, well, there were perhaps six houses there at one time. And there was a wharf there where the boat was taking shelter, and getting water, and that sort of thing, on the other side.
SM: Was there a spring or well?
RM: Yes. It was easy to get water.)

Often times, historical legends are also anchored by place names. Located in Rear Big Beach, Rathad nam Frangach, for example, is named after a crude road discovered by the pioneers upon their arrival in the region. According to the late Murdock MacNeil, early settlers concluded the road was a remnant of one taken decades earlier by the French exiled from Louisburg. A related series of legends describes a treasure buried along the way, 20th-century efforts to retrieve it and spirits charged with preventing that from happening.[6]

Even seemingly mundane place names can reveal links to interesting oral traditions. An t-Allt Buidhe (The Yellow Brook) is a small, nondescript brook in the Highlands of Christmas Island. Local tradition maintains that the brook was so named because a small quantity of gold was once found in its waters. Significantly, stories like this are often fixed in place, but fluid in time. A specific location is provided, but the era remains vague. In this way, the primacy of place over period is made clear. In many ways, personal connections to parts of the natural and built environment inform much place name knowledge. In Barra Glen, for example, the crossroads is remembered as a meeting place for youth, while Drochaid Iain Thom (John Tom's Bridge) brings back memories of informal dances on summer evenings in Benacadie Glen. In the following, Mickey John H. MacNeil provides a fitting example of the manner in which local tradition bearers link place names and memories:

Tha sinn a' tighinn gu Bruthach Shèba a-nisd. Tha cuimhne agamsa nuair bha seo uileadh glan. Cha robh craobh, cha robh weed, no sgàth ann. Seo agad Bruthach Shèba. (Mickey MacNeil 2009)

(We're coming to Jamie's Hill now. I remember when this was all clear. There wasn't a tree, there wasn't a weed, or anything on it. Here's Jamie's Hill.)

Perhaps as a consequence of personal connections like these, place name research can also illuminate regional identities. Even within small rural communities, a strong sense of connection to smaller parts of that community can often be observed. Regional identities like these can be revealed through the number of place names an informant knows in a given part of the community. For example, Peter Jack MacLean, from Rear Christmas Island, appears to be more familiar with place names in Benacadie Glen and a now-abandoned area of the backlands than those nearer the parish centre. Perhaps this is not surprising considering that the late Daniel M. R. MacNeil of Benacadie Pond once described regional identities within the parish as being so pronounced during his youth they were discernible within individual song repertoires (D. MacNeil 2004).

As we might expect, former occupations and activities are also recalled in the place name tradition. Abhainn na Nigheadaireachd (Laundry River) is the brook in which some residents of Jamesville washed their laundry. Nearby, Rathad an Tàilleir (The Tailor's Road) is named for a family known as tailors. Cnoc na Ceàrdaich (Smithy Hill) brings to mind the former presence of a blacksmith shop near Castle Bay while Pòn a' Chupair (Cooper's Pond) is a reminder of a former cooper in the area.

Located downstream from the location of a former gristmill and sawmill, Drochaid a' Mhuilinn (Mill Bridge) demonstrates the occasional flexibility of the place name tradition. The structure is also known as Drochaid Eòs Thom (Joe Tom's Bridge) after the man who established the original mill, and Drochaid Aonghais Anndra (Angus Andrew's Bridge) after his son who operated the mill well into the 20th century. A certain degree of generational change is expected in toponymy. The static nature of many of the place names uncovered through this research is best understood within the historical and linguistic context of the region. They have been collected from the last generation in the community to be raised within a primarily Gaelic-speaking environment. Subsequent changes to the regional place name lexicon, initiated by the next generation, would have occurred in English. In many cases, however, this did not occur.

As a result, many of these places have once again become anonymous aspects of the landscape. Language shift has drawn a curtain over them and a changing relationship with the land has made their presence less important to younger generations. Small brooks, hollows and hills lose their prominence when travelling quickly through the countryside. In addition, residents are no longer as closely connected through their lifestyle to the natural resources that immediately surround them. Indeed, an increased familiarity with a larger geographic area has sacrificed a depth of knowledge associated with smaller places like these.

However, with the renewed interest in the well-being of the Gaelic language, all aspects its oral culture, including local place names, should be seen as essential elements in its revitalization in Nova Scotia. Gaelic place names are portals to rich oral traditions, language and local history. The promotion and recognition of these names is also powerful and effective tool in preventing cultural amnesia by providing clear evidence of the extent of Gaelic settlement in the province. By exploring place names found in one area, and extending these results to areas where the language was formally spoken, the density and diversity of minor place names soon becomes clear. Taken as a whole, the presence of these names demonstrates the extent to which a sense of Gaelic identity was imprinted on parts of Nova Scotia. For these reasons, the legacy of Gaelic toponymy in Christmas Island, Iona and other parts of the province should be seen as a rich and exciting source of strength for the future of Gaelic Nova Scotia.

Notes

Thanks are extended to Angus MacLeod for proofreading portions of the transcriptions and translations used herein.

1. The benefits of in situ fieldwork have been noted by others. See, for instance, Cruikshank 1990: 25; Martin 1993: 9.

2. The name Iona was officially adopted in 1891. It seems clear this process privileged place names in English. Despite their apparent prevalence, few Gaelic place names were ever made official in Nova Scotia. Considering the bias that existed against unofficial languages, this is not surprising.

3. For examples of Mi'kmaw place names, see Rand 1919.

4. International motifs associated with this complex of ideas include F211 (fairyland under hollow knoll) and F217.1 (Congregating place of fairies).

5. Thompson motif E421.1.2 (Ghost visible to horses alone).

6. These stories include several international motifs, including N500 (Treasure trove), N550 (Unearthing hidden treasure), N553 (Tabus in effect while treasure is being unearthed) and N570 (Guardian of treasure).

References

Cruikshank, Julie. 1990. *Life Lived Like A Story: Life Stories of Three Native Yukon Elders*. Lincoln: University of Nebraska Press.

Fergusson, Charles Bruce, ed. 1967. *Place-Names and Places of Nova Scotia*. Halifax: The Public Archives of Nova Scotia.

MacDonald, Jeff. 1992. Bràighe na h-Aibhne: Iarmad Mo Shluaigh. BA thesis, St. Francis Xavier University.

MacLennan, Gordon. 1984. Bòcan Brook. *Béaloideas* 52:1-8.

Martin, Charles. 1993. *Hollybush: Folk Building and Social Change in an Appalachian Community*. Knoxville: University of Tennessee Press.

Nilsen, Kenneth. 1991. The Gaelic Placenames of Mainland Nova Scotia: a Preliminary Survey. *Ainm: the Journal of the Ulster Placename Society* 4:220-23.

Office of Gaelic Affairs. 2010. Gaelic Awareness. http://www.gov.ns.ca/oga/awareness.asp?lang=en (accessed 2 December 2012).

Rand, Rev. S. T. 1919. Micmac place-names in the Maritime Provinces and Gaspe Peninsula. Ottawa: Geographical Board of Canada.

Fieldwork

MacKinnon, Cathee. 2009. Interview with the author. Christmas Island. 2 September.

MacNeil, Catherine. 2009. Interview with the author. Christmas Island. 28 August.

MacNeil, Daniel. 2004. Interview with the author. Sydney River. 3 January.

MacNeil, Jimmy. 2006. Interview with the author. Benacadie Pond. 12 February.

MacNeil, Maxie. 2010. Interview with the author. Iona. 3 June.

MacNeil, Mickey. 2009. Interview with the author. Iona. 2 September.

MacNeil, Roddie. 2010. Interview with the author. Iona. 22 May.

Natasha Sumner

The Ceudach Tale in Scotland and Cape Breton

In the late 18th and early 19th centuries, Gaelic-speaking Scottish settlers poured into Cape Breton Island to form Canada's largest and most resilient Scottish Gaelic community (Dunn 1953: 11-23). Amid new surroundings, it was through their cultural heritage—their stories and their songs—that these immigrant Scots preserved their identity during the harsh early years of settlement and beyond. The stories that took pride of place were the "long tales," as the renowned Cape Breton storyteller, Joe Neil MacNeil refers to them, i.e., Fenian and hero tales. As in Scotland, the reciter of this genre of lore was ever a welcome *céilidh* guest (Shaw 1987: xxvii; MacNeil 1987: 24-29).

One such tale in particular merits close examination by reason of its popularity among Cape Breton Islanders to a very late date. This tale has been classified in each instance as a variant of the well-known Fenian story of the "helper" character Ceudach. Three different Cape Breton versions were collected during the 20th century, all of which display significant variation. In fact, not only is each one an independent version of the tale, the Cape Breton versions exhibit several features that set them apart from published variants from Scotland and evidence a degree of creativity and innovation not often recognized in studies of Nova Scotian Gaelic folklore. Because of this variation and innovation, we are here presented with an excellent opportunity to study the development of a common folktale that has been displaced from its geographical point of origin. Placing the Ceudach tale in its historical context, this article begins with an overview of the earliest mentions of the character in Irish sources.[1] I then proceed to discuss the oral tales collected in Scotland, and the Cape Breton tales in relationship with them.[2]

The story of Ceudach is, according to Alan Bruford, "probably the most popular of all Fenian folk-tales" (1969: 123). More than one hundred oral versions of the story have been collected in Ireland, eighteen in Scotland and three in Cape Breton.³ The tale's modern popularity suggests that it has been in circulation for quite some time. Literary references indicate that a similar form of the tale was known by the early modern period, and the name is evidenced in older texts. The earliest use of the name "Cétach" occurs in *Acallam na Senórach* (ca. 1200), although this does not appear to be the same character (Dooley and Roe 1999: 167). A 13th-century lament for several Fenian heroes proclaims simply that "Céadach, man of delight, is no more" (*Ní mhair Cedach fear go n-aoibh*; MacNeill 1908: 48, 152). Dáithí Ó hÓgáin asserts that this is "the first real reference we have to our Céadach," which is true insofar as the character is here associated with the Fianna, but nothing more definite can be claimed about the body of story to which this poet was referring (1988: 257).

The first substantial reference to a character with this name can be found in the late medieval tale, "The Chase of *Síd na mBan Finn* and the Death of Finn" (composed prior to 1419), where "Cétach Cithach mac rí[g] Lochlann" is described as a powerful Fenian "helper" character, much like in the modern tale,⁴ although the details of his coming to the Fianna do not agree with modern versions. In the early tale, we are told that Cétach intended to avenge his brothers' deaths, but instead he fell in love with the heroic Fenian lifestyle of hunting and fighting and chose to join them (Meyer 1910: 76-77). In the modern versions, Ceudach generally seeks out the Fianna to join them, rather than to harm them. From the 15th until the 19th century, scattered references to the character can be found, and he plays a role in the ca. 18th-century literary Ulster Cycle tale, *Eachtra na gCuradh* (Bruford 1969: 123).

Irish and Scottish Recensions

There is no extant early literary tale about Ceudach with which any of the oral versions or literary references might be compared, but there is a 19th-century manuscript version of the story, of which we have four recensions that all likely originated in Cork (Bruford 1969: 130n1).⁵ Bruford suspects that this version is actually a literary rendering of a southern Irish variant of the oral tale, rather than a new composition, and he posits a lost post-medieval manuscript source for the modern folktales (126-27). Because the manuscript version "is obviously not the source of all the current folk versions," however, Bruford seems somewhat dismissive of it, noting further that "the telling of the story [is] rather confused" (1969: 123). While I do not think it is an excellent literary specimen, I do not perceive an extraordinary amount of confusion in the manuscript text. More importantly, though, I think it shares some interesting commonalities with the Scottish Gaelic versions on which this article focuses, for which reason it will be useful to give an overview of the plot of the manuscript version.

In the Irish manuscripts, the tale opens with a large young warrior (*óglach*) approaching the Fianna and seeking to enter into service with Fionn. Fionn takes him on and the next morning they go out hunting, at which the new man excels; at midday when they break from hunting, he has killed as many deer as all the rest of the Fianna. He takes them home and is able to prepare the meal and set it out for the Fianna before they arrive, at which point everyone gets more than enough. Diarmuid becomes jealous of the new man, however, and begins to suspect that he has been sent to spy on the Fianna and will turn on them. Diarmuid reveals his suspicions to a wise man (*draoi*), who recommends that Fionn should have the new man attempt to capture a particular bull that Fionn is not powerful enough to overcome. Upon the very mention of the bull, the man volunteers to capture it and bring it to Fionn, which he does. As soon as the bull is in Fionn's possession, however, a hag takes interest and challenges Fionn to gamble for it. He loses twice, and thus forfeits the bull and is required to undertake certain tasks. First, he must wrestle with her, which causes him some broken bones. Next he is instructed to fetch a drinking horn belonging to the three sons of the Hag of Combat and to lodge for a night with *Rudaire na Finna Féinne*.

Before the Fianna set out to accomplish these tasks, Fionn's new man fetches a bottle of water from Tobur na Sláinte which heals Fionn's injuries. They then depart over the sea. They stop first at an island residence that turns out to belong to the new man. Here, his name is revealed for the first time—"Céadach Mór mac Righ na Sorach" (Sgéal Chéaduig 375)—and we meet his wife, who makes Fionn promise that if Céadach accompanies him, when they return they will put up a white sail if he is alive and a black sail if he is dead. They set sail again and the next stop is the fort where they are to steal the drinking horn. While on a scouting mission for the Fianna, Céadach accomplishes the task, killing the hag and her sons. We are told that this is the same hag who charged Fionn to perform the tasks, which might be one source of the confusion Bruford registers, since despite her death the Fianna continue on their quest. Upon reaching the next location, the abode of Rudaire na Finna Féinne, Céadach's expedient scouting furnishes the Fianna with reluctantly granted hospitality for the night, after which a battle ensues. When the Fianna are nearly defeated, Céadach springs to action, turns the tide of the battle, and kills Rudaire na Finna Féinne, but is then struck and killed by an arrow fired by a small boy. The Fianna bring the body back to his wife, but forget to raise the black sail. Upon their arrival, Céadach's wife is sorrowful, but after the Fianna leave, a figure comes to her in the night and tells her that water from the Well of Life will resurrect Céadach. Once restored to life, Céadach goes to visit the Fianna in Ireland again. Upon his arrival, there is much celebration, and as a mark of honour, Céadach gives his daughter in marriage to Oscar.

As Bruford notes, this tale differs in some aspects from the orally collected versions. In comparison with the Scottish variants, however, some interesting similarities ought to be noted which I contend necessitate a revision of Bruford's analysis of the tale. I am aware of twenty-two Scottish Gaelic versions of the Ceudach tale told by separate tellers, including ten not listed in *Gaelic Folk-Tales and Mediaeval Romances*. I have incorporated these into Bruford's classification system in the chart below;[6] items I have added are marked with an asterisk (*).[7]

	SUTHERLAND
S1	JFC 13:65 = Folk-Lore Journal 6:173 (Eng. trans.)*;[8] Teller: Mrs. Young, Lairg; 1859.
S2	SA 1955.073.B15; SA1958.075.B2 + SA1958.076.A1 (Eng. version)*; Teller: Alexander (Ailidh Dall) Stewart, Lairg.
S3	SA 1955.124.A2; Teller: Alexander (Alec) Stewart, Muir of Ord, Easter Ross.
S4	SA 1957.048.A4 + B1;[9] Teller: Mary (Micki) Stewart, Bonar Bridge (originally from Lairg [Zall 1998: 21-22]).
S5*	SA 1958.072 + 073; LS Tape 956;[10] Teller: Alexander (Brian) Stewart, Culrain (originally from Lairg [Zall 1998: 21-22]).[11]
	ARGYLL[12]
A1	WS 2:376; Teller: Neil Livingston, Oban; latter half of 19th century.
A2	WS 3:27; Teller: Alexander Cameron, Ardnamurchan; 1888 or 1889.
A3	WS 4:225; Teller not named; latter half of 19th century.
A4	WS 4:260; Teller not named; latter half of 19th century.
A5	WS 4:274 (Eng. summary of start of story); Teller not named.
A6	Gille nan Cochall Chraiceann, 7 = JFC 11:133; Teller: Angus Campbell, Rosneath; 1860.
A7	JFC 16:107 (Eng. summary); Teller: a MacLean (male), Mull, 1870.
A8	JFC 16:141 (Eng. summary); Teller: Uilleam Robertson, Tobermory, Mull (learned in Uist); 1870.
A9*	MWHT 2:68 (+ Bodach an Chóta Lachtna); Teller: Miss Jean MacTavish, Islay; 1859 or 1860.
A10*	WS 2:32 (+ The Finding of Bran = ATU 513A); Teller: Archibald MacTavish, Oban/Mull; 1881 or 1882.
	HEBRIDES
H1*	CWP Coll-97/CW106/127: 54v-70r; Teller: John MacInnes, Stillgarry, South Uist; 1875.[13]
H2*	SA Notebook I.XXX.1:1-8 (1952) = Scottish Studies 6.2:184; SA 1965.017. A1; Teller: Neil Gillies, Barra.
H3*	SA 1966.050.B1 + SA 1966.051.A1; Teller: Peter Stewart, Lewis.
H4*	SA 1969.098.B1 (fragmentary); Teller: Angus John MacDonald, North Uist (?)

	CAPE BRETON
CB1*	*Gairm* 15:243 = Sgialachdan a Albainn Nuaidh, 94; Teller: Neil Macintyre, Benacadie Pond, Cape Breton Co.; 1950s.
CB2*	*Luirgean Eachainn Nìll*, 53; Teller: Hector Campbell, Hillsdale, Inverness Co.; 1964.
CB3*	*Sgeul gu Latha*, 46; Teller: Joe Neil MacNeil, Middle Cape, Cape Breton Co.; 1976.

There is, as Bruford asserts, a "range of variation in the actual versions of the story" (1969: 126). The most variation tends to occur in the opening sequences of the different versions, after which point a number of similarities are generally evident in the plot. A comparison of the opening sequences of the Irish manuscript and Scottish versions will therefore enable us to glean a better understanding of the overall structure of the tale than has been available to date. This, in turn, will allow for a more informed analysis of the relationships between the Scottish and Cape Breton versions of the tale. In the Irish manuscript (Sgéal Chéaduig) and the versions from Scotland that I consulted (S1-5, A1-6, A9, A10, H1, H2; see endnote 7), two opening sequences are discernible. One of these, which I will refer to as "Opening A," was noted by Bruford as the most common opening sequence, appearing in "thirty-nine of sixty-two versions [63 per cent], from all areas from Argyll to Cork"; this opening was thus preferenced in his analysis of the tale (1969: 125).

If Scottish and Irish data are isolated, however, it appears that Opening A was a good deal less popular in Scotland than Ireland. Removing the twelve Scottish Gaelic versions Bruford recognized (S1-4, A1-8) from the tally, we can assume that between thirty-three and thirty-five out of fifty Irish versions employ Opening A (roughly 68 per cent).[14] Only four of the fifteen Scottish tales I consulted (27 per cent, all from Argyll) open with a similar sequence, however, indicating that Opening A is the least common opening among tales collected in Scotland. While it is important to recognize Opening A, then, perhaps it ought not to be given primary status in an examination of the Ceudach tale as told in Scottish Gaelic.

The basic theme of Opening A is Ceudach's coming to the Fianna after marrying the intended wife of a companion. This can occur in a couple of different ways in the Scottish tales. In the first, Ceudach and his companions are training under the same instructor and one of them wants to marry the instructor's daughter, but she elopes with Ceudach instead. Ceudach then joins the Fianna after going into exile to avoid his companion-turned-rival (A1).[15] In the other opening episode of type A in the Scottish tales, Ceudach and two companions set out on a mission to entreat a particular woman to marry one of the men. Upon their arrival, a martial contest is set for all of the companions, and when Ceudach wins, the woman chooses him instead of the companion who sought her hand. In two of these versions, having won the woman fairly, he does not elope with her. He goes to Fionn because of a desire to be among the Fianna, not because of any sort of exile (A3 and A4). In A6, however, Ceudach's two companions strongly resent his victory because in this version, he merely accompanied them as their servant (*gille*) and was not meant to participate in the contest for the woman.[16] Ceudach and the woman must therefore flee the two companions. Interestingly, in this version Fionn seeks to sign Ceudach into service after hearing of his superb hunting skills. In all four versions, Ceudach is employed as Fionn's cook.

The most common opening sequence in the Scottish tales (Opening B) is shared by twelve of the fifteen versions I examined (S1-5, A2, A5, A6, A9, A10, H1 and H2) and closely parallels the opening of the manuscript version of the tale summarized above (Sgéal Chéaduig).[17] The common factor in these versions is that they all display an expanded focus on the Ceudach character's early days with the Fianna. If they provide any information about his life prior to joining Fionn's band of warriors, the context is generally different from that in Opening A. Marriage is not a concern; in these tales, he generally leaves home and joins the Fianna to avoid a magical imperative involving prophecy or *geasan* (enchantment). For instance, the Sutherland tales open with a description of the Ceudach character's unusual birth. His father, a king, is delayed in a misty bog on his way home one evening and seeks shelter in what turns out to be a fairy dwelling. While there, he conceives a son with a fairy woman. This son eventually comes to live with the king, who also has another son with his wife, the queen. One day a prophecy is made that one boy will kill the other. Upon hearing this, the Ceudach character departs to join the Fianna in order to prevent the prophecy's realization (S1-5).[18] A5 gives an alternate scenario. In this short, English summary, the young Ceudach challenges his schoolmates to play shinty against him and wins several matches. An onlooking woman then places him under geasan not to marry anyone but her, so he outfits himself in animal skins to appear disagreeable to her. When she still pursues him, he departs to join the Fianna.

In tales with Opening B, the Ceudach character often approaches the Fianna while hunting and is hired by Fionn to carry burdens and/or to prepare and cook the meat. He generally excels over the others in carrying the load of deer corpses back from the hunt (A2, A6, A9, A10, H1, H2) and then prepares them quickly (A2, A5, A6, A9, A10, H1, Sgéal Chéaduig).[19] One of the Fianna, usually Conan, dislikes him, however, and he is sent to perform a difficult task in the hope that he will die (S1, S4, S5, A2, A9, A10, H1, H2, Sgéal Chéaduig). In many versions, the task involves acquiring a particular cup from a powerful foe (often the king of Lochlann) (S1, S4, S5, A2, A6 A10, H1).[20] Upon Ceudach's return, Conan issues a challenge to Ceudach in leaping (S1, S3-5, A2, A10), wrestling (A2, A10), and/or racing (S1-5, A2, A9, H1), which Ceudach wins. In some versions, offended by Conan's continued malice, Ceudach leaves the

Fianna (S1-5, A2, A10, H1).[21] A couple of the tales end here (A5, A9, H2); others continue, and from this point describe incidents commonly found in other Ceudach tales (S1-5, A2, A6, H1, Sgéal Chéaduig). A10 continues into an episode from a different Fenian helper tale, which may help to explain why Bruford does not include it in his list of Ceudach tales.[22] As the above summary shows, however, this tale's opening sequence bears a marked resemblance to those of several Ceudach tales, for which reason I have included it here.[23]

Opening B can be very lengthy, and makes up the whole of some of the tales (A5, A9). An argument could therefore be made for classifying it as a separate tale that has become closely associated with the Ceudach story, particularly in Scotland. A good deal of further research on the Irish sources and other Fenian helper tales would be required to substantiate such a claim. Because the sequence is so strongly associated with Ceudach in the Scottish tales, and because the manuscript version, which is of Munster origin, evidences a greater geographical spread for this association, for the time being I am comfortable classifying all Scottish Gaelic tales of this kind that I have come across as Ceudach tales. My analysis diverges from that of Bruford, who does not consider that Opening B might be a unified sequence of events, let alone a separate tale, and seems not to find many of the traits common to the manuscript and the Scottish tales to be important to the plot. He makes next to no mention of the hunting setting prominent in the manuscript and many of the Scottish versions that employ Opening B, and other consistent similarities, such as the carrying of burdens and the cooking of game also get no particular focus.[24] The only tasks that find a place in the text of Bruford's book, rather than the endnotes, are those assigned as a result of a jealous Fenian aggressor's attempts to get Ceudach killed, and these are presented in such a way that it would appear they can be found in most if not all versions of the tale. The endnote to this discussion only lists twenty-one versions (of the sixty-two Bruford considered) as containing one or more such tasks, however (1969: 130n19), and an analysis of the Scottish versions shows a consistent association of both the Fenian aggressor incident and the hunting setting and tasks with Opening B. By recognizing this relationship, it is thus possible to see the significance of features in the Scottish and manuscript versions of the tale that appeared in Bruford's study as minor and unnoteworthy variations. This in turn enables us to recognize two more related Scottish versions of the tale than were accounted for in Bruford's bibliography (A9, A10).[25]

Bruford's treatment of these details as insignificant seems to stem from an initial assumption about the overall structure of the text which I argue contributes to a misleading interpretation of the central focus of the oral tale. According to Bruford, "The basis of the plot of the story, from which the part involving the Fenians is a long digression, is Céadach's feud with an enemy who eventually catches and kills him" (1969: 124). While this may well have been the basis of the plot of a no-longer-extant literary tale (the existence of which Bruford posits), the Fenian part of the tale is not a digression in the manuscript version, nor in a number of the Scottish oral tales. This is evident from those tales which include no background material whatsoever prior to Ceudach's coming to the Fianna (A2, A9, A10, H1, H2, Sgéal Chéaduig), or give Ceudach a highly conventional personal history in order to manufacture a conflict, as in the stock opening episode of the Sutherland tales (S1-5) (Bruford 1969: 225-26).[26] In fact, Bruford's comments on the lack of a frame tale in some instances (and, we can infer, the consequent primary focus on the Fenian material) illustrate his preferencing of a posited literary plot over the folktale plot(s). Commenting on the fact that a rival who will eventually kill Ceudach is not always established in the tale's opening, Bruford writes, "It is not typical of folktale construction to have such a character waiting in the wings throughout the greater part of the story" (1986/1987: 41).

I would rather opt for a less reductive description of this story's plot which incorporates the large degree of variation in the versions that have been collected. On the basis of the Scottish evidence, I suggest that the story is a Fenian helper tale likely to contain one of two common opening sequences, after which the Ceudach character aids Fionn in a quest (S1-5, A1-4, A6, H1, Sgéal Chéaduig). In this final and often lengthy sequence of events, three incidents occur in all the Scottish versions I examined: the Ceudach character's wife or mother must give permission for him to go on the quest and requests that he be returned to her dead or alive; the Ceudach character dies in battle, often but not always against a rival who reappears from an earlier episode; and the Fianna return his body to his wife or mother, who magically resurrects him.[27] The tale may end at this point, but it may also continue with further episodes (S1-5, A2, H1, Sgéal Chéaduig).[28]

While the quest is often an important element of the story, its nature is not fixed.[29] H1 is the most unique of this group of Fenian tales. Its quest consists of a series of events that bear little resemblance to those found in the other Scottish Ceudach tales, although such a string of adventures is not uncommon of long hero tales. As we will see, a comparison can be drawn between H1 and one of the Cape Breton tales, and it is also possible that points of correspondence might be found among some of the Irish tales. Similarities with the Irish manuscript tale are evident in all of the other versions of the Scottish tale that include a well-developed quest.[30] We will recall that one of the episodes in the manuscript tale's quest involved securing hospitality for a night from Rudaire na Finna Féinne, an enemy to Fionn and therefore an unwilling host. Upon discovering the identity of his guests, the host is reluctant to acquiesce to Ceudach's demands on behalf of Fionn. He duplicitously directs them to a large residence inhabited by monstrous beings called *amhais*.[31] Ceudach swiftly defeats the amhais, however. He then clears away the bodies, furnishes the house and procures food and drink for the Fianna from his reluctant host's household. Likewise in the Sutherland versions of the tale, Ceudach aids Fionn in obtaining hospitality from a deceitful host. In these, Fionn is placed under geasan by the queen of Eilean nam Muc to pay her a visit. Suspecting a trap, Fionn brings Ceudach along for protection. S1 bears the nearest resemblance. In this tale, the Fianna are directed to lodge in a large barn full of combative giants. Ceudach defeats them, and then orders the other men to clean the barn and fetch fuel for a fire from a location indicated by the hostess. When they cannot accomplish this because every shovelful they try to remove from the barn and every peat they try to pick up magically flies from their hands to hit them in the face, Ceudach performs all the tasks. Upon requesting food from the hostess, they are told to capture a particularly aggressive bull, which only Ceudach is able to do. Later that night, the mother of the giants comes to avenge her sons, and Ceudach must kill her too before they are able to depart the next day. The other Sutherland versions, all told by members of the same traveller family, omit the hostile monsters in the barn, but accord more or less (depending on the degree of detail in this portion of the tale) with S1 in the events that follow, including the nighttime attack by a female adversary.[32]

Similar scenarios are found in some of the versions collected in Argyll, as well. In A6 the daughter of Rìgh a' Mheangain Bhlàthaich puts Fionn under geasan to come and marry her. Upon arrival, they are lodged in a cowshed inhabited by giants, as in S1 and corresponding to the amhais of the Irish manuscript version. Ceudach kills the giants, has the bodies cleared, procures fuel and food (an ox) that are similarly difficult to obtain, furnishes the house with the king's chairs, and brings the king's family to the cowshed to socialize with him and Fionn. At this point, the king's daughter recognizes them and she and Fionn are married. The quest in A2 is related to those described above, but not as closely. In this tale, the Fianna are summoned by a queen who has them choose to lodge in one of two houses. In the house of their choice, they must defeat a number of *amhaisg* (= Irish *amhais*) and clear away their bodies (Cameron 1891: 52). Unlike the other tales, they find an abundance of food in the house and do not have to go to any trouble to access it, but like other versions, Ceudach must fend off a nighttime attack. A scenario like these also appears in one of the Cape Breton tales.

The Cape Breton Variants

The three Cape Breton variants of the tale were collected during the 1950s, 1960s and 1970s from tellers of different family backgrounds residing in different locations on the island. The first variant to be collected in Nova

Scotia was recorded from Neil Macintyre of Benacadie Pond in Cape Breton County in the 1950s by C. I. N. MacLeod (CB1) who gave it the title "Rìgh na Gréige" (The King of Greece) when he published it in *Gairm* 15 in 1956. He reprinted it in *Sgialachdan a Albainn Nuaidh* (1969) and in translation in *Stories from Nova Scotia* (1974). Interestingly, even though Macintyre's locale was first settled by emigrants from the Hebrides, his tale accords closely with the Sutherland versions discussed above (MacLeod 1974: 8). As in S1-5, the Ceudach character is born to a king—here, the king of Greece—by a fairy woman with whom he lodged after going astray in a thick mist one day.

As in the other versions, the king's wife also has a son, and it is prophesied that one boy will kill the other. In most of the Sutherland versions, the prophecy is made by an old beggar man (*bodach baigeir*) after the fairy woman's son has been living with the king and queen for some time (S2, S4, S5). In Macintyre's tale, however, the prophecy is made twice, the first instance occurring before the Ceudach character comes to live with the king; one day a mischievous retainer (*eachlach-ùrlair*) visits the queen to inform her that the king has another son and that boy will grow to bear malice toward her own son, to which she surprisingly responds, "O ... that is not the proper attitude to take. Although it may be true, and although this might disrupt our domestic harmony for a while, I would not predict what you state" (1974: 78; 1969: 95; *O ... chan 'eil an leithid sin ceart idir. Ged a bhiodh, is ged a chailleadh sinn ar rèit uile gu lèir cha bhithinn cho dona riutsa*).[33] The queen insists on incorporating the boy into the family. Some time later, she receives the prophecy again, this time from a seer (*fear fiosachd*) who predicts the death of one boy at the hands of the other. If this reaffirmation disturbs her at all, we are not told of it. While the queen seems to put little store in the prophecy, however, when the Ceudach character finally learns of it as an adolescent, he takes it very seriously. As in the Sutherland versions, he departs immediately in the hope of evading his fate.

Upon reaching the Fianna, the Ceudach character is hired to cook for Fionn's men and to remove their boots when they come home at night. In A6, he is given the similar task of removing, washing and drying the men's stockings, which he does with great alacrity. In Macintyre's tale, however, he displays a weakness not seen elsewhere when he has difficulty removing the men's boots. Rather than inspiring the confidence or even jealousy of the Scottish tales, here, Fionn is worried he has made a poor hiring choice. Further tasks are thus assigned not in the hope of getting the Ceudach character killed, but to give Fionn an excuse to retract his offer of employment on the basis of ability. Yet the Ceudach character proves himself to be the most powerful man of the Fianna in a race against Caoilte (whom he turns to a deer, as in the Sutherland tales), and in a unique task resembling the leaping feat of the Sutherland tales. In S1, S3, S4 and S5, the Ceudach character is required to leap a wide ditch while catching arrows, spears or daggers that are being launched at him. In Macintyre's tale, he must climb over a castle while throwing and catching seventeen spears.

Macintyre's version also includes a quest, and as in all of the Scottish tales with well-developed quest sequences that we have so far seen, the Ceudach character is deemed essential to the completion of the task, but permission for him to come must be sought from the woman closest to him—here, his mother. In this version, however, his return dead or alive is not demanded. As we would expect, given the tale's opening, the story ends with a battle between the Ceudach character and his half-brother, but in this version he is returned dying but not dead. His mother therefore does not have to resurrect him but only nurse him back to health. The only action that occurs after his revival is his return of Caoilte to human form, which sometimes occurs at the end of the Sutherland tales, and sometimes comes earlier. The quest itself in Macintyre's tale also resembles Scottish versions, particularly those that are comparable to the Irish manuscript version. As in the Sutherland tales, Fionn is summoned by the queen of Eilean nam Muc.[34] Upon arrival, the men must catch a bull, clean out a barn to lodge in and build a fire to roast the bull, although, in this version, the Ceudach character must only overcome magical impediments to two tasks for them, catching the bull and cleaning the barn. Also as in the other tales, they are visited overnight, this time by a "little glassy-eyed creature on the threshold playing music" (1974: 84; 1969: 100; *creutair beag gloineach air an starsach, is e a' deanamh ciùil*). Here, however, when the Ceudach character goes after the creature, it gets away, which he takes as a bad omen foreshadowing the outcome of his upcoming battle.

This brief summary of Macintyre's tale has shown that, in keeping with Opening B, attention is paid to the Ceudach character's early days with the Fianna, and the events of his birth and the quest resemble other Scottish Gaelic versions of the text. Although some of the details are different, this Cape Breton version accords well with the Sutherland tales specifically, and the Scottish tales generally. While MacLeod provides no information about either Macintyre's personal heritage or his source for this tale, we might suppose that, despite the most common ancestry in the Benacadie region (Barra and the other Hebrides), a Sutherland version of the tale found its way to him. This is in no way conclusive, however. Given the comparatively small number of Ceudach tales collected in Scottish Gaelic and the lack of representation in many regions, it may only be a coincidence that this particular variant of the tale turns up only in Sutherland and Cape Breton.

In Macintyre's version, the Ceudach character is known not as "Ceudach," but as "the Lad of the Goat-Skin Covering" (Gille a' Chochuill-Chraicinn). The name refers to the skin garment he dons when his clothes wear out after his departure from the king's house. He spends this interim period before joining the Fianna with his fairy mother. As Bruford notes, pseudonyms referring to Ceudach's animal skin garment are especially common among the Scottish variants of the tale (1969: 124). In fact, eleven of the fifteen Scottish tales I consulted refer to Ceudach by a similar pseudonym for at least part of the story.[35] Often in these tales, this pseudonym is adopted in order to conceal Ceudach's identity. For instance, in A3, A4 and A6, Ceudach's wife makes him the suit of skins before he goes to the Fianna and renames him "the Lad / Man with the Skin Covering" (Gille / Fear nan Cochla Craicionn). In A6, his wife explains that she does this to prevent his rivals from recognizing him, which works for some time, although by the end of the tale they have discovered his identity and come for him. Other times, the Ceudach character is known only by a pseudonym and is not given a proper name at all.

In some of these, however, even though the name "Ceudach" is absent, a version of his usual patronymic is evidenced. For instance, in most of the Stewart family versions collected in Sutherland, the enemy addresses the Ceudach character as Mac Rìgh na Sorach when calling him to battle (S2, S4, S5; see endnote 11). This may mean that in a related earlier version of the tale the protagonist was named Ceudach, but that this detail got dropped at some point in the tale's transmission. "Sorach" is not Ceudach's usual patronymic in the Scottish tales, although it is used in the manuscript version and evidenced elsewhere in Ireland (Bruford 1969: 124). In Scotland, Ceudach is more commonly called Mac Rìgh nan Collach (A3-5) or some variation of this.[36] Macintyre's version is the only one of the Scottish tales in which the Ceudach character is the son of the King of Greece, which may likewise indicate that a detail has been altered in transmission. If so, the change is not radical, but adheres to the conventions of the Gaelic hero tale genre: "The hero is in fact often from [foreign] countries: the son of the king of Greece or France, Norway or Spain, but rarely Scotland" (MacInnes 2007: 69).

The only Cape Breton version that names the hero as Ceudach was collected from Hector Campbell of Hillsdale, Inverness Co. in August 1964 by John Shaw (CB2), included in the collection *Luirgean Eachainn Nill* (1984). As the title of Campbell's tale indicates, his hero bears the conventional name and patronymic: Ceudach Mac Rìgh nan Collach (Ceudach Prince of the Collach). The tale also begins in a conventional way, employing a version of Opening A, described above. In Campbell's tale, Ceudach is sent by his father to learn swordsmanship from the King of Mallachan, but soon after his arrival he elopes with his instructor's daughter. In standard versions with Opening A, there are other suitors also vying for the woman's hand—Ceudach's erstwhile companions—whose disappointment over the elopement leads to Ceudach's death in battle near the end of the tale (this is the plot structure deemed primary by Bruford). In Campbell's tale, however, Ceudach has no companions and his elopement with his instructor's daughter is not opposed. Unlike in other versions, then, this opening does not overtly appear to be part of a frame narrative but simply the first of a progression of episodes. As the tale progresses, however, retrospectively added details will hint at the opening episode's origin as a frame tale.

This pattern is played out to a greater or lesser degree throughout Campbell's tale. While some aspects look quite familiar and clearly indicate that this is a version of the Ceudach tale, on the whole we see a greater disparity between Campbell's rendition and the Scottish versions examined above than we did in Macintyre's version. For instance, while in the other Scottish Gaelic cases Ceudach seeks employment with Fionn after eloping, Campbell has the couple flee to an unnamed king's court where, after Ceudach beheads a lion that has been evading the king and twelve of his soldiers, they are invited to stay. The beheading of the lion in Campbell's version might be viewed in a similar light to the tasks assigned to the Ceudach character in Macintyre's tale, in which he must prove his worth in order to gain acceptance into Fionn's group. His voluntary performance of the task upon seeing the king in duress is also comparable to tasks in A6, H2 and the manuscript version. Similarly, the task in the manuscript version involves the pursuit of an animal. The most striking difference in the scenario Campbell presents is that Ceudach does not enter into the service of the king, as he does in all of the other tales. Instead, he and the king become close companions—so close that Ceudach and his wife sleep in the same room as the king and queen in order to have more time together to converse.

The nature of Ceudach's relationship with the king in this tale is highly pertinent in that it alters the power relationship on which the corpus of "Ceudach tales" is based. Whatever variations in plot we may find, the Ceudach tale is in essence a helper tale, with Ceudach as the powerful outsider who comes to the Fianna's aid. Thus, in the Scottish versions of the Ceudach tale, when Fionn is placed under geasan by a messenger to undertake a journey, Ceudach accompanies him as a contracted helper (Bruford 1969: 125). Because Ceudach is the king's equal in Campbell's version, however, it is possible for him to function not as a helper, but as a hero in his own right. In this tale Ceudach is the one placed under geasan, and the king, as his devoted friend, decides to join him in his quest. This is not a role reversal, since the king does not take on a helper role; he is unable to accomplish any of the difficult tasks, and Ceudach must perform them all. Another consequence of the fact that Ceudach is not a helper character is that his wife has no say in whether he goes or not. As he is under geasan, he must go. Her opinion is not asked, and she does not stipulate the return of his body dead or alive, as we are used to seeing in Ceudach tales. Unlike other female characters, though, she accompanies the men on the quest.

The quest that Ceudach is required to undertake is reminiscent of one of the geasan in H1. In that version, Fionn and Ceudach must first fetch the head of an Toman-fheoir, and then the head of Bheagan-blathbheinne. In Campbell's tale, Ceudach is required to get the head of "the Great Turk" (an Turcach Mór). As in conventional versions of the tale, he is attacked by a formidable adversary with whom he engages in single combat. The adversary bears a similar name here as in one of the Scottish tales: Leobhar in Campbell's tale and Leòmhan Cridheach in the Scottish tale (A1). What is unique in this instance is that the enemy is his wife's brother, who is the Great Turk's greatest warrior.[37] Upon their mutual death in battle, Ceudach's wife recognizes her brother and at this point she reveals a prophecy that if both men ever came to Turkey, they would kill each other there. As we have seen, Ceudach's prophesied death is also a common feature in these tales, although the prophecy is usually given in the opening sequence. After the champions' death, Campbell's tale once again displays a similarity with H1. In that version, after Ceudach's death his wife has to be brought to him in order to heal him with a *botal ta bheò[tha]chain* (65r; a bottle of reviving water). In this version, she must go to her father to fetch a similar solution that was intended for her brother in the event of his death in Turkey. Once Ceudach is revived, however, she cannot simply leave her brother lying dead. Unlike in the version where Ceudach's mother heals him and his brother with a special oil or balm (A2; cf. S1, A6), here the bottle Ceudach's wife uses does not contain enough for both men, and so they must undertake a new quest to procure another dose of restorative water.[38] Thus, in an uncommon but not unheard of turn of events (cf. H1), the action of the tale continues after Ceudach's death and resurrection.[39]

The structure of a version of the tale like Campbell's reminds us that, while many of the Scottish versions seem to display a relatively fixed plot, the Ceudach tale is a complex one, and as such its multi-episodic structure is somewhat flexible and has the potential for both expansion and contraction. If the teller was so inclined (and the audience receptive), he or she could employ repetition to add length to a story or even import episodes from other tales. Likewise, the teller might contract repeated sections or drop episodes, either consciously or unconsciously.[40] There is an indication that Campbell may have once been in the habit of telling a longer version of his Ceudach story. Upon Ceudach and the king's return after the revivification of Leobhar, the queen places Ceudach under geasan once again and we expect another lengthy episode to follow. But rather than complete the task (the nature of which is not revealed), in an odd turn of events, Ceudach beheads the queen. While there is some similarity here with Joe Neil MacNeil's version (discussed below), the tale seems to have been unnaturally cut off, as though the teller's memory of this final episode failed him, or perhaps he realized that he introduced it by mistake. It is unfortunate that this tale was only recorded from Campbell on one occasion, as other tellings might contribute to our understanding of this odd closing to the tale.

We have examined two Cape Breton versions of the Ceudach tale. The first of these, told by Neil Macintyre of Benacadie Pond, closely corresponded with versions of the tale collected to date only in Sutherland, despite most people in his region claiming Hebridean ancestry. The second, told by Hector Campbell, displayed an adapted version of the least common opening in Scotland, Opening A, and a much-altered but related plot in which Ceudach is no longer a helper character, but a hero. We will now consider the final Cape Breton version, which was told by Joe Neil MacNeil of Middle Cape, Cape Breton Co. to John Shaw at the considerably late date of February 1976 (CB3). Its connection to the Ceudach group of tales was noted by Shaw in his 1987 collection of MacNeil's stories, *Tales Until Dawn / Sgeul Gu Latha*, but that relationship has until now been perceived as an uncertain one.[41] I argue here that despite a number of apparent irregularities, it is indeed a version of the Ceudach tale.

The opening of MacNeil's tale, which he titles "Fear a' Chòta Liathghlais" (The Man in the Light Grey Coat), incorporates a version of the Fenian helper tale *Bodach an Chóta Lachtna*.[42] The plot of the latter is as follows. A warrior named Cael an Iarainn challenges the Fianna to a competition in exchange for the tribute of the island of Ireland. Fionn goes to ask Caoilte to race against the adversary, but on the way he meets Bodach an Chóta Lachtna, who volunteers to take on the challenge. The Bodach delays a number of times during the race to sleep, pick berries, and mend his coat, and still wins. He then knocks off Cael an Iarainn's head and puts it back on backwards before sending him on his way (O'Grady 1892: 324-31). The race episode in A9 is a version of *Bodach an Chóta Lachtna*, and similar delay tactics can be observed in the races in other Scottish versions of the Ceudach tale (see endnote 21). Indeed, Bruford notes the commonalities between the race episodes in both tales, and it is not difficult to perceive the ease of combining the two.[43] It appears that is precisely what has happened in MacNeil's version, of which the opening parallels one of the Scottish versions (H2) in which the Ceudach character pursues and catches a deer when Fionn's six best men cannot. In MacNeil's tale, the Ceudach character is called "the Man in the Light-Grey Coat" (Fear a' Chóta Liathghlais), which immediately recalls the name "Bodach an Chóta Lachtna." He approaches the Fianna while hunting at the same time as Caoilte starts chasing an unnaturally speedy deer.[44] Like in H2, after they are some distance away, Fear a' Chóta Liathghlais sets off after them, but unlike in H2, he stops twice to have his coat shortened and then lengthened, before finally catching the deer for Fionn.[45] We are then told that "the deer was killed and carried back," but it is not clear whether the Ceudach character is doing the carrying as in H2 and other Scottish tales employing Opening B (MacNeil 1987: 50-51). The beginning of MacNeil's story thus resembles Opening B with its hunting opening and (unassigned) racing task, but it is less detailed and only closely related to one of the other Scottish Gaelic versions.

After this opening sequence resembling *Bodach an Chóta Lachtna*, MacNeil's tale proceeds into a quest sequence similar to those found in Campbell's version, H1 and H2. In MacNeil's tale, Fionn is placed under geasan three times. The first two tasks he must perform, collecting the heads of Feamain-Feòir ("whatever sort of creature it was" [1987: 50-51; *ge b'e gu dé seòrsa beathach a bh'ann*]) and Bogan Balachaidh, closely parallels the collection of the head of Toman-fheoir and Bheagan-blath-bheinne in H1, and resembles the quests for the heads of "the Great Turk" (an Turcach Mór) in Campbell's version and "the Great Youth" (a' Mhacain Mhóir) in H2. The similarity of the names of the beheading targets in MacNeil's version with those in H1 suggests to me a close relationship between the two versions which I think further details below will corroborate. Neither of these tasks is explained in great detail in MacNeil's version, and his memory clearly fails him in parts; for example, when describing the completion of the second task he simply says that "whatever they had to do there—a battle or a fight or some conflict" (*ge b'e b' fheudar a dheanamh ann a' sin—cath neo còmhrag neo cuir-air-n-aghaidh*), they were able to get the head (1987: 52-53). Given such a sparse narration, it is not surprising that MacNeil does not explain Ceudach's role in fetching the heads.

The third task is explained in greatest detail and it is the one for which the most parallels can be found with other versions of the Ceudach tale. This is the collection of "the [Great Smith's] clawed cup" (1987: 52-53; *an cupan ìneach aig a'cheàrd mhór*). As we have seen, Ceudach is often required to fetch a cup in other Scottish Gaelic versions of the tale when he is being tested (or the Fianna are trying to get him killed) (S1, S4, S5, A2, A6 A10, H1).[46] The task is part of the quest sequence in only one version of the tale considered here, the Irish manuscript, in which Fionn is placed under geasan to get a drinking horn belonging to the three sons of the Hag of Combat (Sgéal Chéaduig). Ceudach accomplishes this task for him. Likewise in MacNeil's tale, the Ceudach character (Fear a' Chóta Liathghlais) is the one to enter the smith's place and steal the cup. As in the other versions, he does this by means of deception, gaining the opportunity to handle the cup, and then fleeing with it. Interestingly, MacNeil includes one detail which only occurs in one of the Hebridean versions: the Ceudach character breaks the cup when it is first handed to him and it must be repaired (H1) or reforged (CB3). In both cases, the Ceudach character expresses shame (*lan naire*;[47] MacInnes 1875: fo. 57r) or remorse (*cha mhór nach deachaidh [e] gu caoineadh leis*; MacNeil 1987: 54). That the two tales share this unique detail is another indication that MacNeil's version descends from one similar to this Hebridean one.

The way the tasks are assigned in MacNeil's version and H1 adds further weight to this hypothesis. In both, Fionn's wife develops an attraction to the Ceudach character upon his arrival with the Fianna. Seeking to get Fionn killed, she places him under geasan to accomplish difficult tasks.[48] As in the other versions, Fionn is able to complete these tasks only because he brings the Ceudach character along. In MacNeil's highly condensed version, the Ceudach character's contract details with the Fianna are not discussed and no permission is requested in order for him to join on the quests. His battle with a formidable adversary and resultant death and resurrection are also absent from MacNeil's tale. MacNeil ends with one last point of similarity with both H1 and Campbell's tale: upon the successful warriors' return from questing, Fionn's wife is put to death. In H1, after returning to find that his deceitful wife has remarried, Fionn kills her on Ceudach's advice. In Campbell's version, as we will recall, the king's wife attempts to place Ceudach under geasan and he kills her. MacNeil's version is somewhat similar to Campbell's—having accomplished all the tasks she set, Fionn places his wife under counter-geasan to stand in a particular manner on the roof while he goes away for a time. Upon his return, she has died, although not apparently of punishment, but of rage (MacNeil 1987: 56-57). While this may seem a strange and elaborate punishment, it is not without parallel in the corpus of Ceudach tales. In H2, when the Ceudach character is placed under geasan to fetch the head of the Great Youth, he immediately casts counter-geasan on her to straddle a particular stream until he returns, which reduces her to a pile of bones. Likewise, in a version collected in Kerry (Ireland) by Jeremiah Curtin, Ceudach loses at chess to a mer-hag, is placed under geasan, and assigns counter-geasan to stand on the roof-gables with nothing to eat while he is away. Like Fionn's wife in MacNeil's tale and the hag in H2, the mer-hag does not survive (Lynch 1894: 466).

While there are a number of differences between MacNeil's tale and more standard versions of the Ceudach story, from the many similarities that have emerged in this analysis, I think it is clear that we are dealing with a Ceudach tale here. The final correspondence that I would like to point out concerns the Ceudach character's name. As we have seen, in MacNeil's tale, this character is known by a pseudonym related to that of the principal character in the tale, "Bodach an Chóta Lachtna." Near the end of MacNeil's story, however, this man's patronymic is revealed to be Mac Rìgh nan Collachan Òir. This patronymic differs only slightly from Ceudach's usual epithet, Mac Rìgh nan Collach, which we saw preserved in Campbell's tale, among others. What is more, it is closely aligned with the variation of his name in H1, Ceudach Nan Collachain Oir. Shaw's notes to the tale explain that MacNeil understood his protagonist to be Ceudach (Shaw 1987: 454n8). Given the degree of plot simplification that is evident in MacNeil's rendition of the tale, as well as his own admission that "This is quite a long story ... and I have forgotten a large part of it" (1987: 46-47; *'Se sgeulachd gu math fada a th'ann ... agus tha cuid mhór dhi air a dhol air dìochuimhn' orm*), it seems safe to take MacNeil at his word that his Fear a' Chóta Liathghlais is Ceudach. If we take into account the fact that MacNeil's region was settled by people from South Uist and Barra, and that his source for this tale, Archie Kennedy, was of Canna descent, his version's close relationship with the plot of the Hebridean tales does not appear at all out of the ordinary (Shaw 1987: xviii, 453).

Conclusions

This examination of the Scottish Gaelic versions of the Ceudach tale concludes, not with a claim to the homogeneity or conservatism of the tradition in either Scotland or Cape Breton, but with a celebration of its vibrancy. While I have found it possible to isolate two loosely defined opening sequences and a number of structural similarities among the various versions of the tale, this study in no way accounts for the range of elements that might be productively compared in these tales; much work is yet to be done. My primary focus on plot has clarified the relationships between the tales somewhat, but it has also revealed just how little is known about the development of the Ceudach tale over time in its new, transatlantic localities. We see none of the changes happening, only that they must have happened if we assume the tales to have come from versions something like those recorded in Scotland. Thus, in Neil Macintyre's tale, we recognize a variant most closely related to versions of the story collected in Sutherland, and we are left wondering both how it got to Benacadie, and how localized or widespread the variant may have been in Scotland.

Hector Campbell presents us with the only one of the Cape Breton tales to name the character as Ceudach—yet in a somewhat radical shift in focus, here he becomes a hero in his own right, rather than a helper, and he is unconnected with the Fianna. This shift may have already happened prior to Campbell's storytelling progenitors' departure from Scotland with the tale, but it is also possible that the new Canadian context engendered a new focus. If so, it could be conjectured that this version evidences a degree of structural deterioration within the Fenian genre at a late stage in the storytelling tradition as once-fast norms within the subgenre of Fenian "helper" tales become flexible enough to permit a drastic role change. The most puzzling tale to date has been Joe Neil MacNeil's partially forgotten version, due in part to its contracted nature. Through comparative analysis it has been possible to show the tale's relationship with the Ceudach complex, as well as to highlight some striking similarities with Hebridean versions of the tale.

It is indeed unfortunate that more versions of this tale were not collected in both Cape Breton and Scotland, for we can be certain that there must, at one time, have been a great many. And yet, perhaps the mere fact that three unique versions could be gathered in Cape Breton in the latter half of the 20th century says more about the strength of the storytelling tradition there than any number of earlier versions could. While it would be premature to base any more certain claims about the coherence of the Fenian genre or the cultural memory of 20th-century Cape Bretoners on such scarce data, it is hoped that in the future, comparative historical-geographic analyses of other Cape Breton tales might shed further light on these findings and enable us to say more about the tenacity and development of the tradition in Cape Breton.

Notes

1. Note that his name is alternately spelled Céadach or Céatach in Irish sources and scholarship using Irish sources, such as Bruford.

2. I am grateful to Ken Nilsen, who first introduced me to the study of Gaelic folklore.

3. Due to constraints of time and space this article does not take the Irish oral versions of the tale into account. Several of these are in print, however, should the reader wish to consult them for further comparison. See Bruford's bibliography in *Gaelic Folk-Tales and Mediaeval Romances* for an extensive list of published and unpublished versions of the tale in both Irish and Scottish Gaelic (1969: 258-59).

4. A Fenian "helper" character is a supernaturally powerful character from outside the Fianna who is contracted to perform difficult tasks for Fionn and his men. Gaelic heroic tales (primarily Fenian) organized around such "helper" characters are known as "helper tales" (Bruford 1969: 8; Murphy 1953: xiii-xv).

5. No linguistic analysis has yet been carried out on these texts, but, as Bruford notes, "the language is evidently late"—certainly later than Classical Common Gaelic (1969: 123). I was able to access three of the four recensions on microfilm: RIA 23 G 41, 99-117; RIA 24 C 47, 42r-50v; and RIA 24 C 2, 366-85. All three represent the same version of the tale, but the last is in by far the best condition. All further references to the manuscript tale cite that text, which is titled "Sgéal Chéaduig mac Rígh na Sorach."

6. See Bruford 1969: 258, under the heading "Eachtra Chéadaigh Mhóir." I have also incorporated storytellers' names and additional versions located by Carol Zall (217-19). I am grateful to Carol for sharing a copy of her dissertation with me. Abbreviations used in the chart are as follows: JFC = John Francis Campbell of Islay manuscripts; SA = School of Scottish Studies Archive; LS = Linguistic Survey of Scotland; WS = *Waifs and Strays of Celtic Tradition*; MWHT = *More West Highland Tales*; CWP = the Carmichael Watson Project online database.

7. Those items that I have added are the published English translation of S1, the English version of S2, S5, A9, A10, H1, H2, H3, H4, CB1, CB2 and CB3. Most of these either had not yet been recorded or were unknown to exist at the time of Bruford's research. Bruford categorizes A9 under another tale heading, *Bodach an Chóta Lachtna*. While he does not include it in his Ceudach entry, he writes that "the two stories have actually been combined" (1969: 132n41). I agree that A9 includes aspects of both stories and thus include it in my list. He must have purposefully chosen not to include A10, because he would have read it; I will later justify my inclusion of it. Bruford knew of CB1, referring to it as CB in his discussion of the tale, but it has been overlooked in his bibliography. I did not have the opportunity to consult the John Francis Campbell of Islay manuscripts, so I have not read the Gaelic original of S1 or the two English summaries, A7 and A8. The Gaelic version of S2 could unfortunately not be located when I requested a copy of the recording, but I was able to listen to the English version. I had access to transcriptions of all versions of S5, but base my analysis primarily on the first version listed in the chart, since it is the most complete. Due to time constraints, I was not able to consult H3 and H4.

8. Not having had access to the manuscript, I can only assume from the distinctly Gaelic names and from the fact that Bruford does not list Campbell's manuscript version to be in English that the published English version is a translation.

9. This item is incorrectly recorded in Bruford's bibliography as SA1957.048 A4 + B7.

10. Carol Zall also recorded three versions of this tale from Brian Stewart on April 16, 1993, September 24, 1993 and July 2, 1994 (1998: 217). She provides transcriptions of these and the two earlier versions of S5 listed above in her dissertation (298-336). Zall's study indicates that there is some structural instability in the versions of the tale recorded from this teller (122). SA1958.072 + 073 is the most complete.

11. S2-5 were all told by members of the same traveller family in Sutherland. Mary Stewart was Ailidh Dall's daughter, and Brian Stewart was his nephew. Both Mary and Brian say they learned the tale from their grandmother (Ailidh Dall's mother, Siùsie). Ailidh Dall says he learned it from his maternal uncle (Uncle Jock), but notes that his mother and brother also had the tale. Alec Stewart is Mary and Brian's second cousin—the grandson of Siùsie's sister, Clementina (Clemidh). Alec heard his tales from own grandmother. Zall writes that Siùsie was originally from Argyll (and thus, Clemidh and Jock presumably also were; 1998: 22-24, 110).

12. In addition to these, a discussion about the tale in English was recorded in 1955 from Bella Higgins of Blairgowrie, Perthshire. She explains that she heard the tale told in English at Aberfoyle, Stirlingshire, from an old man named George MacPhee, who also spoke Gaelic (SA 1955.153.B2). She does not remember any specific details.

13. I am grateful to Domhnall Uilleam Stiùbhart for sending me a draft transcription of this lengthy tale prior to its publication in the Carmichael Watson Project's online database.

14. It is unclear whether or not Bruford omits CB1 from his total when enumerating the tales he has consulted. When describing his findings, he writes, "I know of a dozen Scottish Gaelic versions and 116 from Ireland" (1969: 123). He lists twelve Scottish tales in his bibliography, but in his endnote to the quoted statement he mentions also having CB1. His dozen may thus be a "baker's dozen," reducing the number of Irish tales he consulted to forty-nine. Unfortunately, no more accurate data is available at this time.

15. This description of Opening A is similar to, but much less constrictively detailed than, Bruford's summary. Bruford describes the tale opening with "a quarrel between Céadach and his foster-brother or fellow-pupil over his tutor's daughter: her father settles the quarrel by putting them in a room with two doors; each man is to leave by one door, and the one she chooses to follow may leave with her. She chooses Céadach" (1969: 125).

16. A3, A4 and A6 share a similar introductory episode that either prefaces the episode described above (A4, A6) or is retrospectively added (A3). In these, Ceudach and two of his friends are playing as children and one of them hits the ball into an old woman's house, either striking her belongings or herself. The old woman then places a curse on them regarding their deaths; they will either die at each other's hands (A3, A4) or in three distinctive ways: one will be drowned in the ocean, one killed on land and one burned in the sky (A6). In this way, these tales resemble those in which the Ceudach character's death is prophesied in Opening B.

17. A6 is unique in that it contains episodes common to both opening sequences. The English version of S2 is also different from the other tales listed above. Skipping the opening events, Ailidh Dall plunges directly into the Fenian quest incident that usually comes next. He summarizes the opening events at the end of the tale, but references throughout seem to indicate that he is more used to placing them at the beginning.

18. Bruford shows the use of this stock opening (minus the prophecy) in other tales as well, and dubs it "the common brugh opening" (1969: 225). The reception of this particular prophecy is also a shared motif, and Zall notes its use in another tale told by Brian (1998: 124). It is found in all the Sutherland tales except S3 and some of the renditions of S5.

19. These details are primarily found in the versions that do not elaborate on Ceudach's life prior to joining the Fianna. A comical detail sometimes noted is that while following (and soon overtaking) a guide back to Fionn's camp, the lengthy toenail of his big toe tears the guide's clothes, or even cuts the guide's back and legs (A2, A10). A variation of this appears in A5, where Ceudach travels and performs his tasks quickly wearing only one stocking and one shoe. H2 is somewhat exceptional in that the Ceudach character goes

fishing rather than hunting on his first day with Fionn. This soon progresses into a hunting episode in which only he is able to catch a particular deer. He is not the one to prepare and cook this deer, however; instead, he instructs Oscar and Caoilte to do it while he negotiates with the hag who owned the deer.

20. Bruford notes that fetching a cup or horn is a common task set for Ceudach, as is running a race (1969: 125).

21. The Sutherland tales present a slightly different scenario in which the Ceudach character injures or kills some of Fionn's men, prompting Fionn to want to get rid of him (S1, S3-5). A6 and H2 are also somewhat anomalous. In A6, Ceudach is not asked to perform a difficult task in order to get rid of him; rather, he sees that Fionn is under duress and voluntarily completes the task for him. In H2, the aggressor is not one of the Fianna at all, but a hag whose deer the Ceudach character has just killed for Fionn. Similarly to later quests in H1, he is placed under geasan to fetch the head of a particular foe. All of the other versions cited above include a jealous, Fenian aggressor who seeks to get rid of the Ceudach character, but he is not always Conan. In the manuscript tale, Diarmuid is the Fenian aggressor. In H1, the aggressor is Caoilte, who beats the Ceudach character in a game of chess and then requires him to perform a dangerous task. The task involves recovering *cupa Fhionn na Féinne* (the cup of Fionn of the Fianna) from a foe on penalty of having his head cut off by Caoilte; if he succeeds, however, he can remove Caoilte's head (fo. 56v). (Upon the Ceudach character's success, Caoilte negotiates to keep his head [fo. 57v].) Fetching a particular drinking horn is also a task set in the manuscript version (Sgéal Chéaduig), but there it is one of the tasks that the hag requires Fionn to perform. In A9, no task is set. Because this version is a cross with *Bodach an Chóta Lachtna*, the focus in this portion of the tale is on the events of the race between the Ceudach character and Conan. (The topic of *Bodach an Chóta Lachtna* is a race between a large, unkempt, unnamed stranger and a powerful challenger to the Fianna. Despite several seemingly unnecessary delays, the stranger easily wins the race. See also endnote 42.) The race episodes in H1 and the Sutherland versions also display delay tactics reminiscent of Bodach an Chóta Lachtna. In the Sutherland tales, the race is against Caoilte, whom the Ceudach character overtakes and transforms into a deer, after which he leaves the Fianna (S1, S3-5). (Caoilte's transformation and the Ceudach character's leaving is mentioned in the discussion following the English version of S2, but it is omitted from the actual telling of the tale.) In some of the other versions, the Ceudach character ties Conan up and departs, leaving him for the Fianna to discover and free.

22. Bruford categorizes this latter portion of the tale as a version of the *Feis Tighe Chonáin* episode, "The Finding of Bran," although it is one in which the puppies are not actually found. It can also be classed as a version of ATU 513A (1969: 118, 121n12).

23. I am not the first to have noted these similarities; Carol Zall also includes A10 in her tale list (1998: 218).

24. Bruford only refers to the hunting setting of the Ceudach tale in an endnote to a discussion of an entirely different tale (*Bodach an Chóta Lachtna*; 132n41). The carrying of burdens and the cooking of game are trivialized in another endnote as "routine matters of hunting … superlatively well fulfilled as in most such helper-tales" (1969: 130n19). No references to comparable helper tales are provided, but we might uncover some by process of elimination if we compare Bruford's list of Ceudach tales with the representative list of Fenian helper tales compiled by Murphy (a considerable number of which are Ceudach tales). See Bruford 1969: 258-59; Murphy 1953: 177-88.

25. My criticism of Bruford's analysis is not intended to suggest that he was careless or inattentive to detail. In undertaking such a gargantuan task as the comparative consideration of all of the medieval Gaelic romances and the related modern folktales, some structural points were bound to be overlooked. Moreover, as he clearly states, his consideration of the tale is not a definitive study, but rather a broad overview of a representative sample of versions of the tale (1969: iv, 124). Nor do I claim that the categorical method I introduce in this article ought to be taken as definitive. (In essence, all such modes of categorization are artificial academic apparatuses designed primarily for the purpose of comparison; they are subject to fault, and in practice there is often a great degree of variation and flexibility [cf. Dégh 1965: xxx-xxxi; Bruford 1969: 238-40].) By my criticism, I intend to illuminate the way in which the primary assumptions a scholar makes about the structure of a story frame his or her interpretation, and how data outlying that frame can be overshadowed by it, sometimes to the detriment of the interpretation.

26. As Zall notes, the Sutherland background story is not "logically linked with the rest of the story" like the frame stories in Brian's other tales are, which "would … make it easier for the storyteller to forget it, at least temporarily" (1998: 123, 127). In other words, it is something of a commonplace element that is not always considered integral to the tale. It might also be noted that even in some versions that include the particular frame tale that Bruford preferences (Opening A + death at the hands of a disappointed suitor), the Fenian portion is the primary focus of the narrative (A6, for instance).

27. Interestingly, A9 also alludes to a conflict with an enemy something like the sort Bruford takes to be the "basis of the plot" of the Ceudach tale. While A9 contains no quest, and therefore none of the events described above, at the end of the tale the Ceudach character requests that Fionn accompany him home. On the way, he informs Fionn that he is a king's son, and that Fionn's coming will break a curse that caused him and his brother never to agree until Fionn visited their home.

28. In the Sutherland tales, the Ceudach character proceeds to his father's house where he heals his stepbrother and then reveals his identity, explaining that the prophecy that one brother would kill the other has been fulfilled. In A2, Ceudach is resurrected at his mother's house, after which he accompanies Fionn home to prevent Fionn's own men from accidentally killing him

in their excitement to see him. The quest in H1 continues after Ceudach's resurrection. In the manuscript version, Ceudach is resurrected at his mother's house after the Fianna depart, but he decides to return to Ireland to visit them and gives his daughter to Oscar in marriage.

29. In A1, A3 and A4 the quest is secondary to the rivalry with an enemy, corresponding with Bruford's assessment of the tale. (This is unsurprising, given that all three tales display Opening A, which was also taken by Bruford to be primary.) In A3, the quest is announced and the Fianna depart, but the events of their journey are omitted and the teller proceeds directly to the battle with Ceudach's rival on the return journey. In A1 and A4, the battle with the rival occurs upon their arrival at the location of the quest. Because the quest itself is downplayed in these tales, they are omitted from my discussion of the quest.

30. Bruford also notes this similarity (1969: 125-26).

31. The word *amhas* (Irish pl. *amhais*; Scottish Gaelic pl. *amhasan*) has been interpreted in different contexts to mean either a mercenary/hireling or a monster. The first definition, which implies some form of service, looks to be an older usage (cf. the entry for *amus* in the Dictionary of the Irish Language). According to Dinneen in some folktales, *amhas* means "ogre" (1934: 39; cf. Bruford's interpretation of the word in 1969: 15).

32. These are all versions of a stock episode known as *teach na n-amhus* which may have its origins in the 16th century (Bruford 1969:15; Zall 1998: 149).

33. MacLeod's translation of this sentence is fairly loose. S1 is similar in that the queen learns of the fairy woman's son from a hen-wife who is "skilled in enchantment," but no prophecy is made at this time (Young 1888: 173). In Appendices 1 and 2 to J. F. Campbell's *More West Highland Tales*, J. G. MacKay discusses the hen-wife and *eachlach-ùrlair* characters, noting that "in the modern forms of folk-tales [the *eachlach-ùrlair*] strongly resembles the Hen-Wife" (MacKay 1994: 492). Both generally possess magic and/or extraordinary knowledge and often act as troublemakers.

34. MacLeod translates this as "Muck Island" (Macintyre 1974: 82), while Zall renders it "The Isle of Pigs," noting the possibility that the Isle of Muck could be intended (1998: 73). Generally when a hero departs on such an adventure, the action takes place at a faraway and often fictional location. About the Ceudach tale in particular, Bruford notes that Fionn tends to be summoned to the "Eastern World" (1969: 125). The named locations in the other Scottish Gaelic versions I have consulted include Lochlann (A1), the Kingdom of the Big Men (*rìoghachd nam fear mòra*) (A3), the city of Camlisk (*cathair na Camluisg*) (A4) and Turkey (CB2). While Turkey and (arguably) Lochlann may be real physical locations, they reference fantastic ideological constructs not unlike the other places named. In a Gaelic folkloric context, they are all liminal story lands in which heroic or supernatural activity may take place. I am inclined to think that this tale does not break with this

preference for fictional quest locations, and therefore that Zall's interpretation, "The Isle of Pigs" (a decidedly unreal place), is likely the intended meaning.

35. S1-5, A2-6, H2. A2 also calls the helper character "the Big Lad" (an Gille Mór). In A9 he is "the Man with the Slovenly Blue-grey Coat" (Fear a' Chòta Shlibistich Liathghlais) and in A10 he is alternately referred to as "the Bent Grey Lad" (an Gille Crom Glas) or "the Big Lad" (an Gille Mór). Those versions that name the helper character as Ceudach are A1, A3-6 and H1. In H2 he is introduced as Cialla. The English translation of S1 gives the helper's name as Fach-Mòhr-mac-Righ-na-Lirriach, which resembles the *Ceudach (Mór) mac Rìgh na ---ach* pattern. I was unfortunately not able to consult the Gaelic version of S1 to verify this name. H1 is unique in that the helper in the beginning, called "the Grey Lad" (An Gille Glas), seems to be understood as a separate character from the helper who comes to Fionn's aid in the quest that follows the opening sequence—*Ceudach nan Collachain Oir* (glossed by Carmichael as "Ceudach of the Golden Doors").

36. Cf. *Ceudamh Mac Rìgh nan Cola* (A1); *Conn Ceutach Mac Rìgh nan Colachan* (A6); *Ceudach nan Collachain Oir* (H1). In A2 the Ceudach character is known only by pseudonyms, but his brother is called Mac Rìgh an t-Soluis, which sounds like it may be a derivative of Collach. It is possible that some tellers understood Mac Rìgh nan Collach to refer to the inhabitants of an actual Scottish location, the Isle of Coll (Eilean Chola). Collach can indeed mean "a person from Coll," and would be in the genitive plural in the patronymic. J. G. Campbell suspects such a meaning, translating the word as "Son of the King of the Colla Men" in A4-6 and noting the proximity of the Isle of Coll to the region of collection. One of his informants seems skeptical, however, responding to his inquiry, "The Coll men with a King! – they never had and never will have a King to themselves!" (1891c: 277n10). Collach might also be associated in tellers' minds with the three Collas of the 4th-century Irish kingdom of Airgialla, one of whom, Colla Uais, is the legendary Irish ancestor of the MacDonalds. Taking a different perspective, Bruford suggests that whatever linguistic forms it has taken and whatever it has come to mean in the folk mind, the word likely has its origin in the eastern place name, Críoch na gColach (Ir.) "Colchis" (1969: 21, 29n2, 124).

37. Perhaps Campbell intends his listeners to see the adversarial relationship between Ceudach and his brother-in-law, Leobhar, as resultant from Ceudach's unsanctioned elopement with Leobhar's sister. If so, it is not clearly stated in this telling of the tale.

38. MacDonell and Shaw point out that life-restoring water is also used in some Munster versions, and note a Galway version in which healing balsam is used (1984: 89n11, citing Bruford 1969: 131 and Béaloideas 6: 61-71).

39. In H1 a lengthy episode is included after Ceudach's death as the group makes their way homeward. This episode is different from Hector Campbell's in most respects, but there are some minor similarities. Both episodes involve

collecting water with magical properties, and in both they meet an old man along the way who accompanies them in fetching the liquid (water of youth in H1 and healing water in CB2). When the old man in each tale benefits from the special water, however, his wife is displeased. In Campbell's version, she exclaims "he was hard enough to please before, but he will be altogether insufferable now" (1984: 65-66; *Bha e tàireil gu leòr roimhe, ach bithidh an truaigh' uile air a nist*).

40. Expansion by way of repetition is often noted in discussions about Gaelic hero tales (e.g., O'Nolan 1982: 21), and episodes may also be incorporated into a story. With regard to Fenian tales in particular, Bruford states that their organization around a particular group of characters makes them susceptible to being "strung together" (1969: 212). Studies have indicated that structural changes of this sort generally take place when a storyteller is mastering a tale and making it his or her own, after which point the tale's form tends to remain relatively stable in repeated tellings (Holbek 1987: 173-75). In this way, a tale variant specific to a particular teller, a family or a region may come into being. Episodes may also be misremembered, reordered or forgotten. Moreover, as Georges Zimmermann reminds us, "Performance is generally not the mere reproduction of rehearsed material"—there is always "the possibility of deliberate variation or unplanned improvisation in the course of narration" (2001: 445). See also Bruford (1969: 210-45); Zimmermann (2001: 444-45).

41. Shaw notes the connection only in an endnote (1987: 454n8), and, in his review of the collection, Alan Bruford is cautious about making the assignation. In recounting MacNeil's repertoire of hero tales, Bruford writes, "There are elements of *Bodach an Chòta Lachtna* (and *Céadach*?), [etc.]" (1989: 192).

42. *Bodach an Chòta Lachtna* is the name of the manuscript version of the tale, which can be dated back to approximately the 17th century, and which was copied numerous times throughout Ireland (Bruford 1969: 129, 132n40). According to Bruford's data, only two oral versions have been collected in Ireland, in comparison with Scotland's four variants (253). He states speculatively that the Irish manuscript version of the tale may actually be an Irish redaction of the introduction to a longer Scottish folk tale (129). More investigation of this topic is needed.

43. Bruford writes that "even the names are similar [Caol an Iarainn and Caoilte], and the rough dress of the hero" (1969: 132n41). There is also some evidence in Scotland that both tales were common in the same localities and even among the same tellers. For instance, John Francis Campbell collected the outline of a version of Bodach an Chòta Lachtna from a well-known South Uist storyteller named Donald MacPhee (mentioned in J. F. Campbell 1994: 552). This is the same man from whom John MacInnes learned his version of the Ceudach tale (H1). (Biographies of both storytellers are available online in the Carmichael Watson Project database.)

44. Cf. the Sutherland versions of the tale in which Caoilte is transformed into a deer.

45. The language used in MacNeil's tale and H2 indicates that they are clearly related. In both, Fionn determines the distance between the onlookers and the deer using his tooth of knowledge (Jackson 1962: 187; MacNeil 1987: 49). In H2, we are told that the Ceudach character waits until the deer is "six peaks and six glens and six summer sitting-places" (*sia beannan's sia gleannan's sia àiteachan suidhe samhraidh*) away before he takes up the chase, while in MacNeil's version he waits until it is "three mountains and three glens and three summer sitting-places" (*trì bheannaibh agus trì ghlinn agus trì àiteachan-suidhe samhraidh*) (Jackson 1962: 186-87; MacNeil 1987: 48-49).

46. The names of these cups are: *Corn chearach* (S1); *Còrn an Leathraich* (S4, S5); *a' Cupan Ceathraraich* (A2); *cupa ceithir-cheàrnach na Féinne* (A10); *cupa Fhionn na Féinne* "the cup of Fionn of the Fianna" (H1). The cup in A6 has no particular name, but it is accompanied by a tablecloth, both of which are magical items of plenty: "a tablecloth and goblet that I [Fionn] had" (A. Campbell 1955: 13; *anart bùird agus cuach a bh'agam*). See also James MacDougall's discussion of the cup's name (1891: 267).

47. My reading of the text is tentative here. See fo. 57r, lines 12-13.

48. We might compare the versions in which Ceudach is sent to accomplish difficult tasks in the hope that his death will result. It is also worth noting that this scenario is the inverse of one noted in the Irish National Folklore Collection card catalogue record for this tale, which states that there is a version in which Fionn covets Céatach's wife and thus sends Céatach on quests.

References

PRIMARY SOURCES

Cameron, Alexander. 1891. The Lad of the Skin Coverings / Gille nan Cochla-Craicinn. In *Folk and Hero Tales*, vol. 3 of *Waifs and Strays of Celtic Tradition*, ed. and trans. James MacDougall, 27-55. London: David Nutt.

Campbell, Angus. 1955. Gille nan Cochall Chraiceann. In *Sgialachdan Gàilig a Chruinnich Iain Òg Ìle*, ed. K. C. Craig, 7-25. Stirling: Eneas Mackay.

Campbell, Hector. 1984. Ceudach Prince of the Collach / Ceudach Mac Rìgh nan Collach. In *Luirgean Eachainn Nìll: A Collection of Folktales told by Hector Campbell*, ed. and trans. Margaret MacDonell and John Shaw, 53-68. Inverness: John Eccles Printers Ltd.

Campbell, John Gregorson, ed. and trans. 1891a. Ceudach Son of the King of the Colla Men / Ceudach Mac Rìgh nan Collach. In *The Fians, or, Stories, poems and traditions of Fionn and his warrior band*, vol. 4 of *Waifs and Strays of Celtic Tradition*, 225-232. London: David Nutt.

———, ed. and trans. 1891b. The Lad with the Skin Coverings / Gille nan Cochla Craicionn. In *The Fians, or, Stories, poems and traditions of Fionn and his warrior band*, vol. 4 of *Waifs and Strays of Celtic Tradition*, 260-70. London: David Nutt.

———, ed. and trans. 1891c. [no title]. In *The Fians, or, Stories, poems and traditions of Fionn and his warrior band*, vol. 4 of *Waifs and Strays of Celtic Tradition*, 274-77. London: David Nutt.

Jackson, Kenneth. 1962. The Hag of the Red Stream / Cailleach A[n] Struth Ruaidh. *Scottish Studies* 6.2:184-93.

Livingston, Neil. 1890. Leoän Creeäch, Son of the King of Eirin, and Kaytav, Son of the King of Colla / Leòmhan Cridheach, Mac Rìgh Eirinn, agus Ceudamh, mac Rìgh nan Cola. In *Waifs and Strays*, vol. 2, ed. and trans. D. MacInnes, 376-383. London: David Nutt.

Lynch, Maurice. 1894. Fin MacCool, Ceadach Og, and the Fish-Hag. *Hero-Tales of Ireland*, ed. Jeremiah Curtin, 463-83. London: Macmillan.

MacInnes, John (Iain mac Phàdruig). 1875. Ceudach Nan Collachain Oir. Carmichael Watson Project. CW 106/127, http://www.carmichaelwatson.lib.ed.ac.uk/cwatson/en/fulltexttranscription/3235/0/1/1/cw106$002f127/CW106$002f127/score/true (accessed 12 April 2012.)

Macintyre, Neil. 1969. Rìgh na Gréige. In *Sgialachdan a Albainn Nuaidh*, by C. I. N. MacLeod, 94-101. Glasgow: Gairm.

———. 1974. The King of Greece. In *Stories from Nova Scotia*, by C. I. N. MacLeod, 77-85. Antigonish, NS: Formac.

MacNeil, Joe Neil. 1987. The Man in the Light Grey Coat / Fear a' Chòta Liathghlais. In *Tales Until Dawn / Sgeul gu Latha*, ed. and trans. John Shaw, 46-57. Montréal: McGill-Queen's University Press.

MacTavish, Archibald. 1890. Feunn mac Cüail and the Bent Grey Lad / Fionn mac Chumaill's an Gille Crom, Glas. In *Waifs and Strays*, vol. 2, ed. and trans. D. MacInnes, 32-67. London: David Nutt.

MacTavish, Jean. 1994. The Story of the Man with the Slovenly Blue-Grey Coat / Sgeulachd Fear a' Chóta Shlibistich Liathghlais. In *More West Highland Tales*, vol. 2, by John Francis Campbell, trans. John G. MacKay, ed. W. J. Watson et al., 68-76. Edinburgh: Birlinn.

O'Grady, Standish H. 1892. The Carle of the Coat. In *Silva Gadelica*, vol. 1, 324-31. London and Edinburgh: Williams and Norgate.

Sgéal Chéaduig mac Rígh na Sorach. n.d. Windele Manuscripts Collection. 24 C 2: 366-385, Royal Irish Academy, Dublin.

Stewart, Alexander (Ailidh Dall). 1958. *Gille nan Cochulla Craicinn*. School of Scottish Studies Sound Archive, University of Edinburgh. SA1958.075.B2 + SA1958.076.A1.

Stewart, Alexander (Alec). 1955. *Gille nan Cochulla Craicinn*. School of Scottish Studies Sound Archive, University of Edinburgh. SA1955.124.A2.

Stewart, Alexander (Brian). 1958. *Gille nan Cochulla Craicinn*. School of Scottish Studies Sound Archive, University of Edinburgh. SA1958.072 + 073.

Stewart, Mary (Micki). 1957. *Gille nan Cochulla Craicinn*. School of Scottish Studies Sound Archive, University of Edinburgh. SA1957.048.A4 + B1.

Young, Mrs. 1888. The Romance of Gillen a Cochlan Crackenach. In *The Folk-Lore of Sutherlandshire*, by [Charlotte] Dempster. *Folk-Lore Journal* 6 (3): 149-89.

SECONDARY SOURCES

Bruford, Alan. 1969. *Gaelic Folk-Tales and Mediaeval Romances*. Dublin: The Folklore of Ireland Society.

———. 1986/1987. Oral and Literary Fenian Tales. *Béaloideas* 54/55:25-56.

———. 1989. Review of *Tales Until Dawn / Sgeul Gu Latha*, ed. John Shaw. *Béaloideas* 57: 191-95.

Campbell, J. F. 1994. *Popular Tales of the West Highlands*. New ed. Vol. 1. Edinburgh: Birlinn.

Dégh, Linda, ed. 1965. *Folktales of Hungary*. Trans. Judit Halász. Chicago: University of Chicago Press.

Dinneen, Patrick S. 1934. *Foclóir Gaedhilge agus Béarla / An Irish-English Dictionary*. Dublin: Irish Texts Society.

Dooley, Ann and Harry Roe. 1999. *Tales of the Elders of Ireland*. Oxford: Oxford University Press.

Dunn, Charles W. 1953. *The Highland Settler: A Portrait of the Scottish Gael in Nova Scotia*. Toronto: University of Toronto Press.

Holbek, Bengt. 1987. *Interpretations of Fairy Tales: Danish Folklore in a European Perspective. Folklore Fellows Communications* 239. Helsinki: Suomalainen Tiedeakatemia.

MacDonell, Margaret and John Shaw. 1984. Notes. In *Luirgean Eachainn Nìll: A Collection of Folktales told by Hector Campbell*, by Hector Campbell, 81-90. Inverness: John Eccles Printers Ltd.

MacDougall, James. 1891. Notes. *Folk and Hero Tales*, vol. 3 of *Waifs and Strays of Celtic Tradition*, 259-304. London: David Nutt.

MacInnes, John. 2007. The Gaelic Hero-Tales. In *Scottish Life and Society: A Compendium of Scottish Ethnology*, vol. 10 of *Oral Literature and Performance Culture*, ed. John Beech et al., 64-81. Edinburgh: John Donald, Birlinn.

MacKay, John G. 1994. Appendices 1 and 2. In *More West Highland Tales*, vol. 1, J. F. Campbell, trans. John G. MacKay, ed. W. J. Watson et al., 491-99. Edinburgh: Birlinn.

MacLeod, C. I. N. 1974. Brief History of the Settlers. In *Stories from Nova Scotia*, 5-16. Antigonish: Formac, Ltd.

MacNeill, Eoin. 1908. *Duanaire Finn*. Vol. 1. London: Irish Texts Society.

Meyer, Kuno. 1910. *Fianaigecht. Royal Irish Academy Todd Lecture Series*. Dublin: Hodges, Figgis, and Co.

Murphy, Gerard. 1953. *Duanaire Finn*. Vol. 3. Dublin: Irish Texts Society.

Ó hÓgáin, Dáithí. 1988. *Fionn mac Cumhaill: Images of the Gaelic Hero*. Dublin: Gill and Macmillan.

O'Nolan, Kevin. 1982. Introduction. *Eochair, A King's Son in Ireland, by Éamon Bourke*. Dublin: Comhairle Bhéaloideas Éireann.

Shaw, John. 1987. Introduction and Notes. *Tales Until Dawn / Sgeul gu Latha*, ed. and trans. John Shaw, xvii-xli, 443-477. Montreal: McGill-Queen's University Press.

Zall, Carol. 1998. Mar a Chuala Mi – Remembering and Telling Gaelic Stories: A Study of Brian Stewart. PhD diss., University of Edinburgh.

Zimmermann, Georges D. 2001. *The Irish Storyteller*. Dublin: Four Courts Press.

Part IV: Identity and Race

Paul W. Birt

The Earth in a Suitcase: Cultural Hybridization in the Welsh and Cornish Diasporas

It has become practically *de rigueur* for the histories of European migrants to include a description of migrants carrying little more than their language, culture and/or oral traditions. These aspects of intangible heritage are then treated as badges of replanted identity; their survival in the immigrant context is charted as a sign of the overall health of the ethnic group itself. Such approaches may assume that the ethnic culture was pure to begin with and that the maintenance of this purity is an obvious objective of any self-respecting immigrant group, ignoring the complexities of pre-existing hybridity in the European homelands.

We all encounter hybridity in our daily lives; in fact, nothing could be more normal: we are all in some ways the hybridized versions of our parents. Thus, we should try to view hybridity as a positive development. Hybridity has assumed a number of forms in the cultural history of every people. Today it has reached centre stage, and is highlighted as a prominent feature of globalization. The Celtic world has never been immune to such forces, and, as anyone who has traced the evolution of such a festival as Halloween from its mainly Scottish and Irish roots to its subsequent importation to the eastern States and towns of southern Ontario can attest, Halloween's modern version bears little resemblance to the more traditional Halloween. With its popular and exotic forms of horror, the original associations with love and divining seem to have been almost entirely submerged. In this case, the Celtic world no longer has ownership of the festival, and its excessively over-hybridized version has found a permanent and ever-growing place in the popular culture of the globalized world (Rogers 2002).

Such hybridities are very much part of the Western, postmodern, perhaps post-cultural world, and as such help define that world of consumerist mainstream anglophone culture. The postmodern stresses the cultural over the natural, surface over depth and difference over sameness. Such manifestations are the flotsam and jetsam of often fragmented communities whose struggle with hybridity, assimilation and stigmatization of language will be the core areas of investigation in this chapter.

Apart from the generalized use of the term, hybridity in culture and identity has also been the subject of much discussion in the realms of postcolonial studies. Much of what has been discussed could be applied as well to the cultural and linguistic experiences of most of the nations we tend to call "Celtic," both the original homelands in Europe and the immigrant communities in the Americas.

In purely American terms (including the northern, central and southern parts of the continent), the very first examples of cultural hybridity come from Mesoamerica and date from the period of Spanish colonization (Gruzinski 1999: 59-86). Frescos created by indigenous artists for the walls of new convents, the songs and the festivals that they adopted in a Europeanized style, the street names of the new Spanish towns, all reflect how in a bi-directional way the creation of a cultural hybridity was to give way in time to the *métissage* familiar in the various Mexican cultures of today. This so-called disorder of styles became the basis for new identities which remain today (87-104).

Hybrid identities, the subject of this paper, are not easily defined. Homi Bhabha has gone some way toward elucidating the concept in the context of colonized peoples and immigrant communities. Celtic identities are almost by definition anchored to similar historical experiences where status-less languages and a lack of self-governance created a sense of being minoritized. These identities are not automatically lost in the new environment of the Americas. Rather, the new set of identities adopted leads to a hybridity in cultural terms. Aspects of the new culture may become the norm as various generations come and go, but language and other cultural behaviour may persist to varying degrees. The sense of having been minoritized in the homeland may also persist in the hybridized identity that redefines "Celtic" identities in the Americas.

What is Hybridity?

Homi K. Bhabha provided many of the starting points for a consideration of cultural hybridity, predominantly in the field of postcolonial studies. His best-known work, *The Location of Culture*, as well as other essays, contains an analysis that has been applied to many cultures that have experienced periods of colonization. He examined the concept of ambiguous identities created by the colonial experience as early as 1985 in his essay entitled "Signs Taken For Wonders" (2006b: 38-43). He refers to the result of hybridization in a colonial context as the "doubling" of identity. This concept had already been examined by the Algerian Frantz Fanon. In his books *Peau noire masques blancs* and *Les damnés de la terre*, Fanon explored the particular psychological problems that arose from attempted binary identities. In particular, he demonstrated in a clinical manner that a double identity was frequently an impediment in the search for a "totalized" identity—in the early days of cultural and postcolonial studies, the notion of culture as monolithic was being challenged. For Fanon, the monolithic nature of national culture was especially pronounced while Algeria was still part of a French colonial regime. Hybridized identity, illustrated by Fanon's work, assumes a "linguistic, symbolic, historical reality" where the colonizing Other becomes a negation of the identity of the colonized (Bhabha 1994: 74).

Not surprisingly, much of Bhabha's discourse, together with that of others who have examined the concept of hybridization in colonial contexts, tends to be focused on parts of the world that have suffered recent periods of European colonization. However, some of Bhabha's ideas about hybridization can be applied to some of the older nations of Europe, especially those on the western seaboard of the continent, as well as other peoples of Europe such as the Roma and peoples who have lived in quasi-colonial contexts for at least some of their history. On occasion, Bhabha does refer to migrant groups as well as hybridized subjects, especially when they find themselves in European and American contexts as a result of extreme subjugation, such as African slavery or the more benign economic-based population movement to the cities of the Western world (1994: 67). Cultural hybridity of varying forms is a result of such movements:

> In place of the symbolic consciousness that gives the sign of identity its integrity and unity, its *depth*, we are faced with a dimension of doubling; a spatialization of the subject, that is occluded in the illusory perspective of what I have called the "third dimension" of the mimetic frame or visual image of identity. (71)

In fact, the difference between the world of the Other and the indigenous identity of the colonized, or the *migrant*, becomes the starting point of a struggle to bridge the gap with that "third dimension," the hybridized identity that helps create a psychological balance or stability, at least for a while. Bhabha does not focus especially on the world of the migrant for most of his study, but suggests that migration leads to a situation similar to that in a colonial or, indeed, postcolonial world. The cultural and linguistic tensions brought about by migration are self-evident and were presumed to be resolved in the process of "integration" to the larger cultural and linguistic group. However, in reality, the situations in both North and South America were more complex.

Identity

We need to be careful when using the word "identity." We talk about, for instance, a Highland identity, a Welsh Patagonian identity, a Pontiac Outaouais Irish identity. All such identities taken at random are conceptual areas of quicksand, waiting for our tentative footsteps. Without entering into a theoretical discussion, I will merely state that I am using the word to express a person's or persons' idea of themselves, and as such it assumes the form of an ideal, projected psychologically, and is a fiction (i.e., something made or created). Despite the ambiguities inherent in this term, we can usefully examine such concepts to help understand those ideals held by individuals and communities at a given time, remembering that hybridity is the servant of time and that all such ideas, like identities, will slip into oblivion and give way to new concepts.

We are all familiar with those elements that make up new ways of representing an ethnic concept in an ethnic context: a certain range of shared values, a language, a perceived heritage. Sometimes shared identity is conceived of as a sacred flame carried by tradition bearers, especially when a culture or an identity is deemed to be under threat. Today, to warm one's hands on the flame of shared heritage becomes a way of communing with that identity package in a world where alternative identities are vying for our attention. Seeking out those who speak or understand the heritage language becomes part of that search for the authentic touchstone of a time-honoured identity. Of course, not all ethnic groups which become minoritized in a diasporic context follow the same path in the search for survival. The acceptance of some form of hybridity also allows some ethnic groups to accommodate themselves to the majority. A Welsh Patagonian who feels far more Argentine than European Welsh (i.e., the majority) accepts how his ethnic background helps him or her to feel more at home in Argentina and elsewhere. Such a person may well also have Italian, Basque or Spanish heritage. A Canadian Scot will be quick to remind you how much the Scots have contributed to the building of Canada, and will celebrate Canada Day with great pride. The bilingual Welsh-Spanish primary school in Trelew, Chubut holds a ceremony on the Argentine Flag Day to celebrate the fact of being Argentine. The flag day is held in both Welsh and Spanish and clearly celebrates the special contribution of the Welsh in Chubut as well as the state language.

In these kinds of contemporary contexts, it is my contention that what we are seeing is not a confused, ambiguous identity package where a choice needs to be made between two idealized identities, but rather a very central concern, one often historically associated with a monolithic state, or today more likely with the forces of globalization that seek to turn citizens into uniform consumers. My contention is that the so-called hybrid identities in fact have a very powerful effect in strengthening the sense of belonging to the country that was settled perhaps by ancestors several generations ago. In other words, I contend that a Welsh Patagonian, to take an example, by creating a personal identity based on Welsh culture and Argentine cultural norms, becomes in fact more Argentine and not more Welsh. A Canadian Highlander, whether from Nova Scotia or Glengarry County, ON, does much the same, and thereby reinforces his or her sense of belonging to a certain vision of Canada as an individual and citizen. It could even be argued that, for others, the more Gaelic they become in language and culture, the more they see themselves as authentically Canadian.

This sense of hybridity as a cornerstone of a more authentic citizenship seems to have been developed as an idea especially in the Canadian context. One of the most unambiguous expressions of cultural and national hybridity in the Americas comes from the Canadian writer John Ralston Saul in his book *A Fair Country: Telling Truths About Canada* (2008). His emphasis is on the interaction between the settler peoples and First Nations. Again, the newcomers—the francophones from the 17th century, the Scots from the late 18th and 19th centuries and the German religious minorities from the 18th century—all settled here in difficult, isolating circumstances and survived thanks to the First Nations and, later, the Métis. Their relationships evolved over time, often for the worse. But it was a slow evolution, a matter of centuries. Ways of relating to the Other and of doing things once settled in, became habit, became culture (57).

The hybridizing dynamic that Saul suggests was found in early Canada, and which has implications for today, means that, as he puts it, "Canadians carry both the Aboriginal and the European tradition" (63), and that there is a conflict between the "western Manichaean drive" and those Aboriginal foundations. But that fundamental dynamic of cultural change affects all sides. "Both parties were changed. Both gained. Both lost. But our deep roots are indigenous, and there lie the most interesting explanations for what we are and what we can be" (63). This controversial concept of national hybridity could be applied in a number of contexts. To what extent, for instance, did Aboriginal culture influence the early Welsh communities of Patagonia and leave a permanent imprint on that culture? Certainly Tehuelche and Mapuche communities have been changed by their interaction in the past with the first Europeans they really knew, the Welsh. This would give a further dimension to the concept of hybridity in a Welsh-Patagonian setting.

Part of the hybridity process today in "Celtic" communities in the Americas includes a reaffirmation of "heritage" languages. One sees in the Americas a variety of projects devoted to the revival or renewal of ethnic languages. Among these one could cite Yiddish, Scottish Gaelic, Irish, Basque and several indigenous languages in Argentina. The peripatetic organization Cymdeithas Madog has for some thirty years provided North Americans the opportunity to begin or perfect their knowledge of the Welsh language. Moving from city to city in the U.S. and Canada allows Cymdeithas Madog to mirror the movement of the National Eisteddfod in Wales itself, an organization which is in many ways the very symbol of Welsh culture and language.

Language revitalization of this kind in the Americas is more likely to be connected with individuals' desire to emphasize a hybrid identity as a means of offsetting the powerful influences of globalization which draw the individual toward new identities based on mercantile forces. Although we could contend that revitalization in the homelands implies a renewal of the language's territory and the recreation of a population, however small or large, speaking that language, it would seem that this is not generally the case in the Americas (even if some might harbour such views on Cape Breton Island or in certain parts of Chubut Province, Argentina). In other words, in many cases we have the impression that ethnic languages are learned not necessarily only for communication (i.e., as a social tool), but for communing with an actual or imagined cultural world. Songs in the heritage language are transformed from being elements that weld the language community together in work and express communal emotion to become a means of communing with the culture itself. In this way a new idea of one's own identity is created. This dynamic of self-representation is of course very much a feature of the postmodern world, the fragmentation of familiar cultural boundaries. The person becomes an insider (sometimes a "virtual" insider), having formerly been an outsider to the culture.

Although superficially we might think of hybridity as being a very modern phenomenon, the study of identity and hybridity among the Welsh in both North and South America allows us to see the possibility of nascent hybridities already at work among Welsh migrants in the 19th century. These same processes can also be clearly seen among the Cornish for the same period. The inappropriateness of attempting to use the word "Celtic" except in a strictly linguistic or early cultural context becomes very clear when we look at the six nations traditionally labelled with this marker during the period of the highest percentages of emigration in the 19th century. Irish and Scottish Gaelic speakers were able to express their vibrant civilizations in terms of oral culture when they settled in relatively large numbers in specific areas of North America. These oral forms of culture depended upon the intergenerational transmission of the language, which continued in relatively isolated areas like Cape Breton.

Among the Welsh and the Cornish, orality of this kind was not an especially defining characteristic. The Protestant non-conformity of most of the Welsh migrants was accompanied by a strong sense that Welsh literacy was a core value of Welsh culture, based on reading the Welsh translation of the Bible, and singing a wide range of original hymns in the Welsh language. This, together with a highly specific culture associated with the chapel system, meant that outside of the work context, the Welsh were a clearly separate cultural group.

Another important element that defines both Welsh and Cornish identity in the 19th and 20th centuries is the relationship of the two peoples to the British State. The ideology of the British State pervades many Welsh attitudes during this period, even if these attitudes were often ambiguous. I believe this experience in political terms made the hybridization of Welsh-American identity all the more predictable. Much the same could be claimed for the Cornish in the 19th century, whose specific national identity at that time was far from being coherently articulated in imperial Britain.

I would like now to examine the processes of hybridization in two localities that attracted Welsh emigration, Chubut Province, Argentina, and Pennsylvania, U.S. The Patagonian experience from its earliest period from ca. 1865 reflects a utopian desire to create a new Wales far from the vicissitudes of life in Victorian U.K. Much emphasis was laid on religious freedom and the generalized use of the Welsh language in all aspects of life in Chubut. For many, though, after the initial settlement period and the beginnings of an economically viable *colonia*, Patagonia offered the chance to escape the perils of rural poverty and the equally uncertain nature of the industrial world. It can be suggested that although the organizers of this far-flung settlement in Argentina adhered ideologically to this Patagonian dream, only a minority of those who actually went had particularly clear ideas about how this would be realized, and old political and class structures were later to challenge this dream, especially with the advent of late Victorian settlers from Wales. Many other Celtic-language settlements could be mentioned for the Americas, some relatively small, yet quite successful for a period of time. The Saskatchewan settlements of Bangor, Glyndwr and Llewelyn, although in fact an offshoot of the Patagonian project, were vibrant and successful Welsh-speaking rural communities in Canada. The fact that they eventually attracted Welsh speakers from parts of the U.S. (Dakota) and eastern Canada suggests that they had become culturally and economically vibrant.

19th-Century Chubut, Argentina

Hybridization can take a variety of forms. Adopting new social behaviour can be an important survival strategy in a new environment; changed language habits, or even language shift, may be a result of a range of factors, most importantly the adoption of new values which define the majority Other. In early Welsh Patagonia until the end of the 19th century, certain new skills were necessary for survival, and their adoption redefined how the Welsh might think of themselves in that new society.

The necessary economic adaptation in the late 1860s-1870s to a new environment depended on the interaction between the Welsh (mainly male) population and the wandering indigenous population. This led the Welsh (mostly from urban areas) to adopt the use of horses in a way largely unknown to a mainly semi-urban migrant group. Learning to ride and to hunt for wild animals such as the guanaco or the rhea led the Welsh to adopting indigenous methods, especially methods of lassoing the animal (*bolas*). Early photographs show how Welshmen adopted very quickly a form of dress which derives from norms found among the wandering mestizo cowboys frequently known as *gauchos*. The classic photographs that express this rapid integration of some of the customs of the new country date from the 1880s and were taken by John Murray Thomas. In Figure 1, Thomas, an important figure in the exploration of the route west to the Andes, is seen seated on the ground with his fellow travellers. He wears the typical riding boots of a *gaucho* and holds ceremoniously a gourd for *mate* (Paraguayan tea) in one hand and a pipe in the other. Some of his companions are dressed in gaucho costume. In Figure 2, a picture taken at the same time, Harry Jones together with Antonio Miguens, two prominent early settlers, are seen imbibing *mate*, with the kettle carefully placed in front of them. Jones too has the traditional Argentine riding boots and a colourful muffler around his neck (Bjerg, Jones and Priamo 2003: 50, 51).

Not everyone evidently dressed in such extravagant outfits, and in fact such gauchoesque outfits become a kind of postcard version of Europeans in this desert region of Patagonia, expressing a heroic outward-bound experience. It expressed more than just an adaptation of the necessary clothing for riding in the harsh environment of the semi-desert in the manner of the other indigenous gauchos: it was also an expression of freedom which went against the traditional Victorian values to be found in the early Welsh settlements.

In this sense, we can see the very important role played by the myth of the gaucho in early Argentine literature and oral tradition, emerging to some extent in the Welsh community. Jorge Luis Borges analyzed this poetry in his article "La Poesia Gauchesca" (1996: 179-97). This hybridized Welsh gaucho persona became the subject of a well-known satirical poem in Welsh from Patagonia written by D. R. Daniel toward the end of the 19th century entitled "*Yr Archentwr Cymreig*" (The Welsh Argentine) (Williams 1960: 62-63). The description of the Welsh gaucho suggests some of the characteristics of the free-wheeling spirit who gave rise to this poem, especially the shift from the chapel-based monolingual type of Welsh culture that was being nurtured in the Chubut Valley and Cwm Hyfryd. This is a Welshman who does not work for a living on a regular basis, is bilingual in Welsh and Spanish, after a fashion, does not go to chapel or the *eisteddfod*, is an accomplished horseman and enjoys the pleasures of the *asado* (roasted meat prepared outside on a large spit). In addition, he smokes, which was usually considered as pernicious a vice as drinking in the Welsh community. The poem gives a strong suggestion that some

Figures 1 and 2. Photographs taken in the 1880s by John Murray Thomas of Welshmen in Patagonia. (University of Bangor, Archives and Special Collections)

male members of the new community were assuming a hybridized identity that by definition tended to be unstable and would lead in some cases to complete integration. Although the poet seems to be satirizing his subject, he does at the same time seem to admire the lifestyle of the Welsh gaucho. By the end of the 20th century and into the 21st century the idea of the "Welsh Gaucho" had assumed an exotic status, and could be used as a way of attracting potential tourists to Patagonia. Even if the romanticized gaucho was a thing of the past, the outfit worn by such figures survived, as some of the portraits by the noted artist Sir Kyffin Williams show (Joyner 2004: 95).

The "Welsh Gaucho" topos was not necessarily typical, except among those who left the Chubut valley and ventured toward the Andean west. Other pictures from the turn-of-the-century period show other forms of hybridity. One such photograph conveys a heroic version of the successful farmer. Thomas Davies, on his farm called Tal-y-Sarn near the Atlantic port of Rawson, is shown holding his hayfork as he stands proudly next to a haystack he has just constructed. His outfit is fully Argentine, especially the typical *chiripá* (work trousers) and his wide leather belt. Davies's gaze into the distance is also an expression of optimism and belief in the new world he has created around himself. He has become the very essence of the Welsh Argentine (Roberts, Jones de Zampini and Dodd 1987: 19).

As this example suggests, not all examples of hybridization were potentially threatening in terms of the survival of Welsh culture in Patagonia. One such "hybridized" Welshman was John Daniel Evans. His easy relations with both the indigenous people and the settled Welsh colonists in the Chubut Valley give us a sense that he was a Welshman who was comfortable in these very different worlds. Because of his interaction with roaming indigenous horsemen west of the Welsh settlement in the early 1880s, he became a *baqueano*, a guide who led soldiers and settlers to the Andean west of Patagonia. In his youth, at least, he became a superb example of someone who integrated fully into the environment and social norms of Patagonia while remaining a member of the linguistic and cultural world of the Welsh settler world. Early interaction between the largely wandering indigenous population and the Welsh brought about stages of hybridization among the Tehuelche peoples themselves. Some chieftains sent their sons to the elementary Welsh schools to learn to read and write.

Although images of the Welsh-speaking gaucho have now been subsumed in the exoticism of the growing vacation culture aimed at visitors from Wales and beyond, they should not be trivialized or misunderstood. They represent, then and now, evidence of the necessary adaptations for survival and, at a certain level, the contemporary Welsh-speaking Argentine sees this development as part of the central myth of the early settlers and their exploits. As such, it is a dynamic part of their identity-package whose roots are in the formative period of the 19th century.

The Welsh of Patagonia demonstrate in their accent the interplay between regional forms of Welsh and the Spanish of Argentina. Welsh words coined in Patagonia occasionally survive, but Spanish loanwords reflect new realities. One particular example of linguistic hybridity occurs in the kind of Welsh sometimes used by young people in Patagonia who have learned Welsh as a second language. The term for this hybrid version of Welsh is *Cymrellano*, a combination of the Welsh word for the Welsh language (*Cymraeg*) and the word used in Argentina for Spanish, *Castellano*. An extreme example would be the phrase *"yo siarad Cymrellano"* (I speak Cymrellano).

Sometimes forms of hybridization can be seen at unexpected levels. Certain genres of Welsh writing from the heyday of Welsh Patagonian literature (ca. 1895-1925) bear strong similarities to corresponding Spanish texts from Argentina in the same era. These are usually autobiographical texts which relate the personal and the historical at the same time. In her book on the autobiography in Spanish-speaking America, Sylvia Molloy stated that Spanish American autobiographies are fascinating hybrids, often wielding several discourses at the same time (1991: 159). They seem to aspire to documentary status while promoting the self, and so dwell on the personal experience while still purporting to be bone fide historiography and can become founding texts of a national archive.

This form of autobiography, quite common in the Argentine context, whether in Spanish or Welsh, presents two kinds of memory that are complementary. These hybrid forms, "wielding several discourses," depict first the individual memory, the chosen details of personal life and then the collective memory of the community, of which the author is a privileged tradition-bearing member. The autobiographical documents written by John Daniel Evans (Birt 2004: 64-196) or John Coslett Thomas (Birt forthcoming) fit very well into these categories. The figure of John Evans is normally seen in terms of the "heroic" early history of the Welsh in Patagonia after diverging from the world of Wales, a people's history reinvented from the time of the first landing in New Bay in 1865. His eyewitness accounts as a participant in some of these key events that ensured the very survival of the settlements assumed a special status for people in Patagonia in a way that does not correspond to anything in the Welsh literature of Wales. At the same time, he concentrates on his family's history which integrates with the key moments in early narrative of the Welsh Patagonians as a community.

Taken together, such writings represent a kind of secularized narrative of "sacred" events. This might seem a somewhat exaggerated claim, but the documents written by John Daniel Evans, *El Baqueano* (Birt 2004), whose early life as an explorer and guide along the pathways only known by the indigenous peoples of Patagonia was always in danger of being re-invented as a patriarchal hero of the early colony, have traditionally been revered by many in exactly these terms. It was as if his writings, at first only available in a Spanish adaptation, represented an unadulterated narrative woven around a new Welsh identity in a new land. The "truth" enshrined in such documents was only intensified by being inaccessible for many decades. Another element where Spanish American autobiographies and those in Welsh from Chubut seem to coincide rests on the particularly reverential sense of place, making places into physical moments in the history of a new identity. These are privileged locations, and sites of memory described in the context of significant communal events, and recognized as such by the real or potential readership.

The significance of such events becomes part of the ideological mythology of the community. If the Welsh history of earlier centuries seems either forgotten or disregarded in the minds of the early settlers, the often traumatic or deeply significant events that took place in the 1860-1890 period seem to have assumed the role of a new history. The psychological impact of such episodes and incidents raises them to a mythic level. The narratives of such events as the murder of Aaron Jenkins (1877), or the killing of three Welshmen at Kil-Kein (1884), give those texts a "relic status" for the mythic power of certain localities. Such a range of identities associated with the small community of Welsh people was a consequence of their experiences in southern Argentina, but perhaps also a result of a deprived sense of Welsh historiography where a non-conformist working-class religious upbringing afforded a more abiding sense of belonging and cultural identity in Welsh terms. It was this latter that they brought on board the *Mimosa* in 1865, becoming the basis for a renewed range of identities forged by their experiences and encounters on the banks of the River Chubut. It was in essence a hybridized spectrum of identities based on purely Argentine experiences in a new land and interaction with the indigenous peoples there.

Patagonian-Welsh Identity in the Early 20th Century

There is no doubt that by the end of the 19th century Welsh men and women in Chubut had forged a new relationship with the land and had imbued it with their old and new identities. New Welsh names frequently gave a normative imprint to the geographic features of the land—the administrative divisions on the north and south of the dividing Chubut River—and to the sixteen Welsh-medium non-conformist chapels that were dotted along it. These new largely rural settlements were almost entirely Welsh speaking.

The Welsh created their own memories from the moment they arrived in New Bay in 1865. The events of 1865-ca. 1890 generated a new historical narrative, one that was no longer based on that of forebears in Wales but set entirely in Patagonia. A new cluster of identities was being built, aided by leaders such as Lewis Jones and his influential Welsh-language newspaper *Y Drafod* which played a key role in moulding a sense of community and promoting the Patagonian ideology. Yet, by the end of the 19th century the Welsh were no longer the sole European ethnic group in the region: 40 per cent of the population of Argentina had been born outside the country. The slow migration from Spain and Italy as well as other European countries meant that the critical mass needed to create a Welsh ethnic territory in Chubut was increasingly under threat and in danger of receding as a nationalist dream. This increased the likelihood of a more hybrid range of identities in Chubut which eventually would change the nature of what had been an almost purely Welsh enclave. Some Welshmen like John Murray Thomas, a prominent local businessman, former explorer and influential member of the Welsh community, had taken out Argentine citizenship at an early date and had, typically for his class, never entirely accepted the idea of a separate Welsh colony.

The Welsh slowly lost administrative power in Chubut, partly because the non-conformist church system was practically the only formal institution that had been developed by the Welsh in Wales. Although it was replicated to some extent in Patagonia, little attempt was made to extend Welsh political influence in the secular sphere which was mainly dominated by Argentine state appointees and army representatives. Self-governance had developed in the very first years of the Welsh settlements, but had not prepared members of the community for the more demanding forms of political activity under a more direct Argentine administration. Further, Welsh identity in the mid- to late 19th century was an amalgam of inherited identity patterns. Partly this identity drew its strength from the Welsh non-conformist tradition, but there was also, and increasingly in the 1890s, an overlay of Britishness that was still evolving during this period. This poses a major problem when we come to examine the vivacity of the so-called "Patagonian ideal." Even if Lewis Jones and a small coterie of ideologues were clear in their minds that the Welsh Patagonian settlements were a new beginning, there was no real certainty the three thousand colonists were all in agreement. There was never any doubt that the territory with its colony would not be part of Argentina.

At its heart, Welsh-Patagonian identity was ambiguous and unstable. Perhaps significantly, there is hardly any suggestion in the writings of two of the major Welsh-language authors of the period—John Daniel Evans and John Coslett Thomas—that they adhered to any central idea about Welshness. In fact, others such as the Reverend William Casnodyn Rhys was avowedly pro-British, even going as far as to claim that the Welsh settlers shouted *"Duw Gatwo Shon Darw [sic]"* (God Save John Bull) at the arrival of the British naval ship *Triton* in Puerto Madryn in 1866 (Rhys 2000: 88). Another writer (mainly in the field of journalism) and poet, Gutyn Ebrill, also wrote an article in Welsh for the local Welsh-Patagonian newspaper *Y Drafod* entitled *"Hwre i Brydain Fawr"* (Hoorah for Great Britain), and in the same paper he describes the Welsh colonists from Chubut who relocated to a new location in Buenos Aires Province as being "British" (Birt 2002: 25).

It is difficult to gauge just how typical such ideas were in late 19th-century Patagonia. The apparent certainties that accompanied the first *Mimosa* contingent in 1865 were considerably weakened by economic disasters at the end of the century brought about by extensive flooding of the Chubut Valley, as well as the loss of some of the population in emigration to Canada (1902) and Australia. Further challenges came with increasing confrontation between the Welsh settlers and the central and local Argentine administration. The end of Welsh-medium primary schooling together with the attempted enforcement of military drilling on Sundays demonstrated that some of the cultural gains for Welsh culture were under serious threat as Argentina became increasingly aware of its nationhood. Economic success in the Welsh colonies attracted a wider range of European immigrants into the valley and beyond, resulting in a shift toward a more pluralistic range of identities. This, in turn, provoked some Welsh people there to reaffirm their allegiance toward a specifically British identity. Hybridization in cultural and identity terms becomes more apparent in this era of Welsh Patagonian history, extending into the first two decades of the 20th century.

The anglophone presence in Trelew (the largest urban centre in Chubut) had increased partly as a consequence of greater contacts with the Anglo-Argentine mercantile community in Buenos Aires. The Anglican church of St. Marks saw a period of expansion in Trelew, and an associated church school was opened where instruction was given in English. Some of the first pupils were from Welsh-speaking families. Photographs from this period taken at such events as the eisteddfod began to include national flags, and we see not only the Argentine flag but, perhaps somewhat surprisingly, the British Union Jack. There had been some talk in 1899 during a tense period between the Welsh settlement leaders and the administration in Buenos Aires that the Welsh colony should become a British Protectorate. This clearly suggests that the Welsh had not succeeded on their own in creating a political ideology and infrastructure that would prevent them from being reduced to a minority ethnic group, and one which had little say in the governance of the province of Chubut. It was clear that there was some deep-seated ambiguity about the viability of an independent Welsh identity at this period, and as such it comes as no surprise that with a newly sanctioned national education system in Spanish, the Welsh of

Chubut gradually assumed an Argentine identity whose national language would be exclusively Spanish while Welsh would remain the predominant language of home, chapel and the farm until well into the 20th century.

The creation of another tier of identity did not imply the loss of Welsh identity as such. For most of the 20th century, the Welsh communities continued to express their ethnic identity in a number of structures outside of the home and farm, especially the non-conformist chapels, the eisteddfod and the agricultural co-operative society (CCC). All of these institutions saw a decline by the Second World War, and the younger generations identified less and less with the Welsh language and its institutions. Only after 1965, and especially after 1998, was there a significant change in the fortunes of Welsh culture in the Chubut valley.

The Welsh in North America: Pennsylvania

The 1890 U.S. census indicated that some 100,000 people in the country were born in Wales. Of that number 37 per cent lived in Pennsylvania, either in rural or semi-rural industrial communities. The Welsh, in common with several ethnic groups, tended to settle in areas with a high density of their compatriots. In Pennsylvania those areas were Wilkes-Barre, Scranton and Pittsburgh. Other figures have suggested that there were some 115,000 Welsh speakers in the U.S., with some 33,000 in Pennsylvania and 5,000 in Hyde Park and Scranton (W. D. Jones 1998: 256; Matthews in this volume).

Although the first generation of Welsh settlers was keen to ensure the use of Welsh in the public sphere, and to live much as they had in industrial Wales, by the second generation there was already such a shift in the kind of Welsh identity adopted by much of that community that we can claim that it had become hybridized: a Welsh American identity that would lead eventually to assimilation (or near-assimilation). Many of the purely Welsh-medium organizations and societies (literary circles, etc.) gave way to new organizations whose emphasis was entirely on ethnic holidays, especially St. David's Day (March 1st) and Welsh Day. The second and, certainly, third generations in Welsh-American families tended to switch from Welsh to English, accelerating the decline of elements of Welsh identity that were expressed through the language. The newer and more dynamic Welsh-American identity was one which showed pride in Welsh ancestry, but was thoroughly Americanized. This tendency in North America, whether in the U.S. or Canada, became a norm.

Henry M. Edwards, a prominent Welsh American of the late 19th century who in many ways exemplifies this new hybrid identity said, "A Welshman loves his native country, loves his father and mother, his language, his Welsh Day because he is a good American citizen. No race ever comes to America that gets into the American spirit more quickly than a Welshman" (W. D. Jones 1998: 274).

One might suggest that this view, or variations of it, was held in many Welsh American circles. But it could be suggested that this rapid hybridity may well reflect the underlying ambiguity perceived by many Welsh about their ethnic identity at the time. As reflected in other writings, Henry Edwards saw the Welsh language as not being entirely necessary to his definition of Welshness (W. D. Jones 1998: 275). Even the Eisteddfod, that most Welsh of cultural institutions, was seen increasingly as a celebration that should welcome participants from other ethnic groups. On several occasions during the first three decades of the 20th century, the Eisteddfod seems to have been intentionally hybridized as a statement about American identity. This kind of laissez-faire fusion most probably attracted the upwardly mobile. However, this loosening of constraints must have raised some hackles: there seems to have been a rearguard action from other elites. The renewal of Welsh organizations in the 1890s, the advent of the Gymanfa Ganu and countless St. David's Societies with their seeming rejection of the Welsh language as a defining marker also seem to have left some of the cultural elite determined to soldier on, using Welsh for all aspects of their cultural life.

Central to this vast networking between the various Welsh communities of the U.S., Canada and, later, Argentina was the Welsh American weekly *Y Drych*. Like other ethnic-language periodicals of the time, it gave its readers and contributors a voice which made them feel included in the larger yet dispersed Welsh community, without at the same time excluding them from their new country. Cultural survival and integration become two sides of the same coin. Culture, to use Bhabha's expression, is used as a strategy of survival. With the cooperation of *Y Drych*, Welsh-speaking communities in the first three decades of the 20th century built a cultural edifice where theology, politics, poetry, autobiography and debate on Welsh affairs become the order of the day. This meant that those like the indomitable Gabriel Lewis of Saskatchewan could argue at length in the Welsh language about atheism with entirely opposite-minded Welshmen in New York state.

This newspaper also shared the experience of the various Eisteddfodau in the U.S. and Canada with all its Welsh-speaking readers. Highly detailed accounts of these highlights of Welsh-American life could be seen in *Y Drych*, such as the 1925 Eisteddfod in Utica, NY, illustrated by a picture of the archdruid Cynonfardd. The main eisteddfodau in Toronto, Los Angeles, San Francisco and Utica, and even the smaller events held in Bangor and Saskatchewan, were given similar coverage. Through the columns of this newspaper, the vibrancy of the Welsh world of the U.S. and Canada became increasingly evident. Yet, this rearguard action was relatively short-lived; by 1933, a long series of articles discussed the fate of the language in North America in gloomy tones.

This period of some three decades was the heyday of North American Welsh culture, with its rich network of chapels, the American National Eisteddfod and "Welsh Days" in Utica or Los Angeles (A. Jones and B. Jones 2001: 76, 86). Eisteddfodau attracted competitors from a wide variety of locations. Undoubtedly part of the success was the continuing existence of a large proportion of first generation Welsh speakers on the continent, and that generation was not replaced by newcomers in sufficient numbers. Nor was the next generation committed in the same way to promoting the culture of its parents and grandparents. The resistance to hybridity and assimilation in the first generation gave way to a thoroughly Anglo-American or Anglo-Canadian identity in later generations, often without the ethnic language.

Many Welsh American institutions survived past the Second World War, including the important Gymanfa Ganu, which took the place of the American National Eisteddfod. The Gymanfa Ganu took on a specifically North American form since it provided a meeting place for Welsh people from all over the continent. Although there was a focus on traditional hymn singing in Welsh, it was also to some extent a showplace for Welsh culture in general.

A certain kind of Welshness survives in almost all American and Canadian cities but it is more a set of variations on American or Canadian identities than a particularly Welsh identity or outlook (Greenslade 1986). Initiatives to restore this residual identity have been attempted, such as that of Cymdeithas Madog in 1977. This peripatetic course (Cwrs Cymraeg) visits a different city in North America each year, providing Welsh language instruction together with a Welsh cultural experience. Most of the first students had connections with Welsh societies and, although that still remains true, many are in a sense "new" Welsh Americans with no prior association with Welsh societies or their activities. They are individuals for whom a recreated Welshness and hybridity becomes a comfortable way of being Canadian, American or Argentine.

The Cornish: Galvanizing Cousin Jack

There is an unfortunate tendency to relegate the Cornish to the category of the "also ran," an unjustifiable stance in any discussion of "Celtic" peoples in the Americas. The "Cousin Jacks," as they were affectionately known, are frequently the subject of stereotyping when viewed in a North American context (Payton 2005: 403-405; Deacon in this volume). Although the Cornish might be imagined to have survived into modern times with only a veneer of indigenous culture, and to be easily confused as English, their culture and lifestyle seems to have been distinctive enough to make them a significant ethnic group in the areas to which they immigrated (Deacon

2007: 229). Although there were Cornish settlements in Mexico and other parts of Latin America, they seem to have adopted Hispanic names and lifestyles. There are, however, tantalizing reports of a Cornish Society in Mexico City in the 1940s (Payton 2005: 97-113).

In other parts of North America, California, in particular, Cornish workers were to be found in relatively large numbers: in the late 19th century the population of such places as Soulsbyville near Sonora was 80 per cent Cornish. In 1880, Cornishtown, a small township created during the Californian Gold Rush, was described as a haven of Cornish culture. The absence of saloons and dance halls fostered the performance of music and singing in small houses. The non-conformist self-improvement ideology of the Cousin Jacks merged well with the paternalistic and interventionist ideologies of the mining companies.

Although many Cornish people came to North America as prospective farmers, it was in the field of mining that they created a distinct identity for themselves and earned a special reputation. One description from the 1870s gives a succinct outline of what was perceived as the distinctive Cornish identity: Cornish miners "are mostly stalwart, good-looking fellows, dress better than any other class of miners and are very fond of women. They also appear more clannish than any other foreigners and a majority of them are very good singers" (Payton 2005: 216). These stereotypical features seem to have defined the Cornish for outsiders. Other sources make it clear that the Cornish were renowned as staunch Methodists. Cornish wrestling was also an important badge of identity and decisive contests were held in Grass Valley, California. They formed choirs such as the Butte Carol choir (in Montana) and the Grass Valley Cornish Choir.

The Cornish typically immigrated as family units, so kinship must be recognized as a key aspect of communities in the immigrant context. Although the Cornish did not retain their original Celtic language by the time they emigrated in large numbers, anglophone Americans perceived the Cornish as speaking a distinctive dialect of Western English which prevented them from being confused with the English at the local level. Their specialized skills and technological know-how in mining also contributed to their identity. This repertoire of identity markers remained vibrant until the decline of Cornish mining technology (which was abandoned in Cornwall itself). It was only at this point, when emigration waned, that Cornishness as defined here began to yield to Anglo-Americanization.

Hybridization became a feature of the Cornish experience several decades after the last waves of the so-called Great Migration were over. As part of the pan-Celtic reconstruction of identity, Cornish Americans (like their cousins in Australia) began to recreate or even invent Cornish culture and an associated set of identity items (Payton 2005: 408).

The rediscovery of roots—initially in California, especially in the Grass Valley area—gave rise to the expression "galvanized Cousin Jacks."

In effect "people of a variety of backgrounds came together to cherish, preserve and even assert the district's Cornishness" (Payton 2005: 403). Such appropriation of Cornish identity, a hybridity that would have seemed inexplicable to the original Cousin Jacks a century earlier but which became a dynamic force in the latter 20th century, brought people of diverse ethnic origins into the Cornish American fold, many of whom would have worn badges and emblems with "Cornish person" on them. It is in that period that the real dynamism of modern hybridity can be perceived in the sense that a clearly defined identity comes to the fore, easily claimed and comfortably worn.

A similar dynamic has been observed in Australia where hundreds of thousands of people have claimed Cornish descent. Cornish ethnicity has evolved enormously in the last few decades, and the ambiguity of Britishness has opened the door to those who wish to develop or recreate their ancestral roots (often very selectively). This creativity facilitates re-inventing aspects of historical Cornishness that were entirely absent during the last two hundred years. The Cornish language is certainly part of this hybrid identity in the Americas. Although there is evidence that some early Cornish immigrants had knowledge of the language (see Deacon in this volume), the interest in Cornish in California and other parts of the Americas reflects the need to embrace language as the ultimate marker of ethnicity. The California-based website cousinjack.org lists online Cornish language courses (run by Maga in Cornwall) as part of the menu for Cornish culture. Another modern invention is the Cornish festivals both in California and Australia known as Kernewek Lowender Cornish Festival. Here again hybridization works with an ethnic recreation of identity as a mode of reinforcing pre-existing American identities and conceptions of identity.

Reasserting Hybridity, Creating Cultures

Bhabha refers to hybridity as a "third space" (2006a: 157). He suggests the possibility of merged identities, moving away from the "exoticism or multi-culturalism of the *diversity* of cultures, but on the inscription and articulation of culture's *hybridity*" (157; emphasis in original). Earlier in the same article he elucidates this idea by imagining this "third space" as a challenge to "our sense of the historical identity of culture as a homogenizing, unifying force, authenticated by the originary Past, kept alive in the national tradition of the People" (156). The emphasis then shifts away from what has been the experience of many migrant peoples for unambiguous cultural values (language, lifestyle) toward a contradictory and ambivalent "space" in cultural terms. Among the many smaller nations who came to the Americas, we can see, albeit in relatively small numbers, declarations of difference and renewals of deliberate minoritization.

The major element in the process of hybridization in a modern context is that of the revitalization of lesser-used languages in a diasporic setting: such activity tends to create hybrid forms of identity and culture. Although identity and language are usually deemed to be intertwined, the attempt to revitalize a language in a diasporic context may well be different to that found in the "home" country. In this sense one can compare the various attempts to revitalize Irish in North America and in Ireland, Scottish Gaelic in Cape Breton and Scotland, Welsh in Patagonia and Wales, Basque in Argentina and the Basque Country, even Cornish in California and Australia. Revitalization in the Americas is more likely to be associated with an individual's desire to express a hybrid identity in a mainstreamed, globalized world. In some ways we could define language revivalist movements as anti-mainstream culture: such initiatives appear to reject globalized culture as it influences indigenous culture (Martel 2011; see especially chapter 16).

Greater comparative study is needed of the various language-revitalization schemes throughout the Americas. Even within the Celtic language group, different emphases can be perceived. Language classes and pre-secondary education in Patagonia are attempting to recreate some of the domains of Welsh in the pre-1920 period. The pursuit of Welsh language and culture is not seen as being in any way detrimental to an Argentine national identity, and in fact suggests the beginnings of a local hybridity. Such hybrid identities, although officially ignored, are a part of the Argentine ethnic make-up, which includes Basque Argentines, Irish Argentines and Anglo-Argentines. The Welsh-language enclaves in North America were not so geographically focused, however.

The various hybrid forms of Welsh culture in the Americas over the last century-and-a-half reflect an unstable and ever changing environment. In earlier times, the tendency for a hybrid identity was to surrender to assimilation and mainstream cultural norms. This, of course, was not always entirely voluntary. In more recent years, state ideologies such as multiculturalism have endorsed and facilitated multiple cultural identities and hybridity. At the same time, individuals and communities have sought to redefine their place in such mainstream societies by adopting the use of "rediscovered" heritage languages which open the way to a sense of authenticity and provide an alternative to monolingual mainstream culture. Individuals, once forced by family units or social pressures to limit themselves to a single set of ethnic and linguistic allegiances, now more than ever, are free to choose from a vast array of possibilities which are not exclusive of one another but can in fact be exercised simultaneously and openly. Such multiple "virtual" passports invite membership in many ethnic communities which now co-exist and interpenetrate and interact with one another, in ways that early Celtic migrants could not have imagined.

References

Bhabha, Homi K. 1994. *The Location of Culture*. London and New York: Routledge.

———. 2006a. Cultural Diversity and Cultural Differences. In *The Post-Colonial Studies Reader*, ed. Bill Ashcroft, Gareth Griffiths and Helen Tiffin, 155-57. London: Routledge.

———. 2006b Signs Taken for Wonders. In *The Post-Colonial Studies Reader*, ed. Bill Ashcroft, Gareth Griffiths and Helen Tiffin, 38-43. London: Routledge.

Birt, Paul W. 2002. La Communidad Galesa en la Argentina: Construcción o desconstructión de la identidad. In *Los Galeses en la Patagonia* 11- 34. Puerto Madryn: Fundación Ameghino.

———. 2004. *Bywyd a Gwaith John Daniel Evans El Baqueano*. Llanrwst: Gwasg Carreg Gwalch.

———. Forthcoming. *Hanes Rhyw Americanwr: Hunan-gofiant ac Erthyglau John Coslett Thomas (1863-1936)*. (The Welsh American: The Autobiography and Articles of John Coslett Thomas [1863-1936]).

Bjerg, Maria, Bill Jones and Luis Priamo. 2003. *Una Frontera Lejana: La colonización galesa del Chubut*. Buenos Aires: Ediciones Fundación Antorchas.

Borges, Jorge Luis. 1996. *Obras Completas I*. Buenos Aires: Emecé.

Deacon, Bernard. 2007. *Cornwall: A Concise History*. Cardiff: University of Wales Press.

Greenslade, David. 1986. *Welsh Fever: Welsh Activities in the United States and Canada Today*. Bridgend, Mid Glamorgan: D. Brown & Sons Ltd.

Gruzinski, Serge. 1999. *La pensée métisse*. Paris: Fayard.

Jones, Aled and Bill Jones. 2001. *Welsh Reflections:* Y Drych *and America 1851-2001*. Llandysul: Gomer Press.

Jones, William D. 1998. Y Gymraeg a Hunaniaeth Gymreig mewn Cymuned ym Mhennsylvania. In *Iaith Carreg Fy Aelwyd*, ed. Geraint H Jenkins, 255-80. Cardiff: University of Wales Press.

Joyner, Paul, ed. 2004. *Gwladfa Kyffin/Kyffin in Patagonia*. Aberystwyth: The National Library of Wales.

Martel, Frédéric. 2011. *Mainstream: Enquête sur la guerre globale de la culture et des médias*. Paris: Éditions Flammarion.

Molloy, Sylvia. 1991. *At Face Value: Autobiographical Writing in Spanish America*. Cambridge: Cambridge University Press.

Payton, Philip. 2005. *The Cornish Overseas*. Fowey, Cornwall: Cornwall editions Ltd.

Rhys, William C. 2000. *La Patagonia que canta*. Buenos Aires: Emecé.

Roberts, Tegai, Albina Jones de Zampini and Stella Dodd, eds. 1987. *Los Galeses en Chubut*. Chubut: Secretaria de Cultura de la Nación.

Rogers, Nicholas. 2002. *Halloween: From Pagan Ritual to Party Night*. Oxford: Oxford University Press.

Saul, John Ralston. 2008. *A Fair Country: Telling Truths About Canada*. Toronto: Viking Canada.

Williams, R. Bryn. 1960. *Awen Ariannin*. Llandybie, U.K.: Llyfrau'r Dryw.

Rhiannon Heledd Williams

Whose Friend from the Old Country?
The Welsh-Language American Press and National Identity in the 19th Century

When I am asked about my research topic, I am often met with a mixed response ranging from bewilderment to disbelief, some even skeptical as to whether a Welsh-language press existed thousands of miles from the homeland. People are usually fascinated to learn that there was a flourishing Welsh-language press in the United States of America during the 19th century, which is evident in a mass of virtually untouched journals in various archives. As opposed to the mountain of texts published on Welsh migrations to Patagonia in South America due to the prolonged connection maintained with Wales to this day, the history of the Welsh in North America has been largely sidelined—even though larger numbers emigrated to this part of the Americas. It may not be the same romantic story of adventure conveyed of the attempts to establish a colony in Argentina, but the Welsh in North America also deserve their place in the nation's diasporic history. This period of Welsh history, which saw many transformations in national identity, cannot be fully understood without raising greater awareness of these forgotten people.

Academic research has concentrated on large-scale migration that resulted in lasting and perceptible impacts on the social patterns of America. Setting aside quantitative studies, we see that the qualitative approach is extremely lacking—especially in terms of literature—and more surprising is the neglect of the periodical press, which offers an insight into a rich diversity of information. Despite its practical usability as a genre displaying a vast range of cultural and social habits spanning a number of years, a need remains for an analytic exploration of this primary resource material. In terms of academic research in the field of Welsh diasporas, the periodical press has generally been used rather arbitrarily to explore other topics, but has rarely been considered a resource in its own right. As the body of literature on Victorian periodicals develops, Beetham has argued that they represent more than historical records; they were also part of a complex social process. Such considerations are significant as we attempt to determine the multifaceted nature of the immigrant Welsh communities: "Each article, each periodical number, was and is part of a complex process in which writers, editors, publishers and readers engaged in trying to understand themselves and their society; that is, they struggled to make their world meaningful" (Beetham 1990: 20). The periodical press not only serves the target audience, but also becomes actively entwined in this social web as it responds to the group's changing needs and interprets meanings on their part.

The discourse becomes witness to the era's engine of thought as the literature reproduces meanings in relation to the readers, authors and editors. The variety of evidence these narratives provide opens endless possibilities for the neglected field of periodical press studies. Using the periodical press as a starting point offers a potent resource to assess various religious, political, linguistic and cultural attitudes, given its role as the main communication system of the period to unite over two hundred scattered Welsh American communities.

Several questions naturally arise when using these texts as a springboard for study in the wider context of nationality: How did the press express prominent features of emigrants' Welsh identity in the 19th century? To what extent was it possible to preserve ethnic ties and adapt to novel conditions? How did the press unite the nation's members and define or sustain the identity of Welsh American communities in the 19th century?

The definition of national identity continues to be contested. Modernist theories in the field are particularly useful as they consider different approaches and allow for ambiguity. Gellner's idea of national identity as a social creation allows for consideration of the self-conscious act of preserving nationalistic traits in another country (1983: 50). However, primordic elements are also supported by Nairn, as the Janus metaphor envisages the tendency to cling to past values based on distinguishing features while simultaneously reinventing a new sense of identity adapted to modern conditions (1977), a notion suitable to assess the establishment of the Welsh American press.

The growth of literacy from the 18th century onward indicates that modern communication, especially through the medium of print, enabled membership of a community based on a distinct language and culture. Anderson's revolutionary theory in the field of communication contemplated the power of literary devices and their social implications, maintaining that the ritual of reading creates an invisible network, or what he calls an "imagined community," to which the members of a nation can aspire to belong. This community "is imagined because the members of even the smallest nation will never know most of their fellow members, meet them, or even know of them, yet in the minds of each lives the image of their communion" (1983: 5). This collective consciousness is grounded in the reality of a particular way of life represented by various texts that transcend their territorial dislocation.

Incomplete documentation makes it impossible to determine how many of the Welsh crossed the Atlantic during the first decades of the 19th century, but it is indisputable that Wales saw an outward migration at an unprecedented rate as a result of a harsh industrial and agricultural climate that led to great social unrest. Cultural concerns motivated the establishment of Welsh communities in America during the 18th century, but in the 19th century migration was driven primarily by economic hardship.

Approximately thirty thousand people of Welsh origin were found in the United States by 1850, with 89 per cent concentrated in the states of New York, Pennsylvania, Ohio and Wisconsin (Knowles 1997: 4). Literature hastened the desire to break free from oppression in the homeland, but many of the Welsh were prompted to migrate out of desperation, and transplanted their religious and cultural institutions in the process. The main features that denoted their Welsh identity were their nonconformist beliefs, the Welsh language and unique cultural traditions (Jenkins 1933). The periodical press, which also witnessed a boom in Wales during the same period, gave expression to many of the components that formed their sense of nationality.

As the number of Welsh emigrants, most of whom were largely monolingual, grew in the 1830s, a staggering sixty-five Welsh publications were established on the continent during the 19th century. Some were short-lived, especially literary or special interest periodicals, while others, of a religious nature, and newspapers prospered—some until the 20th century. The 1840s and 1850s represent the golden age in terms of the Welsh periodical press as it proliferated with attempts to establish wide-ranging publications such as those of a political or educational nature. A sizeable portion of the Welsh population was clustered around the city of Utica in upper New York, and it is estimated that fifteen to twenty thousand lived in the city or its surrounding villages and towns by 1860. Subsequently, it became their cultural hub and the heart of Welsh-language publishing in North America.

The year 1838 heralded the true beginning of the Welsh American periodical press as the monthly publication with a religious focus, *Y Cyfaill o'r Hen Wlad* (Friend from the Old Country),[1] saw light. It represents the first successful attempt to provide a publication entirely in the Welsh language to address the needs of the Welsh population, a periodical that would, surprisingly, survive until 1933. The pioneer was a Calvinistic Methodist minister, William Rowlands, who was born in London and raised in

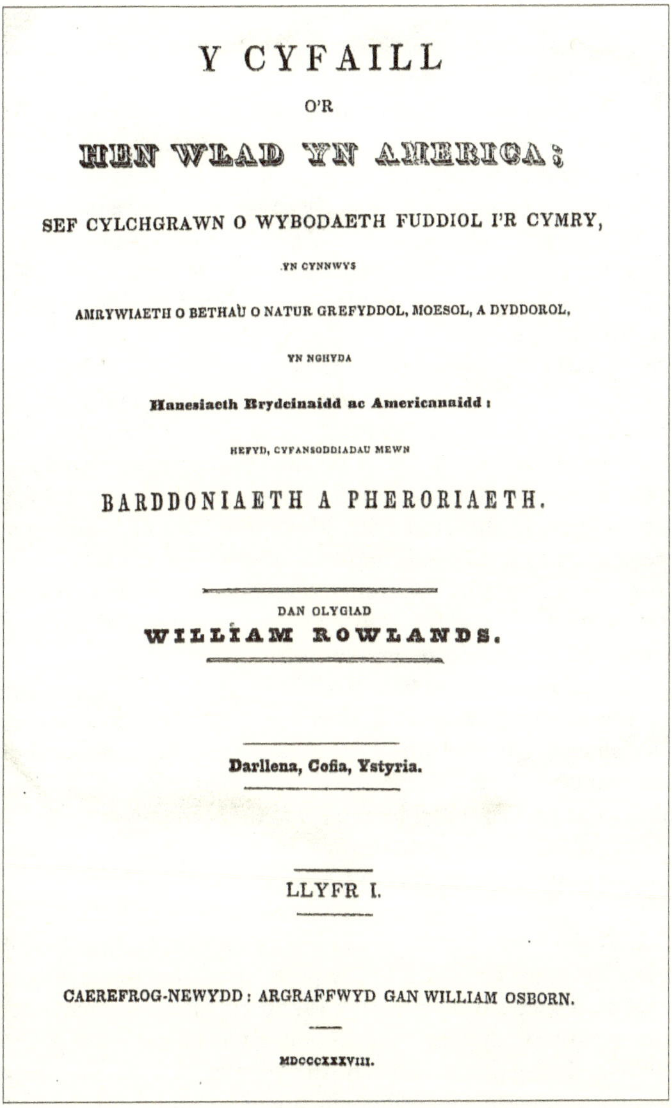

Y CYFAILL

O'R

HEN WLAD YN AMERICA;

SEF CYLCHGRAWN O WYBODAETH FUDDIOL I'R CYMRY,

YN CYNNWYS

AMRYWIAETH O BETHAU O NATUR GREFYDDOL, MOESOL, A DYDDOROL,

YN NGHYDA

Hanesiaeth Brydeinaidd ac Americanaidd:

HEFYD, CYFANSODDIADAU MEWN

BARDDONIAETH A PHERORIAETH.

DAN OLYGIAD

WILLIAM ROWLANDS.

Darllena, Cofia, Ystyria.

LLYFR I.

CAEREFROG-NEWYDD: ARGRAFFWYD GAN WILLIAM OSBORN.

MDCCCXXXVIII.

Figure 1. Y Cyfaill *Welsh newspaper title page, 1838. (Rhiannon Williams)*

English until he learned Welsh through relations in Carmarthenshire, South Wales at a young age. He would remain the editor until his death in 1866.

Rowlands was an entrepreneur in the book publishing and printing trade in Wales, and moved to New York in 1837 following many tribulations. One of his main ambitions was to be productive; he immediately embarked on a long-distance journey around the Welsh American communities to assess their literary needs, and found a great desire for a publication in their mother tongue.

The first edition was released in January 1838, printed by William Osborn in New York City (and in later years at Utica). It stated that its core purpose was to infuse the Welsh with religious values transported from the homeland, a theme repeated frequently in subsequent years in his editorial addresses: "*cynhyrchu gogoniant i Dduw, lleshad ysbrydol i anfarwolion, gwasgaru goleuni iachusawl yn mhlith cenedl allwladedig y Cymry*" (1841; to praise God, provide spiritual sustenance, to spread the light amongst the emigrant Welsh nation).

Although it was consistent with the ethos of the denominational press in Wales, this new publication was not solely devoted to pursuing the doctrinal beliefs of its founder. In light of the infancy of the press, the editor, in a bid to foster national autonomy, decided to satisfy the ambitious aim of serving the Welsh-language population in its entirety, a typical feature of the diasporic press in this era (Tyler 2008). The character of the press was therefore shaped by a cultural, linguistic and religious exclusiveness that would function as their cornerstone of independence from the English-language press; in this respect its aim was to construct and represent their unique national culture in the broadest sense possible.

In the first issue, we receive a vivid impression of the relationship between the character *Cyfaill* (friend) and his compatriots through a fictional dialogue. The Welshman is eager to taste the newfound freedom of America and the adventures it holds, while his "friend" warns him to be mindful not to forget his heritage amid the excitement and wonder of the New World. He promises comfort and support to the estranged Welshman, reminding him that America has an abundance of treasures, but also begs the Welshman not to forget his roots—a plea that epitomizes the paradoxical nature of the double identity of immigrants.

One of the main functions of the periodical press in the 19th century was to act as a guide in social, moral and cultural matters, and one of the editor's most prominent visions—intertwined with his nationalistic and religious aims—was to educate the readers. Many came from poor backgrounds without formal education, and Rowlands was a great believer in its ability to purify souls. As he was himself very well educated, he was qualified to select literature from a vast array of sources, including translations of English texts.

The content and format of the monthly periodical displays a variety of topics, although it was mainly affiliated with religion, and attempted to satisfy the audience's needs intellectually as well as morally. Each edition contains pieces on topics such as theology, art, genealogy and science, along with essays on social and political matters. The factual material is supplemented with culture, including musical lessons, mathematical puzzles, poetry and hymns, as summarized on the front page:

Y Cyfaill o'r Hen Wlad yn America ... cylchgrawn o wybodaeth fuddiol i'r Cymry, yn cynnwys amrywiaeth o bethau o natur grefyddol, moesol a dyddorol, yn nghyda Hanesiaeth Brydeinaidd ac Americanaidd; hefyd, cyfansoddiadau mewn barddoniaeth a pheroriaeth. (January 1838)

(A Friend from the Old Country in America ... a magazine consisting of beneficial information for the Welsh, including a variety of religious, moral and interesting things, along with British and American news; also, poetry and hymnal compositions.)

As well as providing education and promoting cultural creativity, it also functioned as an ordinary newspaper, encompassing a Welsh, American and Welsh American outlook. Welsh American news detailed cultural, political, religious and general activities, while American news mainly addressed constitutional proceedings. Practical information such as market prices and advertisements was also provided. Most significantly, news from Wales was included, strengthening the "transatlantic" connection that was maintained further through the medium of literature. Books and periodicals were frequently exchanged across the Atlantic by ships travelling back and forth, and that is indeed the significance of the monthly periodical's title.

There is evidence that the *Cyfaill* was read in Wales, and it regularly used extracts from various periodicals published in the homeland. Furthermore, it was also read by members of other Welsh diasporic communities, as evident from the numerous letters and greetings addressed to Welsh Americans, mainly discussing religion and language and encouraging people to support print culture. News from Britain as a whole indicates that their identity was inclusive of Britishness, and a summary of worldwide news suggests the need for a comprehensive provider in the Welsh language. Welsh Americans were therefore not isolated, as the periodical press afforded entry to a wider network of communities. One reader commented: "*cyfaill yw, a chyfrwng cyfeillgarwch rhwng cyfeillion gwasgaredig yn America a'u gilydd*" (January 1845; *Cyfaill* is a friend, and a medium of friendship between and amongst scattered friends in America).

The achievement of this task of tying together disparate communities in a national, transatlantic and a diasporic sense contributed to the multifaceted nature of the Welsh American identity. Furthermore, its broad range of republished material from a vast array of periodicals—in both Welsh and English, from America and Britain—indicates the sheer magnitude of the editor's interests and thus the monthly's ability to cross denominational, geographical and linguistic domains.

At the core of the publication's existence—the first to appear at this time—was an effort to unite the print community based on the language.

The editor frequently emphasized that he aimed to serve the national community despite its differences, and therefore does not favour a particular party or denomination:

> Gwnaethom ein goreu i ochelyd gosod dim i mewn a ddoluriai deimladau neb, o ba farn grefyddol bynag y byddai, os byddai ganddo barch i'r Beibl, gan na fwriadwyd y Cyfaill yn offeryn plaid, ond yn gyfrwng o wybodaeth fuddiol i'r genedl yn gyffredinol. (January 1838)

> (We tried our best to refrain from including anything that would offend anybody of any religious conviction, as long as he respects the Bible, as the Friend was not established as a sectarian organ, but rather a medium of beneficial information for the whole nation.)

Cyfaill attempted to gloss over the denominational divisions that were rife in Wales during this period by publishing the activities of the different denominations, thus appealing to the nation as a whole and reinforcing a unifying effect afforded by the deep-seated religiosity of the Welsh as one of their main markers of identity.

Rowlands frequently stressed his plans to support cooperation that would bridge doctrinal differences for the greater good of the religious cause, and would boast his neutral standpoint repeatedly. In an economic sense, at least, he remained loyal to his promise for the greater part of his editorship as he had personally invested in the venture and sacrificed a great deal to ensure that he didn't rely on the support of his personal denomination for funding. Establishing a periodical at this time was a high-risk decision as publications often failed; and his success may be attested to his careful planning beforehand. A number of poems welcome the appearance of the periodical, often as a "friend" in the metaphorical sense:

> Er gadel Cymru lawn ei breintiau
> Ei lloer, ei ser, a'i goleuadau
> Wele'n dod, er difa'n alaeth
> A'r colledion, Gyfaill odiaeth. (February 1838)

> (Although leaving Wales and her blessings,
> Her moon, her stars and her lights,
> Alas, appearing, to ease our longing
> And losses, comes a Friend.)

Rowlands attempted to ensure a wide appeal in his editorial introductions by excluding any quarrelling and attacks of a personal nature. Nevertheless, he was also a great believer in justice, and one of the cornerstones of his policy was to offer an open forum to discuss a wide range of topics, as he pinpointed immediately that the success of the periodical depended largely on the contributions of the readers. In this way, the range of narratives permitted entry to the attitudes of the readership, which—aligned with those of the editor—contributed to determining the course of the periodical. Debates would be tolerated provided they were entertained in a logical and reasonable manner. Exchanging correspondence—what is called "encounters" by Brake and Codell (2005: 3)—acted as a stimulant for preserving the unity of the emigrant community, and provided the opportunity to discuss current affairs of relevance to their new identity.

Reception theory can be employed to consider the active role of the reader as he interprets the meanings embedded in the texts. Of particular note are the ideas of Stanley Fish, who believes that an individual belongs to "interpretive communities," "not as a free agent making literature in any old way, but as a member of a community whose assumptions about literature determine the kind of attention he pays and thus the kind of literature 'he' 'makes'" (1980: 11). The periodical can constitute a battleground of competing ideologies as it can divide the united community, underlined by Anderson, into many sub-communities, especially considering the editor's attempt to appeal to the Welsh as a nation consisting of different religious and political convictions. Brake and Codell emphasize the "false unity" present in a journal: "A journal title promises a false unity, appearing to present, despite its many articles, topics, and illustrations, a unified policy, or set of beliefs, as if the journal itself were a single author" (2005: 1-2).

Brake and Codell outline the importance of considering the "multivocal discourse of periodical text" if we are to develop an understanding of the genre. Fish also stresses the importance of boundaries between the different parties, "independent competing entities whose spheres of influence and responsibility must be defined and controlled" (1980: 12) and therefore due consideration should be given to the editor's role as mediator between the readers and text.

William Rowlands frequently attempted to diminish his editorial role and profess impartiality. Although he strived to refrain from commenting or entering a debate on the pages of the *Cyfaill*, he also desired to become a member of the same interpretive community as that of his readers by publishing articles under a pseudonym. This shows that he possessed certain personal convictions, and this process enabled him to share them in an indirect manner even as his frequent statements of objectivity gained the audience's trust and protected his editorial integrity. Although he professed complete neutrality, his personal contributions coupled with his editorial monopoly to guide the periodical's agenda by selecting material to be published, and this coupling demonstrates a great awareness of his role as a leader who guided the community's opinion.

The growth of the Welsh-language periodical press in North America (Price and Smith 1995) heralded a change in the functions of the *Cyfaill* and transformed the denominational, political and economic boundaries that it had previously monopolized. Although a degree of intertextuality existed between these publications as cultural entities, bitter and long-running debates clearly demonstrate the effect of the print culture context on individual periodicals and their internal processes as tensions surfaced between editors and readers.

As an ardently Calvinistic Methodist minister, it was inevitable that Rowlands's defence of his doctrinal beliefs were numerous, and undoubtedly influence the periodical's ethos. His commitment to revealing the "truth" justified his discourse, and he often surrendered to printing scathing and libellous attacks, despite efforts to keep the peace. But were his political affiliations as apparent as the spiritual beliefs he printed in the *Cyfaill*, and to what extent did these narratives reflect his personal standpoint?

As new settlements were formed, the *Cyfaill* satisfied the needs of readers by providing practical information to increase familiarity with the political arena of their new country and advice on becoming American citizens. William Rowlands was very aware of his role in educating his readers in this context, and he included political news from America and Britain. The public forum of the periodical enabled the Welsh community to comment, in their mother tongue, on social matters affecting their adopted country, especially slavery. The power of the printed word enabled the Welsh to openly declare their unanimous opposition, accompanied by a large body of creative and factual contributions, as this problem increasingly integrated itself into their culture.

Despite William Rowlands's concerns over slavery, he adopted an indirect editorial agenda by using subtle means of persuasion, for which he was harshly judged at times. As opposed to his frank views in safeguarding his personal doctrine, he remained loyal to his neutral political stance during most of his editorship. He published essays of a political nature under pseudonyms until the end of the 1840s, and even then was hesitant to advise on political matters, despite opportunities as a social leader to explicitly influence public opinion.

The means of emancipation posed moral dilemmas and provoked bitter debate rooted largely in doctrinal differences, and it is probable that William Rowlands did not desire to openly declare his alternative ideas on the means of emancipation, which were unpopular at the time. His political views were greatly entangled with his individual religious beliefs, and affected his personal contributions and his editorial decisions to include or refuse articles. Furthermore, examining other publications shows the wider dynamic of print culture at this time, as personal differences highlight a hidden agenda which often comes to the fore in heated political and religious debates, along with the relationship between the publications as social commentary was exchanged.

The aptness of the Welsh language to vent such discussions indicates the importance of the periodical press in acting as a common link between social, religious and cultural institutions that supported the basis of their identity. The lack of status in an official capacity was compensated by the printed word which ensured the visibility of the lively Welsh language culture, while also acting as a bridge with the past and its historical significance.

The periodical press was actively involved in campaigns to aid the preservation of the Welsh language, and is considered one of the main institutions in this respect as it underlined linguistic solidarity. It proved a useful resource to bastion the Welsh language by publishing a wealth of literature in various forms, thereby underscoring the duty of preserving the language within an English-language environment. Creative and factual material such as addresses, poems and essays expressed their linguistic attachment to Welsh, usually in the same sentimental terms that characterized nationalist discourse in Europe at the time.

Subscribing to the *Cyfaill* is also repeatedly portrayed as synonymous with participating in the linguistic mission as an integral cultural institution. Efforts were made to plan ahead, with an emphasis on raising future generations bilingually, stressing the excellence of the language in comparison with others and providing grammar lessons in order to maintain a high standard of Welsh. Feminine and familial metaphors were often employed to describe attachment to the language, especially that of a mother. Another recurrent theme was the praise of the abstract power of the Welsh language, praise which was tempered by the acknowledgement that it wasn't key to progress—a dominant preoccupation of the time.

The press also acted as a pillar for the Welsh language by devoting space to cultural activities such as St. David's day celebrations, *eisteddfodau*, literary meetings and social gatherings. On the one hand, St. David's day celebrations of the patron saint of Wales on March 1 would remind communities of their ancestral heritage, but they also celebrated Independence Day on July 4 as they absorbed new traditions. The toasts declared in these celebrations suggest that their identity was gradually accumulating greater complexity and layers, as they saluted the Welsh language, Wales, Welsh poets, Britain, Queen Victoria, North America and the president of the United States.

The print medium also reinforced the social aspect of literature composed for festivals and cultural gatherings as it expanded the audience. Literature as an engine of patriotic sentiment enriched the content of the periodical press and enhanced its success, while the press alternately functioned as fertile ground for the growth of authors. The amount of literature included on the pages of the *Cyfaill* and other publications of the period can be taken as a measure of the cultural vitality of Welsh settlements.

The *Cyfaill* immediately sought to fill a cultural void by appealing for literary independence and shows an early awareness of a clearly defined literature devised to meet the expectations of Welsh American readers as a separate national community. Although they depended heavily on their counterparts in Wales for literary sustenance in this early period, William Rowlands was confident in the first edition of their creative energy and appeals for regeneration in their artistic talents to reflect their changing circumstances. This call to create an original literature may echo Emerson's 1837 lecture "The American Scholar" in order to enhance their credibility as a nation. This awakening came into fruition in the 1850s as the tradition was canonized by bardic circles, authors and literary critics. This new literary sphere signalled the strength of the press as institutions such as the eisteddfod and literary meetings boomed.

The *Cyfaill* contained not only translations of Anglo-American literature, but also Welsh-language literature centred on American topics, such as American culture, politics and developments, which indicates that its readers were enmeshed in numerous "interpretive communities" rooted in the language. The subjects of literary competitions underline how American culture was encompassed within Welsh tradition, as essays and poems on the electric telegraph, the concept of manifest destiny and American presidents were composed in Welsh.

The *Cyfaill* also maintained literary standards by offering guidance on poetic matters, and a lively forum between poets aided the evolving tradition immensely by voicing debates, questions and concerns. The tradition was supplemented by book reviews and commentary on publications and periodicals that ensured a healthy system of criticism that accentuated the need for high standards.

It is impossible to generalize about the influence of the periodical press in America, but in the case of Welsh, it certainly made the language visible in their culture as one of its main institutions. Evidence suggests that no more than 2,000 copies of any issue of *Cyfaill* were ever printed, but its significance must not be judged by its low print run as it is probable that the publication was read and shared between families and chapel members (R. O. Jones 1997: 257-58) The periodical press certainly slowed the process of assimilation for the most culturally loyal members of the audience.

Despite its representation of a small portion of the Welsh American population and its activities, periodicals offer great potential for examining the interplay of ideologies within this particular community. Consideration of the narratives in their historical context accentuates their importance as a valued medium of communication; text constantly evolves to produce meanings in an ongoing dialogue with readers and editors. Ultimately, this transformative power of the press epitomizes the processes of constructing, maintaining and redefining a dual or even multiple national identity of Welsh Americans.

Editorial discourse often exemplifies the complexity of the inner processes at work in the relationship with the readers and contributors to the periodical as readers react to debates and correspondence from other readers, thereby becoming part of the wider interpretive community of Welsh-language print culture. Contextualizing the *Cyfaill* further against the backdrop of the periodical press enables deeper insights into the interpretive communities and their fluid nature, as they react to the impact of religious, political and economic factors on their boundaries. As de Tocqueville writes, "each separate journal exercises but little authority but the power of the periodical press is second only to people" (de Toqueville 1998: 81).

The fusion of Welsh and American themes in the diasporic discourse ensured that a parallel identity was formed, the Welsh American. Nevertheless, Welsh Americans were divided into sub-communities as a result of opposing beliefs and the influence of editorial policy on these beliefs. The developing print culture was constantly adapting the goals of the *Cyfaill*.

A huge body of essays and poems attests to the ability of the readers to respond according to the literature they consumed, which makes the periodical press a timely resource: "Welsh newspapers, then, were appreciated critically by their contemporaries as a form of literature, and were the subjects of active discussion as well as objects to be read" (A. Jones 2000: 21).

Furthermore, although every periodical possesses a unique viewpoint and editorial principles, the similarity of the *Cyfaill* to the periodical press in Wales—and even English-language denominational journals in America—indicates that we can place this particular publication within the broader milieu of contemporary print culture.

The main strength of the periodical as a resource lies in its broadness, and this strength highlights the need for interdisciplinary studies to engage with its complexity, in fields as diverse as semiology, linguistics, psychology and anthropology. In order to fully grasp the complexity of the periodical press as a literary genre, theoretical groundings are needed to analyze editorial roles explicitly within a triangular framework—rather than as a dialogue—with the text and audience. Further research should also be devoted to an extended consideration of ethnic literature in collaboration with the existing Welsh societies in America today, which may raise awareness of Welsh history and provide insights about our identity. In the words of M. Wynn Thomas, a poet who wrote of the Welsh American dual identity, "the United States in one respect is our echo" (2001: 27).

Notes

1. All translations mine.

References

PRIMARY SOURCE

Y Cyfaill o'r Hen Wlad. 1838. New York: William Osborn Press. Bangor University Archives, Bangor, U.K.

SECONDARY SOURCES

Anderson, Benedict. 1983. *Imagined Communities: Reflections on the origin and spread of nationalism*. London: Verso.

Beetham, Margaret. 1990. *Towards a theory of the periodical as a publishing genre*. In *Investigating Victorian Journalism*, ed. Laurel Brake, Aled Jones and Lionel Madden, 19-32. New York: Palgrave Macmillan.

Brake, Laurel and Julie Codell. 2005. Introduction: Encountering the Press. In *Encounters in the Victorian Press: editors, authors and readers*, ed. Laurel Brake, and Julie Codell, 1-10. New York: Palgrave Macmillan.

Fish, Stanley. 1980. *Is There a Text in this class?: The Authority of Interpretive Communities*. Cambridge, MA: Harvard University Press.

Gellner, Ernest. 1983. *Nations and Nationalism*. Oxford: Basil Blackwell.

Jenkins, R. T. 1933. *Hanes Cymru yn y Bedwaredd Ganrif ar Bymtheg*. Caerdydd, U.K.: Gwasg Prifysgol Cymru.

Jones, Aled. 2000. The Welsh Newspaper Press. In *A Guide to Welsh Literature, 1800-1900*, vol. 5, ed. Hywel Teifi Edwards, 1-23. Cardiff: University of Wales Press.

Jones, Robert Owen. 1997. *"Hir Oes i'r Iaith": Agweddau ar hanes y Gymraeg a'r Gymdeithas*. Llandysul, U.K.: Gomer.

Knowles, Anne Kelly. 1997. *Calvinists Incorporated: Welsh Immigrants on Ohio's Industrial Frontier*. Chicago: University of Chicago Press.

Nairn, Tom. 1977. *The Break-up of Britain: Crisis and neo-nationalism*. London: New Left Books.

Price, Kenneth and Susan Smith. 1995. Periodical Literature in Social and Historical Context. In *Periodical Literature in Nineteenth-Century America*, ed. Kenneth Price and Susan Smith, 3-16. Charlottesville, U.S.: Virginia University Press.

Thomas, M. Wynn. 2001. America: Cân fy Hunan. In *Gweld Sêr: Cymru a Chanrif America*, ed. Thomas, M. Wynn, 1-28. Caerdydd, U.K.: Gwasg Prifysgol Cymru.

de Tocqueville, Alexis. 1998. *Democracy in America*. Ware, Hertfordshire: Wordsworth Editions Ltd.

Tyler, Robert. 2008. Y Wasg Gymraeg yn Nhrefedigaeth Awstralia. *Llafur* 10 (1): 21-32.

Michael Newton

How Scottish Highlanders Became White: The Introduction of Racialism to Gaelic Literature and Culture

If you were to pluck a European peasant from his medieval village and plop him down in the middle of a 19th-century North American city, issues crucial to his prosperity would confound him. He would need a number of concepts explained to him which are central to the structure and operation of anglophone North American society, including the means by which power, privilege and wealth are distributed and justified. Perhaps the most important of these concepts is racialism, the concept of discrete races whose differences are rooted in biology, which can be arranged in a hierarchical pecking order, and whose physical and intellectual characteristics are intertwined and permanently fixed.[1]

Race was represented in popular and academic discourse as an omnipotent force which pervaded the grand narrative of the human condition, explaining not just physical difference but intellectual capacity, social virtues and ills, economic and religious distinctions and political institutions. While few people doubted the reality of race and the ramifications resulting from the inherent abilities and limitations of biological endowments, what was up for debate, sometimes incendiary dispute, was the definition of those racial classifications. Matthew Jacobson has remarked on the construction of whiteness in the United States:

> The contest over whiteness – its definition, proper boundaries, and its rightful claimants – has been critical to American culture throughout the nation's history, and it has been a fairly untidy affair. Conflicting or overlapping racial designations such as *white*, *Caucasian* and *Celt* may operate in popular perception and

discussion simultaneously, despite their contradictions.... One of the tasks of the historian is to discover which racial categories are useful to whom at a given moment and why.... Racial categories themselves – their vicissitudes and the contests over them – reflect the competing notions of history, peoplehood, and collective destiny by which power has been organized and contested on the American scene. (1998: 5, 9)

It would be naive to assume that racialism did not have cultural currency or political relevance in Canada or the British Isles as well. The idea of race, particularly the innate superiority of the Anglo-Saxon, was asserted by many to be at the very core of the inexorable rise of the British Empire and its dominance over the rest of the world. Motivated by the anxiety that they might be left out of the boundaries of the master race, Scottish Lowlanders were prominent in advancing a scientific rationale for race (Kidd 2003). A complete examination of these issues would compare and contrast the discourse between North America and Britain and the differences between contexts; that, however, is not my present aim. Gaelic communities existed in all of these contexts and the ongoing migration of peoples and ideas between these regions allowed for the transference of concepts about race as well. Given this connectivity, it is not possible to study the notion of race in any one community in isolation, even if the rhetoric of racialism was applied differently in different contexts and changed over time, responding to contemporary events and perceptions.

I hope, instead, to determine what surviving evidence can be recovered about how racialism was introduced into Gaelic culture and how consciousness of the concept of race is reflected in Gaelic literature, relating these texts to efforts to secure privileges by the conscious manipulations of racial categories and boundaries. Among other things, it can be demonstrated that particular Gaelic culture-brokers made conspicuous public claims to an external anglophone audience about Highland affinities to Anglo-Saxon races and distance from the peoples of Africa, Ireland and Indigenous America in an effort to clear the path to privilege for themselves and that these discursive practices were internalized by Gaelic communities.

Background

Highlanders had already been exposed to cultural and linguistic oppression in Scotland for several generations before finding themselves once again in an anglocentric environment in North America with the same anti-Celtic prejudices. Although this historical experience provided the ability to identify with other subalterns or join forces with them, this was only one of many options available. I have elsewhere described the sympathetic and cooperative responses of some Gaels to the plight of native peoples and enslaved people of African descent (Newton 2001: 199-209; 2010; 2011). Other Gaels considered resistance to anglocentric hegemony a less advantageous route than capitulation and earning the racial dividends of "whiteness."

From the first planned settlement in North America, in the colony of Georgia, Scottish Gaelic immigrants became conscious of racial categories and their contested nature. Even though they were allowed into the colony on the implicit premise that they were white (Plank 2011: 233-37), an account by the colony's governor in 1742 did not recognize them as belonging to the same racial category as other "white people" (he put them in a category of their own) (Newton 2001: 225), and settlement in the colony was expected to be a process that would "civilize" them (Plank 2011: 234). A battalion of seventy Highland soldiers was raised from the Georgian settlement in 1739 to defend slavery in British colonies from Spanish threats, and while the anti-slavery petition written by Gaels the same year reflects sympathetic sentiments about the injustices of slavery, it also reflects racialist assumptions and shows that they thought of themselves as white (Newton 2001: 201-202; Plank 2011: 236-37).

There were many Gaelic communities that had early and direct contact with racialist ideology and racist institutions but which left insufficient evidence to analyze thoroughly how this trickled through communication networks to influence the perceptions and discourse of Gaels elsewhere. Here are just a few illustrative examples. Gaelic communities of the Cape Fear Valley of the Carolinas owned slaves as early as the 1760s (albeit generally on a small scale). As is well-known, some of the Gaels settled in the Cape Fear Valley fought as Loyalists during the American Revolutionary War and emigrated afterwards, whether returning to Scotland or moving north into Canada. At the same time and for the same reason, some of the Gaels who had been in Georgia migrated to Glengarry, Ontario (Newton 2001: 164-65). As late as the 1840s, some families that had been in the Cape Fear Valley migrated to Canada (Campey 2005: 101), and there is at least one example of a Gaelic-speaking slave being brought with them. As will be clear below, escaped slaves and former slaves passed through Gaelic-speaking communities in Canada. Numerous Gaelic-speaking ministers were involved in the abolition movement from the 1780s onwards (Newton 2001: 202-208). Most important of all, however, was print media, especially newspapers, which maintained ongoing connections between Gaelic-speaking communities across continents and facilitated the communication of ideas across decades.

Disputes over the racial category and characteristics of Scottish Gaels into the 20th century reflect the contested nature of political and cultural life. The eviction of Highlanders from their homes in the 19th century was justified by asserting their supposed racial inferiority (Fenyo 2000), and echoes of these claims resound in Scottish popular discourse to the present day. On the other hand, non-English immigrant communities in North America strived to earn "respectability" in the eyes of the anglophone ascendancy in order to access privilege but maintained their individual ethnic identities by extending the bounds of "whiteness" (Jacobson 1998).

It is useful to recognize that texts can reflect two different processes, with different spokespeople and audiences: internally, especially within the Gaelic speech community, the precepts, strategies and privileges of racialism had to be explained; externally, the racial identity of Gaeldom needed to be defined favourably, especially for the dominant anglophone majority, by asserting affinities with the Anglo-Saxons and distance from the "inferior races."

Evidence of External Declarations

Whatever else we can say about texts in English making declarations about Scottish Highlanders as a race, it is clear that a number of key terms were highly contested, especially "Gael," "Celt" and "Scot." Because these texts are not difficult for a non-Gaelic-speaking researcher to find and analyze, I will only present three examples here.

Organizations created to advance an independent nation-state of Ireland and associated with the legendary warrior band the Fian(na) were established in the 1850s. Imperialists naturally condemned Fenianism not only as a dangerous political movement but as a reversion of civilized values; some Scottish Gaelic elite were quick to pronounce their rejection of it. Given that Fenianism was an active force in the British Isles as well as the United States, Gaelic responses were given in both contexts. The editor of *The Scottish-American Journal* printed a public speech made in Scotland in 1866 by the Reverend Norman MacLeod which manipulates the various racial labels and boundaries so as to assert that Irish and Scottish Gaels are mutually genetically exclusive:

> Speaking of Highlandmen, let me say—whatever may be said to the contrary—that the Celts are not Irish, and the Irish are not Celts. (Applause.) With all our defects, we have always been a loyal people. You never saw anything, and you never will see anything, like that despicable Fenianism in the Highlands of Scotland. (Cheers) (MacLeod 1866)

We see here an attempt to make the labels "Celt" and "Irish" non-overlapping, presumably so that Highlanders can continue to be labelled "Celtic" without being guilty by association with the Irish.

As is well known, Celtic genes were strongly associated in popular discourse with an excess of emotions and the lack of discipline and self-control necessary for any civilized, self-governing people (Jacobson 1998: 13-19). Rather than being a black-and-white matter, however, some Highland elite asserted that Celticity was a matter of degree. An article reprinted in *The Scottish-American Journal* under the title "Highland Blood Not Celtic" from a Scottish source demonstrates how the historical research of Celtic scholars was interpreted for racial purposes:

> Writing in regard to the late Dr. Skene, Sheriff McKechnie says he is entitled to credit for having had the learning and courage to assert and to prove that there is not one drop of Celtic blood in the veins of Scottish Highlanders. The people of Ireland have Celtic blood rushing wildly in their veins. The people of Wales have it in a less fervid form. The people of the Isle of Man, the Sheriff thinks, have none of it. The people who live in Cornwall are supposed to have Celtic blood. "It cannot be the case," says Sheriff McKechnie, "because they are bold, powerful, generous and just. No man of Celtic blood can understand the idea of justice. I have no name for the blood that runs in the veins of Scottish Highlanders. I call it Highland blood; I think it is better than Norman blood, and I regard a Highland crofter as a gentleman superior to the proudest peer in England." (Anon. 1892)

It is clear here that race is directly correlated to political and social conformity to anglocentric norms, and that racial makeup can be inferred from observations in those arenas. Here we also have accusations of the Irish being so Celtic as to be uncivilized; the Welsh have only a touch of madness, while the Manx, Cornish, and Scottish Gaels were free of such defects.

An American writer, C. H. Farnham, wrote an article about the Gaelic community in Cape Breton which appeared in the March 1886 issue of *Harper's Magazine*. While it plays up the country-bumpkin image, I did not find it nearly as offensive as some contemporary Cape Breton folk obviously did. A letter in *The Scottish-American Journal* protested this portrayal of Gaelic manners:

> A person unacquainted with the facts would imagine after reading the article that the Sioux Indian and the average Cape Bretonian are about on a par, and that no one but a bold and hardy magazine writer would dare to encounter the hardships and dangers consequent on a trip through the uncivilized land known as Cape Breton. (Ross 1886)

While his dismay at the negative tone of the article may be justified, his reference to the Sioux makes the obvious implication that the Native

Americans were uncivilized and that the Cape Breton Gaels were above them on an evolutionary scale.

Evidence of Internal Gaelic Discourse

The first Gaelic-medium newspapers, printed in the 1830s, were heavily indebted to English sources for accounts of people and events and there are obvious influences on the terminology and worldview of the resulting Gaelic texts. As far as I am aware, the first documentary evidence of racialism in a Gaelic text is in an article decrying the evils of slavery in the popular newspaper *Cuairtear nan Gleann* in 1840. Terms classifying distinct races according to presumed skin colour were borrowed directly from English without having had any previous currency in Gaelic usage: *geal* (white), *dubh* (black), *buidhe* (yellow) and *ruadh* (red). What is perhaps ironic about many texts of this nature is that they denounce racism while simultaneously reinforcing the tenets of racialism by reiterating these colour categories.

A later article, appearing in the 1849 issue of the religious newspaper *Fear-Tathaich nam Beann*, carried a similar story directly charging those Highlanders, ministers amongst them, who had profited from the slave trade. This article not only reflects a colour term associated with people of mixed ancestry (*odhar-bhuidhe* "high-yellow"),[2] it criticizes the denial that the "African race" was fully human (*na sealbhadairean ag àicheadh gur h-ann de theaghlach a' chinne-daonna na tràillean agus gum bheil iad ach beag co-ionnan ris na brùidean*) (Anon. 1849: 572; the masters deny that they are of the family of humanity but that they are hardly equal to brutes).[3]

What seems to be the earliest Gaelic literary text reflecting racial classifications was composed by an immigrant (of unknown origin) in the United States during the presidency of Ulysses Grant (1869-1877) (Newton 2001: 197-99). It was printed in a newspaper which I have not yet identified,[4] clearly to amuse fellow Gaels with the strange and foreign eccentricities to be found in the United States. While I take his text to be fully tongue-in-cheek, it provides further proof that Gaels could internalize the ideology of racialism.

After promising to entertain the reader in the first verse with the differences from his native land, he says that his new country has many kinds of people: *iomadh seòrsa dhaoine* and *gach nàisinn*. The first term lacks technical precision, but the second term, *nàisinn*, is related in usage to "nation" in English, which at this time would have been understood similarly to how "ethnic group" is used today. It then mentions "Jews and Gentiles, Israelis and Greeks." These terms seem to reflect national categories as demarcated by a Christian framework.

The first couplet of the third verse states that "*tha daoine dubh á Africa / bho Àisia is bho'n Éiphit*" (Newton 2001: 198; there are black people from Africa, Asia[5] and Egypt), thus identifying one racial category by colour and geographical origin; the second couplet states "there are native red men, and many of them are animals." This statement again links skin colour and geography with one of the five supposed racial categories, and explicitly states their presumed sub-human status.

The next verse names French, Spanish, German and Scandinavian immigrants: no geographical location or skin colour is provided, although they are inferred from the text. The fifth verse narrows in on peoples of the British Isles, naming Scottish, English, Manx and Irish people. In the sixth verse, the author states, "*Tha aon seòrs' eile fhathast ann / 'S cha b' iad bu chòir tréigsinn / Tha Gàidheil bhàigheil chaoimhneil*" (198; There's another group I should not leave out: there are gentle, warm Gaels). That the Gaels appear as a separate group is counter-intuitive in that we might expect the category "Gael" to be covered by the labels Scottish, Manx and Irish. Perhaps Gaels are listed separately because these are overlapping but separate categories. Or, the separation may merely reflect the author's rhetorical strategy of moving from the most distant and foreign categories inward to the most specific label that describes his audience. In any case, what is clear is that he is making use of dominant racial classifications and skin colours.

The first datable text that demonstrates an understanding of all of the ramifications of the ideology of race appeared in the 1875 issue of the popular Gaelic journal *An Gàidheal*. This periodical began its life in Toronto but moved to Scotland after the first issue, retaining a large subscriber base in North America. The author, Iain MacIlleBhàin, was one of the editors and the brother of Gaelic scholar Eanraig MacIlleBhàin (better known by his pen name "Fionn"). The article, titled "*Aonachd a' Chinne-Dhaonna*" (The Unity of the Human Race), was originally delivered as a talk under the auspices of the Glasgow Gaelic Mission. Its aim is to explain contemporary theories about race and racial origins, including the common notion that humans are divided into five distinct racial groups, each with a different biological foundation. After reviewing the evidence and theories, MacIlleBhàin refutes this idea and opts for the essential unity of all humankind.

This particular text is remarkable in a number of respects: first, it presents evidence and contemporary theories about race in Gaelic, using neologisms like *gloine-mheudachaidh* (microscope) in order to explain issues without recourse to English terms or discourse external to the Gaelic community; second, it employs several items of oral lore in order to make analogies about race, so as to explain racial ideology in terms of traditions and verbal texts familiar to a Gaelic audience; thirdly, it discredits the multiple-origin theory while simultaneously reinforcing the ultimate authority of Christianity and several negative racist stereotypes. As was standard for the time, his analysis rests not only on physiological and biological data, but also on research in philology and anthropology.

MacIlleBhàin is a very lucid prose writer whose text is engaging and well suited to being read aloud. He manages to express scientific ideas clearly with appropriate Gaelic terminology for terms like "race," "descent group," etc. In fact, because of the Gaelic penchant for describing and expressing ancestry and kinship, which he explicitly acknowledges (1875: 141), these terms are arguably more precise in Gaelic than in English. Let me provide an example:

Tha an t-eadar-phòsadh agus am measgachadh gun chrìch a gheobh sinn feadh theaghlaichean agus feadh threubhan an t-saoghail 'ga fhàgail 'na nì ro-dheacair agus ro-dhuilich an cinne-daonna a roinn 'nan earrannan eadar-dhealaichte, agus cearcal a chur ma'n cuairt air gach buidhinn diubh a tha gu soilleir a' taisbeanadh chomharran aon chuid 'nan cuirp no 'nan inntinnean a tha 'gan cur air leth bho mhuinntir eile. (143)

(The perpetual intercourse and intermixture that we get throughout the kin-groups and races of the world make it extremely difficult and complex to divide the human race into distinct groups, and to define the boundaries of each one to clearly demarcate the characteristics of either their bodies or their minds which distinguish them from other peoples.)

Given that many of his audience may not have been familiar with all of the aspects of racialism, MacIlleBhàin draws upon secular Gaelic oral tradition for analogies and metaphors.[6] There are, in my reckoning, nine examples of these in the text: three quotations from song-poetry, four proverbs and two oral narratives. One of the most interesting of these is a proverb that characterizes people by colour, which by convention referred to hair colour. MacIlleBhàin implies that tradition endorses the idea that physical traits, behaviour and moral qualities are linked, an idea that is one of the major tenets of racialism. He quotes the proverb: *"Bidh fear dubh dàna / 's fear bàn bleideil / Fear donn dualach / 'S fear ruadh sgeigeil"* (143; A black[-haired] man will be bold, and a fair[-haired] man impertinent; a curly-haired, brown[-haired] man and a red[-haired] man will be sharp-tongued).

As a committed evangelical Christian, MacIlleBhàin does not hesitate to cite Biblical texts as historical evidence or to emphasize the importance of recognizing the brotherhood of humankind in its fallen state and the importance of Christianity in meeting its universal spiritual needs. Despite this, he brings into his Gaelic text many racist conceits of imperial Europe. For example, after providing a list of the presumed classifications and features of the five racial groups, he states of "Caucasians":

C'àit air bith am faighear iad chì sinn gu bheil iad gu h-ealamh a' glacadh uachdranachd agus ceannsalachd thar gach treubh a bha anns na dùthchannan sin romhpa. Cha ruig mi leas innseadh gur ann d'an earrainn so d'an chinne-dhaonna a bhuineas sinn fhéin. (173)

(Wherever they are found, we can see that they skilfully seize superiority and domination over all of the other races who were in those lands before them. I need not say that this is the category of the human race to which we ourselves belong.)

This last statement, then, clearly informs Gaels of their racial category and associated birthright as Caucasians, or "white" people.

The earliest Gaelic literary text reflecting racialist ideology in Nova Scotia I have identified was composed by Domhnall MacGilleFhaolain (nicknamed "Domhnall Gobha") who immigrated from Scotland to Nova Scotia in 1819. The sole purpose of the song (MacLellan 1891: 129-31) seems to be to satirize a man of African descent by exploiting racist stereotypes. This unnamed subject spent a winter between Mabou and Strathlorne looking for work sometime around the 1880s, but whether his lack of success was due to the general poverty (or self-sufficiency) of the people of the area or due to antipathy is not recorded (MacFhionghuin 1938).

The song reflects many racist commonplaces: alien physical features ("your head is as black as the raven, your teeth as white as ivory"), incomprehensible speech, laziness, a lack of Christian morality, a base, animal-like existence ("you sleep on the floor of the barn amongst the brutes"), and the hint of a large sexual appetite ("you were married to six women"). Without further contextual information, it is not possible to determine why the poet gushed with such vitriol about this individual; what is clear is that he is drawing from racist tropes familiar in English.

A set of three articles on race appeared in the Gaelic periodical *Mac-Talla* in 1902 from the pen of the Reverend Alexander Maclean Sinclair, a native of Nova Scotia. *Mac-Talla* was printed in Cape Breton, but had subscribers all over the world. Like many intellectuals of his day, Sinclair was a British imperialist who had absorbed many contemporary theories about race and wanted to find a secure place for the Gaels in the imperial scheme. One of the twenty books he published during his lifetime was entitled *Peoples and Languages of the World* (1894), a synthesis of late 19th-century scholarship about racialism, philology and anthropology (Linkletter 2006: 174-86). He extracted material from this book and translated it into Gaelic for his articles. In contrast to MacIlleBhàin, his text is a dull expository essay summarizing supposed facts.

Sinclair's first article is an overview of ideas about racial categories. Although it does not explicitly discuss Celts or Gaels, it can be inferred that they are to be considered members of the Caucasian group.

> Faodar slòigh an t-saoghail a roinn 'nan trì buidhnean: na Cocàsaich, na Mongolaich, agus na Sudànaich. Tha craicionn geal, donn, no dubh air na Cocàsaich agus tha am bilean tana. Tha craicionn buidhe, donn, no donn-dhearg air na Mongalaich; tha am falt garbh agus dubh; agus tha iad a dh'easbhuidh feusaige. Tha craicionn dubh no dubh-dhonn air na Sudànaich is falt camagach, agus tha am bilean tiugh.... Cha robh dùthaich gus an deach na Ariaich anns nach d'fhuair iad sluagh rompa. Cheannsaich iad gach sluagh a thachair orra, ach cha do sgrios iad ás iad gu tur.... Co-dhiubh, is e sin beachd Shergi, ard-fhear-teagaisg sluagh-eòlais an oilthigh na Roimhe. (Sinclair 1902)

> (The peoples of the world can be divided into three groups: the Caucasians, the Mongolians and the Sudanese. The Caucasians have white, brown or black skins and thin lips. The Mongolians have yellow, brown or red-brown skin; their hair is coarse and black; and they do not grow beards. The Sudanese have black or dark brown skin and curly hair, and have thick lips.... There was never a country to which the Aryans went in which they did not find a pre-existing population. They conquered every people whom they encountered, but they did not completely swipe them out.... Anyway, that is the theory of Shergi, the chief professor of sociology in the University of Rome.)

Being a Christian minister, he rejected the multiple-origins theory of race as well as the theories about evolution promoted by Darwin and his disciples, but still accepted a hierarchy of races from inferior to superior (Linkletter 2006: 177-82). Sinclair's views may seem rather anomalous and contradictory to us now, and did to some of his peers as well. We should understand Sinclair and his ilk as being resigned to the reality of British supremacy but hoping to carve out some niche in the imperial order for the Gaels which would be mutually beneficial. In order to be treated as equals within this regime, this necessarily meant advocating the whiteness of Gaels.

North Americans of diverse European origin could represent themselves as "white" and yet maintain ethnic distinctions between themselves and other European peoples on account of a presumed racial basis. This multivalent stance is demonstrated in the letters of "Am B. A.," a correspondent to Gaelic periodicals residing in San Francisco, California. In two letters he wrote to the *Celtic Monthly* in 1907, he expressed his loyalty to Gaelic and chided the journal for not making more use of Gaelic. In one section, he asserts traditional Gaelic antagonisms towards anglophones (*Goill*)[7] in a swaggering, exaggerated form:

> Tha Seumas Sinclair agus na Gàidheil eile anns a' bhaile gu math. Bidh Seumas gu tric a' spaidsearachd anns an deise Ghaidhealach le chlaidheamh air a shliasaid ach cha bhi e deanamh cron sam bith air na Goill ged nach toil leis iad. (1907a).

(James Sinclair and the other Gaels in the city are [doing] well. James frequently struts around the city in Highland clothing with his sword at his side, but he does not do any harm to the non-Gaels, even though he doesn't like them.)

B. A. wrote a letter in the same year to *Guth na Bliadhna*, a Gaelic periodical published in Scotland espousing radical political and cultural reform. This letter was a lengthy exposition on the dangers of unchecked immigration from Japan to California expressed in racialized terms:

> Ged a tha luchd riaghlaidh de'n dùthaich so miannach gu leòir air an lagh a chur an gnìomh, cha toigh leis na Californaich na Iapaich a tha air a' chòrsa; agus tha iad suidhichte gu'n cùm iad na daoine beaga, buidhe bho'n dùthaich so ma bhitheas e idir comasach dhoibh....
>
> Bho chionn deich bliadhna fichead, bha an teachd a nall o'n Eadailt, Austria, is Ruisia, a bha gu mòr air thoiseach, coimhionnan ris an teachd a nall bho Albainn, Eirinn, Sasunn[,] a' Ghearmailt, agus an t-Suain, ri sin bho'n Roinn Eòrpa air an latha an diugh. Anns an àth [*sic*] dheich bliadhna fichead, an tèid teachd a nall nan Iapach, ma leigear air adhart e, air thoiseach air sin o'n Roinn Eòrpa? ...
>
> Mar chumail os cionn so, chan urrainn sinn na Iapaich a leigeil a staigh gu saor-chomasach gun na riaghailtean a tha cumail a mach nan Sìneach a mhùthadh gu mòr air neo an cur air chùl gu buileach. An àth [*sic*] uair a bhitheas mi sgriobhadh, bi facal no dhà agam mu na daoine geala.

(Although the government leaders of this country are certainly willing to put the law into effect, the Californians do not like the Japanese who are on the coast; and they are determined to keep the little yellow folk from this country if they are at all able....

Thirty years ago, the immigration from Italy, Austria and Russia, which was quite early, was equivalent to the immigration from Scotland, Ireland, England, Germany and Sweden, and equivalent to the contemporary immigration from Europe. If it is allowed to continue, will Japanese immigration in the next thirty years outstrip that of Europe? ...

In order to stay on top of this, we cannot allow the Japanese to come in unchecked without either significantly debilitating or entirely eliminating the laws that are keeping out the Chinese. The next time I write, I will have a thing to say about the white people.)

Unfortunately, I have not been able to find any further correspondence from "Am B. A." It would have been interesting to know, for example, which peoples he considered white and what their relationship vis-à-vis the Gaelic world was perceived to be. In any case, the above letters imply that while old rivalries between Gaelic speakers and English speakers may have persisted, they were not as fundamental in contemporary North America social and political affairs as their common identity as "white people."

Given that no Gaelic community was in complete isolation, and that some were in close quarters with people of African descent, it is perhaps surprising that there is not more comment about race and perceptions of other ethnic groups. I have explored elsewhere a set of variants of folklore about identity, of which race was a key element (Newton 2010). As these reflect upon identity but not on racialism per se, I will not discuss them any further than to say that they indicate that Gaels were aware that race was only one of several kinds of markers of identity, but that race was not necessarily the overriding factor in defining identity or determining innate personal characteristics, as popular discourse in English commonly suggested.

Conclusions

The scarcity of sources makes it difficult if not impossible to reconstruct the full story of how Gaels integrated the ideology of racialism into their worldview. The lack of Gaelic-medium periodicals in the 1850s and 1860s, and the narrow interests of most early publications, is particularly limiting to this line of research. By the 1870s, however, Gaelic texts composed in North American communities were expressing the full set of principles inherent in racialism.

Bilingual culture-brokers were involved in making the innovations of anglophone society comprehensible to Scottish Gaels. Even in the 1870s, writers such as MacIlleBhàin considered it necessary to explain racialism to a Scottish audience by way of Gaelic oral tradition, reminding us that tradition is a versatile resource which can be exploited for any number of purposes. Many of these culture-brokers were attached to the Church in some capacity. Very few dared to question the assumptions of race or empire: this makes those who did all the more interesting and noteworthy.

By the mid-19th century the Highland elite were making clear public pronouncements to the dominant anglophone majority, attempting proactively to devise a racial classification and accompanying narrative which would be as beneficial as possible to their ethnic group. In part, this meant countering the negative consequences of being labelled as "Celtic," particularly by association with the low status suffered by the Irish. Similar spokespeople in the North American context tried to maximize distance from other inferiorized groups, people of African and Native American descent.

Ethnic groups acquired "white" status in North America not by changing the pigmentation of their skin, but by accommodating the expectations of "white" anglophone society and inscribing themselves within it. These two mutually reinforcing processes—growing access to privilege and the shifting of ethnic definitions—were not accidental but intentional manipulations of socially constructed hierarchies and boundaries. It clearly would have been impossible for Gaels to demolish the myths of racialism; some believed that it was more feasible, and more advantageous, to instead transform it in their favour.

The descendants of Scottish Highland immigrants to North America are often proud of their ability to achieve economic success and social respectability, but few appreciate that these forms of success were predicated upon their ability to act as honourary Anglo-Saxons, adopting the English language and associated cultural values and norms. Maintaining a serious allegiance to their ancestral language and culture brought derision from anglophones and sustained their exclusion from the privilege and power in the hands of the dominant anglocentric majority.

Notes

1. On the definition of race, racialism and racism, see Smedley 1993: 27. Thanks to Jonathan Dembling for conversations spanning several years over matters of racialism and identity.

2. This seems to be a genuine neologism attempting to describe the skin colour of people of mixed European and African ancestry, rather than an English *calque*. I have inferred it to be equivalent to the modern usage "high yellow."

3. All translations mine.

4. I was given this text by the late Professor Charles Dunn, who copied it from one of the notebooks of newspaper clippings which belonged to the Rev. Alexander MacLean Sinclair of Nova Scotia.

5. The term "Asia" in British usage corresponds to "the Indian sub-continent."

6. Not including quotations from or references to Biblical texts.

7. This is one of many examples of how the ethnonym "Gall," which specifically refers to Lowlanders in a Scottish context, was extended semantically to refer to all anglophones in a North American context.

References

Am B. A. 1907. Letter to the Editor. *The Celtic Monthly* 15: 38.

———. 1907. Litir: Bagradh nan Iapach do na Stàidean Aonaichte. *Guth na Bliadhna* 4:94-96.

Anon. 1840. Tràilleachd agus Daorsa Dhaoine Dubha ann an America. *Cuairtear nan Gleann* 1:93-95.

———. 1849. Gearr Chunntas mu Thràilleachd, no Daorsa ann an Caochladh Linnean agus Chearnan de'n t-Saoghal. *Fear-Tathaich nam Beann* 19:567-76.

———. 1892. Highland Blood Not Celtic. *The Scottish-American Journal*, 28 September, 5.

Campey, Lucille. 2005. *The Scottish Pioneers of Upper Canada, 1784-1855*. Toronto: National Heritage Books.

Fenyő, Krisztina. 2000. *Contempt, Sympathy and Romance: Lowland Perceptions of the Highlands and the Clearances During the Famine Years, 1845-1855*. East Linton, U.K.: Tuckwell Press.

Jacobson, Matthew. 1998. *Whiteness of a Different Color: European Immigrants and the Alchemy of Race*. Cambridge, MA: Harvard University Press.

Kidd, Colin. 2003. Race and the Scottish Nation 1750 - 1900. 7th BP Prize Lecture, 2003. http://www.royalsoced.org.uk/events/reports/2002-2003/prize lectures.pdf (accessed 29 April 2011).

Linkletter, Michael. 2006. *Bu Dual Dha Sin* (That was His Birthright): Gaelic Scholar Alexander Maclean Sinclair (1840-1924). PhD diss., Harvard University.

MacFhionghuin, Iain. 1938. Òran do Dhuine Dubh. *Sydney Post-Record*, 16 January, 7.

MacIlleBhàin, Iain. 1875. Aonachd a' Chinne-Daonna. *An Gàidheal* 4:140-43, 173-76, 199-203, 231-35, 336-38.

MacLellan, Vincent, ed. 1891. *Fàilte Cheap Breatainn*. Sydney, NS: The Island Reporter.

MacLeod, Norman. 1866. *The Scottish-American Journal*, 31 March, 3.

Newton, Michael. 2001. *We're Indians Sure Enough: The Legacy of the Scottish Highlanders in the United States*. Richmond, VA: Saorsa Media.

———. 2010. "Did you hear about the Gaelic-speaking African?": Scottish Gaelic Folklore about Identity in North America. *Comparative American Studies* 8:88-106.

———. 2011. Celtic Cousins or White Settlers? Scottish Highlanders and First Nations. In *Rannsachadh na Gàidhlig 5 / Fifth Scottish Gaelic Research Conference*, ed. Kenneth Nilsen, 221-37. Sydney, NS: Cape Breton University Press.

Plank, Geoffrey. 2011. Deploying Tribes and Clans: Mohawks in Nova Scotia and Scottish Highlanders in Georgia. In *Empires and Indigenes: Intercultural Alliance, Imperial Expansion and Warfare in the Early Modern World*, ed. Wayne Lee, 221-49. New York: New York University Press.

Ross, John. 1886. Letter to the Editor. *The Scottish-American Journal*, 17 March, 5.

Sinclair, Alexander Maclean. 1902. Slòigh an t-Saoghail. *MacTalla*, 14 March, 196.

Smedley, Audrey. 1993. *Race in North America*. San Francisco: Westview Press.

C. Alexander MacLennan

The "Good Indian" Stories in *Mac-Talla*

The Scottish Gaelic newspaper *Mac-Talla* (Sydney, Nova Scotia, 1892-1904) published during its existence three curiously similar stories concerning a "good Indian"[1] confronted with malice and hostility. The reoccurrence of these stories in such a small paper with a Scottish Gaelic audience suggests that they must have had some special significance for the editor and his readers that warranted their reappearance in the paper. The stories in question are *"An t-Innseanach Math"* (D. C. 1893), *"Sgeul air Innseanach"* (Anon. 1899) and *"Gradh Caraid"* (Anon. 1903). We learn nothing about real Native Americans from these stories, which simply follow a long-established script in American literature; these Gaelic stories are translations of, or inspired by, works in the anglophone tradition. Although authentic stories from the Gaelic oral tradition were printed in *Mac-Talla*, these stories have more in common with the frequent short pieces offering life guidance that were a regular feature in this Victorian-era publication (although these pieces were rarely in story form). The readers of *Mac-Talla* were bound to have taken a different meaning from these stories than an English-speaking audience reading them in English would have taken, due to the historical experience of Gaeldom and its own status in anglophone society. Considering the necessities for self-censorship when making any political statements on Gaelic affairs at the time, and the defensive nature of Gaels themselves in regard to their self-image, these stories in Gaelic likely served the editor as a fortuitous means of subtly communicating with his readership about their own situation in relation to the dominant anglophone majority.

The first story takes place in Pennsylvania and is translated by a certain "D. C."[2] An Indian crossing the property of a rich man (*"troimh fhearainn duine mòir"*)[3] on a hot day is refused a drink of beer and then even water by him, and is called a *"cù Innseanach"* (Indian dog). A little later, hunting in the woods the rich man gets lost and the same Indian he insulted encounters him; he rescues him, feeds him and lets him stay in his home for the night. The next day the Indian leads him home, only admonishing him for his racial slur. The Indian feels he has taught him a good lesson: "*Chaidh an t-Innseanach dhachaidh le gairdeachas an déidh buaidh a thoirt air an olc leis a mhath*" (The Indian went home delighted after defeating evil with goodness). This heartless landowner may have brought to the mind of a Gaelic audience the chieftains-turned-landlords of Scotland that turned their back on their kinsmen and the injustices the Gaels had endured from them.

The second anonymous[4] story is a much more elaborate literary creation in which the author is much more emotionally involved with the hero and his thoughts, although it appears to be associated with the previous tale. An American Indian ("*fear do Innseanaich America*") goes out hunting one day and wounds a deer; he follows it farther and farther into the forest until at nightfall he realizes he is lost. Interestingly, the rich man's fear of the forest creatures in the first story is transferred to the Indian in the second story, a fear that seems unrealistic for a Native with a presumably intimate knowledge of the local fauna and more fitting for displaced Gaels in strange new surroundings. In a panic at the prospect of starving and spending the night in the forest, he barges into the first farmhouse he finds, but is driven out at gunpoint by the farmer. He manages, however, to survive the night and find his way home; two months later the same Indian comes across the same farmer lost in the woods. He briefly thinks of revenge but instead invites the farmer home and feeds him, simply leaving him with a warning the next day—after showing him his way home—not ever again to drive a hungry person from his door. The farmer never directly speaks in this story and the issue of race is not emphasized as much as in the first story; in fact, the farmer's racial identity is only mentioned once at the end and the Indian is simply referred to as a hunter in much of it. The conflict seems to be primarily a clash of values and civilizations, and the forcible expulsion of a guest (whether desired or not) from under one's roof would have been seen immediately by the paper's readership as an unthinkable breach of the Highland code of hospitality (Newton 2009: 154-57). The Indian, significantly, declares himself as "a stranger" in his own land, a predicament exiled Gaels would have readily identified with, and defines white men as being the enemy of the stranger ("*nàmhuid a' choigrich*").

The third story in this mode takes a different tone and is far less upbeat; it has no author indicated and may well have been written by the editor himself. It does not follow the formulae of the previous tales, perhaps because it was inspired by a local incident. A good Indian ("*Innseanach còir*")[5] in this country ("*anns an dùthaich so*"), a few years before, obtains a nice farm from the white people in recognition of his good behaviour and friendliness. The story twice explicitly equates English people and whiteness: "*na daoine geala – na Sasunnaich.*" The white characters of the previous two stories flagrantly violate Gaelic social norms and virtues (i.e., hospitality and kindness). In this the most serious version of the story the identity of the Indian's adversary is now finally revealed to be English, making explicit what readers may have inferred in previous versions. The Indian is shown no friendship by the white community he lives among in this story despite his good behaviour. When his only son dies and none of his neighbours come to console him or help him with the burial it is the last straw, and he gives up his farm and leaves to travel two hundred miles to live with his own people. The story concludes discordantly with an unexpected exposition on the universal need for friendship and how Jesus is the best friend we can have. It is a surprising tangent in a piece that seemed to be leading towards a hard-hitting denunciation of English egocentrism and racism. Apparently the story had gone as far as it could go in that direction and some censorship was required of the expected but unacceptable logical ending, leaving us with the pessimistic suggestion that a retreat into spiritual and political isolationism is our only recourse in such implacable ethnic conflicts. This was a common way for Gaels to react in response to the collapse of their traditional world; it is reflected in the "spiritual awakenings" that happened in Scotland after the Clearances and the concentration on religious rather than linguistic rights and issues among Irish and Scottish Gaels in North America (Newton 2009: 39-40, 218-21).

What then is the significance of an Indian being the hero of these stories? In English, these stories would be interpreted in the received manner as tributes to the goodness of a race of people whose disappearance was seen as inevitable and a historic necessity. Such stories about doomed good Indians have a long tradition in the North American English-speaking world, going back at least to James Fenimore Cooper (whose work was influenced by Walter Scott's depictions of Scottish Highlanders). An English-speaking audience would have been very familiar with such texts and would have instinctively understood both how to read them and what they were saying about their relationship with a problematic figure. An Indian is accepted in this capacity as a bearer of moral instruction only because his certain demise renders him harmless, like a benign ghost, or an eccentric character with charmingly naive ideas unsuited for existence in the everyday modern world. Conversely, we may presume that a "bad" Indian would have been more outraged and actively fighting to preserve his world against European/white despoliation and domination. Even well-read bilingual Gaels surely could not have helped but feel that these stories were speaking to them and their experience in a startlingly direct way when reading them in Gaelic.

The question for anglophone society was not how to resolve co-existence with Indians or Gaels: it was assumed that they would die out or assimilate. With this in mind, it should be noticed that the Indians in these stories are not described as being in any way unusual or aggressive in their manner or appearance: what is unusual about them is their strained relationship with the English/white people in the stories; their ethnic Otherness is only really established by the simple label of "Indian" they are given in the stories. The Indian in each story is just an ordinary person going about his life not making unusual demands but simply expecting respect, civility and compassion, and, as such, he would naturally engage the sympathy of the newspaper's Gaelic readership. The central theme of all three stories is a difficult relationship with a hostile English-speaking/white world, and the parallelism between Native-British relations and Gaelic-anglophone relations would have certainly elicited an empathetic response from Gaelic readers. For someone with no stake in Anglo-American manifest destiny, the first two of these stories would read, in fact, like hopeful reaffirmations of traditional Gaelic values of hospitality and the possibility that with heroic forbearance those values would influence the dominant forces in society and allow them to survive. The "Indian" label on the central outsider figure in these stories was probably recognized by the editor and was likely a convenient way of communicating with his readers without offending their sensibilities by seeing themselves portrayed in similar humiliating fictional encounters with anglophone society.

Lecturing Scottish Gaels, even with the best intentions, can be a delicate matter. *"Aisling Dhomhnuill"* (L. L. 1897), another story that appeared in *Mac-Talla*, illustrates the trepidation with which contemporary writers proceeded when attempting to come to grips with troubling issues in Gaelic society. An innocent young fisherman named Donald awakens to find himself one day in a strange country: the Scotland of reality, not the Scotland of propaganda, romanticism or self-delusion. It is not a picture of themselves or their country that would have pleased Gaels. Donald meets with his counterpart in reality, the craven Ruairidh, who is ashamed of his Gaelic name, birthplace and country, and is a creature of the bailiff. The bailiff, minister, school-teacher and innkeeper are castigated as foreign enemies and corruptors of the people.[6] The unnamed English conquerors are cast as the bloody and merciless savages. The nobility are portrayed as decadent and heartless landlords. This is a concise and blunt portrait of the forces conspiring to destroy Gaelic culture, all the more admirable for its rarity. Disgusted, Donald seeks to start a rebellion by burning the heather and ruining the aristocrats' deer-hunting, but immediately Ruairidh betrays him. He awakens just as he is about to be seized by an angry mob that significantly only sees *him* as a villain. Leaving Donald safely back in the comforting Scotland of fantasy where no such tensions exist, the author then launches into a strange and reassuring denouement in which he denies the anger and whole point of his story, making the current situation in Scotland out to be really not so bad after all. The contradictory narration of the tale is as troubling as the injustice it portrays; the author (credited only as "L. L.") is clearly labouring under some duress to mollify what he is trying to say.

Formulating and propagating a radical defence of Gaelic culture and critique of its subordination required questioning the legitimacy of a triumphant British Empire and its narrative of anglocentric progress; these were intellectual and cultural exercises that by necessity required contradicting the assumptions enshrined in the empire's formal institutions and transcending entrenched localized allegiances. In Scotland, the establishment that approved the Clearances was still largely in place and powerful. Open criticism in Scotland could have negative real-life consequences and had little chance of affecting political reform.

In this light, a member of a marginalized ethnic group with a similar social and historical background would make an acceptable and necessary stand-in for a Gael in *Mac-Talla*'s discrete socio-political allegories. Such a replacement could serve to promote Christian virtues such as forgiveness and meekness to a people who might be more apt to respond with retribution and anger for personal and ethnic insults. An example from the Gaelic oral tradition of how a Highlander might respond to disrespectful inhospitality is spelled out in the grisly *An Saighdear a Chaidh Deochan Uisge a Dhiùltadh Dha* (The Soldier that was Refused a Drink of Water) from Cape Breton's Joe Neil MacNeil (MacNeil 1987: 294-301). In it, a soldier requesting a drink of water, as in our first story, is insultingly refused it. In revenge he progressively terrorizes and kills off a whole family. There is no sense in the narrative that the reciter felt that a member of the traditional audience for this story would find the extreme retribution the soldier metes out for this violation of the Highland code of hospitality unusual, although the sentiments of the story may be troubling for the modern reader.

The Mi'kmaq of the Maritimes, incidentally, have similar stories of humiliation and out-of-proportion vengeance, such as in the following story about the 1910 Campbellton fire. Significantly, in this Eastern Canadian tale, the bad man is again specified as an Englishman (as opposed to a Scotchman or Frenchman):

> An Indian was waiting for a train in Campbellton but the train was delayed and would not get in that night. He asked an Englishman to take him into his house for the night. The Englishman was proud, and would not take him. The Indian who had been refused shelter said, "I wish that after a few days he may have to stay out in the open as I do now." Three days after this the fire came, and none of the people had shelter. (Wallis and Wallis 1955: 479-80)

In this instance a curse replaces personal physical violence, but the anger and satisfaction in the resulting destruction is understood and clear. The nobility of a stoic acceptance of defeat and humiliation is obviously best appreciated and admired when exhibited by people other than your own; although it may have eased the consciences of English-speaking readers to read that such rivals were resigned to their humiliation and imminent extinction, such dire prospects were difficult to reconcile in reality. For the readers of *Mac-Talla* the Indian in the "good Indian" stories would have represented a noble Other or distanced version of themselves that could suffer insults without the obligation of responding in kind.

Mac-Talla's mission was both symbolic and educational. A paper of its size and staff was no serious competitor to the English-language dailies of the time and it did not intend to be. Its modest but ground-breaking role was to show that Gaelic could be used in modern daily life to comment on and describe modern events and ideas and that Gaelic was not an outmoded language only appropriate as a medium for folk tales. Just by its existence, it was making a political statement. By extension, the paper allowed people the opportunity to read and learn Gaelic, and raised the consciousness of Gaels about their history and cultural achievements. Therefore, it is highly unlikely that the editor did not encode some cultural message in the "good Indian" stories in *Mac-Talla*, as indeed was standard practice for periodicals of the time. Only that can explain why he allocated space in his newspaper to print three versions of a not-very-original story (for most of its duration, issues had eight tabloid-sized pages), when poems and narratives recovered from oral tradition, letters from subscribers and serious academic pieces from Scottish scholars were competing for space. It seems the message the editor was hoping his readers would take from the first two stories would have been of an upbeat and confident tone at a time when *Mac-Talla* was blazing new trails; the editor perhaps saw himself, as many of his letter-writers and readers seemed to think at the time, as part of a resurgence in the language. The message of the last story in the series appears to be a pessimistic re-evaluation of the situation of the Gaels in light of the coming demise of the newspaper, of which the editor by then must have had some inkling, given that the call for subscribers to pay up had become a regular tiresome feature of the newspaper. The tone of the Indian stories going from confidence to despair definitely mirrors the fortunes of the newspaper.

It is hard to accept that the recurrence of the "good Indian" stories in *Mac-Talla* was due simply to coincidence or to a need for filler. If there was a purpose for the inclusion of these stories in the newspaper it must be due to the fact that these clichéd tales paradoxically became vehicles for reflection on the Gaelic experience. Modern readers can only understand the true purpose of the presence of these stories in this publication by first making themselves aware of the climate of censorship that existed at the time they were published, the mindset of Gaelic exiles and the need of a convenient "Indian" hero to communicate otherwise uncomfortable truths and suppressed sentiments.

Notes

1. I will be using the term "Indian" in this paper because it is a literal translation of the Gaelic term (itself a borrowing from English) and is the term used in American literature of the period. The characters in the stories are all fictional creations.

2. Authors and letter-writers to *Mac-Talla* routinely used initials or nicknames to sign what they wrote. The editor, however, seemed to know their true identities.

3. Literally the "big" or "important" man, it also has the meaning of the "great man," suggesting nobility or the gentry. He is referred to in the story once as a gentleman ("*duin' uasal*").

4. Not all translated items in *Mac-Talla* are noted as such, though some are obviously are based on English-language sources. Such items include foreign news items, jokes about Irishmen and short filler items offering advice that originated from the anglophone world. Translations of the *Arabian Nights* in *Mac-Talla* also appear without credit.

5. Though this phrase may be translated into the "good Indian" in modern English, in Gaelic the word *còir* actually connotes much more affection and sympathy.

6. The innkeeper in this list is a less political figure than the others (who represent naked forces of oppression and control) and can be seen to represent capitalism and the commercialization of tradition social activities such as drinking.

References

Anon. 1899. Sgeul air Innseannach. *MacTalla* 8 (17): 134.

———. 1903. Gradh Caraid. *MacTalla* 12 (10): 79.

D. C., trans. 1893. An t-Innseanach Math. *MacTalla* 2 (25): 4.

L. L. 1897. Aisling Dhomhnuill. *MacTalla* 6 (1): 6-7.

MacNeil, Joe Neil. 1987. *Tales until Dawn: The World of a Cape Breton Gaelic Story-Teller*. Montréal and Kingston: McGill-Queen's University Press.

Newton, Michael. 2009. *Warriors of the Word: The World of the Scottish Highlanders*. Edinburgh: Birlinn.

Wallis, Wilson D. and Ruth Sawtell Wallis. 1955. *The Micmac Indians of Eastern Canada*. Minneapolis: University of Minnesota Press.

Simon Brooks

The Indigenous Atlantic: Welsh-Language Poetry and Indigenous Peoples in the Americas

Paul Gilroy's influential book, *The Black Atlantic*, is important on both sides of the Atlantic. The central idea, that a stateless culture can also be a transnational and trans-Atlantic culture, is a useful one. Gilroy's claim that double consciousness, or "doubleness," as he calls it, comes from being "in an expanded West but not completely of it" (1993: 58) pertains also to those minoritized European cultures that were marginalized by Enlightenment attitudes toward their languages and cultures. This claim raises an interesting question for the most significant of the non-English autochthonous peoples of the British archipelago: the Celtic-speaking peoples. If there is a Black Atlantic, can there be a Celtic Atlantic? Certainly it exists as a geographical reality. Between Gaelic communities in Nova Scotia and Gaelic communities on the western seaboard of the Scottish Highlands and Islands there lies nothing but sea. Nor is there much but ocean between Port Madryn on the coast of Patagonia and the seaboard of Wales. There is a physical Gaelic and Welsh Atlantic, but does it exist too in the mind?

The Celtic-speaking peoples have crossed the Atlantic physically, but they also created a culture that exchanged ideas back and forth across the ocean. New forms of Celtic identities in the Americas impacted identity and culture in Wales, Ireland and Scotland. The idea of a Welsh Atlantic, for example, released Welsh-speaking culture from the clutches of the nation-state. It showed, in Patagonia in particular, what was possible outside the narrow, and culturally specific, confines of Victorian Britain.

But there is another Atlantic that is both an extension to and also a part of this Celtic Atlantic. Perhaps it could be called the Atlantic of the Dispossessed. This is the Atlantic across which the Celtic-speaking peoples seek out subaltern groups in the Americas who they believe reflect their own historical experience in Europe. The most obvious example of a group whose situation has affinities to that of the Celtic Atlantic group is African Americans. An important reason that African American culture—as opposed to other subaltern groups such as the submerged stateless nations of eastern Europe, which might have been more appropriate models—appealed to the Welsh in Wales during the 19th century was simply the physical presence of Welsh-speaking communities in North America. Although these connections between the Welsh in Wales and African Americans are often imagined and discursive, one cannot separate them from the reality of real-time contact in the New World with culturally or socio-economically marginalized groups.

In particular, Celtic-language cultures have sought out similarity between themselves and others in one particular branch of the subaltern: indigeneity. I am not arguing that the comparison between Celtic-language cultures and indigenous cultures is necessarily historically valid. Many indigenous groups in the Americas have been exposed to genocide and colonization in a way that is radically different from the experiences of most stateless ethnic groups in Europe. However, there is ample evidence that whether historically accurate or not, the concept of an autochthonous Atlantic in which settler cultures in the Americas with roots in European stateless nations believe that they share some similarities with indigenous cultures in the Americas is quite common in writings in various Celtic languages. This then is another Atlantic: the indigenous Atlantic. This chapter will concentrate on Welsh-language examples of this phenomenon. Hopefully the material will show that some of the Gaelic accounts of intercultural dialogue with indigenous peoples in the Americas (Newton 2012), as well as motifs of language survival and contact with other ethnic groups (Newton 2001: 195-208, 216-252), can be studied in a comparative context. The Gaelic experience of colonization and ethnic cleansing was more traumatic than anything experienced by the Welsh, and there will be crucial differences between the Welsh and the Gaelic response. But there will also be similarities, some of which are common to other minoritized ethnic groups.

Canadian critics of postcolonialism have argued that "the exclusion of the so-called settler colonies" (Lawson 2004: 152) within postcolonial theory ignores how settlers and their descendants became distanced from the original European homelands of their languages and cultures, and took on some of the trappings of New World indigeneity. This absorption occurred as the indigenous peoples of the Americas were themselves being gradually displaced (158). But while indigeneity may appeal to many European settler societies, it has peculiar relevance for smaller ethnic groups who are fearful of assimilation and disappearance.

In Welsh-language culture there is particular interest in the indigeneity of those ethnic groups that are presumed to be somewhat further along the road to language death than the Welsh themselves. In a British context, therefore, there is a certain amount of poetry in Welsh about the Cornish (Crwys 1935: 113; Hughes 1972: 5), in which the Welsh themselves are rarely mentioned, but the demise of the Cornish language becomes a metaphor for the predicated death of the Welsh language itself.

By far the largest body of contemporary Welsh-language prose and poetry devoted to indigeneity deals with Native American culture. There are songs in Welsh about the Navaho (Ifan 1977), and poetry about the Arawak (R. G. Jones 1968: 7), who were the first Native Americans to be exposed to European contact. The greatest Welsh-language poet of the 20th century, Waldo Williams, has a poem entitled "Sequoya (1760-1843)," dedicated to Sequoya, who developed the Cherokee script (1934: 186). It is significant that much of this material is part of Welsh nationalist discourse. The 1970s in Wales in particular saw the development of ethnolinguistic nationalism, with a strong emphasis on indigeneity and territorial integrity. Those artists most closely connected with this movement, such as the folk singer Tecwyn Ifan, sang most often about the indigenous peoples of the Americas. Nationalist journals in Wales regularly carried items on the fate of Native American culture (G. Morgan 1975-1976: 12-17). There have been critical studies too, most recently Jerry Hunter's book-length study of attitudes in the American Welsh-speaking community and press ca. 1820-1850 toward Native Americans and the Cherokee in particular (Hunter 2012). His evaluation of the Welsh missionary, Evan Jones, who both learned and published in Cherokee and was in many ways hybridized by his experiences, is particularly valuable.

The motif of American indigeneity was useful too for cultures that were hegemonic in a European context, but that had been marginalized in the Americas by the gradual rise of the anglophone tide. In a fine article on the fears that the U.S.'s German-language culture internalized about its own possible ethnic death, the critic Marc Shell writes that:

> Many German-Americans anticipated or mourned the loss of their own culture by projecting that loss onto other peoples and their languages. Native American peoples provided an especially important screen. A brilliant German and German-American scholarly tradition focuses on the loss of "Amerindian" languages and adds to it, sometimes wittingly and sometimes not, a concern with German-Americans' loss of their own language. Much German-American anthropology ventriloquistically transforms Americans' general silence about Amerindian genocide into something like a self-reflexive whisper. (1998: 260)

This "self-reflexive whisper" among minoritized peoples in their reflections on the indigenous population of the Americas does not mean that such thoughts are not ethnocentric. Indeed, in their use of the Amerindian example to illuminate the trauma of immigrant language loss in the Americas, they can be peculiarly so. The 1904 classic, *Dringo'r Andes* (Climbing the Andes), by the most important Patagonian Welsh-language author, Eluned Morgan, places a humanistic and anti-colonial emphasis on the rights of the indigenous population to be free from Spanish cultural imperialism. But it also contains examples of essentialist discourse about the native population, which are typical of majoritarian imaginings about marginalized, and supposedly romantic, peoples.

Climbing the Andes is a colonial, or perhaps postcolonial, book designed mainly for a Welsh audience. Its many protestations that the Welsh are themselves not colonists, but are in fact "friends" of the Indians, are only necessary because of the inherently European and colonial nature of the Welsh intervention in Patagonia. But claiming that the Welsh occupy a sort of "Third Space" (Bhabha 1994: 37) between colonist and colonizer enables Eluned Morgan to make explicit comparisons between oppressed "small nations," an obvious reference to Wales and the fate of indigenous peoples. Her comparison transcends the idea of an absolute divide between the European and Native American experience:

> mor anrhaethol drist yw meddwl fod y dyn gwyn gyda'i Gristionog-aeth a'i ddiod ddamniol yn ysu ac yn difa fel tân pa le bynag yr elo. A raid i'r pethau hyn fod? Dyna gwestiwn sydd wedi dwys-lithro drwy'm calon ganwaith wrth synfyfyrio ar hanes brodorion crwydrol pob gwlad; Indiaid Cochion Gogledd America, Maories swynhudol Awstralia [*sic*], a hen gyfeillion fy mebyd inau yn Ne America. Nid yw'r Hispaenwr un gronyn gwaeth na'r Ianci a'r Sais yn hyn o beth; difa brodorion a chenedloedd bychain yw pechod parod pob un o honynt. (1904: 49)

> (It's incredibly sad to think that the white man with his Christianity and damned drink consumes and destroys wherever he goes. Does this have to be the case? That's the question which has worried me a hundred times in thinking of the history of the wandering natives of every land: the Red Indians of North America, the alluring Maories [*sic*] of Australia, and old friends of my youth in South America. The Spaniard is no worse than the Yankee or the English-man in this regard; destroying natives and small nations is the ready sin of them all.)[1]

It is revealing too that Eluned Morgan makes a connection between indigeneity and the racially oppressed subaltern and interprets the sufferings of indigenous peoples through the prism of the African American experience. In a striking passage commenting on the Argentinian State's genocidal campaigns of the 1870s and 1880s, she compares the so-called "Conquest of the Desert," which aimed to subdue and replace Patagonia's indigenous population, the forced transfer of indigenous peoples to Buenos Aires, with the slave trade carriage from Africa to America:

> A phe ysgrifenid hanes y teithio tros y môr garw mewn llongau bychain caethiwus, a'r creulonderau gyflawnwyd, a'r golygfeydd

ar ddec y llongau yn mhorthladd y ddinas pan wahenid y plentyn sugno oddiar fron ei fam, i fod yn degan mewn rhyw balas gwych lle'r oedd pechod a moethau wedi lladd yr enaid, ac y cipid bychan llygad-ddu, gydiai mor dyn yn llaw ei dad, gan ryw goegyn i'w roi ar flaen ei gerbyd o fewn cyrhaedd hwylus ei chwip ... pe ysgrifenid ond y ganfed ran o'r pethau hyn, byddai yna *"Gaban F'ewyrth Twm"* yn Ne America hefyd, eithr ysywaeth nid oes eto un i'w ysgrifenu. (1904: 50)

(And if the history of the journey across rough seas in small enslaved ships, and of the cruelties inflicted was written, as well as the scenes on the ships' decks in the city's port when the suckling child is taken from his mother's breast, to be a toy in some fine palace where sin and luxury have killed the soul, and of the black-eyed child, who clung so tightly to his father's hand, taken by some vain man to be put at the front of his carriage within easy reach of his whip ... if only a hundredth part of these things was written, there would be an *Uncle Tom's Cabin* in South America as well, but unfortunately there is no one yet to write it.)

The indigenous experience now becomes part of a multi-faceted trans-Atlantic network of exploitation, in which suppression of indigeneity is part of a wider globalized economy. But resistance is also trans-Atlantic and trans-national. The Welsh-language versions of *Uncle Tom's Cabin*, such as *Aelwyd F'Ewythr Robert* (Rees 1853), number among the most iconic Welsh-language texts of radical 19th-century Wales, and their popularity serves as an echo of the perceived oppression of the Welsh. What Eluned Morgan is constructing is a three-way dialogue in which Welsh identity in the Americas stands somewhere between the autochthonous, represented by the indigenous population; the subaltern, represented by African Americans; and the stateless European nation, which is both colonizer, being European, and colonized, because it has been minoritized within state power structures. The fate of Patagonia's indigenous identities, although important identities themselves, is a reflection of the likely fate of the Welsh. The vociferous condemnation in *Climbing the Andes* of the Argentinian nation-state for its attacks on indigenous culture and identity must surely be linked to the antipathy felt by some in the Welsh-speaking elite that the state is trying to Hispanicize Welsh-speaking culture in Patagonia as well.

This discursive triangle connecting the colonizer, the colonized colonizer and the indigenous is quite persistent in Welsh-language culture from and about the Americas, occurring as it does in a variety of national contexts, far removed in time and place from early 20th-century Patagonia. One sees it, for example, in Welsh-language poetry about indigenous peoples in both anglophone and francophone Canada. In many ways, *Dan Ddylanwad [:] Cerddi 'Mericia, Canada a Chymru* (Under the Influence [:]

Poems from America, Canada and Wales) by Iwan Llwyd (1997), whom many regard as the greatest poet of 1980s and 1990s Wales, is a less significant text for the history of the Welsh in the Americas than *Climbing the Andes*. Llwyd was a Wales-based poet who wrote about Canadian indigeneity as an outsider (he was invited to speak at the Saskatchewan Literary Festival), rather than as a member of the Welsh-language community in the New World. The indigenous peoples of the Americas are nevertheless a constant theme in his work, and meditations about the Quechua language of the central Andes, and Inca culture, appear in a later volume, *Eldorado* (2000: 8-9, 14-21).

Iwan Llwyd is a good poet, and his poem, "Chwarae Golff" (Playing Golf), published in *Under the Influence*, is an accessible and well-written example of this sub-genre in Welsh literature which shows very well the intellectual and emotional structure of appeals to indigeneity in Welsh-language thought.

> Dyma wareiddiad:
> cwrs golff ar gyrion Saskatoon
> a'r paith wedi'i gaethiwo
> i'n gwasanaethu:
>
> eto yma y daethost,
> i'r tir ffiniol yma,
> rhwng y ddinas a'r gwastadedd,
> i ail-ddechrau byw;
> . . . .
> fe ei allan –
> tresbasu ar y cwrs golff,
> dwyn aeron o'r llwyni bychain
> sy'n weddill o gynhaeaf y paith. (1997: 63)
>
> (So this is civilization
> A golf course on the edge of Saskatoon
> where the plains are trapped
> to service us:
>
> yet here you came,
> to this border country,
> between the city and the plains,
> to start living once again;
> . . . .
> you go out –
> trespass on the golf course
> steal berries from the small bushes
> which remain of the plain's harvest.)

Without mentioning Wales, Iwan Llwyd is discussing not only the Cree themselves, but also the Welsh. Welsh-language culture is itself hemmed in by Anglo-American colonialism, represented here by an arid and sterile golf course (golf courses are a minor bugbear for some cultural nationalists in rural Welsh-speaking Wales). Welsh-language culture, too, leads a liminal existence in border country, and cultural disinheritance and economic disadvantage face the Welsh as well. The Welsh must themselves "steal berries" from what was once a more plentiful cultural harvest.

A number of other poems by Iwan Llwyd also explore the consequences of disinheritance on both sides of the Atlantic. "Far Rockaway" is superficially a melancholic eulogy to the Queens neighbourhood on New York's Atlantic seaboard (1997: 17). Yet the location is chosen because of Llwyd's fascination with the etymology of the word "Rockaway." According to a local guidebook, "the original landholders, the Native American Canarsie Indians, called this peninsula 'Rechouwacky,' which translates to 'the place of our people.' White settlers changed the name to Rockaway" (Copquin 2007: 167). The significance for Llwyd is that the name "Cymru" (the Welsh name for Wales) could also be broadly translated as "place of our people." The ethnonym Cymro consists of the substantive *bro* (border, boundary), to which is attached the prefix *com-*, denoting a connection or relationship, giving a meaning of "one residing within the same border," "compatriot." These similar etymologies—signifying ethnic belonging and possession of land—enable Llwyd to make the claim that the Welsh have been exposed to the same process of acculturation as Native Americans.

This is a theme picked up in "Playing Golf" as well, as the closing stanzas suggest that both the Welsh and the Cree have been uprooted by Anglo-American modernity. The only proper response can be an alliance of the dispossessed:

> buom yn gwrando lleisiau'r Cree
> yn llawn angladdau a drychiolaethau,
> a gwrando dy ddagrau dithau
> am dy genedl goll:
>
> ac am awr neu ddwy
> doedd dim twyni rhyngom a'r gorwel,
> dim cwrs golff rhyngom a'r cof –
> dim ond gwareiddiad. (1997: 64)

> (we listened to the voices of the Cree
> full of funerals and apparitions,
> and listened to your tears
> for your lost nation:
>
> and for an hour or two
> there were no hillocks between us and the horizon,

no golf course between us and the memory –
only civilization.)

None of this is without irony, or naïve, as his quizzical "*Ga'i fod yn indian, mam?*" (1997: 46-47; Can I be an indian, mum?), a poetic treatise on the Western lust for indigeneity, shows. The world for Llwyd is never black and white, and if indeed a Native American singer can "trace his lineage to Sitting Bull/ like all of us to Llywelyn" (1997: 31; *olrhain ei linach i Sitting Bull, / fel pawb ohonom ninnau i Lywelyn*), it is more significant that he sings "she's a barmaid in a West Texas dancehall."

Iwan Llwyd's poetry is at its most perceptive in its exploration of hybridity, and of the role of the colonized colonizer—of the minoritized descendents of European settlers whose cultural universe was created, but is now threatened, by the process of linguistic displacement. This role is played out in the Saskatchewan poems by the province's francophone minority. In Llwyd's poem, "Jean Marie," a French-speaking woman sunbathes naked on the plains, carelessly throwing her clothes on the ground:

mor wahanol i'r cerrig gofalus
a osodwyd rhyw dro i gyfeirio

rhai a ddaeth yma
ganrifoedd cyn ei thad a'i thylwyth. (1997: 65)

(so different to the stones
carefully placed once to direct

those who came here
centuries before her father and family.)

This woman's way of life, marked out as that of a European colonizer, is threatened as she listens to her husband's tractor "humming in the heat" (*[yn] hymian yn y gwres*):

yn troi'r tir cyn i'r haf
ddiflasu ar undonedd y paith,
diflasu ar acenion Ffrengig Jean Marie,
. . . .
cyn i'r gwastadedd hawlio'r cyfan yn ôl. (1997: 65)

(turning the earth before the summer
gets bored with the monotony of the plains
gets tired with Jean Marie's French accents,
. . . .
before the plain claims everything back.)

The tractor, which is emblematic of a rural Francophonie, stops, and Jean Marie, whose corporality is a physical embodiment of this culture, lies naked, exposed, under a hot sun.

> mae Jean Marie yn gorwedd yn noeth
> ac yn boeth rhwng y cerrig,
> ac mae'r tractor wedi stopio. (1997: 65)

(Jean Marie lies naked
and hot between the stones,
and the tractor has stopped.)

Although discrete cultural entities, neither the francophone nor the Cree community should be regarded as essentialist; certainly not in any ethnic sense. Hybridity within minoritized communities is a useful tool for Iwan Llwyd to explore the blurring between the colonizer and colonized, which in his poem "Monica" he personalizes in a meditation about a Métis girl of Cree and French background who lives, in the poet's words, "in the borderland between two worlds" (1997: 68; *ar dir y ffin rhwng dau fyd*).

In Welsh nationalist discourse, the Québécois are almost always presented in a positive light, as an example of a people who have attained cultural autonomy, normalized a minoritized language and moved toward the cusp of statehood. Published in 1965, the volume *Man Gwyn: Caneuon Quebec*, which one might translate as *Promised Land: Québec Poems*, reflects on a year spent in Montréal by the nationalist poet and academic from Wales, Bobi Jones. Like Iwan Llwyd, Bobi Jones has poems about other parts of the Americas that use the Native American experience as a metaphor for the Welsh. In "Condor," published in a later volume, the bird of prey looks down on a people "who were here building cairns" (1976: 71; *a fu yma'n carneddu*). The word *carnedd* (cairns, mounds) in Welsh carries specifically Celtic connotations. Its use as an embodiment of the indigenous experience in the Andes suggests that the Celts constitute a sort of First Nation of the British Isles. These claims are carried over to the Québec poems, where in "*Portread o Hen Indiad*" (Portrait of an Old Indian), more direct comparisons between Native Americans and the Welsh are made. The poet is told that the Native American is an "Indian" (*Indiad*) as "he had no label" (*nad oedd label arno*), a play on the colonial and post-colonial politics of un-naming and re-naming ethnicities, which reminds Jones of the lack of recognition, outside his own culture, of the Welsh: "Outside Britain I'm nothing but an Englishman / Although I claim to be Welsh" (1965: 11; *Tu fa's i Brydain nid wyf ond Sais / Er brochi mod i'n Gymro*).

Other poems are more complicated as they can only be understood within the context of contact between the Québécois and indigenous peoples, thus challenging the nationalist claim that some European settler societies are "good" (Québecois, Celtic) and others "bad" (anglophone). In

"*Rhag-Lethrau'r Laurentides*" (The Foothills of the Laurentides), the Canadian winter is a symbol of colonization, with indigenous peoples displaced by French-speaking colonists:

> Ar draws estyniad gau mynwesau'r gaeaf
> Mae marciau mân yn arwain,
> . . . .
> Lle byddai'r helwyr gynt yn crafu gwaed
> Er mwyn ymlenwi'n feddw, mae'r rhythmau bach
> Yn symud, yn ôl a gwrthol, i fyny ac i waered,
> Mor bert fan acw. Fe all mai Indiaid ŷnt. (1965: 42)

> (Across winter's false embrace
> Small marks lead,
> . . . .
> Where the hunters used to scratch blood
> And fill up drunk, small rhythms
> Move, back and forth, up and down,
> So pretty. Perhaps they are Indians.)

The coupling of the indigenous culture of Québec with nature is typical of many nationalist texts in Wales in which Welsh-language culture is portrayed as interconnected with the natural environment, and in which ecology becomes a representation of indigeneity (Foster Evans 2006: 41-79; H. Williams 2008: 1-28). These Native American cultures reveal that there were

> Un tro'n benaethiaid trwm yn rheol yma,
> A hwy oedd biau'r bore: eiddynt dyn
> Ac elfen, planhigyn ac anifail. Crynai'r afon
> Mewn cyfrin gydnabyddiaeth rhwng ei brwyn.
> Eithr disgynnodd y Dynion Gwyn: ac nid ŷnt mwy
> Ond rhacs neu ymyrraeth led yr eira.
> ... Ond ar riw
> Mor rhyfedd y mae crwydro'n bêr i synnwyr;
> A balch yw ôl ar eira, a'r eira'n toddi. (Jones 1965: 42)

> (Once weighty chiefs in control here,
> And they owned the morning: they owned man
> And element, plant and animal. The river bent
> In secret acknowledgement between its rushes.
> But the White Men came: and they are nothing more
> But an interference in the snow.

... But on a hill
So strange is to wander sweetly into sense;
And a mark on snow is proud, and the snow is melting.)

Inherent in the poem is the idea that it could be read as a metaphor for Wales, or at least for indigenous cultures in general. The white winter of colonization, brought to Québec by white men (compare with Iwan Llwyd's choice of location in "Far Rockaway" with its allusion to "white settlers"), is an "interference" with the "natural" world of pre-European contact Québec. Yet eventually the thaw comes, and the indigenous footprints, which had become mere marks in the snow, are consumed by the natural environment again, as the dulled blanket of colonialism recedes. The fate of the colonized group in this snowless, postcolonial New World is ambiguous, and a double reading could be suggested here. Although a poem about the Québecois as a colonizing force, "The Foothills of the Laurentides" could also be read as a metaphor for both Québecois and indigenous culture, resisting acculturation in the face of anglophone power.

It is doubtful whether the Indigenous Atlantic is a reciprocal process; the indigenous peoples of the Americas have not colonized the stateless peoples of the European periphery in their own homelands. However, all small peoples seek out internationally acknowledged examples of injustice in order to legitimize their own ethnic complaints. Indigeneity is an important element in Welsh, and Celtic, thought for it positions them within a global network of those peoples who "deserve justice." Empowered by the vocabulary and syntax of indigeneity, Welsh- or Gaelic-language communities can rebut laissez-faire arguments that their continued existence is "illiberal"—xenophobic even—and a barrier to progress. The rights associated with first (or even second or third) claims to land can justify the desire to associate a named culture with particular territories. In the Americas, this claim to indigeneity extends support to Celtic cultures, which have become important markers of identity in regions like Nova Scotia and Patagonia.

Notes

1. All translations mine.

References

Bhabha, Homi K. 1994. *The Location of Culture*. London: Routledge.

Copquin, Claudia Gryvatz. 2007. *The Neighborhoods of Queens*. New York: Citizens Committee for New York City.

Crwys [Williams, William]. 1935. *Trydydd Cerddi Crwys*. Wrecsam: Hughes a'i Fab.

Foster Evans, Dylan. 2006. "Cyngor y Bioden": Ecoleg a Llenyddiaeth Gymraeg. *Llenyddiaeth mewn Theori* 1:41-79.

Gilroy, Paul. 1993. *The Blank Atlantic: Modernity and Double Consciousness.* Cambridge, MA: Harvard University Press.

Hughes, Gwilym Rees. 1972. Baled Dolly Pentraeth. *Y Traethodydd* 541 (January): 4-5.

Hunter, Jerry. 2012. *Llwybrau Cenhedloedd: Cyd-destunoli'r Genhadaeth Gymreig i'r Tsalagi.* Caerdydd, U.K.: Gwasg Prifysgol Cymru.

Ifan, Tecwyn, performer. 1977. *Y Dref Wen.* Penygroes, U.K.: Cyhoeddiadau Sain. LP Record (33 1/3 rpm).

Jones, Bobi. 1965. *Man Gwyn: Caneuon Quebec.* Llandybie, U.K.: Llyfrau'r Dryw.

———. 1976. *Gwlad Llun.* Abertawe, U.K.: Christopher Davies.

Jones, R. Gerallt. 1968. *Y Golau Gwyn: Detholiad o gerddi Jamaica.* Llanystumdwy, U.K.: Gwasg y Moresg.

Lawson, Alan. 2004. Postcolonial Theory and the "Settler" Subject. In *Unhomely States: theorizing English-Canadian postcolonialism*, ed. Cynthia Sugars, 151-64. Peterborough, ON: Broadview Press.

Llwyd, Iwan. 1997. *Dan Ddylanwad Cerddi: 'Mericia, Canada a Chymru.* Bodedern: Gwasg Taf.

———. 2000. *Eldorado.* Published by the author.

[Morgan], Eluned. 1904. *Dringo'r Andes.* Y Fenni, U.K.: Y Brodyr Owen.

Morgan, Gerald. 1975-1976. Yr Indiaid Cochion Heddiw. *Mabon* 1 (9): 12-17.

Newton, Michael. 2001. *We're Indians sure enough: The Legacy of the Scottish Highlanders in the United States.* Saorsa Media.

———. 2012. The Macs meet the "Micmacs": Scottish Gaelic First Encounter Narratives from Nova Scotia. *Journal of Irish and Scottish Studies* 5 (1): 67-96.

Rees, William. 1853. *Aelwyd F'Ewythr Robert: neu, Hanes Caban F'Ewythr Tomos.* Dinbych: Thomas Gee.

Shell, Marc. 1998. Hyphens Between Deitsch and Americans. In *Multilingual America: Transnationalism, Ethnicity, and the Languages of American Literature*, ed. Werner Sollors, 258-71. New York: New York University Press.

Williams, Heather. 2008. Ecofeirniadaeth i'r Celtiaid. *Llenyddiaeth mewn Theori* 3:1-28.

Williams, Waldo. 1934. Sequoya (1760-1843). *Y Ford Gron* 4 (8): 186.

Part V: Interethnic Interactions

Daniel G. Williams

Is the "Pan-" in Pan-Celticism the "Pan-" in Pan-Africanism? Language, Race and Diaspora

The title of this chapter is an adaptation of the title of Kwame Anthony Appiah's well-known article, in which he addresses the question of whether the "post" in postmodernism is the same as the "post" in postcolonialism.[1] He argued that postcolonialism was the product of a *"comprador* intelligentsia: a relatively small, Western-style, Western-trained group of writers and thinkers" who mediated the worldwide "trade in cultural commodities" that constituted the postmodern milieu of late capitalism (Appiah 1991: 348). In the sphere of culture, the "post" in postcolonial, like the "post" in postmodern, shared a "space-clearing" gesture; a rejection of the modernist grand narrative that "the economization of the world was the triumph of reason," and an embrace of a proliferation of narratives, histories and possible outcomes (348).

The intricacies of Appiah's argument do not concern me here, but among those multifarious narratives born in the age of modernism and wedded to an Enlightenment commitment to human emancipation now questioned by postmodern relativism, were the struggles of many colonized African nations for independence. These struggles had been drawn together under the banner of "pan-Africanism" (at least since 1945 when pan-Africanists embraced a more overtly political, as opposed to cultural, philosophy and practice). Appiah's article eventually appeared in a book that attempted to explore, and move beyond, "the racialist history that has dogged pan-Africanism from its inception" (1992: xi). If the "post" in postcolonialism involved a clearing of space following a period of revolutionary activism, then the "pan" in pan-Africanism signified a different gesture; a reaching out to make transnational connections. The question, asked by pan-Africanists throughout the 20th century, was on what basis could a pan-African movement be forged? What common principle underpinned the "pan" in "pan-Africanism"?

Appiah argued influentially that, despite the best intentions of many of its proponents, pan-Africanism was ultimately based on a notion of racial, biological kinship. In a postmodernist milieu that rejected all such claims to rootedness and belonging, and in which the older language of rights, justice, exploitation and political legitimacy had been replaced by an enthusiasm for margins, borders and hybridities, was there any basis for pan-African solidarity? These questions are also relevant to the study of the Celtic peoples and their cultures, perhaps especially when we include the Celts in the Americas in our discussions.

The African American man of letters and activist W. E. B. Du Bois is widely acknowledged to be the "father of Pan Africanism" (Nwafor 1972: xvi). At the first Pan-African Congress, held in London in 1900, Du Bois opened a speech entitled "To the Nations of the World" by noting that "in the metropolis of the modern world, in the closing years of the nineteenth century there has been assembled a congress of men and women of African blood," ready to engage with "the problem of the twentieth century," the "problem of the color line" (1982 [1900]: 11). That imperial metropolis also housed many members of the Celtic diaspora who, as we shall see, were also engaged in a process of cultural revivalism and who held their own inaugural pan-Celtic conference in Dublin a year later (Schneer 1999: 162-83). Toward the end of his seminal analysis of the pan-African movement, Imanuel Geiss called for a comparative analysis of pan-movements and initiated such a project by noting that most "pan" movements appeared in "underdeveloped countries which possessed no states of their own, or whose statehood was only partial" (430).

In pursuing Geiss's lead, my attempt here is to step back from the particular experiences of Celtic communities in the Americas (discussed by many other contributors to this volume), to offer a more theoretical meditation on the ways in which the Celts have conceptualized their own experiences, and to explore the question of which models and methodologies may be most appropriate for exploring those experiences today. In an era characterized by the transnational nature of modes of production, social movements and informational exchanges, is there anything useful still to be found in the "pan"? [2]

Literature

In his autobiography, *Dusk of Dawn*, Du Bois begins the account of his pan-African activities by quoting lines from Countée Cullen's poem of 1925, "Heritage" (Du Bois 1986 [1940]: 639). Cullen was an African American poet, and the initiating question of his poem—"What is Africa to Me?"—was to reverberate throughout the literature of what was to become known as the Harlem Renaissance. The question is initially asked with some skepticism. For "one three centuries removed / from the scenes his fathers loved," Africa can be little more than "a book one thumbs / Listlessly, till slumber comes" (Cullen 1925: 1312). It seems that the answer to the opening question is "nothing." Three hundred years have passed since his ancestors were transported from Africa. The poet is now an American.

But that answer is not allowed to stand. For although the scenes his father loved are initially presented as "unremembered" by the son, the tendency to forget (as if Africa is too distant to matter) is reinterpreted as a requirement to repress (as if Africa is in fact too present to be forgotten):

> One thing only must I do
> Quench my pride and cool my blood
> Lest I perish in their flood ...
> Lest the grave restore its dead. (1314)

That is, lest an apparently lost ancestral Africa turns out not only to be present, but to be a force as strong or stronger than the African's Americanization. And this attempt to repress the African past is now seen to be a failure, for the metaphor that represents the way in which Africa is supposed to be kept out becomes a representation of the way in which it is discovered that Africa is already inside:

> So I lie, who always hear,
> Though I cram against my ear
> Both my thumbs and keep them there,
> Great drums throbbing through the air. (1312)

The poet puts his fingers in his ears to hide external noises, but hears the beating of his heart in his ears instead. Despite the pressure to conform and to assimilate, the African American poet cannot escape the fact of his African ancestry, cannot get away from an essential identity that lies within, beneath the surface.

A famous poem by the Welsh modernist T. H. Parry-Williams shares the same narrative structure as Cullen's "Heritage." "What is Africa to Me?" takes the form of *"Beth yw'r ots gennyf fi am Gymru"* (What do I care about Wales? or What is Wales to me?)[3] in *"Hon"* (This One) (1974 [1949]:

60). Unlike Cullen, Parry-Williams clearly knew and grew up in the Wales of which he speaks, but the structure of the poem is very similar, and it constructs a Wales of the imagination, more than an actual place. Parry-Williams begins by speaking in the voice of an assimilationist. We're told that Wales is no more than a patch of earth harbouring "*gwehilion o boblach*" (the refuse of humanity), and hear of the tiresome debates regarding nation and language that are the bread and butter of nationalist politics. Like Cullen, Parry-Williams turns his back on the noise of the Wales outside, only to discover a Wales on the inside.

> Mi af am dro ...
> Yn ol i'm cynefin gynt a'm dychymyg yn dren.
> Rwy'n dechrau simasanu braidd; ac meddaf i chwi
> Mae rhyw ysictod fel petai'n dod drosof i;
> Ac mi glywaf grafangau Cymru'n dirdynnu fy mron.
> Duw a'm gwaredo, ni allaf ddianc rhag hon. (60-61)

> (I will take a walk, back to my childhood haunts
> In the train of my imagination...
> I'm uncertain and now, I tell you
> I feel a kind of instability creeping over me
> And the claws of Wales clutching at my breast
> God preserve me, I cannot escape from her.)

The power of the poem derives from the expectation that the educated Welshman will assimilate to a British norm and deny the cultural characteristics of the benighted people among whom he grew up. But as the poem proceeds, the assimilationist desire to forget and reject is reinterpreted, as with Cullen, as a requirement to repress. Both poems enact a Freudian narrative in which that which is being repressed reappears in uncanny and ghostly forms in the imagination. In Parry-Williams's "*Hon*," "*Mae lleisiau a drychiolaethau ar hyd y lle*" (60-61; There are voices and phantoms all over the place), while the fear in Cullen's poem is that "the grave restore its dead." These are haunted landscapes for both poems enact a return of the repressed. This desire to access internal memories is perhaps also reflected in the fact that both Cullen and Parry-Williams shared an uncommon fondness for rhyming couplets, a form that evokes children's nursery rhymes and, by extension, a yearning for a lost past or innocence.

Perhaps not surprisingly, both poems have been read in cultural nationalist terms, as poems that ultimately express a resistance to assimilation and the celebration of a forgotten, marginalized or colonized homeland. Such readings have also been offered of W. B. Yeats's "The Lake Isle of Innisfree," a widely canonized poem that shares a somewhat similar narrative trajectory to Cullen's "Heritage" and Parry-Williams's "*Hon*."

> I will arise and go now, and go to Innisfree,
> And a small cabin build there, of clay and wattles made;
> Nine bean rows will I have there, a hive for the honeybee,
> And live alone in the bee-loud glade.
>
> ....
>
> I will arise and go now, for always night and day
> I hear lake water lapping with low sounds by the shore;
> While I stand on the roadway, or on the pavements gray,
> I hear it in the deep heart's core. (1983 [1890]: 39)

Against nationalistic readings that view the island as a metonym for Ireland itself and consider the nation's yearning for freedom to be embodied in the poem's title, Michael North emphasizes that "The Lake Isle of Innisfree" communicates a sense of individualism more than nationalism (1991: 22-25). The freedom sought in the poem is not the freedom desired by a national community, but an individual's freedom from having to interact with other people. The longing in "The Lake Isle of Innisfree" is not for the close face-to-face community of Ireland, but for a life of Thoreau-like isolation in a hut on the water.

Something similar can be said of Cullen's Africa and Parry-Williams's Wales, for the places they evoke in their poems contain no other people. These are profoundly individualistic poems which locate identity deep within the self. Yeats, Cullen and Parry-Williams travel in their imaginations. "Wales," "Ireland" and "Africa" are not political, civic entities in these poems; they are internalized entities that continue to exist within the imagination, within the self, despite external social pressures. Cullen tells us that his "beating heart" has in no way realized that it is civilized; Yeats hears the water lapping "in the deep heart's core"; and Parry-Williams senses "the claws of Wales clutching at [his] breast" (*mi glywaf grafangau Cymru'n dirdynnu fy mron*). In each poem the speaker turns away from the social world to an internal world. The response to assimilation and homogeneity is to turn inwards to an essential, prior, distinctive self that resides in the heart or the soul or the breast. It is on this process of conceiving of identity as something internal, and the cultural and political consequences of thinking of identity in these terms, that I wish to focus. I begin with these comparative examples because I think that this process of internalization is replicated in many minority literatures, and forms the basis for the emergence of a transnational way of thinking about identity which became embodied within the pan-movements.

History

Countée Cullen's "Heritage," T. H. Parry-Willams's "*Hon*," and Yeats's "The Lake Isle of Innisfree" all evoke places in the imagination being described by speakers living in exile. The speaker in Cullen's poem has literally never been to Africa, and encounters the continent through books. The speaker in Yeats's poem wishes to arise and go, but never actually does so, and in his semi-autobiographical novel, *John Sherman* (1991 [1891]), Yeats described the gestation of the themes and images of "The Lake Isle of Innisfree" while wandering the "pavements grey" of London (57). T. H. Parry-Williams knew the *Eryri* (Snowdonia) of which he writes, but he is one of the most well-travelled of Welsh modernist poets. The speaker in "*Hon*" is in the process of travelling back to Wales, and the poem captures a longing which Parry-Williams also evokes in the essays deriving from his travels in South America.

The poems can be seen as representative of a broader truth in this respect, for pan-Celticism and pan-Africanism are to a considerable extent constructed concepts imposed from outside the groups that they try to contain. Azinan Nwafor noted that the "Pan-Africanist movement was for a long period a movement outside Africa before it became a movement within Africa" (1972: xxxi), and histories of the pan-African movement usually begin with the dispersal of slaves torn from their African homelands. Similarly, Joep Leerssen notes that the classification "Celtic" was imposed from outside and is similar to "the construction of concepts like 'the Negro' or 'the Oriental' as analysed in its hegemonistic intent by critics such as Frantz Fanon and Edward Said" (1994: 6). Nevertheless, in the last century the notions of pan-Africanism and pan-Celticism have been adopted by those groups themselves and have come to be uttered in the first person.

Writing in the mid-1920s, Du Bois recognized that "the Pan-African idea was still American rather than African, but it was growing, and it expressed a real demand for examination of the African situation and a plan of treatment from the native African point of view" (1947: 242). In the Americas, as Stephen Howe has noted, both access to education and publishing, and "experience of cultural insecurity born from the destruction of or displacement from 'traditional' African modes of life and from long exposure to racist calumny, were greater than they were on the African continent" (1999: 24). It is possible to trace diasporic responses to this condition, which asserted a specific pan-African cultural ethos and racial destiny, back to figures such as Martin Delany in the pre-Civil War years. Writing in the United States, Delany espoused a separatist nationalism and helped the leading abolitionist Frederick Douglass to found the journal *The North Star* in 1847. Unlike the more broadly assimilationist Douglass, Delany was a powerful advocate for black emigrationism. He consistently sought to compare the situation of Blacks in America with the minorities of Europe:

> That there have in all ages, in almost every nation, existed a nation within a nation – a people who although forming a part and parcel of the population, yet were from force of circumstances, known by the peculiar position they occupied, forming in fact, by deprivation of political equality with others, no part, and if any, but a restricted part of the body politics of such nations, is also true. Such then are the Poles in Russia, the Hungarians in Austria, the Scotch, Irish and Welsh in the United Kingdom, and such also are the Jews scattered throughout not only the length and breadth of Europe but almost the habitable globe, maintaining their national characteristics, and looking forward in high hopes of seeing the day when they may return to their former national position of self-government and independence let that be in whatever part of the habitable world it may.... Such then is the condition of various classes in Europe; yes, nations, for centuries within nations, even without the hope of redemption among those who oppress them. And however unfavorable their condition, there is none more so than that of the colored people of the United States. (Delany 1852: 12-13)

Here Delany places African Americans within the context of other stateless peoples, and includes the Celts in his list of the dispossessed. The African Americans and the Celts are placed within a litany of "nations ... within nations" who yearn for "redemption." Delany was fully aware that a political nationalism was developing among other nationalities and diasporic peoples in Europe whose languages and cultures were not recognized by the states of which they formed a part, and regretted that African Americans were not engaged in the kind of political nationalist movements that were developing in parts of Eastern Europe. The nationalism developed by African Americans in the 19th century tended to take transnational forms. By the 1890s Du Bois was explicitly thinking of forms of identity that look beyond the boundaries of the nation-state. In "The Conservation of Races" he argued that

> the advance guard of the Negro people – the 8,000,000 people of Negro blood in the United States of America – must soon come to realize that if they are to take their just place in the van of Pan-Negroism, then their destiny is not absorption by the white Americans. That if in America it is to be proven for the first time in the modern world that not only Negroes are capable of evolving individual men like Toussaint the Saviour, but are a nation stored with wonderful possibilities of culture, then their destiny is not a servile imitation of Anglo-Saxon culture, but a stalwart originality which shall unswervingly follow Negro ideals. (1986 [1897]: 820)

Du Bois conceived of "Pan-Negroism" less as a vehicle for decolonization than as a means of persuading the leaders of Europe—representatives of the "world of culture"—to bend down to assist in the uplift of their fellow human beings. In his conclusion to *The Philadelphia Negro* Du Bois noted that:

> [W]e grant full citizenship in World Commonwealth to the "Anglo-Saxon" (whatever that may mean), the Teuton and the Latin; then with just a shade of reluctance we extend it to the Celt and Slav. We half deny it to the yellow races of Asia, admit the brown Indians to an ante-room only on the strength of an undeniable past; but with the Negroes of Africa we come to a full stop, and in its heart the civilised world with one accord denies that these come within the pale of nineteenth-century Humanity. (1967 [1899]: 387)

If race is used to justify human disenfranchisement, then in the hands of Du Bois it is recast as a vehicle for African American advancement. "Race" for Du Bois offers a basis for developing a conservationist argument that values the distinctiveness of black culture, and for placing the predicament of African Americans on the world stage at a time of increasing lynchings and segregation. "Race" and "nation" are always invoked in Du Bois's writings as part of a wider cultural and political strategy. If Du Bois's pan-Negroism is partly based on an idea of racial heredity, it also appeals to human values that transcend racial divisions—what he called "the high ideals of justice, freedom and culture" (1982 [1900]: 11). Walter Benn Michaels, following Anthony Appiah, describes Du Bois as attempting to "save the idea of racial identity by redescribing it as historical identity" (1995: 223), yet the idea of race hardly needed "saving" in 1890s America; it was a central component in the way that society was structured and part of Du Bois's everyday reality. "Race is a cultural, sometimes a historical fact," noted Du Bois some years later; "the black man is a person who must ride 'Jim Crow' in Georgia" (1986 [1940]: 666). Inherent in the construction of a pan-African idea lies a tension between racial distinctiveness and universal values.

This tension between universalism and particularism was also of concern to those engaged in nationalist movements in the Celtic countries. If, as I noted, the first pan-African Conference took place in London in 1900, that year also saw the establishment of the pan-Celtic Congress which held its first Conference in Dublin a year later. Like its pan-African counterpart, pan-Celticism has a long history, but it's interesting that both movements begin to envisage themselves in political terms at the turn of the 20th century. The last ten years of the 19th century was a time when, despite considerable historical, social and cultural differences, the national question in Ireland, Wales and Scotland had a simultaneous impact on the political life of Britain. In the cultural sphere this took the form of an emergent pan-Celticism, and if Wales and Scotland generally followed Ireland in politics, the cultural influence travelled both ways. Scottish Gaelic books were frequently reviewed in Irish journals, aided by the similarities between the two languages, and Welsh cultural events were widely reported in the Gaelic press (O'Leary 1994: 376). The Welsh *eisteddfod* was admired by cultural revivalists in both Scotland and Ireland. The Scots established their equivalent festival, the Mòd (Assembly), in 1892, and if it was difficult in 1892 to imagine any Irish organization capable of arranging such an institution, that changed with the birth of Connradh na Gaeilge (The Gaelic League) in 1893. By 1897 the Oireachtas had been born, and the editor of the journal *Irisleabhar na Gaedhilge* (The Gaelic Journal) paid tribute to the inspiration of the Welsh eisteddfod: "We hope to see the Oireachtas, in course of time, do for Irish what the Eisteddfod has done for Welsh" (O'Leary 1994: 377).

It was in this period that what Philip O'Leary calls "lower case pan-celticism"—a pragmatic awareness of similar objectives and shared obstacles by the leaders of Ireland, Wales, Scotland and Brittany—was challenged by an acrimonious row within the Gaelic movement in Ireland regarding its relations to an emergent pan-Celtic movement (1994: 377). One of the chief advocates of pan-Celticism in Ireland was the unlikely Bernard Edward Barnaby Fitzpatrick, or Lord Castletown, one of the country's wealthiest land owners, a fluent Irish speaker and staunch Unionist. Ruth Dudley Edwards suggests that pan-Celticism was identified with the Protestant Ascendancy and aristocracy, and was held in considerable suspicion by nationalists in general and the Gaelic League in particular (1977: 31-38). The movement did, however, have considerable support among influential figures within The Gaelic League, such as Patrick Pearse, who visited the eisteddfod on its behalf in 1899, and Douglas Hyde. Indeed *Fainne an Lae* (literally, "the rise of day"), the official organ of the Gaelic League, was pan-Celtic in its sympathies, committing its allegiance to a vision of "Celtia" in its January 6, 1899 edition:

> "Celtia" or "Keltia" is the name adopted at Cardiff last year for the aggregate territory of the Five Celtic Nations, i.e., those nationalities whose surviving, or rather reviving, national language belongs to the Celtic family of Indo-European languages. That definition leaves the question of blood-relationship, of historical connection, of racial purity, and of political status altogether on one side. "Celtia" has an actual existence in the hearts of those who speak and love their Celtic language, and are in sympathy with the parallel efforts of their kinsfolk across the sea.... The five nations are linked together, however far apart may lie their political or religious tendencies. (Qtd. in O'Leary 1994: 378)

While language is the basis for a common Celticism here, linguistic and racial definitions often become confused in the writings of the period, and those who opposed the pan-Celtic idea noted that the "innate racial sympathy" that united "Celtia" was a fabrication for, with the exception of Scots Gaelic, the other Celtic languages that were unintelligible to Irish speakers. An anonymous Gaelic Leaguer commented in 1907 that

> we are not Pan-Celts ourselves – and for this reason. We are working for the building up of the Irish nation – a nation which will be an Irish Ireland rather than a Celtic Ireland – a nation in which the Irish-born Celt and Saxon, the Irish-born Dane and the Irish-born Norman, shall live together as brothers. The Irishman of Saxon or Norman or Danish blood is of vastly more importance to the Gaelic League than the man of Celtic origin who belongs to any other nation. Our objects are national, not (in the narrow sense of the word) racial. (Qtd. in O'Leary 1986: 109)

These debates, which were ultimately concerned with the very basis of Celtic identity, were to reverberate throughout the 1890s and 1900s. If pan-Celticism represented a dangerously racial definition of identity for some, it offered a model of a multi-national movement for others, thus providing a space in which support for the Irish language could be expressed without that inevitably entailing a commitment to the goals of Irish nationalism. Putting the question of historical context to one side, these debates ask us to consider whether it is ultimately possible to conceive of a philosophically coherent pan-Africanism or pan-Celticism in non-chauvinistic, non-racial, terms.

Theory

An original approach to this question is offered by Hannah Arendt in *The Origins of Totalitarianism* (1973 [1951]). Writing in the aftermath of the Second World War, Arendt identified the rise of modern European racism with the "decline of the European nation-state" and the rise of movements that sought to transcend "the narrow bounds of a national community" by asserting the primacy of "a folk community that would remain a political factor even if its members were dispersed all over the earth" (232). For stateless peoples, argued Arendt, or people who did not conceive of their national aspirations in political terms,

> their national character appeared to be much more a portable private matter, inherent in their very personality, than a matter of public concern and civilization. If they wanted to match the national pride

of Western traditions, they had no country, no state, no historic achievement to show but could only point to themselves, and that meant at best their language – as though language by itself were already an achievement – at worst, to their Slavic, or Germanic, or God-knows-what soul. (231-32)

The result of this emphasis on the "soul," on the internal aspects of an identity (as emphasized in the poems with which I began) that can be measured in terms of what someone is due to ancestry, rather than what someone does through individual choice, was the emergence of a form of racism that from its beginning

> deliberately cut across all national boundaries, whether defined by geographical, linguistic, traditional, or any other standards, and denied national-political existence as such.... Tribal nationalism, spreading through all oppressed nationalities in Eastern and Southern Europe, developed into a new form of organization, the pan-movements, among those peoples who combined some kind of national home country, Germany and Russia, with a large, dispersed irredenta, Germans and Slavs abroad. In contrast to overseas imperialism, which was content with relative superiority, a national mission, or a white man's burden, the pan-movements started with absolute claims to chosenness. Nationalism has been frequently described as an emotional surrogate of religion, but only the tribalism of the pan-movements offered a new religious theory and a new concept of holiness.... Nazism and Bolshevism owe more to Pan-Germanism and Pan-Slavism (respectively) than to any other ideology or political movement. (161, 232, 222)

Arendt constructs a narrative whereby the oppressed peoples of Austria-Hungary, Czarist Russia and the Balkan countries developed pan-movements as a result of the fact that "the Western national trinity of people-territory-state" was not an option for them. Their emphasis on the soul, on the internal dimension of identity, led to the attempt at constructing transnational conceptions of identity, which transcended the structures of the nation-states to which they did not fully belong. The literature of "soul," manifested in the three poems discussed above, underpinned a transnational consciousness that replaced the political, civic space of the nation with a racial conception of a dispersed people. In this respect, according to Arendt, the pan- movements created a context in which totalitarianism could flourish.

Writing in response to the mass murders of the Second World War, Arendt argued bravely that race and nation were distinct and could be separated. This is an interesting stance because the tendency among those who are vehemently opposed to nationalism is to suggest that all nationalisms hide a racial or atavistic essence. That is, even when attempts are made to put some civic lipstick on the ethnic gorilla, all nationalisms ultimately share a desire to keep the race pure and to keep others out. Indeed, the rejection or transcendence of the nation is widely regarded as wholly beneficial by those cultural critics espousing transnational, transatlantic, diasporic and post-national approaches in political, literary and historical studies. Paul Gilroy is typical of many in proceeding to think beyond what he describes as "the moribund categories of national histories" and, in contradistinction to Arendt, turns increasingly and influentially toward the idea of "diaspora" as an alternative to "nation":

> The idea of diaspora offers a ready alternative to the stern discipline of primordial kinship and rooted belonging. It rejects the popular image of natural nations spontaneously endowed with self-consciousness, tidily composed of uniform families.... It disrupts the fundamental power of territory to determine identity by breaking the simple sequence of explanatory links between place, location, and consciousness.... The term opens up a historical and experiential rift between the location of residence and the locations of belonging. Consciousness of diaspora affiliation stands opposed to the distinctively modern structures and modes of power orchestrated by the institutional complexity of nation-states. (2000: 123-24)

But if "diaspora" does away with the problem of "rooted belonging" (to use Gilroy's phrase), what, other than some sense of "primordial kinship," allows one to identify with a diaspora in the first place? Anthony Appiah has noted that sharing a common national history cannot be a criterion for being members of the same nation, for we would have to be members of the same "nation" in order to identify with its history in the first place (1992: 32). In his forensic analysis of the thought of W. E. B. Du Bois, Appiah suggests that the attempt to substitute "history" or "culture" for "race" is never wholly successful.

> In his early work, Du Bois takes race for granted and seeks to revalue one pole of the opposition of white to black. The received concept is a hierarchy, a vertical structure, and Du Bois wishes to rotate the axis, to give race a "horizontal" reading. Challenge the assumption that there can be an axis, however orientated in the space of values, and the project fails for loss of presuppositions. In his later writings, Du Bois – whose life's work was, in a sense, an attempt at just this impossible project – was unable to escape the notion of race he explicitly rejected. (46)

Returning to the passage by Gilroy quoted above, it would seem that this critique of Du Bois could be made—with added force given the absence of a political or territorial dimension—regarding the espousal of diaspora as the frame for cultural and historical analysis. What is the "presupposition" that allows us to claim membership of a diaspora? It can't be sharing a common national history or culture, for we would have to be members of the "nation" or "culture" in order to identify with it in the first place. Appiah seems to have identified a tension, or aporia, that necessarily afflicts all anti-essentialist conceptions of collective identity—including his own attempt at defining a non-racial pan-Africanism. Is there any way out of this apparent stalemate? Is it inevitably a case of, to adapt Marx, race and superstructure? Is it ultimately impossible to conceive of a pan-movement that does not, in the final analysis, rely on a racial base?

However, this is perhaps where pan-Celticism becomes a significant example in the comparative analysis of "pan" movements. The philosopher Étienne Balibar usefully identifies "two great competing routes" to the production of ethnic difference: language and race (Balibar and Wallerstein 1995: 96). While both routes may at times be articulated simultaneously—such as when individuals' "foreign" accent or language marks them as belonging to a specific hereditary group or "race"—for analytical purposes the two routes must be separated. Balibar notes that while the language community seems the "more abstract notion," in reality "it is the more concrete since it connects individuals up with an origin which ... has as its content the common act of their own exchanges" (97). The linguistic community thus "possesses a strange plasticity: it immediately naturalizes new acquisitions" (98). If the linguistic community is inherently open (since anyone can learn a language) the racial community is inherently closed (since no one can change his or her ancestors). This is a distinction of central relevance to the Celtic languages, and to the analysis of pan-movements.

A progressive contemporary pan-Celticism requires communities that live their lives in the Celtic languages. Once a language dies, it can move from being a mode of communication to becoming a symbolic marker of ethnicity. Symbolic language functions like race: it is a practice or characteristic of past generations that cannot be opened up to new members in the present. A living language, however, in Balibar's terms, "immediately naturalizes new acquisitions" (98-99). This is not to say that racism doesn't exist in minority language communities. But the fact remains that the implications for multicultural tolerance are very different for forms of identity rooted in language and forms of identity rooted in race.

A tolerant Celticism thus requires the preservation of the Celtic languages as modes of communication. A genuine multiculturalism in the contemporary nations of the British Isles, and I would tend to think that this would be true of the Americas, must register the reality of multilingualism.

The danger for those of us who live in minority language communities and value linguistic plurality and difference is that our languages are perceived to belong to a specific racial group, and are therefore closed to outsiders. Even those supportive of linguistic difference will tend to conceive of the speakers of the Celtic languages as belonging to an ethnic minority within their respective countries, with English (or, in the case of Breton, French) functioning as the civic language of the nation, as the universal language in which a multicultural society communicates. The Celtic languages are seen as inextricably linked to specific cultural practices, and are thus seen to be incapable of becoming modes of communication for multicultural societies. An Anglo-American form of multiculturalism is used in Wales today, for instance, as a vehicle for undermining that which is actually most multicultural about the place: the Welsh language. A monolingual "multiculturalism" thus becomes a vehicle for linguistic intolerance (Brooks 2006). Anglophone multiculturalism is, for example, different from Welsh *aml-ddiwyllianaeth*, a point made forcefully by Ned Thomas when he argues that we must ask "what is the meaning of multiculturalism within a particular discourse, and within a given language and culture":

> What is often meant within English-language discourse in Britain is tolerance and even encouragement of a number of background cultures and languages within a society which has English as the foreground language – or to be plain, the dominant language. Many speakers of immigrant languages are happy to accept such a place for themselves, always providing that sufficient resources are made available to support their background culture and that it is respected. Welsh speakers on the other hand, like other European territorial minorities, claim a historic space in which their culture too can be a foreground culture, allowing people of different backgrounds to participate. This yields a more European view of Britain, like continental Europe, as a mosaic rather than a melting pot, and requires a rather different account of multiculturalism. (2003: 325)

Ned Thomas speaks from Britain, but his point may also relate to Celtic communities, and our understanding of those communities, in the Americas. It is, as John Koch notes, "the scientific fact of a Celtic family of languages that has weathered unscathed the Celtosceptic controversy" (2007: 3). While traditional area-based studies of Wales, Ireland, Nova Scotia and so forth can explore the diversity of languages and cultures that have occupied a geographical space through history, a transnational, diasporic approach of the kind suggested by a project entitled "Celts in the Americas" needs to develop a meaningful contemporary pan-Celticism that is based on linguistic, not racial, difference.

Conclusion

We might conclude, therefore, that the "pan" in pan-Celticism is different from the "pan" in pan-Africanism, for the former is based on a linguistic difference that offers an alternative to the racial basis on which the latter inevitably relies. But could there also be a linguistically based pan-Africanism? Anthony Appiah thinks not, for he notes that

> few black African states have the privilege of corresponding to a single traditional linguistic community. And for this reason alone, most of the writers who have sought to create a national tradition, transcending the ethnic divisions of Africa's new states, have had to write in European languages or risk being seen as particularists, identifying with old rather than new loyalties.... In a sense we have used Europe's languages because in the task of nation building we could not afford politically to use each other's. (1992: 4)

Kwesi Kwaa Prah however, sees the discussion of African languages in these terms as a continuation of colonial attitudes. It is not surprising that the second largest continent in the world would house many languages, but Prah argues that the notion "that it is impossible to move a few kilometers from one place to the next without coming into another language area" is pure myth (1998: 90). For him, the development and use of indigenous languages for mass education and as the basis for mass culture is a central contemporary challenge. He advocates the reclassification of African languages on the basis of mutual intelligibility so that "it will be possible to create demographic matrices for large literary communities which, with economies of scale will be rational as markets for literature and other media forms" (94).

In an argument that runs parallel to mine in this chapter, Prah describes language difference as the "missing link" in the history of pan-Africanism. There is little doubt that discussions and arguments conducted in dominant European languages, perhaps especially English, are astonishingly blind to issues of linguistic difference. In this respect, the idea of pan-Celticism is useful in that it exposes the intolerance of anglophone and francophone multiculturalism. The monolingual form of multiculturalism informing much cultural debate today is rooted in the belief that the English language, or the French language, is the only legitimate bearer of all civic-democratic nationality, and that those lying beyond its generously catholic embrace are little better than atavistic racists. The construction of a truly tolerant multiculturalism must be predicated on the rejection of this pernicious ideology. A transnational "pan" perspective may still have a role to play in cultural politics.

Notes

1. My attendance at the conference was partly funded by a British Academy Overseas Conference Grant.

2. As this chapter has grown from a keynote paper delivered at the Celts in the Americas conference held in Antigonish, it is worth noting that one of the sites where the histories of pan-Africanism and pan-Celticism overlap is Nova Scotia. As other contributors to this volume attest, the province was a significant area of Scots-Gaelic settlement, and was also home to Irish-speaking communities. Nova Scotia thus has a place of some importance in the history of the Celtic diaspora. Less well known is the fact the several historians trace the origins of pan-Africanism to the linkages established by those escaped southern slaves who settled in Canada, enlisted in the Royalist armies in the American War of Independence, but were ultimately profoundly disappointed by the way they were treated by the British. In 1792, 1,131 African Americans were transported from Nova Scotia to Sierra Leone. Sixty-three died on the journey. See Padmore (1972: 9) and Geiss (1974: 37).

3. All translations mine.

References

Appiah, Kwame Anthony. 1991. Is the Post- in Postmodernism the Post- in Postcolonial? *Critical Inquiry* 17 (2): 336-57.

———. 1992. *In My Father's House: Africa in the Philosophy of Culture*. Oxford: Oxford University Press.

Arendt, Hannah. 1973 [1951]. *The Origins of Totalitarianism*. New York: Harcourt Brace.

Balibar, Étienne and Immanuel Wallerstein. 1995. *Race, Nation, Class: Ambiguous Identities*. London: Verso.

Brooks, Simon. 2006. The Idioms of Race: The "Racist Nationalist" in Wales. In *The Idiom of Dissent: Protest and Propaganda in Wales*, ed. T. Robin Chapman, 139-63. Llandysul, U.K.: Gomer.

Cullen, Countée. 1925. Heritage. In *The Norton Anthology of African American Literature*, ed. Henry Louis Gates et al. New York: Norton.

Delany, Martin. 1852. *The Condition, Elevation, Emigration and Destiny of the Colored People of the United States Politically Considered*. Philadelphia: published by the author.

Du Bois, W. E. B. 1947. *The World and Africa: an inquiry into the part which Africa has played in world history*. New York: The Viking Press.

———. 1967 [1899]. *The Philadelphia Negro: A Social Study*. New York: Shocken Books.

———. 1982 [1900]. To the Nations of the World. In *Writings in Non-Periodical Literature*, ed. Herbert Aptheker, 11-12. Millwood, NY: Kraus-Thompson.

———. 1986 [1897]. The Conservation of Races. In *Writings*, ed. Nathan A. Huggins, 815-26. New York: Library of America.

———. 1986 [1940]. Dusk of Dawn: An Essay Toward and Autobiography of a Race Concept. In *Writings*, ed. Nathan A. Huggins, 549-802. New York: Library of America.

Edwards, Ruth Dudley. 1977. *Patrick Pearse: The Triumph of Failure*. London: Gollancz Ltd.

Geiss, Imanuel. 1974. *The Pan-African Movement*. Trans. Ann Keep. New York: Holmes and Meier.

Gilroy, Paul. 2000. *Between Camps: Nations, Cultures and the Allure of Race*. London: Penguin.

Howe, Stephen. 1999. *Afrocentrism: Mythical Pasts and Imagined Homes*. London: Verso.

Koch, John T. 2007. *An Atlas for Celtic Studies*. Oxford: Oxbow Books.

Leerssen, Joep. 1994. Celticism. In *Celticism*, ed. Terence Brown, 1-19. Atlanta, GA: Rodopi.

Michaels, Walter Benn. 1995. *Our America: Nativism, Modernism and Pluralism*. Durham, NC: Duke University Press.

North, Michael. 1991. *The Political Aesthetic of Yeats, Eliot and Pound*. Cambridge: Cambridge University Press.

Nwafor, Azinna. 1972. *Introduction to George Padmore, Pan-Africanism or Communism*. New York: Doubleday.

O'Leary, Philip. 1986. "Children of the Same Mother": Gaelic Relations with the other Celtic Revival Movements 1882-1916. *Proceedings of the Harvard Celtic Colloquium* 6:101-30.

———. 1994. *The Prose Literature of the Gaelic Revival 1881-1921: Ideology and Innovation*. Pennsylvania: Pennsylvania State University Press.

Padmore, George. 1972. *Pan-Africanism or Communism*. New York: Doubleday.

Parry-Williams, T. H. 1974 [1949]. Hon. In *Poetry of Wales 1939-1970*, ed. R. Gerallt Jones, 60-1. Llandysul: Gwasg Gomer.

Prah, Kwesi Kwaa. 1998. *Beyond the Color Line: Pan-Africanist Disputations, Selected Sketches, Letters, Papers and Reviews*. Trenton, NJ: Africa World Press.

Schneer, Jonathan. 1999. *London 1900: The Imperial Metropolis*. New Haven, CT: Yale University Press.

Thomas, Ned. 2003. Parallels and Paradigms. In *Welsh Writing in English: A Guide to Welsh Literature*, vol. 8, ed. M. Wynn Thomas, 310-26. Cardiff: University of Wales Press.

Yeats, W. B. 1983 [1890]. The Lake Isle of Innisfree. In *Collected Poems*, ed. Richard Finneran, 39. New York: Macmillan.

———. 1991 [1891]. John Sherman. In *John Sherman and Dhoya*, ed. Richard Finneran. New York: Macmillan.

Éva Guillorel

Speaking Mi'kmaw or Gaelic? The Linguistic Policy of the Catholic Church toward Missionaries Sent to Eastern Canada, 17th-19th Centuries

The major moral justification of European colonization in America was to evangelize among Native communities. For this purpose, since the 17th century, learning Amerindian languages lay at the heart of French missionary strategy. At first sight, there seems to be no link between Celtic and Amerindian languages in this missionary context. However, the very rich documentation related to eastern Canada between the 17th and 19th centuries demonstrates that the policy of the church towards native languages was partly connected to the evolving situation of Celtic languages. Valuable Catholic sources on this topic include both linguistic manuscripts left by French missionaries and correspondence between missionaries located in the Maritime provinces and their superiors, especially the bishop of the diocese of Québec, on which eastern missions depended during the French regime and the first decades of the British.

Celtic and Amerindian Languages in Catholic Missions under the French Regime: the Role of Breton Missionaries

Colonization and evangelization started very early in Acadia once the first missionary, Jessé Fléché, landed in 1611 at Port Royal. Jesuits, Sulpicians, Recollets and other secular priests continued this work, especially among Mi'kmaw communities. We know, thanks to *Relations* and letters, that missionaries such as Pierre Biard and Enemond Massé, Chrestien Leclercq, Louis-Pierre Thury and Antoine Gaulin wrote down linguistic observations about the Mi'kmaw language and started to write dictionaries, catechisms and translations of prayers into that language, but we possess few traces of these manuscripts (Thwaites 1959: 140-55; Hanzeli 1969; Leclercq 1999 [1691]).

The major and best-documented figure among these linguists and priests under the French regime was Pierre Maillard, who lived among the Mi'kmaq of Cape Breton and the Acadian peninsula between 1735 and 1762. A secular priest from the diocese of Chartres in central France and educated at the Seminary of the Holy Spirit in Paris before being sent to New France by the Seminary of Foreign Missions, Pierre Maillard became the best French specialist on the Mi'kmaw language under the French regime: he had perfectly understood how a very good knowledge of this language might be decisive in influencing the Mi'kmaw community both spiritually and politically (above all for military alliances against the British) (Dumont-Johnson 1970; Morin 2009). Pierre Maillard translated into Mi'kmaq all the religious texts that a Catholic missionary might need for his apostolate: grammar, catechism, plain-chant songs and hymns, prayers and extracts of the Bible. He also developed a detailed teaching method to learn Mi'kmaw for the benefit of future generations of missionaries, based on oral and written exercises (Maillard 1863; Bellenger 1864; Dubois 1999: 19-26).[1]

Pierre Maillard was much concerned by the idea of training young priests, and he regularly asked his superiors for new missionaries gifted in languages to aid him in his task. He was highly selective in the choice of these disciples and refused two candidates before accepting three young men for training: first Jean-Louis Le Loutre, then Jean Manach and Joseph Gueguen (Le Loutre 1931; Brun 1984; Koren 2002: 37-75). All of them came from the Breton-speaking part of Brittany. It is true that, compared to other places in France, Brittany produced a lot of priests, but it was surely more than mere coincidence that Pierre Maillard chose priests who were already trilingual (Breton-French-Latin). It is certain that a personal experience of multilingualism in Europe helped one become rapidly familiar with native languages. This was also observed in Canada in secular contexts involving immigrants who spoke other Celtic languages, such as Patrick Campbell's testimony concerning Highlanders working in the fur trade who were able to learn native American languages faster than English monoglots (Mitchell 1976: 32; Newton 2001: 195).

In a letter from 1738, Jean-Louis Le Loutre proposed a parallel between the spelling of Breton, his native language, and the spelling of Mi'kmaw (CRAF ASQ, sme 2.1/r/087, 1st October 1738). Of course, the links between these two languages are very narrow, excepting perhaps the pronunciation of guttural sounds (with the Breton letter *c'h*) not found in French. But this comparison must be placed in a wider context: since the 17th century, parallels were made between internal missions in Brittany (in the context of the Counter-Reformation) and external missions in New

France, and the same methods were used to evangelize or re-evangelize both territories (Croix 1988; Deslandres 2003: 306-55). Breton speakers were considered as the Iroquois of France: the anonymous biographer of the forerunner missionary Michel Le Nobletz wrote that the people of Cornouaille (southwestern Brittany) *"ne différait des Canadois que du seul baptême"* (Pérennès 1934: 313; differed from Amerindians in Canada only by baptism).

The ambition of the most famous missionary in Breton-speaking Brittany in the 17th century, the Jesuit Julien Maunoir, was to learn Amerindian languages in order to convert Canada,[2] following the precedent of the first Jesuit martyrs in Huronie. However, because of his poor health, Maunoir was urged to stay in France and was restricted to Brittany and the Breton language (Le Menn 1984: 272).

Such connections between Breton and Amerindian languages can be usefully compared to other Celtic areas. An extensive literature evokes similarities between Welsh and North Amerindian languages in the 17th and 18th centuries, focusing on common linguistic roots (connected to the legend of Prince Madoc and his journey to an unknown western land beyond the sea), pre-Babelian languages and "Welsh Indians," those Amerindians who, according to various testimonies, spoke a perfect Welsh (Lauzon 2008). Many writings from the same period draw parallels between Celtic people and Amerindians: in his *Enquiry into the History of Scotland* (1789), John Pinkerton stressed the point that Celts—and especially the Scottish Gaels—were the most ancient race in Europe and were "to the others what the savages of America are to the European settlers there" (Richards 1994: 123; Williamson 1996). As for Ireland, the proximity between English methods of colonization in the island and those in North America was facilitated by the invention and spreading of stereotypes against the Irish during the 16th century, assimilating this people to pagan and debauched savages: in doing so, the "civilizing process" of colonization was similarly justified on both continents (Canny 1973; Muldoon 1975; Morgan 1999; Rawson 1998; Elliott 2006).

Eastern Missions under the British Regime: Mi'kmaw and Gaelic

Under the French regime, Celtic and Amerindian languages in eastern missions were, as expected, mainly connected through the only Celtic language spoken in the French kingdom: Breton. It is just as logical to notice that such links concern more and more Irish and Scottish Gaelic after Acadia was definitively ceded to the British, most of it in 1713 and Cape Breton in 1763.

At that time, contacts between Celtic and Amerindian languages became stronger in missions, together with a more complex linguistic situation in eastern Canada. In the second half of the 18th century, the balance of power between the different vernacular languages spoken evolved rapidly. The founding of Halifax in 1749, followed by other British settlements, attracted more and more English, German, Scottish Gaelic and Irish speakers. In 1755 and the following years, the number of French speakers decreased dramatically with the deportation of Acadians, whereas Mi'kmaw, Abenaki and Maliseet were still spoken by Natives (Landry and Lang 2001).

This linguistic shake-up jeopardized the efficiency of religious activity and the ability of missionaries to serve all Catholics in their own languages. Between 1812 and 1815, Mgr. Plessis, bishop of Québec, visited at length the eastern part of his diocese and wrote very precious and numerous linguistic remarks in the diary of his journey.[3] He made several observations. First of all, most Catholic missionaries were able to speak in either French or English, but not in both. Moreover, in spite of clear instructions given to these priests requesting that they learn Amerindian languages, few were able to speak or even to understand these languages.

A more disturbing observation he made was that many inhabitants of eastern Canada, even those in Gaspesia, could understand *neither* French nor English, and translators were rare. Some of these monolingual speakers were Natives, but they were more often Irish or Scottish Gaelic speakers.[4] As a consequence, Mgr. Plessis had to find missionaries speaking four different languages—French, English, Mi'kmaw and Gaelic—to hear the confessions of the inhabitants of Prince Edward Island in 1812. During this mission, he preached in French in the morning and in English in the afternoon *"dans l'espoir d'être entendu d'une partie des Écossais qui paraissaient fort ennuyés de ses instructions Françaises"* (with the hope that he would be understood by part of the Scottish that seemed to be very bored by his French instructions), but he had to employ a local Gaelic-speaking priest since this language was by far the most understood (Plessis 1980: 82-97). In 1815, during his last pastoral visitation in Cape Breton, he realized when celebrating Mass in English that nobody among the Irish audience could understand him (Plessis 1980: 167). A few days later, as he was visiting Maliseet and Abenaki missions on the Saint John River, he came up with the same linguistic difficulty, this time with Amerindians (Plessis 1980: 228).

Letters exchanged between bishops and missionaries confirm this problematic situation and show that the Church had to define linguistic priorities so as to preserve Catholicism in the politically tense context of Protestant activism. Missionaries sent to Nova Scotia and New Brunswick often served multilingual communities but could not speak three or four languages; which should they learn? In theory, Amerindian languages were strongly recommended; but, in practice, Catholic missionaries increasingly claimed that learning Mi'kmaw had become less important than having English and Gaelic-speaking priests.[5]

Three major reasons to favour English and Gaelic were given. First, from a demographic point of view, Natives had become far less numerous than the Irish and Scottish. The 1827 census made in Nova Scotia records that the Amerindian community made up less than 1 per cent of the population (Moorson 1830: 71). In 1800, the French missionary Jacques de Calonne wrote a linguistic description of his mission on Prince Edward Island; he distinguished between three categories of Catholics (French and Acadians, Irish, Scottish), but he did not even mention the Mi'kmaq living on the island (AAQ, 312 CN, Nouvelle-Écosse, V-2, Letter to Mgr Denaut, 26 May 1800); it is true that this community probably did not exceed four thousand people spread over all eastern missions (Pacifique de Valigny 1907: 318-19). The second reason was that Natives accepted confession via a translator—this was customary, since almost no missionaries understood their language—but the Irish categorically refused this practice. Thus, if missionaries wanted to hear Irish or Scottish confessions, they had to know their language; that is why Joseph Rinsella, missionary on Prince Edward Island, wrote to the bishop in 1832 to ask "young, strong, active and tongue gifted priests" (AAQ, 311 CN, Nouveau-Brunswick, V-52, Antoine Gagnon, letter to Mgr Plessis, 25 September 1820; AAQ, 310 CN, Île-du-Prince-Édouard, I-123, Joseph Rinsella to Mgr Panet, 8 February 1832).[6] Thirdly, according to the missionaries, Natives had been converted to Catholicism around two centuries earlier, and seemed disinclined to accept a new conversion to Protestantism.

In spite of numerous missionaries, a large amount of money and facilities given to Baptist or Anglican missionaries—above all via the Society of the Propagation of the Gospel in Foreign Parts—Protestants never managed to convert the Mi'kmaq (Pascoe 1901: 107-24; Upton 1979: 153-70; Bickham 2005: 210-40). The situation of Scottish and Irish people seemed less clear. They were surrounded by English-speaking Protestant migrants, with whom they developed economic and even matrimonial alliances; English-speaking ministers approached them. Hence they would have been more tempted to get in touch with Protestant missionaries if there was no French Catholic priest able to speak their language around them, which was often the case (AAQ, 311 CN, Nouveau-Brunswick, V-52, Antoine Gagnon, letter to Mgr Plessis, 25 September 1820; AAQ, 310 CN, Île-du-Prince-Édouard, I-123, Joseph Rinsella to Mgr Panet, 8 February 1832).

All these arguments given by Catholic missionaries were in favour of setting Amerindian languages aside to give preference to Gaelic[7] and, above all, to English. For some of them, supporting the use of English or Gaelic was clearly a strategy to neglect Amerindian languages, considered too difficult to learn.[8] As a consequence, a linguistic specialization occurred among missionaries. On one hand, English and Gaelic native speakers were in charge of Irish, Scottish and English Catholic communities whereas

French-speaking priests served Acadian people. On the other hand, very few missionaries, such as Jean-Marie Bellenger in the 1810s, made much of an effort to learn Mi'kmaw: they moved from one native community to another during the summer, to preach and receive confession at least once a year, trying to coincide with both the religious calendar and native meetings connected to trade (AAQ, Registre des Lettres, 9, Correspondence between Mgr Plessis and Joseph-Marie Bellenger, 1816-1818). In such a situation, many missionaries made a pretext of their linguistic incapacity in English to ask for a more attractive position near the Saint Lawrence valley.[9]

Since the end of the 18th century, the growing presence of Irish priests sent by the bishop of Cork to serve American migrants with the authorization of the bishop of Québec and the unsolicited arrival of Scottish and Irish priests with emigrants to America were very important factors in compensating for the lack of English- and Gaelic-speaking missionaries and even for the lack of French-speaking missionaries. In 1787, an Irish Capuchin monk, James Jones, was nominated by the bishop of Québec to be the supervisor of all eastern missions. This choice did not please the French and Acadians (AAQ, Registre d'Insinuations ecclésiastiques, D-95, Lettre pastorale de Monseigneur l'évêque de Québec aux Catholiques de la Nouvelle-Écosse, 19 October 1787), but it showed how it had become important to take Irish and Scottish communities into account in the management of eastern missions. James Jones's role was to inform the bishop of all difficulties encountered in this territory: among various problems related to the lack of priests and material facilities, the linguistic questions and the problem of Protestant activism were often mentioned in his letters (Murphy 1981; AAQ, 312 CN, Nouvelle-Écosse, I, letters to Mgr d'Esgly, Hubert and Denaut between 1785 and 1799).

Catholic and Protestant Missionaries: Two Different Linguistic Strategies Toward Native Languages

The purpose of Catholics and Protestants was both to support European communities belonging to their religion and to convert Natives. With a similar goal, two different approaches were developed under the British regime with a significant impact on policies concerning vernacular languages.

On the Catholic side, the main goal was to preserve Amerindians from the harmful influence of Europeans. Missionaries had to adapt themselves to the way of the life of Natives, to learn their languages and to encourage them to keep their traditions—even if they tried to make nomadic groups settle. They wanted to keep them from learning English or French and from learning how to read and write (or only by using pictographic writings with which they could read selected sacred books proposed by their priests) (Maillard 1863; Schmidt and Marshall 1995; Dubois 1999; Greenfield 2000; Déléage 2009: 45-111).[10] This strategy was very different from that which had prevailed at the beginning of colonization in the first decades of the 17th century. At that time, a discourse of "civilizing Gallicization," based on the idea of cultural assimilation, had prevailed. But almost all attempts at assimilation failed, causing French authorities to renounce this approach (Dubois 1997: 12-16).

On the Protestant side, the conversion of Natives, and especially Mi'kmaw communities in eastern Canada, was at the heart of the strategy. In the second half of the 18th century, learning native languages was considered a necessary but transitional step on the way to a complete anglicization of Amerindians, which should happen very soon. The preface of the Mi'kmaw-English grammar written in 1766 by the Anglican missionary Thomas Wood of Halifax, typified this perspective:[11]

> The tribe of Mickmak Indians who Reside Chiefly in this your Majesty's Province of Nova Scotia, have for many years part been instructed by French Roman Catholick Priests, & consequently have been taught that infernal diabolical doctrine, that it is meritorious to destroy and murder all whom they are pleased to still hereticks, viz. all Protestants. ... If some Protestant Clergymen & schoolmasters could learn their language, and be sent among them to teach their children English and instruct them in the articles of our pure religion and worship we might reasonably hope by God blessing on our Endeavour, that your Majesty (whom God grant long to reign over us !) may live to see this tribe of Indians added to your faithful subjects, and they and their posterity will probably continue such to your royal descendants to latest posterity. (Wood 1766)

Indeed, the choice of the vernacular language spoken and taught to Mi'kmaw children was central to political and cultural obedience to the British crown, and the cultural assimilation of Natives.

This policy was strongly criticized by French missionaries, as was to be expected,[12] but also by a few secular scholars. The most intriguing figure among these was an Irish schoolmaster called Thomas Irwin. Irwin migrated to Prince Edward Island after spending a short time in the south of Nova Scotia. He decided to devote his life to defending the Mi'kmaw language and culture. In the years 1830-1840, he conducted a fierce battle against the government, attempting to alert public opinion and policy and to improve the cultural and economic situation of the Mi'kmaq. He wrote petitions to the House of Assembly, articles and pamphlets in local newspapers and letters to the commissar of Indian affairs (Upton 1976-1977;

1977). One of his goals was to open a school for Amerindian children in which they would be educated in their own language with books written in Mi'kmaw, in total opposition to the British policy (Ralston 1981). All of his attempts failed. In the reasons he gave in defense of native cultures and languages, he made a direct parallel between the forced anglicization of Celtic people, of which he presented himself as a victim, and the proposed assimilation of the Mi'kmaq. His most interesting pamphlet on this point was published in the *Colonial Herald and Prince Edward Island Advertiser* in 1843 (see Appendix). In Irwin's mind, Celts and Amerindians shared a same destiny of oppression due to the assimilative policy of the British Empire and, thus, they had to support each other to defend their languages and cultures.

Although Irwin was a secular scholar, he played an essential role in the transmission of knowledge of the Mi'kmaw language between French Catholic and British Protestant missionaries. He had obtained manuscripts written by Pierre Maillard—in particular a book on Mi'kmaw grammar, thanks to Jean-Mandé Sigogne, an active Catholic priest who lived in the Acadian community of Baie Sainte-Marie in the south of Nova Scotia. Sigogne himself had obtained these manuscripts from Joseph Gueguen, one of Maillard's direct disciples (Boudreau 1997: 33). Irwin published an English translation of part of this grammar in 1830 in two journals, the *Prince Edward Island Register* and the *Royal Gazette*. A young Baptist missionary sent to Prince Edward Island, Silas Tertius Rand started to learn Mi'kmaw thanks to Irwin's translations. In the second half of the 19th century, Rand became the most accomplished English-speaking linguist, ethnographer and missionary among the Mi'kmaw and Maliseet communities (Rand 1902: v-viii; Abler 1992). Ironically, Thomas Irwin's attempts to save Mi'kmaw, which seemed to have failed during his life, were key to transmitting knowledge of Amerindian languages in eastern Canada across generations and confessions.

In conclusion, connections between Celtic and Amerindian languages are really more important than one could expect at first sight, when one considers the linguistic policy of the Church under both the French and, above all, the British regime in eastern Canada. The rapidly evolving balance of power between various vernacular languages led to two different situations. In the first case, Amerindian and Celtic languages were in competition: in a context where missionaries could not learn too many languages, they had to make a choice between mastering Mi'kmaw, English or Gaelic. In the second case, Amerindian and Celtic languages were presented as sister cultures that had to fight together against British domination. In any case, the interactions between Celtic and Amerindian languages in a religious context in Canada are a fascinating and very promising topic for further research.

Notes

This postdoctoral research, realized at the Centre interuniversitaire d'études québécoises (Université Laval, Québec) under the supervision of Pr. Paul-André Dubois, has been supported by the Fonds Gérard-Dion and Bibliothèque et Archives nationales du Québec. I would also like to thank Oskar Cox Jensen for his help in preparing the English version of this article.

1. Many of his remaining manuscripts are conserved at the Archives de l'Archidiocèse de Québec, especially his *Eucologe*, 1759 (AAQ, 11 UZ).

2. "*Vous sçavez que ma classe est ma mission, & que pour la bien faire, les langues que je dois apprendre, sont la Latine & la Grecque. Si j'en étudiois une autre, ce seroit celle du Canada, où je crois que Dieu m'appelle.*" (Boschet 1697: 39).

3. His comments on multilingualism in Gaspesia are a good summary of the situation: "*Croirait-on que dans une population aussi peu nombreuse que celle de Matane, il se trouve des Canadiens, des Ecossais, des Allemands, des Acadiens, des Irlandais, des Anglo-Américains, des Micmaks ? C'est néanmoins la pure vérité. Aussi rien n'est-il plus ordinaire que d'y entendre la même personne parler trois ou quatre langues*" (Plessis 1980: 60).

4. In French-Canadian sources, a unique word, *gallic*, is used to describe these two Celtic languages.

5. The very rich documentation conserved at the Archives de l'Archidiocèse de Québec has been used for this analysis (AAQ, Registre des lettres; Registre des insinuations ecclésiastiques).

6. Gagnon himself underlined the word "tongue."

7. In 1786, William Phelan insisted on the necessity of knowing Irish not only for missionaries located in Nova Scotia but also for those working in the Gaspesian Baie-des-Chaleurs, in order to serve poor and monolingual Irish immigrants (AAQ, 312 CN, Nouvelle-Écosse, VI-I, Letter to the bishop, 13 June 1786). On Prince Edward Island, the missionary Jacques de Calonne admitted in 1800 that "*la plupart des Écossais ne parlent que celte, je ne puis les entendre, ni par conséquent leur être d'aucune utilité*" (Pineau 1967: 69).

8. For example Joseph-Édouard Morisset, who justified himself in letters sent to the bishop, 31 January 1817 (AAQ, 311 CN, Nouveau-Brunswick, VI-148).

9. Among others, this was the case of Louis-Joseph Desjardins in Percé in 1796, François Lejamtel in Cape Breton in 1800, Ferdinand Belleau in Fredericton in 1830 and Élie-Silvestre Sirois in Madawaska the same year (AAQ, Registre des Lettres).

10. This strategy was clearly exposed by Mgr. Plessis in a letter written August 31, 1816, to the Protestant minister Jonathan Odell (AAQ, Registre des Lettres, 8-668).

11. Photostat conserved at the Archives nationales du Québec in Rimouski.

12. Among many others, see for example the letters sent by the missionary François Ciquart to Mgr. Hubert in the 1790s (AAQ, 311 CN, Nouveau-Brunswick).

References

PRIMARY SOURCES
Manuscript Collections

Archives de l'Archidicocèse de Québec (AAQ).

Centre de référence de l'Amérique française (CRAF), Archives du Séminaire de Québec (ASQ).

Archives nationales du Québec à Rimouski (ANQR).

Printed Sources

Bellenger, Joseph-Marie. 1864. *Grammaire de la langue mikmaque, par M. l'abbé Maillard, rédigée et mise en ordre par Joseph M. Bellenger. Grammar of the Mikmaque Language of Nova Scotia, edited from the manuscripts of the abbé Maillard.* New York: Cramoisy Press.

Boschet, Antoine. 1697. *Le parfait missionnaire, ou La Vie du Révérend Père Julien Maunoir.* Paris: Jean Anisson.

Leclercq, Chrestien. 1999 [1691]. *Nouvelle Relation de la Gaspésie.* Éd. Réal Ouellet. Montréal: Presses de l'Université de Montréal.

Le Loutre, Jean-Louis. 1931. *Une autobiographie de l'abbé Le Loutre.* Nova Francia 6:1-34.

Maillard, Pierre. 1863. Lettre à M. de Lalane. *Soirées canadiennes* 3:289-426.

Moorson, W. 1830. *Letters from Nova Scotia comprising sketches of a young country.* London: Colburn and Bentley.

Pérennès, Henri, ed. 1934. *La vie du vénérable Dom Michel Le Nobletz par le vénérable Père Maunoir de la Compagnie de Jésus.* Saint-Brieuc.

Plessis, Joseph-Octave. 1980. Le journal des visites pastorales de Mgr. Joseph-Octave Plessis (évêque de Québec) 1811-1812-1815. *Les cahiers de la société historique acadienne* 11.

Rand, Silas Tertius. 1902. *Rand's Micmac Dictionary, transcribed and alphabetically arranged by Jeremiah S. Clark.* Charlottetown: Patriot Publishing Company.

Thwaites, Reuben Gold, ed. 1959. *The Jesuit Relations and Allied Documents. Travels and Explorations of the Jesuit Missionaries in New France 3, Acadia 1611-1616.* New York: Pageant Book Company.

Wood, Thomas. 1766. *An Essay towards Bringing the Savage Indian Mickmak Language to be Learnt Grammatically.* ANQR, P9.34.

SECONDARY SOURCES

Abler, Thomas S. 1992. Protestant missionaries and native culture: Parallel careers of Asher Wright and Silas T. Rand. *American Indian Quarterly* 16 (1): 25-38.

Bickham, Troy O. 2005. *Savages within the Empire: Representations of American Indians in Eighteenth-Century Britain*. Oxford: Oxford University Press.

Boudreau, Gérald C. 1997. *Sigogne par les sources*. Moncton: Éditions d'Acadie.

Brun, Régis. 1984. *Pionnier de la nouvelle Acadie, Joseph Gueguen, 1741-1825*. Moncton: Éditions d'Acadie.

Canny, Nicholas P. 1973. The Ideology of English Colonization: From Ireland to America. *The William and Mary Quarterly* 30 (4): 575-98.

Croix, Alain. 1988. Missions, Hurons et Bas-Bretons au XVIIe siècle. *Annales de Bretagne et des Pays de l'Ouest* 95 (4): 487-98.

Déléage, Pierre. 2009. *La croix et les hiéroglyphes. Écritures et objets rituels chez les Amérindiens de Nouvelle-France (XVIIe-XVIIIe siècles)*. Paris: Musée du quai Branly, ENS.

Deslandres, Dominique. 2003. *Croire et faire croire: Les missions françaises au XVIIe siècle*. Paris: Fayard.

Dubois, Paul-André. 1997. *De l'oreille au cœur. Naissance du chant religieux en langues amérindiennes dans les missions en Nouvelle-France, 1600-1650*. Québec: Septentrion.

———. 1999. Tradition missionnaire et innovations pastorales aux XVIIe et XVIIIe siècles : lecture et écriture dans les missions canadiennes. *Études d'histoire religieuse* 65:7-27.

Dumont-Johnson, Micheline. 1970. *Apôtres ou agitateurs: la France missionnaire en Acadie*. Trois-Rivières: Boréal Express.

Elliott, John H. 2006. *Empires of the Atlantic World: Britain and Spain in America*. New Haven, CT: Yale University Press.

Greenfield, Bruce. 2000. The Mi'kmaq Hieroglyphic Prayer Book: Writing and Christianity in Maritime Canada, 1675-1921. In *The Language Encounter in the Americas, 1492-1800: A Collection of Essays*, ed. Edward G. Gray and Norman Fiering, 189-211. New York: Berghahn Books.

Hanzeli, Victor Egon. 1969. *Missionary Linguistics in New France: A Study of Seventeenth- and Eighteenth-Century Descriptions of American Indian Languages*. The Hague: Mouton, 1969.

Koren, Henry J. 2002. *Aventuriers de la mission. Les spiritains en Acadie et en Amérique du Nord 1732-1839*. Paris: Karthala.

Landry, Nicolas and Nicole Lang. 2001. *Histoire de l'Acadie*. Québec: Septentrion.

Lauzon, Matthew. 2008. Welsh Indians and savage Scots: History, antiquarianism, and Indian languages in 18th-century Britain. *History of European Ideas* 34:250-69.

Le Menn, Gwennole. 1984. Le père Julien Maunoir (1606-1683) et la langue bretonne. *Bulletin de la Société Archéologique du Finistère* 113:271-97.

Mitchell, Elaine Allan. 1976. The Scot in the Fur Trade. In *The Scottish Tradition in Canada*, ed. Stanford W. Reid, 27-48. Toronto: McClelland & Stewart.

Morgan, Philip D. 1999. Encounters between British and "Indigenous" peoples, c. 1500-1800. In *Empire and others. British encounters with indigenous peoples 1600-1850*, ed. Martin Daunton and Rick Halpern, 42-78. London: University of Pennsylvania Press.

Morin, Maxime. 2009. L'abbé Pierre Maillard: une figure missionnaire emblématique du XVIIIe siècle acadien. *Études d'histoire religieuse* 75:39-54.

Muldoon James. 1975. *The Indian as Irishman*. Essex Institute Historical Collections 111:267-89.

Murphy, Terrence. 1981. James Jones and the establishment of Roman Catholic Church government in the Maritime provinces. *Société canadienne d'histoire de l'Église catholique* 48:26-42.

Newton, Michael. 2001. *We're Indians Sure Enough: The Legacy of the Scottish Highlanders in the United States*. Richmond, VA: Saorsa Media.

Pacifique de Valigny. 1907. Quelques traits caractéristiques de la tribu des Micmacs. *Congrès international des Américanistes*, Xe session, Québec City, QC.

Pascoe, Charles Frederick. 1901. *Two hundred years of the S.P.G.: a historical account of the Society for the Propagation of the Gospel in Foreign parts, 1701-1900 (based on a digest of the Society's records)*. London: S.P.G.

Pineau, Wilfrid. 1967. *Le clergé français dans l'Île-du-Prince-Édouard, 1721-1821*. Québec: Ferland.

Ralston, Helen. 1981. Religion, Public Policy, and the Education of Micmac Indians of Nova Scotia, 1605-1872. *Canadian Review of Sociology and Anthropology / Revue canadienne de sociologie et d'anthropologie* 18 (4): 470-98.

Rawson, Claude. 1998. "Indiens" et Irlandais: Montaigne, Swift et la question du cannibalisme. La France-Amérique (XVIe-XVIIIe siècles). Ed. Franck Lestringant. Paris: Honoré Champion.

Richards, David. 1994. *Masks of Difference: Cultural Representations in Literature, Anthropology and Art*. Cambridge: Cambridge University Press.

Schmidt, David L. and Murdena Marshall, eds. 1995. *Mi'kmaq hieroglyphic prayers. Readings in North America's first indigenous script*. Halifax, NS: Nimbus Publishing.

Upton, Leslie F. S. 1976-1977. Indians and Islanders: The Micmacs in Colonial Prince Edward Island. *Acadiensis* 6 (1): 21-42.

———. 1977. Thomas Irwin: Champion of the Micmacs. *Island Magazine (Charlottetown)* 3:13-16.

———. 1979. *Micmacs and Colonists: Indian-White relations in the Maritime Provinces, 1713-1867*. Vancouver: University of British Columbia Press.

Williamson, Arthur H. 1996. Scots, Indians and empire: the Scottish politics of civilization 1519-1609. *Past and Present* 150:46-83.

Appendix

Thomas Irwin, Letter sent to the editor of the *Colonial Herald and Prince Edward Island Advertiser* and published April 1, 1843 (extract; emphases and italics in original):

The proposal to give the Indians an English Education is all of a piece with that spirit of English domination that pervades even the sickly suckers of the domineering Saxons to every nation that ever had the misfortune to fall under their sway. In my own country – unfortunate Ireland – law after law was passed by the ruthless subjugators of the country, for the purpose of preventing the natives from speaking their vernacular idiom; and of this tyranny I am myself a living witness, for many a stripe the despotic English dominie inflicted on my own shoulders, for breathing my wants in my native language, lest it should interfere with the jargon of the conqueror.

When the loyal Clans of the mountains and glens essayed to place the last of his race on the throne of his fathers, was not the first act of the heroes of Glocoe [*sic*] an effort to deprive the Gael of his garb, his arms, and his language, that he might the more cheerfully sit down in his degradation? Such has ever been the barbarous policy of England. Witness the murder of the Welsh bards, and the plundering [of] the records of Scotland. Such has been the effort lately made in Canada to obliterate the French; and such the motion under our consideration, only on a *small, very small scale*! But if the Mickmac must pass away from this transitory scene, let him carry with him his noble dialect. The mongrel medley of his conqueror shall never supplant that pure, that melifluous [*sic*] language in which he once addressed the brave and powerful warriors of the woods, – that enkindled their souls to assert the freedom of their country! I, in his name, protest against any measure tending to deprive him of the use of his language.

Suppose you teach an Indian to read English – and from the irregularity of its orthography, and the uncertainty of its component sounds, the difficulty of the task can be known only by those who have taught foreigners – you must then teach him, *in his own language*, the *idea* expressed by every English word, and *vice versa* – a task that few are competent to undertake. Whereas, if they are taught the elements of reading in their own language, the labour is all over, as they instantly comprehend what they read.

The hon. gentleman who condemned it for not possessing such masterpieces as Ossian's poems, and as not being a language, must labour under a *lapsus memoriæ*. Surely a philologist and theologian should recollect that a TONGUE is in Latin "LINGUA;" and from this comes the French words "*langue*" and "*language*", from whence is derived our "*language*". So that, if Mickmac is a "*tongue*", it is also a "*language*". As to the comparative merits of Mickmac and Gaelic, he can be no judge, as he understands but *one* of them; but as I happen to understand *both*, I assure him the Mickmac as far surpasses the Gaelic in copiousness, richness of expression, and elegance of grammatical construction, as the ancient Greek does the dialect of the Calmuc Tartars! As to Ossian, it is well known to be an imposture of his countryman Macpherson: and, even admitting it to be genuine, it would belong to the Irish and not to this country!

Notes on Contributors

Paul W. Birt was awarded an MA by the University of Wales, Lampeter and a PhD by the University of Wales, Bangor. He holds the Chair of Celtic Studies at the University of Ottawa and, since 1998, he has been researching the writings of the first generation of Welsh settlers in Patagonia, Argentina, from 1875 to 1900. The aim of his research is to make primary texts by Patagonian Welsh writers of the period more available and to reassess the identity shift and cultural survival reflected in their writings. The first of these texts, *Gwaith a Bywyd John Daniel Evans*, appeared in 2004.

Simon Brooks is a Lecturer at the School of Welsh, Cardiff University where he teaches 20th-century Welsh literature and cultural history. He is currently working on a book-length study of ethnic diversity within the Welsh-language community, which includes material on concepts of indigeneity and is to be published in the near future. Previous publications include *O dan Lygaid y Gestapo* (Under the Eyes of the Gestapo) (2004), a study of Welsh-language literary criticism and longlisted for Wales Book of the Year, and *Yr Hawl i Oroesi* (The Right to Survive) (2009), a collection of his political journalism.

Bernard Deacon was from 2001 to 2011 Senior Lecturer at the Institute of Cornish Studies, a part of the University of Exeter's Cornwall Campus. While there, he managed the Institute's taught postgraduate degree program and was Director of Education for the History Department's undergraduate programs. He is now Honourary Research Associate at the Institute. He has written extensively on Cornish topics including *Cornwall: A Concise History* (2007), *The Cornish Family* (2004) and *MK and the History of Cornish Nationalism* (2003). He has also published in a range of journals and series, including *Cornish Studies*, *European Urban and Regional Studies*, *Family & Community History*, *Global Networks*, *The International Journal of Regional and Local Studies*, *Local Population Studies* and *Rural History*.

Robert Dunbar is a Research Professor at Sabhal Mòr Ostaig/University of the Highlands and Islands and is Director of "Soillse," a seven-year, £5.29 million research project involving UHI, and the Universities of Aberdeen, Edinburgh and Glasgow whose focus will be public policy toward the maintenance and revitalization of Gaelic language and culture. Dunbar is one of the world's foremost experts on law and minority language maintenance and revitalization, language planning for minority languages, and language policy and planning for Gaelic. A Gaelic-speaking Canadian, he also did his doctorate on the secular poetry of John MacLean, one of the most important Gaelic poets to have emigrated to North America. He is an expert of the Council of Europe and works regularly with the Secretariat for the European Charter for Regional or Minority Languages. He is also a Senior Non-Resident Research Associate of the European Centre for Minority Issues.

Éva Guillorel is Lecturer in early modern history at the University of Caen Basse-Normandie. Her research focuses on orality and cultural history in Europe and French Canada. Éva Guillorel completed a Master's degree in Breton and Celtic studies and another one in Ethnology at the Université de Bretagne occidentale in Brest. After completing a PhD on the use of Breton folksongs as a source for early modern historians at the University of Rennes, she was hosted as a Postdoctoral Fellow at Harvard University (Department of Celtic Languages and Literatures) and at the Université Laval (Québec, Centre interuniversitaire d'études québécoises), where she worked on the use of vernacular languages by missionaries sent to eastern Canada. She is currently hosted at the University of Oxford as a Newton International Fellow (funded by the British Academy) researching the depiction of early modern revolts in oral tradition. Her PhD was published in 2010 as *La complainte et la plainte : chanson, justice, cultures en Bretagne (XVIe-XVIIIe siècles)*.

Ian Johnson is a special political advisor to Plaid Cymru—the Party of Wales in the National Assembly for Wales. His doctoral thesis, "Subjective Ethnolinguistic Vitality of Welsh in the Chubut Province, Argentina," was completed at Cardiff University, Wales in 2007, with the support of the Economic and Social Research Council, and included a term at the Canadian Institute for Research into Linguistic Minorities at the Université de Moncton, New Brunswick, Canada. Ian also writes on minority languages and social media, and social and economic policy issues.

Josette Jouas was born in Brittany but raised in the United States. She was Associate Professor in English at Télécom Bretagne, Brest (formerly École Nationale Supérieure des Télécommunications de Bretagne), where she worked in the domain of Interculturality and United States History and Civilization. Her main academic research focused on Breton Immigration to the United States at the beginning of the 20th Century, which led to her book *Ces Bretons d'Amérique du Nord*, published in 2005. She is now retired and lives in France. She is vice-president of Bretagne-TransAmerica.

Shamus Y. MacDonald is a graduate of St. Francis Xavier University and the University of Edinburgh. He has conducted extensive personal and professional fieldwork in Gaelic Nova Scotia. While living in Nunavut, he also organized oral history research with Inuit elders for the territorial government. Currently based in Newfoundland, MacDonald is pursuing a PhD in Folklore at Memorial University.

C. Alexander MacLennan was born in a French-speaking area of Québec to parents from Gaelic-speaking areas of Cape Breton. He is currently working on an index of the Gaelic newspaper *Mac-Talla* for Cape Breton University's Beaton Institute, a series of scholarly articles on Gaelic traditional tales and a short story collection in Gaelic. He lives in Ottawa and currently works in the Archives and Research Collections Department of Carleton University's Library

Gethin Matthews was born in Wales but brought up in the Welsh community in London. After graduating in psychology he worked in the television business for fifteen years before completing a PhD in Welsh history at Cardiff University, studying the rise and fall of the Welsh community in the gold-fields of British Columbia in the 1860s. After two years lecturing at Cardiff, he took a Welsh-medium lectureship at Swansea University funded by the *Coleg Cymraeg Cenedlaethol*. He is continuing his research into both Welsh communities overseas and the impact of the First World War on Welsh society and culture.

Emily McEwan-Fujita is a linguistic anthropologist specializing in the study of Gaelic revitalization efforts in Scotland and Nova Scotia. She obtained her PhD in anthropology from the University of Chicago. She has conducted research and published on the contemporary construction of Gaelic identity, media discourses about Gaelic, the emergence of a "professional" register of Gaelic and the role of ideology and affect in the experiences of adult Gaelic learners in Uist. Dr. McEwan-Fujita recently succeeded Nancy Dorian as the editor of the Small Languages and Small Language Communities section of the *International Journal of the Sociology of Language*.

Michael Newton is an Assistant Professor in the Celtic Studies Department of St. Francis Xavier University in Nova Scotia. He was awarded a PhD in Celtic Studies from the University of Edinburgh in 1998. He has written several books and numerous articles on many aspects of Highland tradition and history in Scotland and North America. He was the editor of *Dùthchas nan Gaidheal: Selected Essays of John MacInnes*, which won the

Saltire Society's Research Book award of 2006, and is the author of *Warriors of the Word: The World of the Scottish Highlanders*, which was nominated for the 2009 Katharine Briggs Award for folklore research.

Gearóid Ó hAllmhuráin, a native of County Clare and a world-renowned musician, is the inaugural holder of the Johnson Chair in Québec and Canadian Irish Studies at Concordia University, Montréal. A graduate of University College Cork, Trinity College Dublin, and Université du Sud-Toulon-Var, France, he received a PhD in Social Anthropology and Ethnomusicology from Queen's University Belfast in 1990. Author of *A Pocket History of Irish Traditional Music* (O'Brien Press, 2003[1998]) and numerous monographs on Irish music and folk culture, his work has been featured on PBS, CBC, RTE, BBC, TF1 and NPR. An internationally acclaimed music author, lecturer, producer and editor, he holds five world titles in Irish traditional music as a concertina player, uilleann piper and former member of the Kilfenora Céilí Band, the oldest traditional ensemble in Ireland. As a professional musician, he has presented over one thousand concerts on four continents during the past thirty years.

Tomás Ó h-Íde (Ihde) is Associate Professor of Irish in the Department of Languages and Literatures at Lehman College, the City University of New York. He took his MPhil and PhD in Applied Linguistics at Trinity College Dublin and successfully sat the *Dioplóma sa Ghaeilge* examination at the National University of Ireland, Galway. He has published numerous articles and two books, *The Irish Language in the United States* and *Colloquial Irish*. He has served on the executive board of the American Conference for Irish Studies as Irish Language Representative and was co-founder of the North American Association for Celtic Language Teachers. Tomás was born and still lives in Essex County, New Jersey, the area to which his Irish-speaking grandfather immigrated. Both of his children have been raised bilingually and enjoy speaking the language at home.

Natasha Sumner is a PhD candidate in Celtic Languages and Literatures at Harvard University. She holds an AM in Celtic from Harvard, as well as a BA Honours in Celtic Studies and an equivalent BA Honours in English from St. Francis Xavier University. Her ongoing research interests include gender positioning in Irish and Scottish Gaelic folklore and intertextuality in 18th-century Gaelic literatures. She has taught introductory and intermediate Irish language courses at Harvard University and she is active on the Executive Committee of *Cumann na Gaeilge i mBoston*.

Daniel G. Williams is Senior Lecturer in English and Director of the Richard Burton Centre for the Study of Wales at Swansea University. His projects as an editor have included a special edition of *Comparative*

American Studies on "The Celts and the African Americas" and *Canu Caeth*, a Welsh-language collection of essays on connections between Wales and African America. He is the author of *Ethnicity and Cultural Authority: From Matthew Arnold to W. E. B. Du Bois* (Edinburgh University Press, 2006) and *Black Skin, Blue Books: African Americans and Wales* (University of Wales Press, 2012)

Rhiannon Heledd Williams studied her PhD at Bangor University's Welsh Department, exploring the concept of national identity and the Welsh-language press in 19th-century North America. She spent a semester at Harvard University on an exchange program and during her research there she visited different Welsh-American communities. Dr. Williams currently works for the Coleg Cymraeg Cenedlaethol (National Welsh College), developing Welsh as a university subject. She recently undertook sabbatical leave to teach Welsh at the Department of Linguistics at Vienna University.

Other Conference Abstracts

Margaret Bennett, The Royal Scottish Academy of Music and Drama
"Deoch-slàinte a' chuairtear a ghluais à Albainn!": Generational Changes and Evolution of Scottish Gaelic Identity in Newfoundland

This paper is based on fieldwork recordings from 1969 to 2009 of four generations of a Newfoundland family whose Scottish Gaelic-speaking forebears emigrated from the Isle of Canna and Moidart in the first half of the 19th century. While vibrant traditions of song, music, storytelling and dance endure into the 21st century, only a few of the oldest generation speak Gaelic. Questions of identity are addressed, particularly in terms of "Gaelic," "Highland" and "Celtic," not only as they apply to the Scottish Newfoundlanders but also in the much wider context of all Celts in the "Old and New Worlds." Illustrated with examples from fieldwork recordings.

Jonathan Dembling, Independent Scholar
Representations of Nova Scotian Gaels in Feature Films

Cinematic portrayals of Gaelic life in Nova Scotia are anything but common; however, there have been a number of films produced over the last half century that purport to take place in the province's Gaelic-speaking communities. This paper examines the content of four feature films: *Johnny Belinda*, *Wedding in White*, *Life Classes* and *Margaret's Museum*, with a particular focus on the latter two. It also traces the evolution of the strategic deployment of Gaelic Nova Scotia as a pre-modern "other," with which modern Anglo-North American society—the real focus of these films—is contrasted. In the cases of *Johnny Belinda* and *Wedding in White*, Gaeldom is a brutish backwater where superstition and chauvinism remind the rest of "us" how far we've come. In contrast, *Life Classes* and *Margaret's Museum* look to the *Gàidhealtachd* for an alternative to the brutality and ennui of life in a world run by money and technology. In each case, the specifics of Gaelic life are passed over in favour of its symbolic value, and the few attempts to include actual spoken Gaelic or other representations of Gaelic culture are often problematic.

Tiber F. M. Falzett, University of Edinburgh
New Oralities in the Cape Breton Gàidhealtachd: The Nature of Fieldwork in the 21st Century

This paper focuses on new and emerging trends in ethnographic fieldwork, namely from recording verbal art texts to conversational narratives on local tradition or *seanchas*, due in part to shifts in local knowledge extant within the Cape Breton *Gàidhealtachd* in the Scottish Gaelic language. The current generation of first-language speakers is fully capable of illuminating and further contextualizing our understanding of transmission and the creation of communal identity through local cultural forms of expression. Written almost twenty-five years after the First North American Congress of Celtic Studies and its panel "The Celts in North America" in 1986, this paper intends to re-examine the preliminary discussions offered at the time by Dr. John Shaw (1988) and Professor Kenneth Nilsen (1988) on conducting fieldwork concerning the living Celtic language traditions of this continent a quarter of a century later. Portions of personal fieldwork along with supplementary field-notes are employed to demonstrate the importance of such research not only within the discipline of Celtic Studies but as an area of enquiry that is equally important to furthering current theory in the field of cultural anthropology.

Ernest Gilchrist, Independent Scholar
The Fusion of Cultures: The Hybridization of North Carolina's Highland Cape Fear Settlement

The Thistle, the most notable immigrant ship to bring Highlanders from Argyllshire, Scotland, to the shores of eastern North Carolina, landed in Wilmington in 1739 and formed the Argyll Colony, ninety miles inland. This Gaelic settlement provided one strand of several cultures that contributed to the hybrid character of the region. This melding of peoples can be seen as a model, not only for the American South, but for all of the Americas. I have defined "ArgyllAmerica" as a dual hybrid reflecting the multicultural relationships developed by the various peoples in the Upper Cape Fear River Valley and Sandhills from the 18th century to the present. I focus in particular on Cameron Hill, a Presbyterian church founded by the descendants of Scottish Highlanders where my paternal grandfather and great grandfather lie buried in unmarked graves in the "black section" of the cemetery; the amazing life and influence of Paul Green, Pulitzer Prize-winning playwright, poet and humanitarian; and the spiritual beginnings of Campbell University (formerly Buies Creek Academy) by founder and first President, James Archibald Campbell.

Discussed from the perspective of a descendant of Gaelic-speaking African Americans, this paper was presented in a manner that is respectful of the legacy of the Argyll Colony and other peoples, i.e., descendants of Highlanders and Native American Indians who shared the same region. The fusion of these cultures created a peculiar spirit once agrarian in nature, whose influence is also transferable to more populous areas of the United States like Atlanta, Georgia, and Charlotte, North Carolina. Underscored in this paper is the point that the development of the history and culture of "ArgyllAmerica" cannot be credited to one group of people only but must shed light on the fact that its uniqueness was and still is today a reciprocal relationship.

Lynda Harling Stalker, St. Francis Xavier University
Knitting Kilt Hose: Learning About Highland Dance in Northeastern Nova Scotia

The image of the Highland dancer, a young lass dressed in a kilt and ghillies doing the fling, is a ubiquitous symbol of "Scottishness" in northeastern Nova Scotia. This paper sets out to explore how the author learned about Highland dance and its problematic relationship to Gaelic culture through knitting kilt hose for her daughter. It looks at the social history of the dance, its prominence in northeastern Nova Scotia and its connection to wool and knitting. The question put forth is whether or not the celebration of Celtic heritage, as exemplified by Highland dance, is an inclusive exercise or one that puts up barriers not only to those who come from away but even to those who identify with Gaelic-speaking communities.

Michael Hornsby, Deptartment of Celtic Languages and Literature and Adam Mickiewicz, University Poznań, Poland
Changes in the Welsh Language in the 21st Century: Any Lessons for Gaelic in Nova Scotia?

Harri Webb's poem *Colli Iaith* (1974) refers to "*colli iaith a cholli urddas ... ac yn eu lle cael bratiaith fas*" (losing language and losing dignity ... and in their place, acquiring a shallow, debased language). The view that Welsh is somehow "deteriorating" into a "shallow, debased language" is shared by some popular commentators, such as Vaughan Roderick (2009), who considers that the language spoken by children in Welsh-medium schools is *"rhwng rhyw fath o Gymraeg ddeheuol safonol a'r hyn yr oedd pobol arfer dilorni fel 'Rhydfeleneg'"* (between some sort of standard southern Welsh and that which people used to denigrate as "Rhydfelen Welsh," [Rhydfelen being one of the first Welsh-medium secondary schools in the Cardiff area]). It is also a view taken by some academics, such as Jenkins, who comments on the passive nature of the linguistic ability of students who have been educated through the medium of Welsh. This situation is illustrated through reference to a television series broadcast in Wales in the 1990s and 2000s and from associated novels and other publications, and while the language used is obviously scripted, it does display the main features associated with this new variety.

The second half of the paper discusses the sociolinguistic implications of these changes and investigates the claim that such changes are indicative of language demise. By way of conclusion, the lessons from the Welsh experience are used to draw out comparisons with the revitalization of Gaelic in Nova Scotia and to examine the potential mismatch between revitalizers' expectations and actual linguistic output.

Michael Linkletter, St. Francis Xavier University
"An t-Eilean Fada: Eilean Eòin 's Eilean a' Phrionnsa" *The Gaelic Toponomy of Prince Edward Island*"

Highland Settlers came to Prince Edward Island in large numbers beginning in the late 18th century and continuing into the 19th. Even today, their descendants are reckoned the largest ethnic group in the province. Because of the decline in the language over the past century, however, very few place names now in use on the island reveal an origin that reflects the historical strength of the Gaelic community there. This paper discusses the use of Gaelic place names in PEI historically and relies on evidence from early Gaelic books and newspapers as well as on the oral tradition. The Gaelic term for PEI itself is also a significant point of discussion.

Goiridh MacDhomhnaill, Comunn Gàidhlig is Eachdraidh a' Bhràigh
Cuimhnich gur i an ite as àirde 'na do churrac! A Learner's/Instructor's/Parent's Perspective on Successful Gaelic Language Transmission and Acquisition in 21st-Century Nova Scotia

As someone who grew up in a traditional Gaelic community (Bràigh na h-Aibhneadh, Cape Breton) and began learning Gaelic over two decades ago, I, Goiridh mac Alasdair Dhùghaill, have seen the good and the bad in Gaelic language transmission. This paper gives a simple overview of what may be very valuable to us in Gaeldom, and indeed to other minority language communities, in what is to be found in language revitalization theories and practices of some other linguistic groups that seem to be successful. Much is to be learned as well from our own tradition where transmission always occurred naturally in the homes and communities through interaction, history, songs, sayings, prayers, stories and *sgeulachdan*. We need to resurrect the *taigh-céilidh*! The majority of what I have learned about what works best and what doesn't in language intergenerational transmission and instruction comes from being the parent of a nine-year-old native Gaelic speaker being raised in a strongly English-language dominant setting. This paper was presented in Gaelic and English.

Lodaidh MacFhionghain / Lewis MacKinnon, Oifis Iomairtean na Gàidhlig / Nova Scotia Office of Gaelic Affairs
A' Ghàidhlig a Dh'Ionnsaich Mo Chlann Dhomh

Tha iomadach fiosraiche a sgrìobhar is a bhruidhnear air ciamar a thogas clann cànan. Chan e rud ealant' a théid a mhothachadh 's a' phàipear ghoirid seo. O chionn ghoirid fhuair mi fhìn is mo bhean an deagh fhortan dithist bhràithrean a thoirt a-staigh dhan teaghlach againn mar dhaltan. O'n a thàinig an dithist ghillean seo 'nar beatha, thòisich mi air a' Ghàidhlig a chur 'uca cho tric is a 's urrainn dhomh. An dà-rìribh, 's e Gàidhlig an t-suidheachaidh a bhios sinn a' cleachdadh.

Bidh am pàipear seo a' cur sùil air ciamar a théid a' Ghàidhlig a thoirt dhan chloinn againn is na modhannan a chuireas mi gu feum gus a thogas iad a' Ghàidhlig is gus a chuireas iad gu feum i. Aig ceann a' ghnothaich, seallaidh am pàipear seo ciamar tha suidheachadh ann an aon teaghlach far a bheil pàrant a' fiachainn ris a' Ghàidhlig a thoirt dhan chloinn. Ged nach e rud ealant' a th'ann, thathas adhartas a' dèanadh. Cuiridh am pàipear feairt air a' seo gu h-àraid is dearbhaidh am pàipear seo gun gabhadh seo dèanadh ann an teaghlaichean eile.

Daniel MacInnes, St. Francis Xavier University
The One Hundred Thousand Nova Scotian Gaels in the 1901 Canadian Census: Why Did They Disappear So Quickly?

In successive decades since the late John Lorne Campbell's seminal article on Gaelic in Nova Scotia published in 1936, scholars (such as Charles Dunn, Ray Maclean and Doug Campbell, Stephen Hornsby, Jonathan Dembling and Michael Kennedy) have revisited the issue of the extent of Gaelic use and its decline in Cape Breton. More recently, the one hundred thousand Gaels in the census of 1901 have become a touchstone for marking the apogee of Gaelic usage in the extended Cape Breton *Gàidhealtachd*.

This paper first explores the quantitative dimension: was the reputed count correct? It then proceeds to the substantive issue of decline. Frequently, the combination of enforced English and the absence of Gaelic medium education has been blamed. This paper asks questions about the experience of the Gael. What role did emigration and industrialization play in the bilingual Gaels' acceptance of modernization? How was this collective metanoia conditioned by the earlier Victorian embrace of the "reconstructed" Gael, the ongoing emergence of a Scottish/British elite in Canada, the growing infrastructure ties to both local and distant industrialization and the embrace of social liberalism over the pervasive parochial Jansenistic/Calvinistic interpretation of one's existence? Was the rejection of Gaelic a mere predilection asserted by one's gender and level of education or did it speak to something far more universal? Was it yet another in a continuing series of utilitarian repudiations of a rural way of life?

Richard MacKinnon, Cape Breton University
UNESCO's Convention for the Safeguarding of Intangible Cultural Heritage, Digitization and Gaelic Culture in Cape Breton Island

UNESCO's Convention for the Safeguarding of Intangible Cultural Heritage, initiated in 2003, defines intangible cultural heritage (ICH) as "the practices, representations, expressions, as well as the knowledge and skills, that communities, groups and, in some cases, individuals recognize as part of their cultural heritage." As of January 11, 2011, 133 countries have signed this international treaty; Canada, however, is not a party to the convention. The purposes of UNESCO's Convention are "(a) to safeguard the intangible cultural heritage; (b) to ensure respect for the intangible cultural heritage of the communities, groups and individuals concerned; (c) to raise awareness at the local, national and international levels of the importance of the intangible cultural heritage, and of ensuring mutual appreciation thereof; (d) to provide for international cooperation and assistance." The convention seeks to provide and update inventories of a region's ICH, develop representative lists and identify the ICH of a country or region that is in need of urgent safeguarding.

In some countries that have signed the convention, important research projects have been undertaken. Such research focuses on documenting, reviving and revitalizing; education about and safeguarding of traditional practices; and the inter-generational transmission of traditions. These are all pertinent issues for Gaelic culture scholars around the world. This paper closely examines this international convention and its implications for Gaelic culture in eastern Canada. Further, the paper discusses a number of community-based Gaelic ICH research projects supported by the Centre for Cape Breton Studies at Cape Breton University.

Iain MacPherson, University of Ulster
Seanchas air astar: òrain is naidheachdan às "Machraichean Mòra" Chanada / Distance Discourse: Songs and Anecdotes from the "Great Plains" of Canada

This paper draws on research work undertaken through the project "Displaced Poets: Migrant Writing from the Margins in a Scottish Gaelic Context: 1780-1930 and Beyond" at the University of Ulster, which traces the colonial and postcolonial discourse in the written and transcribed record of Scottish Gaelic song-poems of emigration and immigration from the beginning of the Highland Clearances to the inter-war years of the 20th century, with an especial focus on the Canadian prairie provinces and, to a lesser degree, British Columbia.

Combined with this close reading of western Canadian Gaelic texts, which are found in both the pro and contra registers regarding the debate on the merits of emigration or the lack thereof, the paper also focuses attention on disparate and previously unrecorded (or unpublished) Gaelic songs and anecdotes collected by the writer in the first half of the 1990s in Alberta among the surviving members of the prairie pioneering Gaelic-speaking community, which had seen its genesis, in this particular instance, in the 1922-1923 planned emigrations from the Western Isles to the Indian School in Red Deer, Alberta. By the 1990s, the remaining members of this community, who were children at the time of the emigration or born shortly afterward in Canada, were typically in their 70s and 80s, (one was in her 90s) when the writer recorded their stories.

And so, the paper proposes to excavate this rich vein of a little-studied Canadian *Gàidhealtachd* in the part of the country that had seen both a pre- and post-Confederation Gaelic-speaking presence (from the Gaels of the North-West Company in the 1780s to the Selkirk settlers in the Red River country—who, from the 1820s up to the 1880s planned emigration schemes such as those at Saltcoats, etc.—not to mention the Canadian-born Maritime Gaels and their work forays "out west").

By referencing the pro-emigration publication from 1907 *Machraichean Mòra Chanada* in the title, the paper also aims to disentangle the rhetoric of dominion governments' drive to populate the prairie provinces from the lived experiences of the Gaelic-speaking settlers, both positive and negative, evidenced in the *seanchas* (storytelling/rhetoric/discourse) the writer intends to use as his primary source material.

Anna Matheson, University of Cambridge / Dublin Institute for Advanced Studies
The Herring as Buffoon in the Folktale "Am Peata Sgadain"

Among the tales collected last century from Angus Cù MacDonald of Mabou, Cape Breton, is the seemingly odd story of a fisherman who caught a herring and retained it for years as a pet until it accidentally slipped off a bridge and fell into a brook. This story is classified as a "humorous tale," the apparent punch line being that the herring drowned when returned to the water. But for many unfamiliar with such herring tales, it is difficult to grasp the hilarity of the plot.

In this paper, aided by a medieval description of the herring in the 9th-century Irish text known as *Cormac's Glossary (Sanas Cormaic)*, as well as by insight gained from modern terms for herring such as the Welsh *penwaig*, whose etymology reflects traditional perceptions of this fish, I explain the joke contained in our tale.

Trueman and Laurinda Matheson, St. Francis Xavier University
Lesser-Known Early Antigonish Gaelic Bards

Antigonish County maintains today a rich Highland heritage, which it celebrates every year in the longest continually run Highland Games in North America. However, it has taken second fiddle to Cape Breton when viewed as a home of a strong Gaelic culture and bards. Names such as the Bard MacLean, Keppoch Bard and the Ridge MacDonalds do come to mind but these are just a small fraction of the number of bards to be found on Cape Breton Island. However, early in the history of Antigonish there were a number of bards of the highest quality who came to this county. This paper touches on a few of them—Iain am Pìobaire, Dòmhnull Gobha, Iain Boid and others—and shows that as rich a Gaelic tradition existed in this county as in any on Cape Breton.

Patricia A. McCormack, University of Alberta
Lewismen and Aboriginal People of the Canadian Northwest—the Talamh Fuar

Men from the Island of Lewis began to work in the Canadian fur trade in the late 18th century, thereby playing a foundational role in the later development of the Canadian nation-state and its Métis people. As a group, they have been little thought about in either Canada or Lewis. Some of the early Lewis immigrants to the British colonies along the eastern seaboard of North America eventually found their way into the fur trade run by Montréal companies, especially after 1763, when Québec became a British possession and the fur trade was reconstituted by Highland Scots. Beginning ca. 1810, the Hudson's Bay Company began recruiting men directly from Lewis, as a location secondary to the Company's main recruiting centre in Stromness, in the Orkney Islands. Recruitment from Lewis intensified after 1821, and many men signed contracts with the HBC to travel to the *Talamh Fuar* for a fixed period as wage labourers.

While they were not emigrants, some of them did end up staying in Canada or the northwest following the end of their formal employment, becoming "freemen." Many—probably most—of those who remained contributed to the developing Métis population in the northwest. The men who returned home to Lewis brought with them income they used to buy crofts and improve their situations both financially and socially. A few of these men brought home their Native wives and children and were concentrated at Tolsta and Borve, in the northern end of the island. These families were assimilated into the Lewis population.

Chris McDonald, Cape Breton University
Singer-Songwriters in Cape Breton: Marking Ground Between Celtic and Popular

Cape Breton Island has a lively Celtic traditional music scene and independent pop-rock scene. Lying somewhere in between is the category of performer—the singer-songwriter—that has supplied many of Cape Breton's most renowned musical acts. This paper looks at the history of singer-songwriters in Cape Breton from the 1970s to the 2000s, focusing on how many of the most successful performers find ways to connect traditional Celtic idioms (which have a strong sense of geographical place) to a very loose and open construction of genre. This connection allows the singer-songwriter to fit in commercially across a number of categories—folk, adult contemporary, rock and country—while retaining a very specific geographic identity tied to the island and all that it represents.

Drawing on notions of de-territorialization and re-territorialization, the paper examines the use of the word *Celtic* to describe many of these artists, since it seems to play a role in the "emplacement" of the singer-songwriter while still allowing for generic ambiguity. The paper looks to the music and careers of John Allan Cameron, Rita MacNeil, Alistair MacGillivray, JP Cormier, Gordie Sampson, Aselin Debison, as well as family-based groups such as the Rankin Family, the Barra MacNeils and the Cottars, as key components of this history. Cape Breton's popular music has often been overlooked in favour of its fiddle and folksong traditions, and this paper provides some much-needed attention to the former.

Helen Mórag M. McKinnon (née Leland), Independent Scholar
A Voice in the Wilderness: A Modern Tale of Gaelic Isolation and Perseverance in an Anglo-Franco Canadian Province

The continued existence of the Scottish Gaelic language in Canada is dependent upon the ongoing support of groups of Gaelic speakers, influential individuals, academic institutions and enlightened branches of governments. There is strength in numbers and where a sufficient critical mass of the above elements exist, a culture and its language may flourish. This paper narrates a personal history of struggle and success of a family disconnected from the Gaelic Diaspora yet surrounded by all the iconic elements of Scottish culture in New Brunswick. It includes a description of early childhood in a Gaelic-speaking household. This particular household's native-Gaelic-speaking mother was a war bride from Stornoway, Isle of Lewis, whereas the household's father, a multi-linguist, was a fluent speaker, although he was a learner of Gaelic. His two passions outside his family and church were helping to preserve both the Gaelic and Maliseet languages, which, during his adult life, were in peril of becoming extinct.

The family also included the author, a sister and a younger brother. A synopsis shows the family and the author's personal success in dealing with the powerful prejudice of the school system and its attempt to deny students of different cultural backgrounds the right to a chosen education because of apparent negative consequences at school. Music, a powerful tool, was woven into this author's presentation of this paper with examples of how music is used, to potent success, through teaching. Projects undertaken by the author and her father, the late Lloyd George Leland, are introduced through anecdotes, to show what they felt was a challenge yet a boon to the preservation and spreading of a minority language in danger of becoming extinct.

This paper endeavours to show, through the presenter's own personal linguistic history, that the preservation of a culture through its language is not only possible but, despite great odds and challenges, a worthy and fulfilling life's work. It is an imperative that language be preserved; for if a language dies, its culture vanishes also.

Kevin McLaughlin, St. Francis Xavier University
Conradh na Gaeilge, Craobh Bhaile Pitt/*The Gaelic League of Pittsburgh: A Brief History of Irish Language Preservation Efforts in Pittsburgh, Pennsylvania*

The Gaelic League (*Conradh na Gaeilge*) was founded in Ireland in 1893 by Dr. Douglas Hyde (Dubhghlas de hÍde) and others. From the beginning, one of the League's primary functions has been to preserve and promote the Irish Language (*An Ghaeilge*) through participation in, and the sponsoring of, educational and cultural activities. Irish immigrants throughout the 20th century brought the Irish Language, as well as their native music, dancing and sports traditions to the United States. The Gaelic League was founded in Pittsburgh, Pennsylvania, in the 1970s to preserve the language in this New World setting. Unlike other American cities such as Boston or New York, Pittsburgh, Pennsylvania, is not usually perceived as being a leading centre for the Celtic Cultural Renaissance. The predominant white ethnic stereotype is that of an eastern or southern European milieu. Nevertheless, the Gaelic League has kept the Irish language very much to the foreground among the Irish-American community in Pittsburgh. This is a very brief historical sketch of Pittsburgh's Gaelic League and its efforts to promote and preserve an immigrant language in the United States.

Sulien Morgan, Centre for Welsh American Studies, School of Welsh, Cardiff University
The Response of the Welsh in the United States to the Formation of the Welsh Nationalist Party, Plaid Cymru

The formation of Plaid Cymru in 1925 heralded a political movement that called for the creation of a self-governing and Welsh-speaking Wales. Receiving a lukewarm response in Wales, partly due to its eccentric leader Saunders Lewis, Plaid Cymru struggled for support for its cause in Wales. However, the American Welsh prided themselves on being more patriotically Welsh than the people of Wales. So how did they receive the new political party?

Using the two Welsh-American newspapers, *Y Drych* and *The Druid*, as sources, this paper aims to explore the reaction of both newspapers and their audience to the formation and activities of Plaid Cymru from its founding in 1925 until the Second World War.

Sandra Muse, McMaster University
The Nikwasi Sacred Mound: Celtic Overwriting of a Cherokee Village

Franklin, North Carolina, can be viewed as a microcosm of the troubled and conflicted history of Gaelic and Indigenous relations in the early days of the United States. It is a modern yet quaint town nestled in the heart of the Great Smoky Mountains in the southern United States, which draws upon its history of Scottish and Scots-Irish settlement of this originally Cherokee land. Franklin was literally built on top of the ancient Cherokee middle town of Nikwasi, where many early Scots first met Cherokee people and earned their trust, becoming traders among the tribal villages and often marrying Cherokee women. Sitting in the centre of Main Street is the Nikwasi Mound, the sacred centrepiece of that ancient Cherokee middle town, which is protected by federal historical designation.

The Eastern Cherokee reservation is less than a half hour away, and modern-day Cherokees can only stand and look at this sacred mound through a fence, a mound where spiritual ceremonies had always taken place. Meanwhile, a few blocks away stands the local Masonic lodge, which bears the name of Junaluska, a Cherokee warrior who saved the life of then-General Andrew Jackson, who later committed wide-scale genocide upon the southeastern tribes. Franklin is also home to North America's one and only Tartan Museum, which recently opened a special exhibit based on the Cherokee Nation and the early Scottish immigrants. Given the fact that the English army could not have finally beaten the Cherokee in the Battler of Nikwasi in 1760 had it not been for their Highland warriors, many of whom had been Jacobites, and therefore victims of the Clearances and the subsequent transportations, how do we rectify this overwriting and sometimes appropriation of Cherokee culture and history by the newcomers who were Indigenous peoples themselves?

Kenneth Nilsen, St. Francis Xavier University
Bealach Cheanada: *Twentieth-Century* Gaeltacht *Immigration to Canada*

Evidence for Irish speakers in Canada goes back to the early days of British settlement in Newfoundland. During the course of the 19th century, Irish speakers continued to settle in the Maritime Provinces and further west in Québec and Ontario, although evidence for their presence is sparse. Statements such as this one by Scottish-born George M. Douglas, who was the doctor at the quarantine station on Grosse Île, Québec, in 1846 are quite rare: "The number who annually land on our shores varies from 20,000 to 35,000—and one year the number reached to 52,000. Rather more than 3/5ths of these are from the South and West of Ireland, a great proportion of whom speak in no other language than Erse."

As this paper shows, emigration to Canada from the *Gaeltacht*, particularly from Connemara, continued into the 20th century. The paper first uses Irish government statistics, Canadian census records, ships' passengers list and other written sources to delineate a pattern of Irish Gaelic speakers emigrating to Canada. The paper then supplements this material with the details of oral accounts of individuals who emigrated to Canada in the 1920s-1950s, indicating why they came to Canada, where they settled, what occupations they followed and how long they stayed in Canada. The paper concludes with a brief selection of video clips of individuals discussing *Gaeltacht* emigration to Canada.

Catriona NicÌomhair Parsons, Oifis Iomairtean na Gàidhlig, Alba Nuadh
'S gus an càirear anns an ùir mi / Cha chuir mi cùl ri mo Ghàidhlig! *(And Till I'm Buried in the Earth / I Will Not Turn My Back on My Gaelic!)*

'S e a th' anns an òraid seo sùil a-staigh air mar a ghléidh Gàidheil na h-Albann Nuaidhe a' Ghàidhlig's a dualchas an aghaidh iomadh chnap-starraidh; agus air na dh'fhaodas ionnsachadh bho 'n eisimpleir seo a thaobh ath-bheòthachadh cànain. Théid mìn-chunntas de bheachdachadh a dhèanamh air na thachair a thaobh na Gàidhlig 's na deicheadan eadar làithean *MhicTalla* agus an diugh; agus mu dheireadh air na nithean a bu riatanaich do ghléidheadh na cànain.

This paper takes an inside look at how Nova Scotia Gaels preserved the Gaelic and its culture in the face of many impediments and what may be learned from this example about language (re-)vitalization. What occurred concerning Gaelic in the decades between the days of *MacTalla* and the present is briefly considered, concluding with a contemplation of the elements most necessary to its preservation.

Barry Shears, Independent Scholar
It's in the Blood: The MacIntyre Pipers of Cape Breton County, 1828-2010

The past decade has seen unparalleled research into the history, music and playing styles of Highland pipers both in Scotland and the New World *Gàidhealtachd*. The collapse of the Highland clan system in Scotland in the second half of the 18th century led to significant emigration of Gaels from Scotland to the Canadian Maritimes. Included in the estimated 50,000 Scottish immigrants who came to Nova Scotia were almost eight pipers. These musicians came to Nova Scotia for a variety of reasons and were representatives of both the tacksman and tenant class. The tacksman or middle-class pipers included the John Roy MacKay of Gairloch, piper to MacKenzie of Gairloch; Kenneth Chisholm, piper to Chisholm of Strathglas; Robert MacIntyre, piper to both MacDonald of Clan Ranald and Robertson MacDonald of Kinlochmoidart; several sons and grandsons of Rory MacNeil, the Laird of Barra's early 18th-century piper; and MacDonald of Glenalladale's piper and bard, John MacGillivray. In addition, there were dozens of lesser-known pipers, representative of old Highland families who also left Scotland for Nova Scotia, and these included Campbell, Carmichael, Gillis, MacDonald, Nicholson, MacKinnon, MacMillan and MacIntyre.

Included in this rich immigrant tradition of piping were four "piping" MacIntyre families who left South Uist for Cape Breton County between the years 1820 and 1836. They settled in the small farming communities of north side East Bay, Boisdale, Canoe Lake and French Road. Here they continued in their role as community pipers, playing for step-dances, weddings and funerals. In the days before electronic amplification, the volume of the Highland bagpipe made it an ideal instrument for outdoor gatherings and made the Highland piper a popular purveyor of dance music. Piping was critically important to these families and, in keeping with tradition, the art of playing the bagpipes was passed on orally from one generation to the next. This practice was so successful that over forty descendants of these four MacIntyre families were pipers. One family, the French Road MacIntyres, has maintained a tradition of bagpipe-playing to the present day, while piping eventually died out in the other three families. However, the French Road MacIntyres did not escape the changes brought on by 20th-century literate Scottish piping or the influences of the military establishment, and during the second half of the 20th century their performance style moved closer to the Scottish model.

This paper examines the early origins of the MacIntyre pipers in Perthshire, the emigration from South Uist to Cape Breton, the transition from an oral musical tradition to a written one in the 20th century and some of the contributions various members of these MacIntyre families have made to piping in Nova Scotia, through their influences as dance players and teachers. Samples of field recordings and old photographs were used to enhance the presentation.

Heather Sparling, Cape Breton University
Tongue and Toe Twisters: The Relationship between Port-á-Beul *and Dance in Cape Breton*

Port-á-beul is often defined as "vocal music for dancing," but what kind of dancing? In Cape Breton today, it is often assumed to accompany step dancing, a solo form of extemporized dance claimed to have come from Scotland but which was unknown there for a period of time until its recent revival. However, historical sources indicate that *port-á-beul* was not limited to the accompaniment of step dancing on either side of the Atlantic. Neither was it limited to public performance contexts; in fact, *port-á-beul* as dance accompaniment probably occurred most often in domestic environments. For example, women, who were historically excluded from performing as instrumental soloists, would sing *port-á-beul* at home to accompany their children's dancing. Likewise, children would sing *port-á-beul* to accompany their own dancing. Today, *port-á-beul* is rarely performed to accompany dancing except in staged "historical reconstructions" of dancing accompanied by song, usually at concerts designed to educate an audience about Gaelic cultural traditions. *Port-a-beul*'s domestic history is therefore not often apparent. In this paper, I draw on both historical and ethnographic data to explore the relationship between *port-á-beul* and various forms of dance with a particular emphasis on Cape Breton.

Laurie Stanley-Blackwell and John D. Blackwell, St. Francis Xavier Univetsity
The Giant Angus MacAskill and Enshrining "The Mighty Scot"

Even in the 21st century, stories about the extraordinary physical prowess of Cape Breton's Giant MacAskill (1825-1863) continue to exert a timeless fascination. Today, two museums, the Giant MacAskill Museum in Englishtown, Cape Breton and the Giant MacAskill Museum in Dunvegan, Skye, celebrate MacAskill's feats as a heroic spectacle of superior size and strength, and present him as an icon of Scottish physical strength. Wearing this mantle, MacAskill has served a double agenda by simultaneously marketing a public heritage of "tartanism" and celebrating the family honour of the Giant MacAskill Heirs Association—a conflation of the pride of ethnicity and the pride of lineage.

However, despite the popularity of these tourist sites, the storytelling tradition in Cape Breton offers a wider scope of folk narratives that celebrate the role of strength as a cultural marker among Cape Breton's Scots. These folk history tellings reject the ethic of individual performance epitomized by the enshrined MacAskill and alternatively relate the stories of community strong men as more authoritative emanations of their culture. In this sense, Cape Breton's tradition bearers have not been "passive recipients of official memory," nor has MacAskill supplanted their history. In most cases, tradition bearers prefer the multiple and more personalized and localized variants of stories of feats of strength. These are not meant to diminish the significance of MacAskill's achievements but to represent the broader vernacular landscape of memory in Cape Breton.

Peter G. Toner, St. Thomas University
Locating "Celtic" Music in Early 21st-Century New Brunswick

Global musical forms are always made meaningful in local contexts, and there is no doubt that "Celtic" music is a global musical form: transported along with Irish and Scottish migrants to the four corners of the earth, transfigured during the mid-20th century folk revival and commodified and marketed under the auspices of the World Music industry as the 20th century gave way to the 21st. The meanings of these traditions, however, cannot be read in a unitary way. In New Brunswick, despite considerable Scottish and then Irish migration during the 18th and 19th centuries, Celtic musics were not maintained as "pure" forms—possibly because of the lack of continuing immigration after the mid-19th century. Instead, Celtic musics seem to have given way to and combined with emerging mass-mediated genres like old-time and country. The mid-20th century folk revival was fuelled in New Brunswick by persisting Celtic cultural identities and the influence of Celtic music from other parts of Atlantic Canada, leading to today's "second life" of Celtic music in the province.

This paper examines Celtic musics in New Brunswick as everyday practice grounded in local experience, rather than as cultural heritage indexically related to well-defined migrant groups. This requires a recognition of the "inventedness" of musical traditions, the selectiveness and contingency of cultural identities and the diverse and overlapping musical "worlds" of which identifiably "Celtic" musics are only one shifting and sometimes ambiguous part. Although we may be forced to modify hopeful notions of the persistence of these musics in their diasporic contexts, we are repaid with a deeper understanding of the complex ways in which cultural identities are mediated musically.

Peter M. Toner, University of New Brunswick
Irish Language Survival in Canada: Many Questions, Few Answers

For most of my professional career, I have seldom strayed far from the study of the Irish in my native province of New Brunswick. Previous research has called into question and dismissed many "beliefs" about the Irish, in New Brunswick as well as elsewhere. I had known a number of Irish speakers who had been born in New Brunswick, and they had steered my interest in that direction, but there was no hard evidence until the census of 1901 was released. Initial examination of that census produced evidence that flew in the face of established wisdom, making a systematic study imperative. I covered the Maritimes, and small bits of Québec and Ontario before a collapse in health put an end to my work. But what I had discovered put an end to the established wisdom in my mind, and also called into question the standard portrait of the Irish society that had produced this effect in eastern Canada.

Perhaps on a small scale, Irish was nonetheless still a living language in eastern Canada at the beginning of the 20th century. This fact cannot be explained unless the social history of Ireland as it has been written is reconsidered in the light of this evidence. The durability of the Irish language in Canada, as well as its relationship to that other form of Gaelic spoken by neighbours from a Scots background, must also be explained. The questions raised by this evidence are at least as intriguing as many of the potential answers.

Seumas Watson, Nova Scotia Highland Village Museum and Marlene Ivey, NSCAD University
An Drochaid Eadarainn: *Prototyping An Online Social Space for the Nova Scotia Gaelic Community—Concept, Content Parameters and Design*

The creation of an online social space designed to simulate living Gaelic culture is the focus of this paper. *An Drochaid Eadarainn* (The Bridge Between Us), is a prototype that explores the potential for virtual experience to reflect the social reality of living Gaelic culture. *An Drochaid Eadarainn*'s aim, through socially directed technology, is to create an online *caidreabh* (Gaelic fellowship opportunity) framed in virtual expressions of Nova Scotian Gaelic culture.

An Drochaid Eadarainn has evolved from *Stòras a' Bhaile*, a Gaelic immersion folkways program held at Nova Scotia Highland Village, Iona. *An Drochaid Eadarainn* is a technological extension of this event. It includes the capacity to incorporate and advance the use of previously established digital resources for Gaelic Nova Scotia such as *Sruth nan Gàidheal*, hosted by St. Francis Xavier University.

The *An Drochaid Eadarainn* prototype seeks to emulate the vertical, inter and intra-generational transmissions of Gaelic language and culture as social phenomena at local levels. Innovative applications of technology to Gaelic renewal in Nova Scotia may also hold beneficial applications for other cultural-linguistic groups facing similar challenges from issues of maintenance and development.

An Drochaid Eadarainn philosophy rests on the tenet that sustaining a living Gaelic culture is dependent on the internal criteria of its continuum models. Examples of these models are found in the passing on of oral literature such as songs and stories. From this perspective, transmission of living culture inside the *An Drochaid Eadarainn* web portal takes place, not in a pedagogical sense, but rather in an environment informed by immersive social expression maintained through group participation and interaction.

This paper unfolds the concept, content and design development of the project that is rooted in participatory principles and purposefully facilitates inter-activity as a method for developing and disseminating cultural identity through authentic language-based cultural content.

Index

Note that entries refer to the print version.

Aberdare 99, 110-11
Acadia 19, 20, 23, 26, 32, 82, 195, 336-38, 340, 342
African Americans 14, 195, 305-33
aisling tradition 61-62
Alabama 68, 103, 111
Alberta 22, 360
American Civil War 109-110
American Revolutionary War 22, 61, 78, 87, 96, 285, 320
Andes, the 146-50, 53-54, 255, 328, 331
Anglo-Irish 189, 194
Antigonish 15, 77, 84, 169, 179-80
Appadurai, Arjun 193-203
Appalachians 192, 194, 196, 199
Appiah, Kwame Anthony 305-306, 312, 316-17, 319
Arendt, Hannah 314-16
Argentina 56, 79, 94, 145-57, 145-57, 251, 253-63, 267, 270, 326-27
Argyll 221-22, 226, 237
Arnold, Matthew 190-91
Australia 42, 50-51, 61, 65, 261, 266-67

Bard MacLean 77, 80, 84, 122-23
bards. *See* poets
Basque: language 32; people 23, 120; place 253, 267
Benacadie Pond 214-215, 227, 232, 235
Bhabha, Homi 249-51, 263, 266
Bible 49, 83, 199, 254, 276, 336

Bissoondath, Neil 118-19, 125
Borges, Jorge Luis 255
Boston 57-58, 62, 70-72, 79, 89, 192, 195-95, 199, 205
Breton family names 26-27; Bourhis, 22; Carduner, 24, 26; Coyet, 26; Haven, 27; Irvillac, 27; Legault, 27; Le Goff, 27; Kerouac, 27; Rannou, 22
Bretons: language 15, 19, 23-33, 318, 336-37; people 6, 13, 18-33, 120, 126, 192, 318, 336-37
British Columbia 51, 124, 145, 149
Brittany 18-33, 18-89, 313, 336-37
Buenos Aires 57, 261, 326

Caernarfonshire 98-100
California 41-43, 51, 70, 79, 103-104, 111, 201, 265-67, 285, 292
Canadian Charter of Rights and Freedoms 136
Canadian constitution 14, 124, 128
Canadian National Railway 125
Cape Breton Gaelic Society 133-35, 141
Cape Breton University 15, 133, 183
Cape Breton 26, 85, 89, 90, 118-19, 123, 133-35, 161, 169, 179, 180-82, 192, 195, 199, 201-202, 209-16, 218-44, 253, 267, 287-88, 291, 298-304, 336-38, 343; place names in, 209-16
Cardiganshire 100, 102
Carolinas 61, 83, 78-79, 194
Cartier, Jacques 19, 26

Catholicism 19, 21-22, 28, 30, 57, 61-63, 65-66, 78, 83, 121, 181, 189, 335-44; Jesuits, 335, 337. *See also* religion
ceilidh 80, 90, 198, 218
Celtic languages 118-19, 124, 126, 129, 133, 137, 139, 140-41, 161. *See also individual languages*
Celtic music 6, 28, 187-205; Breton 32; Cornish 45, 256; Gaelic 81, 86, 122, 134-35, 193, 197-200, 202, 205n2, 291; Irish 193, 195-99, 202; Welsh 105, 110, 155-56, 190, 254, 264
Celtic studies 9, 11-14, 33, 127, 135-36, 187, 189, 204
Chicago 51, 71, 79, 89, 106, 195, 199
Chubut province 145-57, 153-54, 251, 253-62
Classical Common Gaelic 236
Clearances. *See* Highland Clearances
clothing: Breton 26; Welsh 255, 257; Scottish 293
colonialism. *See* empire
Confederation 121, 124, 126
Connradh na Gaeilge 313-14
Cork 219, 222
Cornish: language 40, 41, 46-51, 265-67, 325; people 6, 13, 39-52, 192, 253-54, 264-67, 287, 324
Cornu-English: communities 50-51; dialect 40, 46, 48
Cornwall 39-51, 188, 265-66
Counter-Reformation 82, 336
Cullen, Countée 307-310
cultural hybridization 248-67
Cwm Hyfryd 149, 256
cymrellano 258

Daltaí na Gaeilge 72
de Champlain, Samuel 26
de Tocqueville, Alexis 281
Detroit 50, 79, 89, 199
d'Hauterives, Countess de Grand-saignes 22

Dolavon 146, 148-49, 153
Donegal 57, 65, 69, 70
drolls 47, 51
Du Bois, W. E. B. 306-307, 310-12, 316-17

education: Gaelic 82, 84, 86, 169-83, 178-79; in Chubut in Spanish 261; Welsh 257, 261
eisteddfodau 104-108, 149, 253, 256, 261-62, 264, 279, 313,
El Pueblo de Luis. *See* Trelew
El Pueblo del Molino. *See* Trevelin
Ellis Island 24, 27
empire 7-9, 13-14: British 5-7, 14, 82, 88, 120-21, 189, 254, 284, 302, 342; French 7, 18, 250; Spanish 249, 326
Enlightenment 8, 189, 194, 197, 305, 323
Esquel 146, 149, 153-54
Evans, John Daniel 257-58, 260

Famine. *See* Great Famine
Fanon, Frantz 250, 310
farming 21-22, 43-44, 49, 57, 62, 96-97, 100-102, 148-49, 257, 265
Feis an Eilein 181, 183
Fenian Trials 56
Fenianism 286
Ferriter, Patrick 62, 68
First Nations 14, 22, 27-30, 60, 82-83, 88-89, 109, 126, 252, 285, 287-88, 298-300, 325, 328-32, 335-44, 347; Béothuks 27; Inuit 27; Métis 252; Mi'kmaw language, 32, 335-44, 348; Mi'kmaw people, 20, 23, 195, 302, 335-44 342, 347; Mi'kmaw place names, 211, 216; Montagnais 27, 34
First World War 102, 104, 110
fishing 19, 23, 26-27, 30, 57, 60
folk music 195, 198-99, 202
folk tales. *See* oral tradition
food: Breton 31; Cornish 45; Welsh 148, 255-56

French language 84, 89, 319, 330-31, 336, 340: in Brittany 18, 20, 23-24, 29; in Canada 19-21, 23-24, 26, 30-31, 82, 84, 121, 124-25, 128-29, 137, 139, 161, 179, 332, 338, 340; in the U.S. 24-25, 29, 61
French people in Canada 65, 121, 124, 126, 252, 338
French Revolution 27
fur trading 89, 336

Gaelic College, NS 119, 181, 183
Gaelic: language 13, 15, 23, 26, 118, 121-24, 126, 139, 160-83, 209-16, 218-44, 253, 267, 298-304, 313-14, 324, 333, 337-40, 342, 348; people 6, 13, 76-91, 120-24, 126, 132, 133-35, 160-83, 188, 190, 192, 193, 140, 194, 198, 201-202, 205n1, 209-16, 218-44, 252, 253, 283-96, 298-304, 320, 313, 323, 324, 333, 337-40
Gàidhlig aig Baile 119, 169, 178-79
Gaiman 146, 148-50, 153-56
Galway county 58-59, 65, 196
gameinschaft 192-93, 195
Gaspesia 30, 338, 343
gauchos 255-57
Georgia 61, 78, 285
German: language 67, 84, 122, 127, 161, 325; people 41, 105, 127, 252, 315, 338
Gilroy, Paul 316-17, 323
Glamorgan 97-99
Glengarry, ON 78, 85, 91, 192, 252, 285
gold 43, 79, 103-104, 265
Gourin City, AB 22, 24, 26
government: of Argentina 146, 154; of Canada 21-22, 31, 118, 122-25, 128-40; of Chubut 148; of Ireland 58; of New York 67; of Nova Scotia 179; of Scotland 83; of the U.K. 157, 189; of the U.S. 108; of Wales 145, 149, 154, 156
government policy, Canadian: on immigration 125, 138; on multiculturalism 117-20, 122, 129-40
Grass Valley 42, 45-47, 50, 265-66
Great Famine 41, 57, 59, 61-68, 190, 194, 196
Gueguen, Joseph 20, 336, 342
Gwernig, Youenn 28-29
Gymanfa Ganu 105, 263-64

Halifax, NS 122, 161, 169, 183, 338, 341
Highland Clearances 79, 192, 195, 198, 300, 302
Highland Games 87-88

indigenous American languages. *See under* Native Americans
indigenous peoples of Argentina 259, 326; Mapuche people, 147, 252; Tehuelche people 147, 252, 257
Inverness county, NS 124, 209-10, 222, 229
Inverness-shire, U.K. 85
Iona 141, 210-12, 214, 216
Ireland 6, 8, 43, 47, 56-72, 97, 124, 188-90, 193-94, 196-99, 201, 203, 205, 220, 222, 229, 232, 234, 238n14, 243n42, 267, 286-87, 309, 313-14, 323, 337, 347
Irish Famine. *See* Great Famine
Irish: language 15, 23, 26, 56-72, 161, 195, 205, 253, 267, 313-14, 320, 337-40; people 3, 13, 46, 56-72, 105, 126, 140, 188, 190, 192, 193, 194, 195, 199, 201-202, 205n1, 211, 251, 286, 287, 289, 295, 300, 304n4, 313-14, 320, 337-38, 339, 340, 341, 343, 348
Irish-American, The 64, 68, 70
Irwin, Thomas 341-342, 347-48

Jacobitism 78, 86, 77, 189

Kerouac, Jack 28
Keweenaw Peninsula 43, 45-46, 48, 51

Killoran, Paddy 201
Killursa 58, 59

Latin 10, 336, 348
Le Loutre, Jean-Louis 20, 23, 336
Lenox Dale 23, 25-26
Lewis Town. *See* Trelew
Lewis, Scotland 79, 89, 198
literature: Argentine 255; Celtic 10; Gaelic 61, 76, 80-82, 85, 86-88, 218-44, 288-94, 298-304, 313; Irish 60-62, 68, 70, 190, 308-310, 313; Welsh 104-109, 110, 255, 258, 260-61, 263, 270-81, 307-10, 323-33, 327-28, 332. *See also under* newspapers
Liverpool 95, 146
Llwyd, Iwan 328-31, 333
Logan, Michael 69-70
Los Angeles 102, 263-64
Louisiana 20, 68
Lowlanders 76, 78, 88, 123, 192, 194, 284, 296
Loyalists 78, 285

Mabou, NS 161, 192, 291
MacGilleain, Iain. *See* Bard MacLean
MacGilleFhaolain, Domhnall 291
MacIlleBhàin, Eanraig 289
MacIlleBhàin, Iain 289-90, 294
MacIntyre, Linden 134
MacKenzie, Hugh F. 133
MacKinnon, Lewis 86
MacNeil, Joe Neil 218, 222, 232, 302
MacNeven, William James 62
Mac-Talla 85, 291, 298-304
Maillard, Pierre 336, 342
Malley, Thomas 58-59
Manach, Jean 20, 336
Manitoba 22, 79
Manx people 6, 13, 15, 192, 287, 289
Maritime provinces 78-79, 83, 335. *See also individual provinces*
Marshall, William 190, 198
Marx, Karl 317

Massachusetts 23, 28, 60
Maunoir, Julien 337
McDonagh, Anne 58
Menter Patagonia 150-51, 156
Michigan 42-43, 47, 50
Mi'kmaq. *See under* First Nations
Mill, John Stuart 120
Milltown, Argentina. *See* Trevelin
Milltown, NJ 23-24
Miltown, Galway 196
Milwaukee 51, 202
Mimosa, the 259, 261
Mineral Point 42-43, 50
mining 21, 42-48, 50, 52, 79, 97-99, 103-104, 265
missionaries 20-23, 28, 325, 335-44. *See also* religion
Montréal 19, 23, 26, 31, 79, 89, 128, 331
Morgan, Eluned 325-27
Mulroney, Brian 118, 136
Munster 63, 65, 224
music. *See* Celtic music

Native Americans. *See* First Nations
New Brunswick 20, 65, 79, 196, 338
New Jersey 23-24, 51, 59, 61-62
New World 15, 40, 51, 72, 76, 95, 160, 192-200, 203-204, 274, 324, 328, 333
New York: state 61-62, 65, 70, 78, 83, 89, 263, 272-73; city 24-25, 28-30, 32, 49, 57, 66-68, 70-72, 79, 102, 107-108, 199, 201, 273-74, 329
Newfoundland 19, 23, 26, 27, 60, 62, 194-96, 201, 205
newspapers: Gaelic 84, 181-82, 285, 288-94, 298-304, 313; Irish 64, 69-70; Welsh 107, 149, 270-81, 325
Nilsen, Kenneth 15, 71-72, 209, 236
North Carolina. *See* Carolinas
North San Juan 104, 112
North Shore, NS 161, 178
Nova Scotia 13-15, 77-79, 82, 84-88, 90-91, 119-23, 127, 132, 135, 139,

160-83, 209-16, 218, 226-27, 291, 298-304, 320, 323, 338-39, 341-43

Ó Lócháin, Mícheál 69-70
Ó Siadhail, Pádraig 15, 72
Office of Gaelic Affairs 14-15, 86, 90, 179, 210
O'Growney, Eugene 70-71
Ohio 100, 102, 105, 107, 272
Old World 76, 81, 188, 191, 194, 197-98, 203-204
Ontario 28, 72, 78-79, 85, 88, 91, 195, 248-49, 252, 285
oral tradition 188, 211-16, 218-44, 248, 253; Gaelic, 80-81, 85, 88-89, 90, 122, 135, 160, 198, 289-91, 294, 298, 302-303, 210; Irish, 198; Welsh, 255
Ossianic tales 62, 348

Paimpol 19, 27
pan-Africanism 305-314, 319-20
pan-Celticism 41, 305-20
Parry-Williams, T. H. 307-310
Patagonia 13, 94, 145-57, 192, 251-52, 254-62, 267, 270, 323, 325-27
Pearse, Patrick 313
Pearson, Lester 125-26, 129
Pennsylvania 51, 61, 84, 95, 99-100, 104, 106, 254, 262-64, 272, 298
periodicals. *See* newspapers
pétanque 30
Pezron, Paul-Yves 189
Philadelphia 49, 59, 62, 107, 200
Phlem, Yves 23
Phoenix 68
Pittsburgh 99, 111, 262
poetry. *See* literature
Port Madryn 146, 149, 153, 261, 323
prairies, Canada 22-23, 79, 101, 127
press. *See* newspapers
priests 20-21, 62, 66, 335-42. *See also* religion
Prince Edward Island 79, 83-84, 88, 342-43, 338-39, 341-42

print culture. *See* newspapers *and under individual newspapers*
Protestantism 72, 83, 180-81, 189, 253-54, 313, 338-43; Anglicans, 261, 339, 341; Baptists, 96, 107, 339, 342; Congregationalists, 107; Methodists, 45, 96, 107, 265, 272, 278; Presbyterians, 189, 192. *See also* religion
Puerto Madryn. *See* Port Madryn

Quakers 95-96, 107
Québec 20, 22, 26, 28, 30-32, 56, 65, 79, 84-85, 88, 91, 121, 125, 195-96, 201, 331-33, 335, 338, 340
Quechua 328

Rand, Silas Tertius 342
Rawson, Chubut 146, 148-49, 153, 257
Red River Valley, MB 79
Redlegs 60
regime: British 23, 26, 337-42; French 19-20, 23, 26, 250, 335-37, 342
religion 78-79, 88, 260, 289-92, 326, 336, 338, 340, 343; in Gaelic communities, 82-83, 88; in Welsh communities, 95-96, 102, 104-108, 145, 147, 274-81. *See also* Catholicism, missionaries, priests, Protestantism, Quakers
Reversing Language Shift 155-56, 162-64, 177-83
Revolutionary War. *See* American Revolutionary War
Rhys, William Casnodyn 260
River Chubut 146, 148, 259
Riverdance 197, 202, 204-205
Roman Catholic Church. *See* Catholicism
Rowlands, William 272-74, 276-78, 280
Royal Commission on Bilingualism and Biculturalism 125-33, 141
Royal National Mòd 86, 197

Sabhal Mòr Ostaig 178
Saint-Malo, Brittany 19-20
San Francisco 68, 70, 107, 192, 263, 292
Saskatchewan 21, 24, 33, 254, 263, 328, 330
Saul, John Ralston 252
Scotland 6, 41, 47, 57, 65, 76, 81-86, 89, 97, 122-23, 160, 178, 181, 188-90, 193-94, 198-99, 210, 218-44, 267, 284-86, 289, 291, 293, 299-302, 313, 323, 347
Scots-Irish 61-62, 192-96, 199
Scottish. *See* Gaelic
Scranton, Pennsylvania 104-105, 108, 110, 262
Second World War 31, 50, 102, 108, 147, 262, 264, 314-15
Sinclair, Alexander Maclean 85, 291, 295n4
slavery 60-61, 96, 109, 192, 250, 278, 285, 288, 310, 320n2, 326-27
societies: Cornish 50-51, 265; Gaelic 83, 122, 133-35, 141n5, 197; Irish 66, 69; Welsh 104-105, 263
South Carolina. *See* Carolinas
Spanish language 145-48, 154-57, 251, 256, 258-59, 261-62
St. David's Day 262, 279
St. Francis Xavier University 15, 127, 135, 181-83
Sydney, NS 89, 133, 180-81, 183n7, 298-304

Tadoussac, QC 19
temperance movement 81
Tennessee 96, 110, 195
Texas 96, 196
Thomas, John Coslett 258, 260
Thomas, John Murray 255-56, 260
Toronto 51, 79, 85, 89, 90, 106, 128, 263, 289
tradition bearers 90, 134, 192, 210-16, 251, 258, 368

Trelew 146, 148-50, 152-54, 251, 261
Trevelin 146, 149, 153-54
Triton, the 261
Trudeau, Pierre 129-34

Ulster Scots. *See* Scots-Irish
UNESCO 140, 164-65, 202
Utica, NY 62, 102, 106-108, 263-64, 272, 274

Vancouver 51, 79, 89
Victoria, BC 42, 51
Victorian era 120, 190-91, 203, 254-55, 323, 358

Wales 6, 41-42, 60, 94-102, 104-105, 107-111, 145-49, 153, 155,157, 188-89, 253-54, 257-58, 260, 262, 267, 270, 272-76, 279, 280-81, 287, 308-10, 313, 318, 323-333
War of Independence. *See* American Revolutionary War
Washington state 96, 103
Welsh: language 13, 15, 23, 26, 102-109, 145-57, 251, 253-64, 267, 270-81, 318, 323-33; people 6, 13, 94-111, 120, 126, 140, 145-57, 183n7, 190, 192, 248-67, 270-81, 287, 307-308, 318, 323-33, 347
Wilkes-Barre, PA 104, 262
Winnipeg 89, 108
Wisconsin 42-43, 46, 50-51, 101, 272
World War I. *See* First World War
World War II. *See* Second World War

Y Cyfaill o'r Hen Wlad 107, 272-81
Y Drafod 260-61
Y Dravod 146-47, 149
Y Drych 103-104, 108, 263
Yeats, W. B. 308-310
Ysgol yr Hendre 148, 152-54, 156

www.ingramcontent.com/pod-product-compliance
Lightning Source LLC
Chambersburg PA
CBHW032015230426
43671CB00005B/96